International Political Economy Series

Series Editor: **Timothy M. Shaw**, Visiting Professor, University of Massachusetts Boston, USA, and Emeritus Professor, University of London, UK

The global political economy is in flux as a series of cumulative crises impacts its organization and governance. The IPE series has tracked its development in both analysis and structure over the last three decades. It has always had a concentration on the global South. Now the South increasingly challenges the North as the centre of development, also reflected in a growing number of submissions and publications on indebted Eurozone economies in Southern Europe.

An indispensable resource for scholars and researchers, the series examines a variety of capitalisms and connections by focusing on emerging economies, companies and sectors, debates and policies. It informs diverse policy communities as the established trans-Atlantic North declines and 'the rest', especially the BRICS, rise.

Titles include:

Caroline Kuzemko
THE ENERGY SECURITY–CLIMATE NEXUS

Hans Löfgren and Owain David Williams (*editors*)
THE NEW POLITICAL ECONOMY OF PHARMACEUTICALS
Production, Innovation and TRIPS in the Global South

Timothy Cadman (*editor*)
CLIMATE CHANGE AND GLOBAL POLICY REGIMES
Towards Institutional Legitimacy

Ian Hudson, Mark Hudson and Mara Fridell
FAIR TRADE, SUSTAINABILITY AND SOCIAL CHANGE

Andrés Rivarola Puntigliano and José Briceño-Ruiz (*editors*)
RESILIENCE OF REGIONALISM IN LATIN AMERICA AND THE CARIBBEAN
Development and Autonomy

Godfrey Baldacchino (*editor*)
THE POLITICAL ECONOMY OF DIVIDED ISLANDS
Unified Geographies, Multiple Polities

Mark Findlay
CONTEMPORARY CHALLENGES IN REGULATING GLOBAL CRISES

Nir Kshetri
CYBERCRIME AND CYBERSECURITY IN THE GLOBAL SOUTH

Kristian Stokke and Olle Törnquist (*editors*)
DEMOCRATIZATION IN THE GLOBAL SOUTH
The Importance of Transformative Politics

Jeffrey Wilson
GOVERNING GLOBAL PRODUCTION
Resource Networks in the Asia-Pacific Steel Industry

International Political Economy Series
Series Standing Order ISBN 978–0–333–71708–0 hardcover
Series Standing Order ISBN 978–0–333–71110–1 paperback
(*outside North America only*)

You can receive future titles in this series as they are published by placing a standing order. Please contact your bookseller or, in case of difficulty, write to us at the address below with your name and address, the title of the series and the ISBN quoted above.

Customer Services Department, Macmillan Distribution Ltd, Houndmills, Basingstoke, Hampshire RG21 6XS, England

The New Political Economy of Pharmaceuticals

Production, Innovation and TRIPS in the Global South

Edited by

Hans Löfgren
Associate Professor, School of Humanities and Social Sciences, Deakin University, Australia

and

Owain David Williams
Research Fellow, Centre for Health and International Relations, Aberystwyth University, UK

Editorial matter, selection, introduction and conclusion © Hans Löfgren and Owain David Williams 2013
Individual chapters © Respective authors 2013

All rights reserved. No reproduction, copy or transmission of this publication may be made without written permission.

No portion of this publication may be reproduced, copied or transmitted save with written permission or in accordance with the provisions of the Copyright, Designs and Patents Act 1988, or under the terms of any licence permitting limited copying issued by the Copyright Licensing Agency, Saffron House, 6–10 Kirby Street, London EC1N 8TS.

Any person who does any unauthorized act in relation to this publication may be liable to criminal prosecution and civil claims for damages.

The authors have asserted their rights to be identified as the authors of this work in accordance with the Copyright, Designs and Patents Act 1988.

First published 2013 by
PALGRAVE MACMILLAN

Palgrave Macmillan in the UK is an imprint of Macmillan Publishers Limited, registered in England, company number 785998, of Houndmills, Basingstoke, Hampshire RG21 6XS.

Palgrave Macmillan in the US is a division of St Martin's Press LLC, 175 Fifth Avenue, New York, NY 10010.

Palgrave Macmillan is the global academic imprint of the above companies and has companies and representatives throughout the world.

Palgrave® and Macmillan® are registered trademarks in the United States, the United Kingdom, Europe and other countries.

ISBN 978–0–230–28463–0

This book is printed on paper suitable for recycling and made from fully managed and sustained forest sources. Logging, pulping and manufacturing processes are expected to conform to the environmental regulations of the country of origin.

A catalogue record for this book is available from the British Library.

A catalog record for this book is available from the Library of Congress.

Contents

List of Tables and Figures	vii
Acknowledgements	ix
Notes on Contributors	x
List of Acronyms and Abbreviations	xii

1. The New Political Economy of Pharmaceuticals: Conformity and Resistance in the Global South — 1
   Owain David Williams and Hans Löfgren

2. The Political Economy of Pharmaceutical Production in Brazil — 29
   Cassandra M. Sweet

3. Pharmaceuticals, Health Policy and Intellectual Property Rights in China — 48
   Chee-Ruey Hsieh

4. Immunity to TRIPS? Vaccine Production and the Biotechnology Industry in Cuba — 70
   Jens Plahte and Simon Reid-Henry

5. TRIPS and Access to Medicines in Egypt — 91
   Dina Iskander

6. The Pharmaceutical Industry in India after TRIPS — 111
   Sudip Chaudhuri

7. The Healthcare System and the Pharmaceutical Industry in Indonesia — 134
   Richard Husada and Raymond R. Tjandrawinata

8. TRIPS, Free Trade Agreements and the Pharmaceutical Industry in Malaysia — 152
   Mohamed Azmi Hassali, Jayabalan Thambyappa, Shankaran Nambiar, Asrul Akmal Shafie and Hans Löfgren

9. The Pharmaceutical Industry, Intellectual Property Rights and Access to Medicines in Pakistan — 167
   Zaheer-Ud-Din Babar, Shazia Qasim Jamshed, Muhammad Ashar Malik, Hans Löfgren and Anwarul-Hassan Gilani

10	TRIPS, Access to Medicines and Local Production in South Africa *Andrew L. Gray and Yousuf A. Vawda*	185
11	TRIPS and New Challenges for the Pharmaceutical Sector in South Korea *Bong-min Yang and Hye-young Kwon*	204
12	Neoliberalism, Intellectual Property Rights and the Turkish Pharmaceutical Industry in the 2000s *Ipek Eren Vural*	221
13	Conclusion: TRIPS, Drug Production in the Global South and Access to Medicines *Hans Löfgren and Owain David Williams*	246

Index   251

Tables and Figures

Tables

2.1	Application of TRIPS changes to Brazilian IPR law	32
3.1	Health and economic indicators in China, 1978–2008	51
3.2	Market share of different drug types in China	58
3.3	Concentration indices of the pharmaceutical market in China	59
3.4	Selected indicators of the Chinese pharmaceutical industry by sector, 1997	60
3.5	Comparisons of R&D capability in China, US and Europe	61
3.6	Total production value of the Chinese pharmaceutical industry by type of products (in billions of RMB)	62
3.7	Ownership structure in China's pharmaceutical industry	65
3.8	Pattern of trade in the Chinese pharmaceutical sector (in billions of US$)	66
4.1	Vaccines marketed by Cuban manufacturers	82
6.1	M&As and tie-ups in Indian pharmaceutical industry, 2006–2010	113
6.2	Patent status of new drugs marketed in India, 1995–2010	117
6.3	Market structure of new drugs, 2010	118
6.4	New drugs marketed by MNCs, 2010	119
6.5	Prices of MNC monopoly drugs	121
12.1	Overview of pharmaceutical IPR in Turkey	225
12.2	Transnational entry and acquisitions in the Turkish pharmaceutical market, 1999–2011	234
12.3	Pharmaceutical imports and exports, 1980–2010, in US$ million	236
12.4	Percentage of imported and locally produced pharmaceuticals in the Turkish pharmaceutical market, 2005–2010	237

Figures

2.1	Trends in trade: Brazil's pharmaceutical import and trade balance, 2005–2011	41
3.1	Number of foreign pharmaceutical patents in China, 1985–2006	50
3.2	Sources of healthcare financing in China, 1978–2008	53
3.3	Percentage of health expenditure spent on pharmaceuticals	55

3.4 Drug expenditure as a percentage of GDP in China, 1990–2008 — 57
3.5 Pharmaceutical price index, 1990–2005 — 64
10.1 Percentage private sector market share by volume (packs), 2006–2010, based on year to September data — 198
10.2 Percentage private sector market share by value (single exit price), 2006–2010, based on year to September data — 199
11.1 South Korea's pharmaceutical industry outputs — 214
11.2 Changes in proportions of over-the-counter and prescription-only medications, 1995–2007 — 215
11.3 Percentage of foreign manufactures in numbers and in drug expenditure, 2002–2005 — 216
11.4 Share of generic drugs in pharmaceutical expenditure (quantity, value) — 217
12.1 Total public health and drug expenditures, 2002–2010, in US$ million — 231
12.2 Turkish prescription market sales, 2003–2010, in US$ billion — 232
12.3 Turkish prescription market sales, 2003–2010, in volume of million boxes — 232
12.4 Pharmaceutical patent applications to the Turkish Patent Institute, 2004–2010 — 239

Acknowledgements

We are grateful for comments and high-quality copy-editing by Alison Caddick, Crissene Fawcett and Michael Leahy, and to Colleen Keane for her fine proof-reading. We are also thankful to Palgrave Macmillan for their support and professionalism. Hans Löfgren would like to acknowledge financial support from the Centre for Citizenship and Globalisation, Deakin University. Owain David Williams' time and research were made possible through funding from the European Research Council under the European Community's Seventh Framework Programme – Ideas Grant 230489 GHG. All views expressed remain those of the contributors, to whom we are indebted for their critical and constructive engagement with the themes and problems addressed in this volume.

Contributors

Zaheer-Ud-Din Babar is a senior lecturer and Head of Pharmacy Practice, School of Pharmacy, University of Auckland, New Zealand.

Sudip Chaudhuri is Professor of Economics, Indian Institute of Management Calcutta, India.

Anwarul-Hassan Gilani is the Noor Mohamed Shamji Professor of Pharmacology, Department of Biological and Biomedical Science, Aga Khan University, Karachi, Pakistan.

Andrew L. Gray is a senior lecturer in the discipline of pharmaceutical sciences, University of KwaZulu-Natal, Durban, South Africa.

Mohamed Azmi Hassali is an associate professor and Programme Chair for Social and Administrative Pharmacy, School of Pharmaceutical Science, Universiti Sains Malaysia.

Chee-Ruey Hsieh is a research fellow in the Institute of Economics, Academia Sinica, Taipei, Taiwan.

Richard Husada is a senior lecturer at Universitas Surabaya, Indonesia.

Dina Iskander works for Oxfam Novib as the Policy and Campaigning Officer for Egypt and Yemen, based in Cairo.

Shazia Qasim Jamshed is an assistant professor at the International Islamic University, Kuantan, Malaysia.

Hye-young Kwon is a pharmacist and PhD in health economics at the Seoul National University.

Hans Löfgren is an associate professor in the School of Humanities and Social Sciences, Deakin University, Melbourne, Australia.

Muhammad Ashar Malik is a senior instructor in the Department of Community Health Sciences, Aga Khan University, Karachi, Pakistan.

Notes on Contributors xi

Shankaran Nambiar is a professor in the School of Business at Manipal International University, Kuala Lumpur, Malaysia.

Jens Plahte holds a PhD in economic geography. His dissertation was on the Cuban biotechnology sector. He operates a consultancy business in Oslo, Norway.

Simon Reid-Henry is a lecturer in geography at Queen Mary, University of London.

Asrul Akmal Shafie is Associate Professor of Social and Administrative Pharmacy, Universiti Sains Malaysia.

Cassandra M. Sweet is Assistant Professor of Public Policy, the Institute of Political Science, PUC, Santiago, Chile.

Jayabalan Thambyappa is a member of the Governing Council of Health Action International, a Technical Committee member of the Malaysian Health Promotion Board and a member of the Academy of Occupational and Environmental Medicine, Malaysia.

Raymond R. Tjandrawinata is the executive director of Dexa Laboratories of Biomolecular Sciences (DLBS), Tangerang, Indonesia.

Yousuf A. Vawda is Professor of Law at the University of KwaZulu Natal, South Africa.

Ipek Eren Vural is Assistant Professor of Political Science in the Department of Political Science and Public Administration, Middle East Technical University (METU), Ankara, Turkey.

Owain David Williams is a research fellow in the Centre for Health and International Relations, Aberystwyth University, Wales.

Bong-min Yang is Professor of Health Economics, School of Public Health at the Seoul National University, South Korea.

Acronyms and Abbreviations

ACTA	Anti-Counterfeiting Trade Agreement
ACTD	ASEAN Common Technical Dossiers
AFTA	Asian Free Trade Area
AIDS	Acquired Immune Deficiency Syndrome
AIOCD	All Indian Origin Chemists & Distributors
ANVISA	Brazilian National Health Surveillance Agency
API	Active Pharmaceutical Ingredient
ARV	Anti-Retroviral Medicines
ASEAN	Association of Southeast Asian Nations
ASJII	*Asuransi Jiwa Inhealth Indonesia* (subsidiary PT of Askes)
Askes	*Asuransi Kesehetan* (Malaysian National Health Insurance scheme)
Askeskin	*Asuransi Kesehetan bagi para miskin* (scheme for free medication for the lowest-income groups through Askes)
BNDES	Brazilian National Development Bank
BPOM	*Badan Pengawas Obat dan Makanan* (see NAFDC)
BRIC	Brazil, Russia, India and China
CBD	Convention on Biological Diversity
CDSCO	Central Drugs Standard Control Organization (India)
CECMED	Cuban National Drug Regulatory Agency
CESCR	International Covenant on Economic, Social and Cultural Rights
CIGB	Centre for Genetic Engineering and Biotechnology (Cuba)
CIM	Cuban Centre for Molecular Immunology
CIPIH	Commission on Intellectual Property Rights, Innovation and Public Health
CLs	Compulsory Licences
CMIE	Central Monitoring for Indian Economy
CMS	Cooperative Medical Scheme
CNS	Central Nervous System
CPT	Consumer Project on Technology
CQB	Cuban Centre for Biomolecular Chemistry
CRAMS	Contract Research and Manufacturing Services
CSDH	Commission on the Social Determinants of Health
CVS	Cardio Vascular System
DAF	Department of Pharmaceutical Assistance and Strategic Raw Materials
DBF	Dedicated Biotechnology Firm

DNDi	Drugs for Neglected Diseases Initiative
DOEN	*Daftar Obat Esensial National* (see NELM)
DPHO	*Daftar Plafon Harga Obat* (list and ceiling of drug prices – Malaysia)
EC	European Commission
ECU	European Customs Union
EFPIA	European Federation of Pharmaceutical Industries and Associations
EGF	Epidermal Growth Factor
EIPICO	Egyptian International Pharmaceutical Industries Company
EPC	European Patent Convention
EU	European Union
EUPI	Employers Union of the Pharmaceutical Industry
FAO	UN Food and Agriculture Organization
FATA	Federally Administered Tribal Areas
FDA	United States Food and Drug Administration
FDI	Foreign Direct Investment
FTA	Free Trade Agreement
FTAA	Free Trade Area of the Americas
G8	Group of Eight
G20	Group of Twenty
GATT	General Agreement on Tariffs and Trade
GAVI	Global Alliance for Vaccines and Immunisation
GCP	Good Clinical Practice
GDP	Gross Domestic Product
GHG	Global Health Governance (literature/discipline of)
GHP	Global Health Partnership
GISN	Global Influenza Surveillance Network
GLI	Green Light Committee Initiative
GLP	Good Laboratory Practice
GMP	Good Manufacturing Practice
GNI	Gross National Income
GSP	General System of Preferences
HAI	Health Action International
HCV	Hepatitis C Virus
HFA	Health for All
HHI	Herfindahl-Hirschman Index
HIV	Human Immunodeficiency Virus
HNP	Health, Nutrition and Population Partnership
HPTF	Health Policy Task Force
IAVI	International AIDS Vaccine Initiative
ICH	International Commission on Harmonisation of Technical Requirements for Registration of Pharmaceuticals for Human Use

xiv List of Acronyms and Abbreviations

IDR	Indonesian Rupiah
IDSC	Information and Decision Support Centre
IEIS	Pharmaceutical Manufacturing Association of Turkey
IFPMA	International Federation of Pharmaceutical Manufacturers and Associations
IIPA	International Intellectual Property Alliance
IMC	Industrial Modernisation Centre (Egypt)
IMD	Incrementally Modified Drugs
IMF	International Monetary Fund
IMPACT	International Medical Counterfeiting Taskforce
IMR	Infant Mortality Rate
INN	International Non-proprietary Name
INPI	Brazilian Patent Office
IP	Intellectual Property
IPC	Intellectual Property Committee
IPE	International Political Economy
IPO	Intellectual Property Organization
IPR	Intellectual Property Rights
IR	International Relations
ISI	Import Substitution Industrialisation
ISO	International Standards Organization
Jamkesmas	*Jaminan Kesehatan Masyarakat* (social health security network – Malaysia)
KFDA	Korea Food and Drug Administration
KIPO	Korea Intellectual Property Office
KODC	Korea Orphan Drug Centre
KOR–US FTA	Korea–US Free Trade Agreement
KRW	Korean Won
LAS	Laboratory for Synthetic Antigens
LDC	Least Developed Country
LMIC	Low to Middle Income Country
M&As	Mergers and Acquisitions
MCC	Medicines Control Council
MDG	Millennium Development Goal
MFA	Multi-Fibre Agreement
MFN	Most Favoured Nation
MMV	Medicines for Malaria Venture
MNC	Multinational Corporation
MoH	Ministry of Health
MOPI	Malaysian Organization of Pharmaceutical Industries
MRP	Maximum Retail Price
MSF	Médicins sans Frontières
NAFDC	National Agency of Food and Drug Control (Malaysia)
NAFTA	North American Free Trade Agreement

NBE	New Biological Entity
NCD	Non-Communicable Disease
NCE	New Chemical Entity
NCMS	New Cooperative Medical Scheme
NEDL	National Essential Drugs List
NELM	National List of Essential Medicine (Malaysia)
NGO	Non-Governmental Organization
OECD	Organisation for Economic Cooperation and Development
OGB	*Obat Generik Berlogo* (unbranded generic medicines – Malaysia)
ONIITEM	Cuban National Office of Inventions and Trademarks
OTC	Over-the-Counter (medicines)
PCT	Patent Cooperation Treaty
PDP	Product Development Partnership
PEPFAR	President's Emergency Plan for AIDS Relief
PhRMA	Pharmaceutical Research and Manufacturers of America
PIC/S	The Pharmaceutical Inspection Convention and Pharmaceutical Inspection Cooperation Scheme
PLT	Patent Law Treaty
PPMA	Pakistan Pharmaceutical Manufacturers Association
PPO	Pakistan Patent Office
R&D	Research and Development
RM	Malaysian Ringgit
SAAFTA	South Asian Free Trade Agreement
SAARC	South Asian Association of Regional Cooperation
SAC	Supreme Administrative Court
SACU	Southern African Customs Union
SAGMA	Southern African Generics Medicines Association
SIPO	State Intellectual Property Office of China
SJSN	National Social Security System – Indonesia
SPLT	Substantive Patent Law Treaty
Super 301	Section 301 of the US Trade Act of 1974
SUS	Sistema Única de Saúde (Brazilian healthcare system)
TAC	Treatment Action Campaign
TAN	Transnational Advocacy Networks
TB	Tuberculosis
TCM	Traditional Chinese Medicine
TNC	Transnational Corporation
TPI	Turkish Patent Institute
TPP	Trans-Pacific Partnership Agreement
TRIPS	Trade Related Aspects of Intellectual Property Rights
UN	United Nations
UNAIDS	Joint United Nations Programme on HIV/AIDS
UNCTAD	United Nations Conference on Trade and Development

UNDP	United Nations Development Programme
UNESCO	United Nations Educational Scientific and Cultural Organization
UNFPA	United Nations Population Fund
UNICEF	United Nations International Children's Emergency Fund
UPOV	International Union for the Protection of New Varieties of Plants Convention
USAID	United States Agency for International Development
USMFTA	US–Malaysia Free Trade Agreement
USTR	Office of the United States Trade Representative
WHA	World Health Assembly
WHO	World Health Organization
WIPO	World Intellectual Property Organization
WTO	World Trade Organization

1
The New Political Economy of Pharmaceuticals: Conformity and Resistance in the Global South

Owain David Williams and Hans Löfgren

Some two decades will shortly have passed since the World Trade Organization's Agreement on Trade Related Aspects of Intellectual Property Rights (henceforth WTO and TRIPS) came into force in 1995 (World Trade Organization, 1994). TRIPS has proven to be one of the most politically charged and divisive multilateral agreements yet negotiated. The agreement has polarized opinion with regard to its effects on knowledge production and consumption in areas as diverse as agriculture and food security, literacy and education, software and the internet economy, and its general implications for capitalist accumulation.

TRIPS has received the greatest critical scrutiny and generated the fiercest opposition in the area of pharmaceutical innovation and access to medicines. TRIPS-mandated minimum intellectual property rights (IPRs), including 20-year patent protection for products and processes in 'all fields of technology', and a cluster of associated practices, rules and trade agreements, now constitute a global regime of private monopoly rights which is widely recognized as an impediment to access to essential medicines. This regime complicates and delays the production and market entry of lower cost generic drugs, with dire implications for affordable access and public health ('t Hoen, 2009).

This volume examines the political economy of pharmaceutical production in the Global South in the aftermath of TRIPS through case studies of developments in Brazil, China, Cuba, Egypt, India, Indonesia, Malaysia, Pakistan, South Africa, South Korea and Turkey. Before 1995 these countries framed national IPR legislation in terms of sovereignly determined social and developmental goals, and most did not recognize pharmaceutical product patents. These are also countries which pre-1995 had relatively significant local pharmaceutical industries (Ballance et al., 1992).

Many studies of pharmaceutical markets have presented powerful critiques of the IPR system in general and the extension of pharmaceutical product patents to low and middle-income countries (LMICs) in particular (see e.g. Hollis, 2007; Love and Hubbard, 2007; Pogge et al., 2010). This volume continues in this vein of work. We promote an approach which examines the interaction of IPRs with other market and policy dynamics in play in the case study countries. Clearly, IPRs are not the sole determinant of the political economy of global drug production. Indeed, critiques of their impact on access to medicines have become more nuanced, with greater appreciation of the underlying 'real world' economics of innovation and generic production. Contributors to this volume have sought to go beyond the academic and policy literatures focused on the minutiae of IPRs, integrating such work with empirical analyses of how the pharmaceutical sector in these countries has evolved over the last several decades, and has often done so in conjunction with policies towards national health systems and population health, or those for economic and technological development.

The global IPR regime has evolved unevenly, with variations in strength and enforcement in different jurisdictions (Williams, 2012). There are also significant pockets of resistance. In particular, countries such as China, India and Brazil bring growing political and economic resources to bear in their interactions with the multinational companies (MNCs) and with the governments of the US and Europe. Also significant is the global coalition of public health advocates, non-governmental organizations and some LMIC governments which, since the mid-1990s, has limited the impact of IPR protection on access to medicines (Sell, 2002). This coalition also contributed to the establishment of new product development partnerships and new health governance institutions such as the Global Fund to Fight Aids, Tuberculosis and Malaria (the Global Fund). Pressure also produced *The Declaration on the TRIPS Agreement and Public Health*—the Doha Declaration—perhaps the major achievement of the international access to medicines campaign. Adopted at the fourth WTO ministerial conference in Doha in 2001, the Declaration confirmed and extended the right of WTO members to utilize a range of 'flexibilities' available under TRIPS, allowing the circumvention of patent rights to meet pressing population health needs (World Trade Organization, 2001).

Subsequent chapters demonstrate the diversity of patterns of pharmaceutical production and supply in key LMIC countries. This diversity is shaped by a range of factors. First, the role of foreign (health aid) donors and the new global health partnership organizations has become apparent in promoting the wider use of generics under the 'select disease' focus of many 'vertical' international health programmes, particularly those targeting HIV/AIDS (Rushton and Williams, 2011; Williams, 2012). This has provided a boon for generic firms and suppliers of active pharmaceutical ingredients (APIs), including production of anti-retrovirals (ARVs) and anti-malarials, particularly in India and China. Second, the distinct composition of local health sectors, including price controls and social insurance arrangements, shapes patterns of consumption and production. Third, joint ventures between MNCs and LMIC firms, as well as North-to-South (and also South–South) mergers and acquisitions, appear to replicate industry consolidation in developed country markets. Fourth, in several of our case studies we find evidence of abuse of TRIPS-compliant IPRs by both foreign and local firms through evergreening (patenting of marginal product modifications) to extend the term of monopoly pricing, patent thickets (multiple patents on a single chemical entity) and excessively broad patenting (with consequent obstruction of follow-on innovation or even basic medical research) through exploitation of low patentability standards. Fifth, studies of the patent landscape of individual LMICs add valuable detail to patterns of foreign pharmaceutical patent filing and litigation in domestic courts. Sixth, much scholarly and political interest is focused on the use of so-called TRIPS flexibilities, including definition of patentability criteria, patent oppositions, 'bolar' and research exceptions, parallel imports and especially compulsory licensing. Finally, it is widely recognized that generic entry, provided for differentially in different jurisdictions, is more effective in lowering of prices and widening access to medicines than philanthropy or the MNC-preferred model of tiered or differential pricing strategies.

Both this chapter and the volume proper, therefore, engage with many of the socio-economic, legal and political forces which are shaping and constraining the pharmaceutical industries in the Global South. The volume aims to provide a more detailed, comparatively framed empirical picture of how generic production and profile of markets have changed since 1995 than has previously been available, but acknowledges that not all of what has transpired in the case study countries is a consequence of the implementation of new forms of IPR protection. In keeping with this approach, we proceed in this introductory chapter to offer a perspective on the wider global strategic environment for drug production and an overview of the responses to changes in this environment by governments and firms in the case study countries.

A changing strategic environment

The pharmaceutical industry consists of thousands of firms engaged in one or several of the functions of discovering, developing, manufacturing and marketing medicines for human use. The industry's strategic environment has recently been dramatically reshaped by economic globalization, which has brought about a wave of mergers and acquisitions, and the re-engineering of corporate structures to achieve greater flexibility and increased capacity to engage in external collaborations. More than ever in a global economy, patents (and exclusive marketing rights) enable research-based companies to charge monopoly prices, and the extension of patent protection often translates into many millions or even billions of dollars.

Yet, the boundary between the research-based and the generics segments of the pharma industry is blurring. Most big pharma companies also supply generics, including so-called pseudo-generics that are identical (not copies but produced at the same production lines) to their branded equivalents (Lofgren, 2007). Conversely, some generics companies also supply patented products.

In this globalized economy, interdependencies, and even competition, between the 'big pharma' MNCs headquartered in the US and Europe, and generics producers in the Global South, is more pronounced than ever before. The MNCs are 'in a period of rapid environmental change and intense competition, following a relatively long period of...stability in which the same business models...dominated for many decades' (Smith, 2011, p. 100). *McKinsey Quarterly* puts it more colloquially: 'The good old days of the pharmaceutical industry are gone forever' (Hunt et al., 2011). Other factors coming together to reshape the industry's strategic environment include steadily falling research and development (R&D) productivity, the expiry of patents on many major products, a shift towards biological medicines, health cost constraints in developed countries, the threat of pandemics, and political mobilizations for access to medicines for all.

Some of these influences are grounded in economic and scientific–technological rationalities, others in relatively autonomous political and social dynamics, such as rising regulatory hurdles and mounting expectations of access to essential medicines as a human right. Reinforcing the volatility is the unfolding of the global economic and financial crisis which commenced in 2008. This crisis puts downward pressures on growth in developed country pharma markets, and possibly it will transpire that these markets 'will contract for the first time in history' (IMAP, 2012, p. 1). Furthermore, the tendency towards relative stagnation in developed country markets forms part of the backdrop to a shift of MNC business strategies to focus more on LMICs; and '[t]here is consensus that future growth in the Pharma Industry will mainly come from emerging markets, most notably China' (IMAP, 2012, p. 1).

For us, the IPR system provides a pivotal strategic tool for the MNCs and the governments of the US and the EU. The IPR regime, intertwined with international trade law, is the principal mechanism by which these dominant actors exercise (political) agency over the global political economy of pharmaceuticals. The IPR regime instituted over the past 20 or so years now encompasses a relatively coherent ensemble of norms, rules, institutions and sets of policies and practices, externalized from the national systems of developed countries. One of the objectives of this volume is to make clearer, in the light of case studies, the centrality of top-down transmission of rules and policies from the global to the domestic level (or from North to South), as well as the responses to them from the South.

TRIPS provides minimum standards for the global regime, which have been overlaid incrementally by other forms of IPR protection and exclusivities (Williams, 2012). Disparate mechanisms are available for the disciplining of recalcitrant members of this regime. These include threats of trade sanctions and power politics, legal challenges to governments for alleged failures to properly enforce patent rights, and even seizures of generic drugs traded internationally (Micara, 2012; Sell, 2011). Conflicts have been played out in many different institutional contexts. For example, the Anti-Counterfeiting Trade Agreement (ACTA), negotiated in secret from 2007, and rejected by the European Parliament in 2012, would, if implemented, provide a means for more stringent IPR enforcement. Public health advocates and generics producers were concerned that ACTA would blur the distinction between piracy/counterfeiting, alleged infringement of patent rights and public health (Love, 2011). Importantly, the global IPR regime also includes a plethora of bilateral and regional free trade agreements (FTAs) entailing so-called TRIPS-plus provisions which have the effect of entrenching and extending patent protection and thus delaying the market entry of cheaper generic drugs (Joint United Nations Programme on HIV/AIDS, 2012).

Any barriers to MNC dominance within the wider IPR regime's provisions is the cause of tensions in the strategic environment, none more so than the compulsory licensing route offered under the TRIPS agreement and subsequent Doha Declaration. A compulsory licence authorizes a third party to manufacture and sell a product without the consent of the patent holder in return for 'adequate' compensation. The Doha Declaration confirmed that '[e]ach member [country] has the right to grant compulsory licences and the freedom to determine the grounds upon which such licences are granted' (World Trade Organization, 2001). Yet the US and other governments in the North exercise strong pressures for compulsory licences to be considered legitimate only in circumstances of national emergency, and as a consequence developing countries have not made extensive use of such licences. Between January 1995 and June 2011 there were only about 24 compulsory licensing episodes in 17 nations, mostly for HIV/AIDS medications (Beall and Kuhn, 2012, p. 1). Notwithstanding such pressures, and further obstacles built into many of the FTAs, compulsory licences are on the policy agenda in many countries and have proven an effective threat to MNCs in some price negotiations, for example in Brazil and Malaysia. The MNCs, however, combat this threat wherever they can, as they did in India in 2012 (see further below).

Above and beyond asserting the right to produce generics for pressing health needs, many now question the basic rationale for the global patent regime. In arguments over IPRs and access to affordable medicines it is endlessly repeated that patent protection is necessary for the financing of the discovery and commercialization of new drugs. Yet many of the new drugs commercialized post-1945 were discovered and introduced before product patents were available in most countries (Boldrin and Levine, 2008; Munos, 2009). It is only in the past 20 years, with TRIPS as a milestone, that the notion of product patents as a basic requirement for pharmaceutical innovation gained the status of common sense, at least in terms of the need for their blanket global availability. Moreover, product patents in this sector are relatively recent even in many developed countries. Japan did not introduce product patents for drugs until 1976, and pharmaceutical powerhouse Switzerland waited until 1977 to introduce patents covering pharmaceutical products. Spain, Portugal, Greece and Norway introduced product patents over drugs as recently as 1992. At the end of the 1980s, at least 40 developing countries, including the most populous, provided no protection for pharmaceuticals (Chien, 2003, p. 864).

Indeed, the unavailability of patents in many countries was not considered important until the 1980s. Then a group of US business groups and corporations, including the big pharma association Pharmaceutical Research and Manufacturers of America (PhRMA), led by Pfizer and Johnson & Johnson, commenced the campaign for the global extension of IPRs (Sell, 2003, p. 107). This campaign succeeded in the reframing of IPRs as a trade issue in the Uruguay Round of General Agreement on Tariffs and Trade (GATT) negotiations which preceded the establishment of the WTO in 1995 (Drahos and Braithwaite, 2001; Sell, 2003). We have therefore taken this date as the start of the post-TRIPS transition to a new legal/political superstructure governing global drug production.

Surging drug markets in the Global South

The MNC business model, which has been premised on profits from sales in developed country markets of patent-protected 'blockbuster' drugs (loosely defined as those generating more than US$1 billion in annual sales), is now faltering. The pipeline of such new products is drying up at the same time as patents expire on major drugs. This is considered in the trade literature to mark 'a fundamental shift in the structure of the research-based industry' (Kaitin and DiMasi, 2011, p. 183). While R&D investments by the world's top 500 pharmaceutical and biotechnology companies are estimated to have increased between 2002 and 2011 by 93 per cent to $133 billion, the number of new drug launches in the US remained stagnant at an annual average of 25 (AstraZeneca, 2011, p. 16). The so-called R&D productivity crisis and declining growth in developed markets are driving consolidation through mergers and acquisitions as well as large-scale plant closures and lay-offs. In 2011 alone, ten top pharma MNCs shed almost 25,000 staff, mostly in developed countries (IMAP, 2012, p. 6). Yet the dominant trend may not be consolidation in the form of giant corporations; *McKinsey Quarterly* reports that 'the number of companies competing for the profit pool has more than doubled' (Hunt et al., 2011, p. 5). Instead, the MNCs are building innovation and production networks linking public research systems, smaller dedicated biotechnology firms and various types of service providers across many locations. The MNCs form the nodal points of these networks, through which promising molecules are in-licensed and some innovation and production activities outsourced. Growing markets for contract research and manufacturing services ('CRAMS') offer opportunities for firms in LMICs, particularly in India and China, to join these networks. In India, recent MNC acquisitions of domestic firms, and a plethora of collaborations and outsourcing arrangements, are a manifestation of this trend (see Chaudhuri in this volume).

The crisis of the established business model explains the MNCs turning to the LMICs for cost savings and because new revenue streams from their growing middle-class markets are becoming too attractive to ignore. Tempest (2010, p. 116) observes that 'Big Pharma have become intrigued by the fact that 88 per cent of the world's pharmaceuticals is shared among only 18 per cent of the world's population.... Here lies a business opportunity.' The world market in 2011 grew by the historically low rate of 4.5 per cent to $839 billion. The US and Western Europe accounted for around 62 per cent of global sales, and per capita spending remains much higher in developed countries than in LMICs. Yet the aggregate growth rate in 'emerging markets' (or 'pharmerging' markets) was 12 per cent in 2011, four times that of 'established markets' at 2.8 per cent (IMS Health data cited in AstraZeneca, 2011). As in so many other areas, China displays particularly strong growth, resulting from the combination of general economic expansion and market growth flowing from the introduction of health insurance for virtually the whole population (see Chee-Ruey Hsieh in this volume).

Emerging markets are becoming more attractive also because of their changing disease burdens through the rise of so-called lifestyle non-communicable diseases such as diabetes, cardiovascular and respiratory conditions, and cancers. For example, '[i]t is estimated that nearly 33% of the world's diabetes patients will come from India and China by 2030, by which date its prevalence in Brazil is expected to have increased by two-thirds' (AstraZeneca, 2011, p. 15). Upper deciles of income earners in these countries are now able to pay 'global' prices for on-patent or branded generic products, while those who remain in the lower deciles cannot afford even basic medicines. What firms would lose by pricing their drugs beyond the reach of the poor, they make up by sales to the rich, avoiding the deadweight losses incurred by excluding the poor priced out of the market (Flynn et al., 2009).

Meanwhile, in the developed countries, public and private insurance providers mandate or provide effective incentives for the use of cheaper generic brands as a means of containing health costs. As patents expire, prices come down radically. In the US—in its own right nearly 40 per cent of the global pharmaceutical market—generics now constitute 80 per cent of the market by volume (AstraZeneca, 2011, p. 18). In the EU and elsewhere, tender-based models of drug procurement deliver a large market share for generics (Kanavos et al., 2009). In contrast, in most LMICs price control systems are patchy, consumers often carry the full cost of medicines, and drug markets are only imperfectly regulated for quality, safety and efficacy. Typically, high-margin 'branded generics', seen as providing quality assurance, predominate (as for example in China); this creates markets quite different from the (sometimes) low-profit commodity generic markets of the US and Europe. Overall, though, the generics segment is expanding across all markets; according to Pfizer, '[b]y 2020, off-patent medicines and their generic equivalents are estimated to account for more than 50 percent of global pharmaceutical sales' (Pfizer, 2012).

Even though most drugs in LMIC markets remain non-patented, profit maximization (and the renewed potential for growth in sales) requires MNCs to reduce the flow of new generics to and from local companies. Thus, the global IPR regime has become their principal strategic tool for achieving this end. For us, TRIPS and associated rights should be considered less an effective incentive structure for innovation than a strategic system of barriers to the entry of competitive alternative product brands. Correa (2011) documents a significant recent proliferation of patents in five developing countries (Argentina, Brazil, Colombia, India and South Africa). Confirming this trend, Eren Vural in this volume reports that in Turkey patent applications submitted by MNCs increased (staggeringly) from 346 in 2004 to 1195 in 2010 (while local pharma applications increased only from 18 to 63). Some analysts identify increased local innovation in emerging economies and view the extension of IPRs as a positive incentive for LMIC innovator firms (Rezaie et al., 2012). This is a promise or theoretical assumption about patents that any LMIC negotiator in the Uruguay Round would recognize, yet, as Correa (2011) shows, patents are issued mostly to foreign companies for incremental modifications of existing drugs, and little innovative activity focused on developing country needs is evident.

Most chapters in this volume provide support for this assessment and for the failure of TRIPS accession to produce the promised leap forward in innovation in the LMIC pharmaceutical sectors. For example, Chaudhuri demonstrates that technologically advanced Indian pharma firms focus on incremental innovation for exports of generics into developed country markets, while efforts to develop new products remain insignificant. The possible exceptions here are the biologics and regenerative medicine sectors of India and China. More generally, to the extent that Indian firms undertake discovery research—and recently such research has been in decline—it is premised on the expectation of outlicensing promising molecules to an MNC. Yet, according to Correa (2011, p. 21), 'most of patenting [in these countries] is motivated by strategic reasons, namely to restrict generic competition, rather than to protect genuine innovations'. Alliances and licensing deals are also cementing this 'stitching up' of innovation.

Desirable though the development of the pharmaceutical industry in the Global South may be, there is a certain perverse feature to such 'progress' as it is currently transpiring: it often services the needs of developed countries and the local middle classes of the affected LMICs, but not necessarily those of the local poor. Some LMIC firms have retargeted production and sales to developed countries, particularly the US market (or home-based markets for lifestyle diseases). This requires investments in quality production facilities for accreditation by external agencies such as the US Food and Drug Administration (FDA), and often in R&D, in order to develop what are only incrementally modified versions of products focused on lucrative disease areas (Bower and Sulej, 2007; Chaudhuri, 2010).

It seems in terms of access to medicines that the new political economy of pharmaceuticals is signalling a looming crisis. While LMIC middle classes are important suppliers of effective demand, there may no longer be the capacity or commercial incentive to produce low value generics for the poor. Thus, for countries such as India and Turkey, it is the value of exports to developed countries (rather than the incentives for genuine innovation ostensibly offered by monopoly patents) that might be the principal reason for pessimism about the future of supply of medicines for the global poor. After all, generics producers are profit maximizers like any other firms, albeit subject to particular market pressures and different national health or international agency purchasing arrangements. This volume is careful to treat these firms as such, and any notion that generic producers are automatically the white knights of access to medicines needs to be quickly disabused. But it is not only companies that play a role in the emerging political economy of pharmaceuticals in the Global South, and the question we now address is how firms as well as states in LMIC countries have responded to pressures from the MNCs and the governments of the North. What has been their response to the strategic environment presaged by TRIPS, and have these responses helped or hindered generic production and access to medicine?

Government strategies

This section provides an overview of conformity and resistance to the new strategic environment on the part of the case study countries and their generic drug sectors. These responses are characterized in some areas by common circumstances and capacities and in others by policy variance or different relative strengths of national economies and pharmaceutical sectors. It is worth noting that, in the terminology of the World Bank, we consider in this volume mainly lower- and upper-middle-income countries (an exception being high-income South Korea) whose typically high economic growth in the last two decades has granted them a degree of international political clout. They are also countries with technological capabilities and pharmaceutical sectors of some significance, and are therefore not completely dependent on foreign sources of essential and other medicines, as is the case with most low- and many lower-middle-income economies.

The majority of the case study countries have individually or collectively sought, by the use of TRIPS flexibilities and other mechanisms available in multilateral fora, to resist the impact of the global IPR regime on their ability to produce or import generics. Their powers of resistance are, of course, limited by their political and economic power, and their policy responses and approaches vary accordingly. It is fair to say, however, that several policies that challenge the norms, rules and basic political economy of the global IPR regime have attained legitimacy as a result of the application of human rights and public goods discourses to the field of health (Williams, 2012).

Yet, successes in changing the rules of the game that characterize the strategic environment—as with the Doha Declaration of 2001—have been tempered by failures and conformity to yet other TRIPS-plus IPR rules and instruments. Even countries such as Brazil and India, which have been most successful in insulating their populations from the negative effects of the IPR regime, have proven susceptible to pressures to conform to the wider system.

Clearly, government policy has an impact on local generics sectors, in terms of providing a legal environment and the conditions under which MNCs and patented drugs enter national markets. Generic firms are also important actors in their own right. This volume and other studies have shown that the generic sectors in the Global South are very different in terms of size, range of medicines produced, orientation to export markets and the extent to which they support domestic health needs (Kaplan and Laing, 2005). Differences are apparent in terms of firms embarking on innovation, and in capacities for the production of APIs. Many countries, having generic sectors with only basic capabilities, concentrate on reformulations and packaging of basic essential drugs (Correa, 2011; see also Kaplan and Laing, 2005).

The capacity of domestic pharmaceutical companies and the size and weight of national markets also shape the ability of governments to resist external pressures (Yu, 2008). In particular, this is an acute problem in countries with little or no manufacturing, as rules for compulsory licensing for imports and parallel importation are complex and intimidating. This creates dependence and vulnerability with respect to drug supply and very limited space for strategies of resistance.

The case study countries have all contributed to the new political economy of pharmaceuticals presaged by TRIPS. In doing so, they have taken into account health needs and crises (especially HIV/AIDS) and strategies for economic and scientific–technological development. Responses to the wider strategic environment do not reflect passivity in relation to the structural and relational power of those agents which have assiduously promoted the global IPR regime, though resistance in areas such as IPR enforcement has been weak, at least until recently (Yu, 2011). In fact, there are multiple instances of willing adoption and enforcement of TRIPS-compliant standards or other market exclusivities. Pakistan, South Korea, Malaysia (with some exceptions) and Turkey are 'TRIPS-maximalist' actors, favouring a strong version of the regime with little use of flexibilities. Yet, when one considers the diversity of policy responses across our case study countries (and in the wider LMIC community), particular strategic actions and policy responses often appear ambiguous or contradictory. A country such as Malaysia may at one juncture enact a compulsory licence for an HIV/AIDS medication, as it did in 2003–2004, but also participate in the negotiations for the Trans Pacific Partnership Agreement. Malaysia is also engaged in FTA negotiations with both the US (as of 2011) and the EU, where measures to forgo the right to such licences are on the agenda (Godwin, 2011). Other instances of similar schizophrenic policy can be found in Indonesia, and even in China and India.

It is clear from many instances of conformity and alignment that domestic politics weigh heavily, as do the strategic preferences of local generic sectors towards national IPR standards. Thus, external pressures—as described, for example, in Deere's (2009) analysis of the US Special 301 Report process—do not always explain conformity and alignment with the global IPR regime. In this volume, we find examples of domestic sources of 'TRIPS maximalism' in Turkey, China, Brazil (though not in relation to medicines), and increasingly in India. Here we explore contradictory strategic and policy responses across our case study countries with the aim of imposing some conceptual and analytic clarity upon the diverse signals and strategies present.

Conformity and alignment

Many studies have been undertaken of the health implications of bilateral and regional TRIPS-plus measures in different regions, for example El Said (2005; M. K. El Said, 2010) on the Middle East and Maghreb, Vivas-Eugui (2003) on Latin America, and Lindstrom (2010) and Sell (2011) on the Asia-Pacific region. It is beyond the remit of this introduction to detail the TRIPS-plus measures adopted in the case study countries. However, some of the more deleterious can be listed to illustrate that the IPR-ratchet continues to be applied.

In China, Article 35 of the Implementing Regulations of the Drug Administration Law 2002 provides six years of data exclusivity from the date of marketing approval. Data exclusivity refers to the right to protect or not disclose publicly the pre-clinical and clinical trial data that originator companies must submit to national drug regulatory authorities for drug approval. Generic companies rely on such data to demonstrate the bioequivalence of their alternative brands, thereby avoiding lengthy duplicate trials to prove safety and efficacy. By permitting data exclusivity for six years, China has slowed down the ability of Chinese generic firms to launch competitor drugs after the expiry of patent protection.

Korea is another of our case study countries providing for this type of TRIPS-plus provision. Data exclusivity was enacted in 2009 in Korea in the context of an FTA with the EU. More recently, as a consequence of the FTA with the US which took effect in 2012, Korea changed the Korean Pharmaceutical Affairs Act to include a patent term restoration provision (in effect a patent term extension) of up to five years, as well as data exclusivity of five years for pharmaceuticals. Korea has also adopted a form of 'patent linkage', that is, marketing approval is provided only if evidence is presented of no breach of patent rights. There are now closer procedural ties between patent filing, the IP office and the Korea Food and Drug Administration, whereby any generic submitted for approval will automatically be sent to the patentee for consent (Lee and Choi, 2012). The US–Korea FTA also triggered Korea's joining the Trans-Pacific Partnership Agreement (TPP) negotiations, which include US proposals for extending patent terms, restrictions on pre-grant patent opposition, longer patent terms in exchange for marketing and registration in developing countries, new customs and other enforcement measures (for drug shipments), and government drug pricing restrictions (Médecins Sans Frontières, 2012).

Korea is joined in the TRIPS-plus TPP negotiations by Malaysia, which is also engaged in FTA negotiations with the EU, where data exclusivity limited to 'less than five years' is on the table. Malaysia has in the past shown willingness to resist patents on drugs by means of compulsory licensing. Both the TPP and the EU negotiations are subject to significant opposition. Yet Malaysia in 2011 caved in to US pressures and introduced five years' data exclusivity for new chemical entities and three years for second indications of a registered drug product (see Hassali et al. in this volume).

Turkey has proven almost completely incapable of defending its generic sector and public health in the face of EU pressures to conform to European TRIPS-plus standards, the most significant of which was the adoption in 2005 of a data exclusivity term of six years. More widely, levels of protection for IPRs in Turkey are generally TRIPS-plus, and weak standards of patentability allow patenting of incremental innovation (see Eren-Vural in this volume). The source of much of Turkey's passivity with respect to TRIPS-plus measures appears to have been twofold. First, we have seen regular deployment of the carrot of EU accession as a means to defuse recalcitrance and resistance. Second, Turkey's domestic pharmaceutical sector is itself bifurcated along lines of export orientation and basic drug supply for local need, and the former group of companies, along with the MNCs, have held sway (Eran-Vural herein).

South Africa, an early resister of TRIPS, recently entered regional trade negotiations with the US under its membership of the Southern African Customs Union. The talks have, thankfully, stalled. However, in key areas such as disclosure standards and procedural requirements for the granting of compulsory licensing, South African patent law is stricter than required by TRIPS (see Grey and Vawda herein). More worryingly for patent standards, South Africa has no system for patent opposition and no system for prior substantive examination of patent applications. Correa (2011) and Grey and Vawda (herein) note that this has engendered a low standard of patentability and a veritable open door for incremental patenting as well as so-called Markush claims, in which a single patent based on a general formula allows coverage of multiple molecules (Correa, 2011, pp. 12–13). Moreover, the South African process for granting patents appears to lack transparency, which compounds the basic problem of not providing for prior examination of patent applications. Unfortunately, almost all TRIPS-compliant African countries also lack a system of prior examination of patent applications (Global Commission on HIV and the Law, 2012), making the continent a free-for-all for abusive patenting practices.

More problematic still is the failure of many LMICS to avail themselves of the full transitional period for TRIPS compliance. Whereas India deferred TRIPS compliance until 2005, and used the transition period to promote a remarkable period of growth in its generic sector, Brazil, South Africa, Pakistan, Cuba, South Korea, China and many other LMICs introduced TRIPS-compliant patent laws prior to the 2005 deadline (Deere, 2009). We also find reluctance in all our case study countries to take full advantage of available TRIPS flexibilities, or the development of rigorous standards of patentability (Hermann, 2011; UNAIDS/WHO/UNDP, 2011). This failure is exactly the reason why UNCTAD and the United Nations Development Programme (UNDP) provide programmes for training LMIC governments in the use of TRIPS flexibilities. As discussed below, however, there are indications that compulsory licensing may at long last emerge as a major strategy of resistance.

Even in ostensibly 'TRIPS-minimalist' countries, there is depressing evidence of conformity and alignment on a legal and technical level. Correa (2011) shows that the MNCs are employing patent and litigation strategies in the emerging economies of Columbia, Argentina, Brazil, South Africa and India. As already noted, there was a substantial increase in foreign patenting activities in each of these countries with a commensurate rise in patent litigation (as is also the case in China; see Chee-Ruey in this volume). Yet higher degrees of compliance and IPR policy alignment are apparent in South Korea, Indonesia and Turkey, which have implemented a broad range of IPR-related policies. If policy conformity is not wholesale, then it is present as an incremental process in our case study countries. As Susan Sell, Peter Drahos and others have argued, such strengthening and deepening of the IPR regime occurs over a number of levels (multilateral or bilateral) and through forum shifting over a plethora of institutions and policy initiatives (Drahos and Braithwaite, 2004; Helfer, 2004; Sell, 2010, 2011). The upward IPR ratchet involves a creeping process of implementation, enforcement measures or other changes. In this sense, as Susan Sell has bluntly put it, 'TRIPS was never enough' for those who sought to advance the global regime and curtail generic entry (Sell, 2011). The initial WTO regime is considered incomplete and ineffective to the extent that it has left open lacunae and policy space for LMICs to continue the production of a wide range of generic medicines, including drugs still under patent in developed markets. TRIPS was not enough in the sense that there were still higher levels of protection and enforcement to be gained and longer durations for monopolies to be enjoyed, with TRIPS seen as the baseline to be extended in complex and technically obtuse areas of IPR law (Sell, 2011; Yu, 2011).

Alignment and conformity are also the result of developed country governments and MNCs exploiting the weaknesses of poorly resourced technical capacities in LMIC countries. Correa (2001, 2011) has shown how low national patent standards encourage incremental patenting and impede generic competition. For him, the right to define the criteria of patentability (novelty, inventive step and industrial application) is a key TRIPS flexibility that developing countries have largely failed to use. Other domestic weaknesses are common, such as poorly resourced patent offices which are often unable or unqualified to examine the volume of pharmaceutical patent applications enabled by TRIPS accession. Moreover, evidence from Turkey and India suggests that some LMIC sectors are becoming polarized between exporters/innovators and traditional generic firms. This creates opportunities for the formation of lobbying coalitions between foreign MNCs and pharmaceutical associations, their local counterparts and globally aligned segments of domestic industry. Together they supply a push towards alignment and higher standards of IPRs (Vural and Chaudhuri herein; see also Baker and Avafia, 2011, p. 13). Additional pressures result from other tools of 'soft diplomacy' such as the training of judiciaries and patent offices by foreign counterparts under bilateral or World Intellectual Property Organization (WIPO)-led technical assistance programmes (Matthews and Munoz-Tellez, 2006; Musungu and Dutfield, 2003). The use of 'hard diplomacy' has also been persistent, as witnessed in the sanctioning and disciplining function of the Office of the United States Trade Representative's (USTR) 301 watch lists and threats of sanctions under the WTO dispute system (Muzaka, 2011, p. 68).

Despite the upward-ratcheting of the IPR regime described above, there is also evidence of sustained resistance. First, we see areas where resistance has been collective, involving many of our case study countries. Second, we see the majority of our case study countries prepared to individually enact or consider compulsory licences and other TRIPS flexibilities. Third, we find strategies by which countries continue to promote domestic generic sectors and the funding and encouragement of the wider use of generics in national health systems, which is an element discussed in the majority of our case study country chapters. Here we concentrate on the first two of these strategies of resistance.

Strategies of resistance

Amid the gloom of conformity, there are grounds for optimism. Collaborative South–South strategies of resistance to the IPR regime have occurred intermittently, yet have been persistent in the post-TRIPS era. Indeed, hard-line early resisters to the regime, most prominently Brazil and India, played the leading role in the Uruguay Round TRIPS negotiations, which resulted in loopholes and flexibilities being present in the final agreement (Drahos and Braithwaite, 2002; Watal, 2001). More recently, resistance has been coordinated by Brazil, India, South Africa and, lately, China, which have spearheaded broader constellations of states seeking better access to medicines, such as between members of the G20 and the G21 and the Group of 77. Major emerging economies with the most advanced pharmaceutical sectors have shown significant economic and political resistance to the global IPR regime (Ganji, 2011). Sizeable local industries and huge internal markets arguably make these countries less vulnerable to pressure and less dependent on the MNCs for imports of drugs. As Peter Yu (2008, p. 358) notes, MNCs and developed country governments, recognizing the changing geopolitical and economic terrain, are less likely to challenge strategies of resistance emanating from the biggest of the emerging economies, especially when access to their pharmaceutical markets is an attractive business opportunity. However, it is possible that their market size and obstinacy also make them a target for disciplining actions, given the economic and political imperatives to bring them into line.

LMICs have frequently challenged aspects of the global IPR regime in multiple fora. Challenges to the IPR regime's effects on health have been lodged not only in the World Health Organization (WHO), but also under both the Convention on Biological Diversity and international human rights bodies. Challenges in such fora, in turn, facilitate the recasting and reframing of the terms of the patent debate from questions of private rights to questions of human rights and public goods (Helfer, 2004; Odell and Sell, 2003; Sell, 2006).

The principal collective strategy of resistance has emerged at the level of WTO Ministerial meetings and, more recently, in the WTO-TRIPS Council and the WTO dispute settlement system (Yu, 2011). Within the WTO system, LMICs have reaffirmed the TRIPS flexibilities for generic production and importation. At the conclusion of the Uruguay Round, many LMICs were already well aware of the relationship between TRIPS, patents and access to medicines. The most obvious reason was that ARV treatment of victims of the HIV/AIDS pandemic would be impossible with on-patent prices of circa US$10,000 per annum per patient (Waning et al., 2010). When the South African government passed its 1997 Medicines and Related Substances Control Amendment Act, which allowed the parallel importation of generic medicines such as ARVs, the MNCs responded with legal action between 1998 and 2000. This case involved 39 companies claiming breach of the TRIPS rules. Also, the USTR included South Africa on its 301 Special Watch List and suspended access to the Generalized System of Preferences (GSP) which provides duty-free entry for a certain range of products from designated beneficiary countries. Due to international pressure by a new Access Coalition of non-governmental organizations (NGOs) (including Médecins Sans Frontières (MSF), Oxfam and Consumer Project on Technology), patient activist groups (such as the Treatment Action Campaign and ACT UP) and LMIC governments, the case was abandoned and sanctions removed (Sell, 2002).

The abandonment of the South African case, and the collapse of the 1999 WTO Seattle Ministerial Meeting following unprecedented developing country solidarity and public protests, enabled LMICs to better prepare for the Doha Ministerial Meeting of 2001. In the period before Doha in 2001, the US had also put particular pressure on Brazil, Argentina and Thailand over separate attempts to use TRIPS flexibilities with respect to generic production or data exclusivity (Baker and Avafia, 2011; Kohr, 2009). The Doha Declaration, however, confirmed the flexibilities in the TRIPS agreement that allowed countries to meet public health needs. Sadly, the Declaration failed to clarify TRIPS Article 30—the basis of exceptions to patent rights—with particular reference to restrictions to the flexibilities present in Article 31(f) (Baker, 2004; Correa, 2002; Muzaka, 2011).

Of particular importance here were attempts to affirm the right to enact compulsory licences for the purposes of export of generics to countries lacking manufacturing capacity, under Paragraph 6 of the Declaration. This particular right was not properly clarified in the Declaration, or in subsequent attempts to amend TRIPS and establish such rights in 2003 and 2005 (at the Hong Kong Ministerial meeting; see especially Muzaka, 2011). To date, compulsory licences for export to countries lacking pharmaceutical capacity have been used only once, in a case involving a Canadian licence for export of generic ARVs to Rwanda in 2007. The amendment to TRIPS itself (under the so-called Article 31bis), proposed to the WTO as a solution to the Paragraph 6 problem, has not yet been ratified by a quorum of members. In fact, the whole environment for use of compulsory licences under TRIPS rules is characterized by complexity and obfuscation, and ultimately subject to the same pressures and constraints to which the Doha Declaration sought to respond (Baker, 2004; Baker and Avafia, 2011).

Nevertheless, the loose coalition of LMICs built around the Doha Declaration remains a thorn in the side of the global IPR regime and its promoters. At least four of our case study countries have been important participants in coalitions of resistance. Notably, Brazil was a leader in the initial activities of the Group of 20 Developing Countries, and South Africa and Egypt, with the African Group, have been prominent at the WTO and WIPO. Expertise and advocacy in the area of trade law and patenting has also expanded hugely in many LMICs, particularly in Brazil and India. Yu (2011) notes that many LMICs have become more active in WTO disputes relating to IPR-linked pharmaceutical issues. He suggests 2010 as a turning point for renewed resistance within the WTO TRIPS Council and the dispute system, with a dispute on the issue of Dutch/EU seizures of generics in transit as its catalyst (see also Micara, 2012). China also appears to have properly entered the fray, after being challenged on its IPR enforcement record in a WTO dispute, and that country now seems ready to respond both within the WTO and in terms of a new stand on the issue of compulsory licences (see below).

WIPO has become an unexpected institutional site for LMIC resistance to drug patents (and biodiversity and copyright issues), most notably in successfully instigating WIPO's Development Agenda process. Brazil, Argentina, South Africa and Egypt led the charge from 2004. With support from a coalition of international NGOs and other LMICs, they achieved the formal adoption of the Development Agenda in 2007. A range of actions and initiatives have been formalized under provisions for 'Developing Tools for Access to Patent Information' and 'Intellectual Property and the Public Domain'. The achievement of the Development Agenda has been to bring about a normative shift in this policy arena: it is now formally recognized that IPRs should promote the welfare of the citizens of the Global South.

Collective resistance has also been mobilized around the WHO, a process that commenced in 1998 with the publication of the *Revised Drug Strategy* (World Health Organization, 1998). A coalition of NGOs, Brazil, South Africa and other LMICs ensured that the strategy included reference to TRIPS flexibilities. A controversial WHO guide to the public health impact of TRIPS was published in the same year (Velasquez and Boulet, 1999). These initiatives were followed in the early 2000s by several critical reports, notably that authored by Carlos Correa in 2002, which focused on the negative impact of bilateral FTAs on the use of TRIPS flexibilities and the ratchet effect of TRIPS-plus provisions (Correa, 2002). From this emerged a momentum for increased access to affordable essential medicines which resulted in the WHO establishing the Commission on Intellectual Property Rights, Innovation and Public Health in 2003. The Commission produced its final report in 2006 (Commission on Intellectual Property Rights, 2006). This report included a huge amount of analytical work on neglected disease areas, innovation, technology transfer and solutions to incentives for innovation, pharmaceutical market and IPR-related problems. The more practical and policy-orientated Intergovernmental Working Group on Public Health Innovation followed next, instigated by the WHO. Its final 2008 report inspired the landmark *Strategy and Plan of Action* (World Health Assembly, 2008). Adopted at the 61st World Health Assembly, this resolution included recommendations on assessment of R&D needs with respect to developing countries and neglected diseases; the need to build alternative pharmaceutical R&D capacities and secure sustainable financing mechanisms to incentivize research; the need to accelerate technology transfer, and monitor and evaluate progress to those ends. The Intergovernmental Working Group provides a normative, ethical and practical touchstone for LMIC engagement with the strategy as it unfolds.

Finally, LMIC collective action has revolved around recasting the terms of debate about access to medicines in terms of basic human rights, which should trump claims to intellectual property. Brazil has been instrumental in garnering wider LMIC support for the UN Covenant on Economic, Social and Cultural Rights (CESCR) and for the WHO joint statement in 2000 which affirmed the 'right to the highest attainable standard of health' (Baker and Avafia, 2011; Committee on Economic Social and Cultural Rights, 2000; Muzaka, 2011). This was followed in the same year by a resolution of the UN Sub-Commission on the Protection and Promotion of Human Rights which stated that TRIPS conflicted with the right to health. Other statements by human rights bodies followed in 2003, with more direct emphasis on the negative impact of IPRs on access to ARVs (Third International Consultation on HIV/AIDS and Human Rights, 2003). In tandem with such resolutions at the multilateral level, South Africa, Brazil and other LMICs have incorporated human rights-based obligations to provide access to medicines and health in their constitutions. In several countries human rights to health have formed the basis of lawsuits against governments for their failure to provide sufficient access (Hogerzeil et al., 2006).

Compulsory licences

Compulsory licensing has figured on the policy agenda in several of the case study countries. Government threats to use compulsory licences, and sometimes even mere consideration of the possibility of such licensing, can on occasion be sufficient to win such concessions from MNCs as price reductions or voluntary licences (Beall and Kuhn, 2012). Compulsory licences are possibly the most controversial of the TRIPS flexibilities, and are likely to be the most significant means available to LMICs of securing generic versions of on-patent drugs in the near future. Under Article 31 of TRIPS, WTO members are able to enact compulsory licensing in cases of national or extreme emergency or for public non-commercial use, subject to requirements such as prior negotiation with the patent holder and adequate remuneration.

Compulsory licences can be awarded to firms, or can be issued for purposes of public non-commercial use. While Article 31(f) of TRIPS limits such licences for the purpose 'predominantly' of the supply of the domestic market, a great deal of effort and political will has been expended in securing the right to export compulsory licensed drugs to third party states with no domestic manufacturing capacities. Analyses of the fallout and nuances of compulsory licensing under TRIPS are legion (Abbott and Reichman, 2007; Ho, 2008; Reichman, 2009). We turn instead to how and when licences have been used as strategies of resistance in the case study countries, before offering some conclusions on their utility and likely future uses for ensuring generic production and access to medicines.

In 2001 Brazil initiated the first of a wave of compulsory licensing actions by declaring its intention to license patents on two ARV drugs held by Merck and Roche (Efavirenz and Nelfinavir, respectively). The compulsory licensing threat became credible when a local government-owned laboratory proved to have the capacity to import APIs and manufacture these drugs. In order not to lose the largest market for anti-AIDS medicines in the developing world, Merck and Roche accepted significant price cuts. Between 2005 and 2007, a similar approach was employed with regard to Abbott's drug Kaletra and Gilead's Viread: in both cases securing almost a 50 per cent price reduction. Finally, in 2007, Brazil enacted a five-year compulsory licence on Efavirenz, the first issued in Latin America. This step was taken, however, only when an acceptable discount could not be obtained from Merck. The generic version of Efavirenz was initially imported from India, and Merck was paid royalties of 1.5 per cent (Sweet herein; see also Mello e Souza, 2013).

In 2001 South Africa followed its renowned competition law action against ARV prices with threats of compulsory licences on eight ARV drugs (Love, 2007). The compulsory licences were denied by the competition regulator, but the threat was sufficient to win both voluntary licences and substantial price discounting. In Malaysia in 2003, compulsory licences were issued for two years for the import of generic ARVs from India for government use, and the suppliers also cut their prices substantially (Correa, 2011; Kohr, 2009). In 2004, Indonesia, by way of a Presidential Decree, issued a compulsory licence to the local firm Kimia Farma for the manufacture of generic versions of two ARVs. Again, price reductions were dramatic. A second Presidential Decree was issued in 2007 for Efavirenz (Hanim & Jhamtani, 2006).

In Korea a civil society and medical professional coalition filed in 2002 for a compulsory licence on the leukaemia drug Glivec, and in 2008 a similar petition was submitted to the Korean authorities for a licence on an HIV drug. In both instances the Korean Patent Office rejected the claims. Elsewhere in Asia, Thailand set the pace, issuing three compulsory licences in 2007 (for AIDS medications sold by Merck and Abbott and a cardiovascular drug sold by Sanofi-Aventis). In 2008, Thailand issued licences on four cancer drugs. Thailand's licensing of drugs for non-communicable diseases set an important precedent by resisting strong pressures from companies and the EU and US not to break the unwritten rule that compulsory licences are only really permissible in the case of HIV/AIDS (Ho, 2008, pp. 167–72).

Despite these and a limited number of other compulsory licences, this strategy has not yet acquired sufficient momentum to seriously shift market dynamics in the Global South (Kohr, 2009; Love, 2007; Reichman, 2009). After a peak between 2003 and 2005, the practice has tailed off, with Thailand responsible for most compulsory licences since then. Only in the case of Rwanda and Canada have compulsory licences been issued for importation to a country with no manufacturing capacity. Compulsory licensing activity remains predominantly associated with ARVs: nearly two-thirds of all cases. It is almost as if ARVs alone are seen as qualifying for exemption from patent rights, and then only in narrowly circumscribed circumstances (see Beall and Kuhn, 2012).

Two events in 2012 may offer ground for new optimism for the compulsory licensing strategy. These involve the two most powerful LMIC economies, India and China, at a time when they seemed content to drift into alignment with the global IPR regime. In March 2012 a compulsory licence was issued in India for the very first time. This compulsory licence was awarded to the Hyderabad-based generic company Natco Pharma, for the production and supply of the patented anti-cancer drug sorafenib, marketed by Bayer as Nexavar. The price of Bayer's version of this drug was Rs 280,000 a month (circa US$5000 in 2012 prices), an astronomical figure for almost all Indian households. Natco committed to selling the same drug at 3 per cent of this price, while paying a licence fee and still expecting to make a profit. The licence was issued essentially on the grounds of Bayer's exorbitant price. Bayer also did not manufacture the drug in India, and imported in such small volumes that only a tiny fraction of potential patients could benefit. This decision sets a precedent both in India and in other countries of the South for possible compulsory licences on other patented products sold at unaffordable prices (Srinivasan, 2012). The Controller General of Patents, Designs and Trademarks, P. H. Kurian, concluded, just prior to retiring from the office, that the drug 'was not bought by the public due to only one reason, that is, its price was not reasonably affordable to them'. Natco Pharma had since signalled its intention to apply for compulsory licences on other exorbitantly priced drugs (Pilla, 2012). Testifying before the House Subcommittee on Intellectual Property on 27 June 2012, the Deputy Director of the US Patent and Trademark Office asserted that US officials are in response 'constantly being there on the ground' pressuring the Indian government to desist from compulsory licensing (YouTube, 2012). After all, such intimidation is pivotal to the interface between the strategic environment promoted by developed countries and LMICs such as those studied in this volume.

Hard on the heels of events in India, China also announced in 2012 that it intends to complete the ongoing process of overhauling its IPR laws to facilitate more widespread use of compulsory licensing. It is reported that the State Intellectual Property Office has produced a revised version of laws under Measures for the Compulsory Licensing for Patent Implementation (coming into force in May 2012). China has apparently prepared meticulously for the change in laws, consulting with Thai counterparts, and is already in the process of considering compulsory licences on several ARVs (see e.g. Lyn, 2012). If India and China are prepared to lead the way in the use of compulsory licences as tools of resistance to the IPR regime, other LMICs may be able to follow that lead. While limited in use to date, the compulsory licensing route has the potential to be the undoing of the global patent regime on drugs, and the means by which generic production for health needs is reasserted.

Conclusion

The chapters which follow highlight how LMICs have found themselves in a changed strategic environment for drug production and consumption 15 years into the post-TRIPS era. Authors detail how TRIPS has been adopted in national systems and the major flashpoints and repercussions that have ensued with regard to domestic production and access to medicines. However, in keeping with the arguments of this introductory chapter, it is clear that IPRs and related rights constitute only one component of the new political economy of pharmaceuticals in the case study countries. First, in particular, national health and medicines policies, in conjunction with generic sector profiles, contribute to a political economy which is still in transition. Furthermore, while it is clear that these dynamics and population health/medicines needs have contributed to instances in which our LMICs have been prepared to resist the pressures to conform to the global IPR regime, it is also certain that the incremental strengthening and deepening of national IPR systems constitute the dominant, if depressing, trend. TRIPS was never enough, and the process of regime consolidation is not over. LMICs and local generic sectors form part of that consolidation process, either by omission or by commission, with respect to their policy choices, vulnerability to pressures or basic reorientation to global markets.

Second, it is clear that the process of legal and policy consolidation and alignment is multilevelled and multinodal. TRIPS is no longer the sole cause of the IPR upward-ratchet (if it ever was), and chapter authors document LMIC engagement in negotiations and agreements at bilateral, regional and multilateral levels. TRIPS was a baseline and not an end point, and the sources of the upward-ratchet are so diverse as to potentially obfuscate comparison (Sell, 2011). Pressure is constant and changing, resulting from FTAs,

ACTA, TPP, WIPO and a plethora of measures such as technical assistance programmes and good old-fashioned lobbying. Domestic firms in a number of countries (such as India and Turkey) are also increasingly vocal in their support of stronger rights and more assiduous enforcement of drug patent standards. Weaknesses in domestic legislation and patent examining bodies also exacerbate vulnerability to erosion of policy space for generic production and use. While comparison is, therefore, difficult, it should not obscure commonality in terms of the general and worrying direction of policy change.

At the same time as the global IPR regime has strengthened and deepened, both the industry and market structures for drugs (generic and innovator) have changed. Generics remain vital sources of essential medicines in all our LMICs, a pattern echoed in yet other developing and, indeed, developed countries. The MNC drive into LMIC markets (via market entry, joint ventures and acquisitions), and the orientation of many domestic firms to niche developed country markets, is in tension with the ongoing need for generics for the poor. MNCs, in tandem with these strategies, also seek to tie up (or stitch up) innovation that is emerging in the most advanced of the developing countries, while at the same time seeking monopolies over innovator drugs where possible or, as Correa (2011) has shown, over what are often very spurious forms of innovation. In each of our countries (with the exception of Cuba) these alliances and corporate strategies are clearly present, but it is in India and China that new alliances and patenting strategies are most troubling, not least because of the early signals that these countries have the ability to develop genuinely innovative national pharmaceutical sectors.

Pessimism should be properly tempered by more optimistic signals. As we have detailed above, resistance to the new political economy of pharmaceuticals is ongoing and equally multilevelled and complex as are the sources of pressures to conform and align. Two decades ago, few would have predicted the economic rise of several of the LMICS studied here. It is clear that all these states have made policy moves to insulate their populations from some of the most negative effects of the global IPR regime, especially in terms of access to HIV/AIDS treatments, and to lead or participate in alliances to roll back the IPR regime at critical junctures. The willingness to resist has often emerged from the foregrounding of domestic health needs, medicines policies, public pressure or constitutional commitments to provide health and drug access. These have in turn been successfully externalized by LMICs in terms of multilateral policies that have shifted the normative terrain by which drug patenting is framed and discussed, and this has produced genuine pro-access global health policies such as the Doha Declaration. If the Brazil, Russia, India, China and South Africa (BRICS) members of our volume are prepared to take the lead in the use of compulsory licences and other instruments they might make a very real difference and tip the balance against blanket global drug patenting. It is also clear that they are not alone, and academics (such as ourselves), civil society, health and medical professionals, and policy makers all now recognize that there is a problem with the global and diverse national political economies of drugs, and that the global patent system is deeply dysfunctional with respect to innovation and price. Nonetheless, that system is presently the only real 'system' in place, operating globally to extend the scope and scale of monopolies and to impede access to affordable medicines. Radical change will be difficult, but it is not impossible to envisage, especially given the scale of manifest needs for wider availability of medicines even in the richest of the LMICs, and for wider supply for those countries which cannot manufacture any category of medicines whatsoever. Signs present in China and India at the time of writing indicate that these countries may be about to mount a challenge to the new political economy of drugs presaged by TRIPS. The authors in this volume would collectively support and encourage any movement in this direction.

Finally, and on a much more grounded level, we hope that this volume will help provide badly needed empirical detail about how different countries have responded to the new political economy of pharmaceuticals. The details are slowly being filled in, and this volume contributes to joining the dots between the global IPR regime, national health systems and generic producers, legal options and strategies, price controls and external constraints, and power political pressures. Hopefully, this volume will prove helpful for public health advocates, academic analysts and policy makers alike.

References

Abbott, F. M. and J. H. Reichman (2007) 'The Doha Round's Public Health Legacy: Strategies for the Production and Diffusion of Patented Medicines under the Amended TRIPS Provisions', *Journal of International Economic Law* 10, 921–87.

AstraZeneca (2011) 'Annual Report and Form 20-F Information', Retrieved from http://www.astrazeneca-annualreports.com/2011/documents/pdfs/annual_report_pdf_entire.pdf, date accessed 20 October 2012.

Baker, B. K. (2004) *Processes and Issues for Improving Access to Medicines Willingness and Ability to Utilise TRIPS Flexibilities in Non-Producing Countries*, Issues paper—Access to medicines (London: DFID Health Systems Resource Centre).

Baker, B. K. and T. Avafia (2011) 'The Evolution of IPRs from Humble Beginnings to the Modern Day TRIPS-Plus Era: Implications for Treatment Access', Working Paper prepared for the Third Meeting of the Technical Advisory Group of the Global Commission on HIV and the Law, 7–9 July 2011, Global Commission on HIV and the Law.

Ballance, R. H., J. Pogány, and H. Forstner (1992) *The World's Pharmaceutical Industries: An International Perspective on Innovation, Competition and Policy* (Aldershot: Edward Elgar).

Beall, R. and R. Kuhn (2012) 'Trends in Compulsory Licensing of Pharmaceuticals since the Doha Declaration: A Database Analysis', *PLoS Med* 9, e1001154.

Boldrin, M. and D. K. Levine (2008) 'Against Intellectual Monopoly', http://www.dklevine.com/general/intellectual/againstfinal.htm, date accessed 11 September 2012.

Bower, D. J. and J. C. Sulej (2007) 'The Indian Challenge: The Evolution of a Successful New Global Strategy in the Pharmaceutical Industry', *Technology Analysis & Strategic Management* 19, 611–24.

Chaudhuri, S. (2010) 'R&D for Development of New Drugs for Neglected Diseases in India', *International Journal of Technology and Globalisation* 5, 61–75.

Chien, C. (2003) 'Cheap Drugs at What Price to Innovation: Does Compulsory Licensing of Pharmaceuticals Hurt Innovation?', *Berkeley Technology Law Journal* 18, 853–907.

Committee on Economic Social and Cultural Rights (2000) *The Right to the Highest Attainable Standard of Health (Art. 12)* (Geneva: United Nations High Commissioner for Human rights).

Correa, C. (2002) *Implications of the Doha Declaration on the TRIPS Agreement and Public Health* (Geneva: World Health Organization).

Correa, C. M. (2001) 'The WTO Dispute Settlement Mechanism: TRIPS Rulings and the Developing Countries', *The Journal of World Intellectual Property* 4, 251–5.

Correa, C. M. (2011) *Pharmaceutical Innovation, Incremental Patenting and Compulsory Licensing*, Research Paper 41 (Geneva: South Centre).

Deere, C. (2009) *The Implementation Game: The TRIPS Agreement and the Global Politics of Intellectual Property Reform in Developing Countries* (Oxford: Oxford University Press).

Drahos, P. and J. Braithwaite (2001) 'Intellectual Property, Corporate Strategy, Globalisation: TRIPS in Context', *Wisconsin International Law Journal* 19, 451–80.

Drahos, P. and J. Braithwaite (2002) *Information Feudalism: Who Owns the Knowledge Economy?* (London: Earthscan).

Drahos, P. and J. Braithwaite (2004) *Who Owns the Knowledge Economy: Political Organising Behind TRIPS*, Briefing Paper 32 (London: The Corner House).

El Said, M. (2005) 'The Road from TRIPS-Minus, to TRIPS, to TRIPS-Plus: Implications of IPRs for the Arab World', *The Journal of World Intellectual Property* 8, 53–65.

El Said, M. K. (2010) *Public Health Related TRIPS-Plus Provisions in Bilateral Trade Agreements: A Policy Guide for Negotiators and Implementers in the Eastern Mediterranean Region* (Cairo: World Health Organization).

Flynn, S., A. Hollis, and M. Palmedo (2009) 'An Economic Justification for Open Access to Essential Medicine Patents in Developing Countries', *The Journal of Law, Medicine & Ethics* 37, 184–208.

Ganji, S. K. (2011) 'TRIPS Implementation and Strategic Health Policy in India and Brazil', *Josef Korbel Journal of Advanced International Studies* 3, 29–58.

Global Commission on HIV and the Law (2012) *Regional Issues Brief: Intellectual Property Rights and Access to Medicines. For the Africa Regional Dialogue of the Global Commission on HIV and the Law* (New York: United Nations Development Programme).

Godwin, J. (2011) *Regional Issues Brief: Intellectual Property Rights and Access to Medicines* (New York: Global Commission on HIV and the Law).

Hanim, L. and H. Jhamtani (2006) 'Indonesia: Manufacturing Generic Aids Medicines under the "Government Use" Approach', *Third World Resurgence 196*. http://www.twnside.org.sg/title2/twr196.htm, date accessed 12 March 2012.

Helfer, L. R. (2004) 'Regime Shifting: The TRIPS Agreement and New Dynamics of International Intellectual Property Lawmaking', *Yale Journal of International Law* 29, 1–84.

Hermann, R. M. (2011) 'Developing Countries Are Not Making the Most of TRIPS Flexibilities Because of Political Pressure', *British Medical Journal* 343, d7706.

Ho, C. M. (2008) 'On Breaking Patents: Separating Strands of Fact from Fiction under TRIPS', http://works.bepress.com/cynthia_ho/2/, date accessed 1 August 2012.

Hogerzeil, H. V., M. Samson, J. V. Casanovas, and L. Rahmani-Ocora (2006) 'Is Access to Essential Medicines as Part of the Fulfilment of the Right to Health Enforceable through the Courts?' *The Lancet* 368, 305–11.

Hollis, A. (2007) 'Drugs for Neglected Diseases: New Incentives for Innovation' In F. A. Sloan and C.-R. Hsieh (eds), *Pharmaceutical Innovation: Incentives, Competition, and Cost-Benefit Analysis in International Perspective* (pp. 75–90, Cambridge: Cambridge University Press).

Hunt, V., N. Manson, and P. Morgan (2011) 'A Wake-up Call for Big Pharma'. *McKinsey Quarterly*, December, https://www.mckinseyquarterly.com/A_wake-up_call_for_Big_Pharma_2897, date accessed 8 July 2012.

IMAP (2012) 'Global Pharma & M&A Report 2012'. http://www.imap.com/imap/media/resources/Pharma_Report_2012_FINAL_2F6C8ADA76680.pdf, date accessed 8 August 2012.

Joint United Nations Programme on HIV/AIDS (2012) *The Potential Impact of Free Trade Agreements on Public Health* (Geneva: UNAIDS).

Kaitin, K. I. and J. A. DiMasi (2011) 'Pharmaceutical Innovation in the 21st Century: New Drug Approvals in the First Decade, 2000–2009', *Clinical Pharmacology and Therapeutics* 89, 183–8.

Kanavos, P., L. Seeley, and S. Vandoros (2009) *Tender Systems for Outpatient Pharmaceuticals in the European Union: Evidence from the Netherlands, Germany and Belgium* (Brussels: European Commission).

Kaplan, W. and R. Laing (2005) *Local Production of Pharmaceuticals: Industrial Policy and Access to Medicines*, Health, Nutrition and Population (HNP) Discussion Paper (Washington, DC: The International Bank for Reconstruction and Development/The World Bank).

Kohr, M. (2009) *Patents, Compulsory Licences and Access to Medicines: Some Recent Experiences*, Intellectual Property Rights Series 10 (Penang: Third World Network). http://www.twnside.org.sg/title2/IPR/pdf/ipr10.pdf, date accessed 13 August 2012.

Lee, S. H. and A. Y. Choi (2012). 'Korean Patent Laws Amended in Order to Implement Korea-US FTA,' Retrieved from http://www.kimchang.com/mailzine.asp?mailzine_no=1110, date accessed 12 September 2012.

Lindstrom, B. (2010) 'Scaling Back TRIPS-Plus: An Analysis of Intellectual Property Provisions in Trade Agreements and Implications for Asia and the Pacific', *New York University Journal of International Law and Politics* 42, 917–80.

Lofgren, H. (2007) 'The Global Biopharma Industry and the Rise of Indian Drug Multinationals: Implications for Australian Generics Policy', *Australia New Zealand Health Policy* 4, 10.

Love, J. (2011) 'What's (Still) Wrong with ACTA, and Why Governments Should Reject the Illegitimate Agreement,' http://keionline.org/node/1369, date accessed 1 July 2012.

Love, J. and T. Hubbard (2007) 'The Big Idea: Prizes to Stimulate R&D for New Medicines', *Chicago-Kent Law Review* 82, 1519–53.

Love, J. P. (2007) 'Recent Examples of the Use of Compulsory Licences on Patents[1]. KEI RN 2007:2', http://keionline.org/content/view/41/1, 4 September 2012.

Lyn, T. E. (2012) 'China Changes Patent Law in Fight for Cheaper Drugs', *Reuters*. http://www.reuters.com/article/2012/06/08/us-china-medicines-patents-idUSBRE8570TY20120608, date accessed 1 September 2012.

Matthews, D. and V. Munoz-Tellez (2006) 'Bilateral Technical Assistance and TRIPS: The United States, Japan and the European Communities in Comparative Perspective', *Journal of World Intellectual Property* 9, 629–53.

Médecins Sans Frontières (2012) 'Trading Away Health: How the U.S. Intellectual Property Demands for the Trans-Pacific Partnership Agreement Threaten Access to Medicines', http://aids2012.msf.org/wp-content/uploads/2012/07/TPP-Issue-Brief-IAC-July2012.pdf, date accessed 18 August 2012.

Mello e Souza, A. (2013) 'The Politics of AIDS Treatment in Brazil: Patents and Access to Medicines'. In H. Löfgren (ed.), *The Politics of Pharmaceuticals and Access to Medicines: World Pharmacy and India* (pp. 272–99, New Delhi: Social Science Press).

Micara, A. G. (2012) 'TRIPS-Plus Border Measures and Access to Medicines', *Journal of World Intellectual Property* 15, 73–101.

Munos, B. (2009) 'Lessons from 60 Years of Pharmaceutical Innovation', [10.1038/nrd2961], *Nature Reviews Drug Discovery* 8, 959–68.

Musungu, S. and G. Dutfield (2003) *Multilateral Agreements and a TRIPS-Plus World: The World Intellectual Property Organisation (Wipo)*, TRIPS Issues Papers 3 (Geneva: QUNO).

Muzaka, V. (2011) *The Politics of Intellectual Property Rights and Access to Medicines* (Basingstoke: Palgrave Macmillan).

Odell, J. S. and S. K. Sell (2003) 'Reframing the Issue: The WTO Coalition on Intellectual Property and Public Health, 2001', Paper presented at the conference on developing countries and the trade negotiation process, UNCTAD, 6–7 November 2003, Geneva.

Pfizer (2012) 'Annual Review 2011', http://www.pfizer.com/investors/financial_reports/annual_reports/2011/biopharmaceutical.jsp, date accessed 30 August 2012.

Pilla, V. (2012) 'Natco Targets Drugs Ripe for Compulsory Licensing', http://www.livemint.com/Companies/ZR7YHsT0xTb6e9ppKDIAuN/Natco-targets-drugs-ripe-for-compulsory-licensing.html, date accessed 4 September 2012.

Pogge, T. W. M., M. Rimmer, and K. Rubenstein (eds) (2010) *Incentives for Global Public Health: Patent Law and Access to Essential Medicines* (Cambridge, UK; New York: Cambridge University Press).

Reichman, J. H. (2009) 'Comment: Compulsory Licensing of Patented Pharmaceutical Inventions: Evaluating the Options', *The Journal of Law, Medicine & Ethics* 37, 247–63.

Report of the Commission on Intellectual Property Rights, Innovation and Public Health (2006) (Geneva: World Health Organization). http://www.who.int/intellectualproperty/report/en/index.html, date accessed 1 January 2012.

Rezaie, R., A. McGahan, S. Frew, A. Daar, and P. Singer (2012) 'Emergence of Biopharmaceutical Innovators in China, India, Brazil, and South Africa as Global Competitors and Collaborators', *Health Research Policy and Systems* 10, 18.

Rushton, S. and O. D. Williams (eds) (2011). *Partnerships and Foundations in Global Health Governance* (Basingstoke: Palgrave Macmillan).

Sell, S. K. (2002) 'TRIPS and the Access to Medicines Campaign', *Wisconsin International Law Journal* 20, 481–522.

Sell, S. K. (2003) *Private Power, Public Law: The Globalization of Intellectual Property Rights* (Cambridge, UK: Cambridge University Press).
Sell, S. K. (2006) 'Books, Drugs and Seeds: The Politics of Access', Paper presented at the Transatlantic Consumer Dialogue The Politics and Ideology of Intellectual Property, 20–21 March 2006, Brussels.
Sell, S. K. (2010) 'The Rise and Rule of a Trade-Based Strategy: Historical Institutionalism and the International Regulation of Intellectual Property', *Review of International Political Economy* 17, 762–90.
Sell, S. K. (2011) 'TRIPS was Never Enough: Vertical Forum Shifting, FTAs, ACTA, and TPP', *Journal of Intellectual Property Law* 18, 447–78.
Smith, B. D. (2011) *The Future of Pharma: Evolutionary Threats and Opportunities* (Farnham: Ashgate).
Srinivasan, S. (2012) 'The Compulsory Licence for Nexavar: A Landmark Order', *Economic and Political Weekly* 47, 10–13.
Tempest, B. (2010) 'A Structural Change in the Global Pharmaceutical Market', *Journal of Generic Medicines* 7, 113–17.
't Hoen, E. F. M. (2009) *The Global Politics of Pharmaceutical Monopoly Power: Drug Patents, Access, Innovation and the Application of the WTO Doha Declaration on Trips and Public Health* (Diemen: AMB Publishers).
Third International Consultation on HIV/AIDS and Human Rights (2003) *HIV/AIDS and Human Rights International Guidelines* (Geneva: Office of the United Nations High Commissioner for Human Rights and the Joint United Nations Programme on HIV/AIDS).
UNAIDS/WHO/UNDP (2011) 'Using TRIPS Flexibilities to Improve Access to HIV Treatment: Policy Brief', http://asia-pacific.undp.org/practices/hivaids/documents/trips/JC2049_PolicyBrief-TRIPS_eng.pdf, date accessed 13 July 2012.
Velasquez, G. and P. Boulet (1999) *Globalization and Access to Drugs: Perspectives on the WTO/TRIPS Agreement*, Health Economics and Drugs DAP Series No. 7 (Geneva: WHO).
Vivas-Eugui, D. (2003) *Regional and Bilateral Agreements and a TRIPS-Plus World: The Free Trade Area of the Americas (FTAA)*, TRIPS Issues Papers 1 (Geneva: Quaker United Nations Office).
Waning, B., M. Kyle, E. Diedrichsen, L. Soucy, J. Hochstadt, T. Barnighausen, and S. Moon (2010) 'Intervening in Global Markets to Improve Access to HIV/AIDS Treatment: An Analysis of International Policies and the Dynamics of Global Antiretroviral Medicines Markets', *Globalization and Health* 6, 9.
Watal, J. (2001) *Intellectual Property Rights in the WTO and Developing Countries* (London: Kluwer Law International).
Williams, O. D. (2012) 'Access to Medicines, Market Failure and Market Intervention: A Tale of Two Regimes', *Global Public Health*, Forthcoming.
World Health Assembly (2008) *Global Strategy and Plan of Action on Public Health, Innovation and Intellectual Property* (Vol. WHA61.21), http://apps.who.int/gb/ebwha/pdf_files/A61/A61_R21-en.pdf, date accessed 14 August 2012.
World Health Organization (1998) *Revised Drug Strategy. WHO's Work in Pharmaceuticals and Essential Drugs* (Geneva: World Health Organization).
World Trade Organization (1994) 'Agreement on Trade-Related Aspects of Intellectual Property Rights', Annex 1C of the Marrakesh Agreement Establishing the World Trade Organization, signed in Marrakesh, Morocco on 15 April. http://www.wto.org/english/tratop_e/trips_e/t_agm0_e.htm, date accessed 10 January 2012.

World Trade Organization (2001) *Declaration on the TRIPS Agreement and Public Health* (WT/MIN(01)/DEC/2 20 November 2001 ed.).

Yu, P. K. (2008) 'Access to Medicines, BRICS Alliances, and Collective Action', *American Journal of Law & Medicine* 34, 345–94.

Yu, P. K. (2011) 'TRIPS and Its Achilles' Heel', *Journal of Intellectual Property Law* 18, 479–531.

YouTube (2012) 'Teresa Stanek Rea Tells Congress USPTO Opposes India Compulsory Licence on Patented Cancer Drug', http://www.youtube.com/watch?v=k9_68z6De9E, date accessed 2 September 2012.

2
The Political Economy of Pharmaceutical Production in Brazil

Cassandra M. Sweet

Over the last two decades global pharmaceutical production has been shaped by a series of profound political, legal and economic changes.[1] On the one hand, the rise of bulk pharmaceutical production in Asia and a wave of mergers and acquisitions throughout the 1990s (Kesic, 2009; Nolan, 2001) has resulted in sector concentration (Abbott and Dukes, 2009; 't Hoen, 2009). On the other hand, industry consolidation has been compounded by increasing standardization of intellectual property law. One hundred and fifty-three countries now adhere to the World Trade Organization's (WTO) Agreement on Trade Related Aspects of Intellectual Property Rights (TRIPS). The Agreement's standard for intellectual property rights (IPR) has been implemented in most developing countries, with significant implications for diffusion of innovation and the range of public health policy options available to local governments. As these global processes have been under way, nation-states have grappled with how to apply new international standards, create fair domestic regulatory frameworks that maintain sufficient levels of competition in the pharmaceutical sector, and ensure access to medicine for their citizens.

This chapter investigates the emerging political economy of the making, and to a lesser extent importation, of medicine in Brazil. Its driving questions are how international intellectual property standards have been applied at a domestic level, and how local production has evolved in the wake of TRIPS implementation. The focus is, therefore, on changing institutional frameworks and their outcomes in local production. The chapter's structure is as follows: the first section introduces the major changes in Brazilian intellectual property law and its use of 'flexibilities' in the TRIPS Agreement; the second examines the creation of a generics category in Brazil and the emergence, post-TRIPS, of a regulatory regime for pharmaceuticals;

and the third examines Brazil's industrial sector, reviewing the contemporary status of local pharmaceutical production. In conclusion, I explore the particularities of the Brazilian case, while putting them in context both regionally and globally.

The legal framework for pharmaceuticals

Before TRIPS, developing and industrialized countries employed highly varied systems for the evaluation of patentability and duration of patents, with a number of products wholly excluded from patentability (Correa, 2000). Brazil, for example, did not consider pharmaceuticals patentable. Brazil's stance that pharmaceuticals should be considered and defended as public goods was maintained at both domestic and international levels. More generally, and throughout the 1980s and 1990s, Brazil's international trade negotiators repeatedly pushed for lower, not higher, global IPR standards (Moreira, 1990; Sell, 1995; Sell, 1998).

Yet, during the WTO's Uruguay Round of negotiations, Brazil, together with other leading developing countries that had originally argued to keep IPR entirely off the negotiating agenda, ultimately accepted a final agreement that set in motion a shift towards global IPR harmonization. Why did developing countries accept the inclusion of intellectual property on the negotiating agenda, a step that would greatly constrain their ability to compete in the general area of knowledge-intensive goods globally, and specifically curtail their ability to produce generics locally?

In the case of Brazil, the move from rejection of any patent standard for medicines to their full acceptance was a result of several factors. First, there was apparent weakness in the coordination of domestic interests and in resistance to TRIPS. For example, Brazil did not have the highly coordinated civil society base that would come to the fore some five years post-1994. Second, mounting threats from industrialized countries (Jawara and Kwa, 2003), combined with the acceptance of agricultural concessions as a trade-off for compliance, were the carrot and stick incentives for general accession to the TRIPS Agreement. Third, there was the perception that creating a set of minimum standards would protect the country from future trade attacks from the US.[2] Fourth, there was overall acceptance that acceding to global IPR standards would encourage greater foreign investment, an argument and linkage that was an important justification of TRIPS during its negotiation (Drahos, 2008). Perhaps most importantly, despite a large local pharmaceutical industry in Brazil, negotiations during the Uruguay Round did not draw on input from this sector. Indeed, the process of negotiation was marked by a lack of coordination among domestic interests (a hallmark of the Brazilian diplomatic approach to certain trade issues after the Uruguay Round). Brazil's foreign trade negotiators simply 'didn't sit down at the table together'—as described by Roberto Jaguaribe, former director of the Brazilian patent-granting agency—with Brazil's domestic industry or local public health agencies (Jaguaribe, 2005). It is not surprising, therefore, that these negotiators failed to incorporate domestic interests into TRIPS negotiations.

As a result of the Uruguay Round negotiations, Brazil entered into the WTO in 1995 and amended its local legislation to full TRIPS compliance in 1996.[3] This made it part of the first wave of TRIPS-compliant national legislation in the Latin American region (Oliveira et al., 2004). All central components of the TRIPS Agreement were adopted, most importantly those regulating the duration of patent protection and what was considered patentable subject matter. Nevertheless, Brazil's overall application of the new IPR standards has been comparatively mixed and uneven. Most clearly, some aspects of Brazil's domestic laws embraced flexibilities inherent in the treaty while others adopted a rigid interpretation of the new intellectual property standards.

One of the key areas in which Brazil's application of the treaty to national law rigidly followed the treaty was in its definition of an invention, which encompassed: 'any object of practical use...that involves an inventive act that results in a functional improvement in its use or manufacture' (Industrial Property Law N. 9279/96, 14/05/96, Section I, Article 9). This understanding of an invention is broad and unspecific, giving the patentee an easier ride in gaining a patent and creating the potential for incremental invention patents. By contrast, other countries adopted definitions that demanded significantly more from patent applications. For example, India's inclusion of the word 'efficacy' in its definition of an invention takes it beyond the generalized pattern of application and implementation of TRIPS patent standards of other developing countries, including those of Brazil, Mexico and Thailand. Brazil's broad definition opened up the possibility of extending patent rights, so-called evergreening, through patent claims that, while able to show an (often marginal) added aspect of novelty, could not show enhanced efficacy.

On the other hand, from a comparative regional perspective, other aspects of Brazil's interpretation and adoption of TRIPS laid the groundwork for policies that have become increasingly restrictive of the broad and powerful IPR that countries like the US have sought globally under the regime. Most notable was Brazil's rather strong statement allowing the right to issue compulsory licenses, when it maintained that instrument in its 1996 industrial property law, and its provisions for parallel imports and exercise of Bolar rights (Cassier and Correa, 2003; Orsi et al., 2003). Brazil's stance in these areas set it apart from a number of countries in the region that, through bilateral trade agreements, have limited their space for action under these so-called TRIPS flexibilities (Jorge, 2004; Roffe, 2004).

Table 2.1 presents the key legal and procedural changes that have been adopted by Brazil.

Table 2.1 Application of TRIPS changes to Brazilian IPR law

Legal and procedural issues	Implications	Corresponding TRIPS article	Corresponding Brazilian law, year
Duration of patent protection	Patents for products and processes, marked from application filing date, minimum of 20 years	Article 33	Law 9279 (1996) Article 40
Patentable subject matter	All inventions, be they products or processes, provided they constitute a new step and have industrial application	Article 27	Law 9279 (1996) Articles 8–15
Granting of 'pipeline' patents	Patent applications that were granted a different standard of review from traditional channels	Not present in TRIPS	Law 9279 (1996) Articles 230–231
Parallel imports	Products imported into a country without the authorization of the rights holder in that country, put on the market in another country by that person or with his consent	Article 6	Law 9279 (1996) Article 68, Section 1
Compulsory licensing	The authorization given by a judicial or administrative authority to a third party for use of a patented invention without the consent of the patent holder	Article 31 (Paragraphs 5 and 6 of Doha Declaration confirmed)	Law 9279 (1996) Article 68 (Permits in the case of a patentee using patent in abusive manner) Article 71 (in cases of national emergency or public interest)
Patent granting mechanism	Amendment to the original Patent Act stipulating that patents granted by Brazil's patent agency would first have to be approved by its regulatory agency, ANVISA	Not present in TRIPS	Law 9279 (1996 amended in 1999) Article 229C

Source: Compiled by author from Brazil's 1996 Industrial Property Law and the 1994 TRIPS Agreement (see Presidência da República, http://www.planalto.gov.br/ccivil_03/leis/L9279.htm and http://www.wto.org/english/tratop_e/trips_e/t_agm0_e.htm for original texts).

Compulsory licences

One of the elements of TRIPS that allowed national interpretation was arguably determination of the criteria for the issuing of compulsory licences (TRIPS Article 31). A compulsory licence suspends the rights of patent holders for exclusive use of the patent for production, although they are compensated for subsequent uses by the state or, indeed, other third parties (Vaughan, 2001). Compulsory licences are an instrument of public policy available to governments when companies refuse to 'exercise' and produce from or otherwise distribute the goods germane to the patent; when they make prices unreasonably unaffordable to consumers (Bird, 2009); or when the patent covers subject matter that is critical in the case of a national health emergency. These grounds for exemptions to patent rights are, therefore, the typical justifications for issue of a compulsory licence, and have an extensive history of use by developed countries ('t Hoen, 2009). Indeed, in one recent example, the US Congress debated legislation that would enable the issuance of a compulsory licence on Swiss company Roche's Tamiflu. The proposed Bill (HR 4392) acknowledged the flexibility within the TRIPS Agreement and mandated that the state would act 'to provide for the importation of pharmaceutical products under a compulsory licence as provided for under the World Trade Organization' (Bill HR 4392, 109th Congress, 1st Session, Page 1, http://www.gpo.gov/). Although the Bill did not become law, the debate it provoked signalled US willingness to use this instrument in public health crises.

By contrast, compulsory licences have been infrequently proposed and rarely applied by developing countries in the post-TRIPS period because of a lack of procedural clarity for establishing their use, and because of the intense political pressure governments face from patent owners based in industrialized countries (Chakraborty and Singhvi, 2009). A handful of exceptions exist, most notably those issued in Brazil, Canada and Thailand (Correa, 2011; Lybecker and Fowler, 2009). Brazil's issuing of a compulsory licence for the anti-retroviral (ARV) Efavirenz in May 2007 made it a particularly unique case as the first country in the region, and one of the few developing countries in the world, to have successfully implemented a compulsory licence in the post-TRIPS era.[4]

More broadly, the harmonization of IPR to the minimum standards set out in the TRIPS Agreement has led to markedly heterogeneous results in Latin America. While in Brazil we have witnessed a move to use TRIPS flexibilities, combined with policies aimed at strengthening the generics sector, other countries in the region have shifted in the opposite direction—towards further extension of patent periods, and rights for what are often foreign patent holders. Most notably, countries such as Chile, Peru and member states in the Central American Free Trade Agreement have joined in bilateral agreements with the US in which IPR standards have been raised beyond those set in TRIPS (Roffe, 2004).

Above all, one central factor explains Brazil's position on TRIPS. Beginning in 1996, Brazil began a free-of-charge treatment programme for all HIV/AIDS patients. By 2004, 180,000 HIV patients were undergoing treatment with a budget of approximately US$371 million a year. While the majority of first-line anti-retrovirals (ARVs) were off patent, and could therefore be manufactured in a generic form, some ARVs provided by the government were on patent, and required purchasing directly from patent owners. The Brazilian government argued that just three of the products—Merck's Efavirenz, Gilead Science's Viread (tenofovir) and Abbot Laboratories' Kaletra (lopinavir and ritonavir)—were responsible for more than 70 per cent of the cost of the programme. The other 13 components of the cocktail administered by the Brazilian government were manufactured in public laboratories, the leading one being Farmanguinhos.

In 2007 Brazil issued a compulsory licence, the culmination of a protracted process of state engagement and negotiation with patent holders. The use of a compulsory licence by Brazil followed over a decade of the country's local and global activities concerned with the goal of providing universal access to HIV/AIDS medicines (as codified in its 1996 Law 9.313). Local production of ARVs in Brazil commenced in 1997, and by the year 2002 it was estimated that production (based in five national laboratories) had resulted in lowering the prices of ARV medicines publicly procured by the government by as much as 83 per cent (Cassier and Correa, 2003; Chequer, 2005). Even with a strong programme of local production, the Brazilian government found itself constrained by the increasing costs of a select number of ARVs.

Pipeline patents

One of the key components of patent policy lies in the institutional design through which a patent is granted. In this respect, Brazil's implementation of a system of patent review rights through a pipeline process provoked great concern in the public health community. The pipeline system existed for a period of one year (from May 1996 to May 1997), during which time owners of patents granted outside Brazil could request their accession into the Brazilian system. Patents granted through the pipeline system were not evaluated with the Brazilian government intellectual property office's (INPI) standards for innovation, which demanded novelty (albeit under the broad definition discussed above).

The argument in favour of the pipeline system was that it provided protection for pre-1995 patent inventions, thus indicating a strong national commitment to patent rights. Opposition to the pipeline system noted that patents were conceded even if the product in question was already part of public knowledge in Brazil, and by some standards could no longer be considered innovative. Total deposits through the pipeline system resulted in 1182 applications (45 per cent from the US, 13 from the UK, 10 from Germany, 9.6 from Japan and 7.7 from France). Of those applications filed, over 700 (or well over half) were granted (Amin, 2010). The result was the protection of at least 340 medicines that would not have been patented in Brazil but for the pipeline mechanism (Associação Brasileira Interdisciplinar de AIDS, 2009).

Ongoing legal conflicts

Brazilian IPR law stipulates that patent approval for pharmaceutical products and processes is interlinked with previous approval by the regulatory authority in charge of sanitary and health norms (known in Brazil as ANVISA, an institution comparable to the US Food and Drug Administration). In this dual track scheme, both ANVISA and the INPI assess patent applications (Barbosa, 2009). Nevertheless, ANVISA's responsibilities are highly contested. Patent-holding firms argue that the regulatory agency's authority should be limited to evaluating the quality of medicines and their production. Public health and local producers view ANVISA's involvement in the patent review process as fundamental, given their inclusion of public health goals and orientation as factors in the granting of patent rights.

Currently ANVISA takes part in the patent-granting process, and a number of cases illustrate how it has played a role in the rejection of patent applications. In 2004, for example, the INPI denied a patent application for the product valganciclovir hydrochloride (the active pharmaceutical ingredient of the HIV drug Valcyte), citing ANVISA's denial of the patent application. Swiss multinational Roche subsequently sued INPI, arguing that ANVISA's opinion was irrelevant to the granting of patents and constituted an infringement of TRIPS. In the first trial the courts ruled for Roche. The INPI has since appealed and the case is currently pending (Original Ruling, Vara Federal do Rio de Janeiro, 2004; see Basso et al., 2011, pp. 75–81, for further discussion of the case).

A similar case arose in 2008 when the INPI denied Aventis' application for a patent, citing an earlier ANVISA rejection. In the first ruling the court's decision had emphasized the impact of illegal granting of patents on access to medicine. The inclusion of a concern for public health and access issues in the consideration of a patent application represents an important development in Brazilian jurisprudence. At stake in both these cases are issues that reach beyond the mere ruling on the Roche or Aventis applications. They go to the very core of the institutional design and balance of rights present in the patents system, and the procedural steps that will determine the future of the system in Brazil.

These procedural disputes highlight the current battle for the future of Brazil's patent system. Indeed, since the implementation of TRIPS in 1996, Brazil's IPR policy has comprised a mixed application of international standards with some use of flexibilities at the domestic level. On the one hand, the country adopted a broad definition of what amounts to an invention, subsequently opening the door to potentially frivolous claims and the practice of evergreening. On the other hand, new research has emphasized the importance of rigid innovation standards, buttressed by rigorous processes of patent application review. A study of patents granted in Argentina, Brazil, Colombia, India and South Africa, for example, has confirmed that a significant portion of recently granted patents 'would not be deemed patentable if more rigorous standards of patentability were applied' (Correa, 2011, p. 22). Despite room for local definition of innovation standards, the rules governing what constitute sufficient levels of novelty and the institutions that implement and enforce such standards remain weak in many developing countries.

The Brazilian case is, therefore, remarkable for its extremes. It is certain that Brazil's continuing use of broad, lax innovation standards—compounded by the historical legacy of its pipeline policy, which granted privileges to patent owners far beyond the scope of TRIPS—has resulted in hundreds of pharmaceutical patents that would not otherwise have been granted. Such policies tilted the balance of rights in favour of patent holders. At the other extreme, Brazil's inclusion of compulsory licences in its application of TRIPS, and its subsequent use of that tool, has made it a model of state-sponsored and protected public health and access to medicines in the region. Brazil's vigorous defence of this right in both domestic and international law is notable (Azevedo, 2010). Nevertheless, the political capital required to issue a compulsory licence restricts its ability to be instituted systematically and globally. Finally, current legal disputes regarding the role of ANVISA and the patent-granting procedure illustrate how definition of IPR in Brazil remains both contentious and ongoing.

Market liberalization and pharmaceutical regulation

During the early 1990s the Brazilian economy underwent a comprehensive programme of liberalization, including the reduction of import taxes, the privatization of state-owned companies, and deregulation. These changes profoundly affected Brazil's national innovation system, especially in the case of local firms and public finance projects (Tigre et al., 2002). One policy that had an immediate effect on the pharmaceutical industry was the swift reduction of tariffs from 1990 to 1994. In this period import taxes in this sector were reduced from 60–70 per cent to approximately 14 per cent (Oliveira, 2006). Facing an influx of competition, many local firms failed to adapt. According to a local industry representative, 'Our sector was forced into suicide. It was dismembered. [President] Collor entered into power and said, tomorrow, we are going to import everything' (Gomes, 2006). In the first half of the decade, over 1000 pharmaceutical manufacturing units went out of business, and over 500 investment projects were terminated.

On the heels of a rapid decrease in competition in the pharmaceutical sector, the price of medicines in Brazil rose sharply. Demand, however, did not decline. According to the General Manager of Medicines for ANVISA, policy makers were increasingly aware of the rigidity of the pharmaceutical market, and by the late 1990s government intervention in the market regained acceptance (Bezerra, 2006). A range of regulatory policies were subsequently implemented with the aim of increasing market competition. Changes that occurred in this period included the complete restructuring of product categories within the pharmaceutical market, the introduction of price controls and the creation of sanitary and surveillance measures. Among many significant changes, two key policies transformed the political economy of making medicine in Brazil in this period: the enactment of a law to regulate public procurement and the formation of the generics category under the stewardship of a newly established pharmacological surveillance agency.

Public procurement

The economic impact of liberalization, or *abertura*, policies pursued during the Collor presidency in the early 1990s has been widely analysed (Amann, 2000; Packenham, 1994). Yet one outcome of the Collor legacy which has been widely overlooked was the passage of a law regulating public procurement. As the first democratically elected president of Brazil, Collor's removal from office via impeachment proceedings had an immediate effect on the public's perception of government. Facing a crisis of legitimacy (Weyland, 1993), Law 8.6666, the Lei de Licitações (literally translated, the Law of Tenders), was enacted in 1993 by Brazil's Congress in an attempt to re-establish transparency in contracting and procurement by public entities (Presidencia da República, 1993). The law stated that public purchases made at municipal, state or federal levels had to be made via open tender systems, with concessions granted to the lowest possible bids. The law did not consider the quality of products offered or the reputation of the service provider, and relied in principle on the lowest price.

Over a quarter of Brazil's pharmaceutical market is procured by government. Despite a federal, unified public healthcare system—the Sistema Única de Saúde (SUS)—public purchases of medicines are 'organized' through a fragmented, decentralized system.[5] Local Brazilian companies found it difficult to compete with low-cost suppliers from India and China, and argued that their price was not competitive, but, rather, 'political'. Public institutions complained that the law forced them to procure 'garbage', with one director of a public laboratory reporting that as many as one-third of all chemical inputs and 10 per cent of finished formulations purchased did not meet minimum quality standards. In response, in recent years there has been increased advocacy by local chemical producers to coordinate production of active pharmaceutical ingredients (APIs) with public laboratories, as well as to increase the quality standards for public purchases (Almeida, 2009). This particular policy dispute reflects the difficult balance facing policy makers in Brazil, who aim to integrate Brazilian industry into the global economy and reduce public procurement costs in an open and transparent manner while avoiding the mistakes that decimated local industry in the 1990s.

Introduction of generics

Around the same time that Brazil was implementing international intellectual property standards, it introduced a number of regulatory reforms that had a significant impact on its generics pharmaceutical sector. In 1999 the Brazilian Congress established ANVISA through Law 9.782 and, shortly thereafter, established a new legal category defining generics medicines (Law 9.787). ANVISA was thus born with a dual regulatory and health mission and entrusted with a range of autonomous powers from the state (including financial independence as well as its own directorship and policing power). ANVISA regulates ports, airports, international borders, medicines, medical devices, food, cleaning products and tobacco products. Its role is not limited to sanitary regulation. ANVISA also influences the pharmaceutical market through price controls. About 800 medicines are unregulated, while 19,000 to 20,000 products have their prices fixed through ANVISA's General Office of Drugs (Bezerra, 2006). ANVISA created new benchmarks in Brazil's pharmaceutical industry, which for most of the 1990s had been highly unregulated:

> Before 1998, the scenario was akin to a pharmaceutical Wild-West. There was no control... ANVISA became very proactive in changing the environment. Some 30–40 companies went out of business the first year because they couldn't meet minimum standards.
>
> (Vijay, 2006)

Before the generics law, medicines in Brazil that claimed the 'generic' label were not expected to meet the technical guarantee of bioequivalence with the original drugs or API. With the creation of ANVISA, the new legislation ensured that generic products would be regulated to a single national standard, with a requirement that they be identical in quality, dosage, safety, therapeutic characteristics and strength. The new generics category (and bioequivalence and other standards) constituted the most dramatic shift in Brazil's institutional control over the pharmaceutical sector. Other important areas covered by the 1999 generics law were in regulation of pricing and public purchase of drugs. The new law stated that the prices of generic medicines should be set at least 33 per cent lower than those of brand-name equivalents. Regulations for generics thus became more stringent in Brazil than in any other Latin American market because bioequivalence tests had to be realized and Good Manufacturing Practice followed (Valente, 2006).

In addition to bioequivalence and pricing rules for generic medicines, the 1999 generics law included other policy changes, such as requirements regarding the promotion, packaging and sale of generics. The role of packaging colour, design and labelling was a key part of generics policy, as approximately 12 per cent of the Brazilian population are illiterate. ANVISA, therefore, sought to create guidelines that would be easily identifiable to all consumers. The generics law also gave the Ministry of Health the task of educating the public about changes in the regulation of generics, and the differences between generic drugs and their brand-name alternatives.[6] The Ministry was successful in fulfilling this task. The Ministry was successful in fulfilling this task. A number of studies conducted by ANVISA in the early 2000s indicated a majority of the Brazilian population were aware of the existence of the generics category; recent studies confirm widespread awareness of generics as an option (Blatt et al., 2012; Vosgerau et al., 2011). In a period of a few short years Brazil had crafted a generics sector that provided quality standards for its citizens and a well-regulated market in which domestic firms could compete.

In all, the 1990s were a turbulent decade for Brazil's pharmaceutical industry. Policies of rapid market liberalization gave firms little time to adjust to new tariff levels. New global intellectual property standards were also hastily implemented, again leaving local firms with little time to adjust to the new patent paradigm. The arrival of low-cost Indian and Chinese API producers cemented the country's dependence on imported organic chemicals. Yet, at the end of the decade, policies shifted. Local production was increasingly promoted and a regulatory regime was introduced, creating a generics category that local firms would soon come to dominate.

The political economy of production: Local pharmaceutical manufacturing

In parallel with the recent rapid expansion of the Brazilian economy, the country's pharmaceutical market has consistently grown in double digits over the last five years, increasing by 20 per cent in 2008 and 13 per cent in 2009. In 2009, sales of pharmaceutical products in Brazil reached US$17 billion and accounted for one-third of the Latin American pharmaceutical market. Growth in Brazil's pharmaceutical market has been buttressed by macroeconomic, demographic and policy factors. Brazil's gross domestic product (GDP) has expanded by approximately 3.3 per cent annually over the last decade (World Bank, 2009). Combined with diminishing levels of inequality, the purchasing power of middle and lower income Brazilians has surged (Lustig and Lopez-Calva, 2010). An urban population of nearly 90 per cent has enabled concentrated logistics and distribution of pharmaceutical products. Moreover, with nine in ten of Brazil's citizens' basic health costs covered through a public programme providing low-cost medicine, access to pharmaceutical products has reached segments of the population excluded in other developing countries (IMS Health, 2010).

Competitors in the Brazilian pharmaceutical market fall into the same two broad categories as in any other country: generics and on-patent/innovator producers. I will now focus on private generics manufacturers. These firms are predominantly owned by local capital, while providers of on-patent medicines are largely foreign multinationals.[7] Recent data indicate that, a decade after the creation of the generics category in 1999, national firms were responsible for over 70 per cent of generics sales (IMS Health, 2009). The strong position held by local firms is also reflected in registrations of products in this category. Of the more than 2790 generics products registered in Brazil, 89 per cent were held by national generics firms in 2008 (ANVISA, 2009). Imported generics registered with the national regulatory authority amount to less than 10 per cent of total market share. Of foreign registrations, almost two-thirds are held by Indian generics pharmaceutical firms (Sweet, 2008).

The strength of Brazil's representation in terms of its share of the local generics market is notable. Yet, beneath the veneer of market representation, the Brazilian model of generics pharmaceutical production is somewhat shallow and misleading. While seven in ten generics products in the country are produced by Brazilian firms, local companies engage in a low level of innovative activity or basic organic chemical production. The majority of APIs, the building blocks of any pharmaceutical product, be it on or off patent, are imported. Furthermore, only a handful of local firms are engaged in innovative research or chemical production. As the market for generics has grown, so has the import of inputs in the pharmaceutical production chain. Figure 2.1 illustrates trends in the importation of both finished formulations and bulk chemicals into the Brazilian market, which reached a combined approximate value of US$6 billion in 2011.

Figure 2.1 shows that Brazil's trade deficit and import of pharmaceutical products appear roughly correlated in increasing divergence. Over the last five years Brazil's import of APIs, or bulk pharmaceutical chemicals, nearly doubled, increasing from US$1.1 billion in 2005 to more than US$2 billion in 2011. Finished pharmaceutical products followed a similar trajectory, increasing from US$1.5 to 3.5 billion. As a result, by 2011, Brazil's balance of trade in this sector reached a combined deficit of US$4.2 billion.

For local pharmaceutical firms, dependence on the key inputs of bulk generics pharmaceutical chemicals has made Brazilian industry vulnerable to currency fluctuations and has limited the value-added qualities of locally produced pharmaceutical goods. More crucially, it highlights that the manufacturing activities of Brazilian generics firms are overwhelmingly concentrated on assembly and packaging and that the capacity to conduct innovation activities is restricted, even at a very basic level.[8]

In addition to increasing dependence on foreign APIs, another trend affecting the Brazilian generics industry has been the acquisition of leading national generics firms by multinationals. Recent examples include

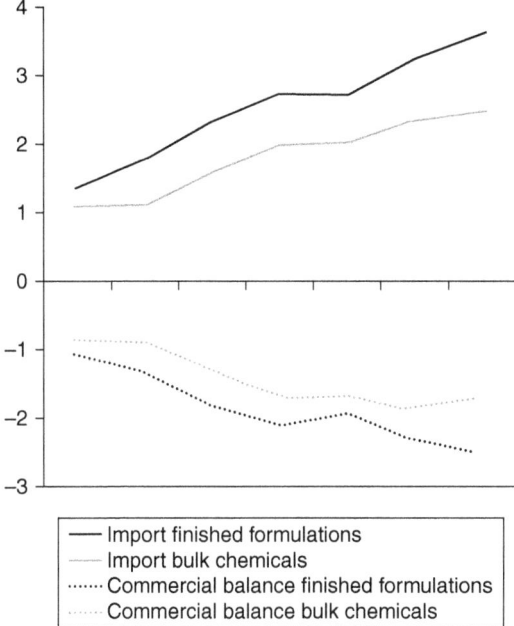

Figure 2.1 Trends in trade: Brazil's pharmaceutical import and trade balance, 2005–2011
Source: Associação Brasileira das Indústrias de Química Fina, Biotecnologia e suas Especialidades, ABFINA (2012), elaborated by the author.

Sanofi-Aventis' acquisition of leading domestic generics producer Medley in 2009, and Pfizer's agreement for generics production with Eurofarma in April 2010. Another leading generics producer, Neo Quimica, was recently purchased by Hypermarcas, signalling a continued consolidation of players in the generics market. Trends in Brazilian pharmaceutical production are consistent with the wave of global consolidation across the pharmaceutical industry over the last decade (Nolan, 2001; Nolan, Sutherland and Zhang, 2002) and specifically in the developing world, Eastern Europe (Kesic, 2009) and India (Yee and Leahy, 2008). In the wake of acquisitions, the three remaining major Brazilian-owned generics firms are EMS, Aché and Eurofarma. There are signals, however, that the current trend towards consolidation is not confined to acquisitions by northern firms. EMS itself has also adopted the strategy, purchasing two other generics producers in Latin America and pursuing regional expansion.

In light of the recent acquisitions, the Brazilian government is reportedly considering imposing restrictions on foreign takeovers in the pharmaceutical sector. This is not a likely policy outcome, given the high level of risk it might provoke in other sectors of the Brazilian economy. What is notable, however, is the consistency with which the pharmaceutical sector has remained an important policy area for the last decade. The linkage of health policy and industrial development has emerged as a single policy platform in the government of President Luiz Ignacio da Silva, who early in his first term identified the pharmaceutical sector as one of four 'strategic sectors' that would be a goal of his administration (Quental et al., 2008, p. 620).

There is clear recent evidence of government support for this sector, as is illustrated in the disbursement of competitive grants and loans for innovative activities. In recent years PROFARMA, a publicly funded programme administered by the state-owned Brazilian Development Bank (BNDES), has allocated over US$697 million in projects directed towards strengthening the national pharmaceutical industry. During the first three quarters of 2009 alone, BNDES distributed over US$ 697 million, aimed at 86 projects. PROFARMA projects fell into four areas: production (51 per cent); exports (3 per cent); restructuring (27 per cent); and innovation (19 per cent). Over 92 per cent of funding was destined for nationally owned firms. One of the challenges the current government has faced is that the PROFARMA programme, charged with increasing national production of pharmaceutical goods and reducing Brazil's deficit in the import of pharmaceuticals and bulk inputs, has meant that the Brazil pharmaceutical sector has become attractive to foreign firms. As such, many Brazilian companies that were recipients of government financing schemes are now targets of foreign takeovers.

Brazilian generics pharmaceutical firms currently control a significant share of the local market. Nevertheless, they lack depth in their manufacturing activities, and few undertake research and development (R&D). As is the case in other countries in the region, Brazilian pharmaceutical producers now find themselves wedged between low-cost bulk chemical suppliers (which are also quickly entering the generics market) on the one side, and innovation-driven patent firms on the other. For Brazilian firms producing generic products, their advantage remains their knowledge of the local regulatory system and local market preferences. For Brazilian policy makers, maintaining a competitive market place that benefits low-income citizens and fosters local innovation has proven a difficult policy balance.

Conclusion

In this chapter I have examined the new political economy of pharmaceutical production in Brazil, analysing key changes in the country's legal, regulatory and industrial structure over the last two decades. Intellectual property standards and rules regarding patents in Brazil have radically changed since the implementation of the TRIPS Agreement. While the country once recognized and promoted pharmaceuticals as public goods, they have now become a patentable and private product. Despite the mixed enforcement of new standards, a slew of policies aimed at ensuring access and increasing the innovative capacity of local firms has acted as a partial counterbalance. These policies, however, have served to foster still wider public debate, and ongoing political conflict, rather than quiet it. As the Brazilian state's judicial system reviews the role of ANVISA in the patent-granting process and the political viability of compulsory licences is tested in future cases, the Brazilian IP system is clearly in flux with enduring disputes regarding access to medicine, regulation of the pharmaceutical market and the standards for granting patents.

In the emblematic case of Brazil's HIV/AIDS programme, we may well ask whether Brazil's use of a compulsory licence provides a wider and replicable policy model for ensuring access to medicines. Brazil's HIV programme has by almost all measures been successful, reducing transmission rates among infected patients, lowering hospitalization costs and, yes, saving lives (Nunn et al., 2009). Nevertheless, even though Ecuador also recently issued a compulsory licence for a HIV/AIDS medicine, it is unlikely that the tool will be widely used by developing countries. In the case of Brazil, the issuing of a compulsory licence followed on the heels of more than a decade of negotiation with patent holders, and was supported by multiple ministers, sophisticated representation in international arenas (in particular at the WTO) and broad, sustained public support among local and international public health groups. Because the potential domestic and international political cost of issuing compulsory licences is high, the tool requires significant political coordination and economic resources in order to be viable.

Crucially, Brazil was able to rally all of these requisite political, diplomatic and economic resources. It is increasingly clear that few other developing countries are likely to be able to do so. As a result, some scholars now emphasize the importance of high standards of innovation in awarding patents and the application of rigorous standards from the application process onwards (Correa, 2011). This upfront approach may help prevent the granting of frivolous patents in the first place, before a 'back door' policy of revoking them is required in instances of compulsory licensing or otherwise.

From an economic and industrial standpoint, the issuing of a compulsory licence in Brazil was made technically feasible because of the country's ability to produce generic alternatives in public laboratories. For countries without strong public production capabilities, sourcing APIs and finished formulations after the issuing of a compulsory licence will become increasingly difficult. This is particularly notable since the adoption of TRIPS standards in India, where the bulk of generic APIs and finished formulations have, up to this point, been produced.

As global pharmaceutical production shifts towards ever more integrated transnational supply chains and harmonized international standards, developing states face an increasingly complex set of policy decisions. How can countries promote local innovation, attract foreign investment and protect the public health interests of their citizens?

Notwithstanding these wider concerns, it is clear that over the past decade Brazil has taken important practical and symbolic strides to tackle these problems. It has used flexibilities available in the TRIPS Agreement, put public health interests and health agencies squarely at the centre of the patent-granting process, and contributed to a generics market that is well structured and competitive. Here the contribution of government funding and grants for innovation undertaken by local firms has also added impetus to the market and local production. Significant challenges remain, but, in the global discussion of public health and access to medicines, Brazil is a country that cannot be overlooked.

Notes

1. Thanks are due for the constructive comments of the editors on earlier versions of this chapter, as well as suggestions from colleagues at the Institute of Political Science, PUC-Chile. This research is framed within FONDECYT's Project N° 1110368 and the Millennium Nucleus for the Study of Stateness and Democracy in Latin America, Project N° NS100014. All caveats apply.
2. One such example was an investigation in 1987 by the USTR. The USTR examined Brazil's patent protections, determining that they infringed the rights of US patent holders. As a result, the US set a temporary policy of 100 per cent tariffs on a number of Brazilian imports.
3. The lack of impact of Brazil's local industry contrasts with the influence the Indian pharmaceutical industry played in its country's negotiations. The Indian industry gained a slower implementation period, with India becoming fully harmonized to the TRIPS provisions only in 2005.
4. In the Latin American region, Ecuador has also issued a compulsory licence. In April 2010 it issued a licence for the HIV/AIDS medicine Ritonavir, held by US Abbott Laboratories.
5. Article 196 of the 1988 Brazilian Constitution makes health services (and access to basic medicine) a right. Financing of this system occurs partly through the SUS, which is connected to the Ministry of Health. Purchases of medicine through this system take place at federal, state and municipal levels. Each year a number of medicines are identified as those that will be acquired by the Ministry of Health through the Secretary of Science, Technology and Strategic Medicines' purchasing unit, known as the 'DAF', Department of Pharmaceutical Assistance and Strategic Raw Materials (*Insumos Estratégicos*).
6. Gonzalez, Fitzgerald and Bermudez (2006) provide an overview of generics regulations in Latin America. They describe three groupings: first, countries which support competing medications, promote the use of INNs (a product's generic chemical name) and have no restrictions on innovative (proprietary) medicines. This category includes Argentina, Columbia, Costa Rica, Ecuador and Paraguay. A second group requires therapeutic equivalence, recognition of generics by their INN and distinctive labelling: Brazil, Mexico, Panama and Venezuela. A third group, Barbados, Bolivia, Guatemala, Nicaragua and Peru, is described as commencing development of regulation.
7. A number of foreign multinational firms operate in Brazil, including Abbott, Pfizer, GlaxoSmithKline, Boehringer Ingelheim, Bristol Myers Squibb, Novartis and

Roche, all of which have production facilities. Like their Brazilian counterparts, the activities of foreign multinationals are focused on the final stages of production, packaging, registration and marketing of products, with little investment in R&D of bulk chemical ingredients.
8. Two firms that are exceptions are medium-sized producers Biolab and Cristália, which have both recently announced plans for the construction of new R&D facilities.

References

Abbott, M. F. and G. Dukes (2009) *Global Pharmaceutical Policy* (London and New York: Edward Elgar).
Almeida, E. N. D. (2009) 'Analise do trabalho de qualificação de fornecedores de insumos farmacêuticos na unidade de Farmanguinhos', Masters Thesis in Public Health, FIOCRUZ, Rio de Janeiro, Brazil.
Amann, E. (2000) *Economic Liberalisation and Industrial Performance in Brazil* (New York: Oxford University Press).
Amin, T. (2010) 'Re-visiting the Patents and Access to Medicines Dichotomy: An Evaluation of TRIPs Implementation and Public Health Safeguards in Developing Countries'. In Yu, O. Aginam and J. Harrington (eds) *Global Governance of HIV/AIDS: Intellectual Property and Access to Essential Medicines* (London: Edward Elgar).
ANVISA, (2009) 'Medicamentos Genéricos.' July, http://portal.anvisa.gov.br/wps/content/Anvisa+Portal/Anvisa/Inicio/Medicamentos/Assunto+de+Interesse/Medicamentos+genericos, accessed September 2012.
Associação Brasileira Interdisciplinar de Aids (2009) 'Perguntas e respostas sobre patentes pipeline: Como afetam sua saúde', Policy paper (Rio de Janeiro ABIA).
Azevedo, R. (2010). 'Brasil ataca acordo de ricos contra falsificação', Estadão line, http://www.estadao.com.br/noticias/impresso,brasil-ataca-acordo-de-ricos-contra-falsificacao,621618,0.htm, date accessed 10 November 2010.
Barbosa, D. (2009) 'O papel da ANVISA na concessão de patentes', http://denisbarbosa.addr.com/papelanvisa.pdf, date accessed 3 December 2010.
Basso, M., B. Edson, J. Rodriguez (2011) *Intellectual Property Law in Brazil* (The Netherlands: Kluwer Law International).
Bezerra, C. A. (2006) *General Manager of Medicines*, ANVISA, Personal interview, Brasilia, 24 June.
Bird, R. (2009) 'Developing Nations and the Compulsory Licence: Maximizing Access to Essential Medicines While Minimizing Investment Side Effects', *Journal of Law, Medicine and Ethics*, 37: 209–21.
Blatt, C. R, S. C Trauthman, E. H. Schmidt, S. Marchesan, L. M. da Silva, and J. L. Martins (2012) 'Conhecimento Popular e Utilização dos Medicamentos Genéricos na População do Município de Tubarão, SC, *Ciênc. saúde coletiva*, 17: 79–87.
Cassier, M. and C. M. Correa (2003) 'Patents, Innovation and Public Health: Brazilian Public-Sector Laboratories' Experience in Copying AIDS Drugs' in J.-P. Moattli, B. Coriat, Y. Soutryran, T. Barnett, J. Dumoulin and V.-A. Fiori (eds) *Economics of AIDS and Access to HIV/AIDS Care in Developing Countries, Issues and Challenges* (Paris: Agence Nationale de Recherches sur le Sida).
Chakraborty, S. and A. Singhvi (2009) 'Compulsory Licensing for Access to Medicines in the Developing World', *International Journal of Intellectual Property Management*, 3, 110–26.

Chequer, P. (2005) 'Access to Treatment and Prevention: Brazil and Beyond', Power point presentation to the International Aids Society 2005 Conference, Rio de Janeiro, http://www.aids.gov.br/en/publicacao/access-treatment-and-prevention-brazil-and-beyond, accessed 12 December 2011.

Correa, M. C. (2000) *Intellectual Property Rights, the WTO and Developing Countries: The TRIPS Agreement and Policy Options* (London: Zed Books).

Correa, M. C. (2011) 'Pharmaceutical Innovation, Incremental Patenting and Compulsory Licensing', South Centre Research Paper, 41.

Drahos, P. (2008) 'Does Dialogue Make a Difference? Structural Change and the Limits of Framing', *The Yale Law Journal*, Pocket Part 117, 268–73.

Gomes, L. (2006) 'Manager of Foreign Trade', *Febrafarma*, personal interview, Sao Pablo, 6 June.

González, C. P. V., J. F. Fitzgerald and J. A. Z. Bermúdez (2006). 'Definición de medicamento genèrico ¿un fin o un medio? Análasis de la regulación en 14 países de la Región de las Américas', *Pan American Journal of Public Health*, 20, 314–23.

IMS Health (2010) *Pharmerging Shake-up: New Imperatives in a Redefined World* (Norwalk, CT: IMS Health Incorporated).

Jaguaribe, R. (2005) Comments at the International Seminar on Contributions to the Development Agenda on Intellectual Property Rights, Maastricht, The Netherlands, 23–24 September. Confirmed in correspondence with author 18 December 2007.

Jawara, F. and A. Kwa (2003) *Behind the Scenes at the WTO* (London: Zed Books).

Jorge, F. M. (2004) 'TRIPS-plus Provisions in Trade Agreements and Their Potential Adverse Effects on Public Health', *Journal of Generic Medicines*, 1, 199–211.

Kesic, D. (2009) 'Strategic Analysis of the World Pharmaceutical Industry', *Management*, 14, 59–76.

Lustig, N. and I. F. Lopez-Calva (2010) *Declining Inequality in Latin America: A Decade of Progress?* (Washington, DC: Brookings Institution Press and UNDP).

Lybecker, M. K. and E. Fowler (2009) 'Compulsory Licensing in Canada and Thailand: Comparing Regimes to Ensure Legitimate Use of WTO Rules', *The Journal of Law, Medicine and Ethics*, 37, 222–39.

Moreira, M. M. (1990) 'The Point of View of an Emerging Trading Nation: Brazil' in J. Bhagwati and H. T. Patrick (eds) *Aggressive Unilateralism: America's 301 Trade Policy and the World Trading System* (Ann Arbor: University of Michigan Press).

Nolan, P. (2001) *China and the Global Business Revolution* (London: Palgrave).

Nolan, P., D. Sutherland and J. Zhang (2002) 'The Challenge of the Global Business Revolution', *Contributions to Political Economy*, 21, 91–110.

Nunn, S. A., E. M. D. Fonseca, F. Bastos and S. Gruskin (2009) 'AIDS Treatment in Brazil: Impacts and Challenge', *Health Affairs*, 28, 1103–13.

Oliveira, A. M., J. A. Z. Bermudez, G. C. Chaves and G. Velasquez (2004) 'Has the Implementation of the TRIPS Agreement in Latin America and the Caribbean Produced Intellectual Property Legislation that Favors Public Health?', *Bulletin of the World Health Organization*, 82, 811–90.

Oliveira, N. B. D. (2006) Vice President of ABIFINA, personal interview, Rio de Janeiro, 26 June.

Orsi, L. F., B. Hasenclever, B. Fialho, P. Tigre and B. Coriat (2003) 'Intellectual Property Right, Anti-AIDS Policy and Generic Drugs: Lessons from the Brazilian Public Health Program' in J.-P. Moattli, B. Coriate, Y. Soutryran, T. Barnett, J. Dumoulin and V.-A. Fiori (eds) *Economics of AIDS and Access to HIV/AIDS Care in Developing Countries, Issues and Challenges* (Paris: Agence Nationale de Recherches sur le Sida).

Packenham, R. (1994) 'The Politics of Economic Liberalization: Argentina and Brazil in Comparative Perspective', Working Paper 206, Kellogg Institute for International Studies.

Presidencia da Republica (1993) Lei N°8.666 de Junho de 1993, Codigo Civil, http://www.planalto.gov.br/ccivil_03/Leis/L8666cons.htm, date accessed 10 December 2011.

Quental, C., J. Abreu, J. Bomtempo and C. Gadelha (2008) 'Medicamentos genéricos no Brasil: impactos das políticas públicas sobre a indústria nacional', *Ciencia e Saúde Coletiva*, 13, 619–28.

Roffe, P. (2004) 'Bilateral Agreements and a TRIPS-plus World: the Chile–USA Free Trade Agreement. QIAP', http://www.quno.org/geneva/pdf/economic/Issues/Bilateral-Agreements-and-TRIPS-plus-English.pdf, date accessed 12 December 2011.

Sell, S. (1995) 'Intellectual Property Protection and Antitrust in the Developing World: Crisis, Coercion and Choice', *International Organization*, 49, 315–50.

Sell, S. (1998) *Power and Ideas: North-Politics of Intellectual Property and Antitrust* (Albany, NY: State University of New York Press).

Sweet, C. (2008) *Indian Multinationals in Brazil: Emerging Multinationals in Emerging Markets. 'Emerging Multinationals': Outward Foreign Direct Investment from Emerging and Developing Economies* (Copenhagen: Copenhagen Business School).

't Hoen, E. (2009) *The Global Politics of Pharmaceutical Monopoly Power* (Diemen, the Netherlands: AMB Publishers).

Tigre, P., J. E. Cassiolato, M. H. D. S. Szapiro and J. C. Ferraz (2002) 'Institutional Change and Technology: Impacts of Deregulation on the National Innovation System' in R. Bauman (ed.) *Brazil in the 1990s: An Economy in Transition* (Basingstoke: Palgrave).

Valente, V. (2006) 'Generics in Latin America: An Analysis of the Brazilian Experience', *Journal of Generic Medicines*, 4, 30–6.

Vara Federal do Rio Janeiro (2004) Ação ordinária n°2004.51.01.506840-0-37[a]

Vaughan, V. S. (2001) 'Compulsory Licensing of Pharmaceuticals under TRIPS: What Standard of Compensation?' *Hastings International and Comparative Law Review*, 25, 87–110.

Vijay, B. (2006) Country Manager, Wockhardt, personal interview, Sao Paulo, 18 May.

Vosgerau, M. Z., R. K. T. de Souza, and D. A. Soares. (2011) 'Utilização de Genéricos em área de Atuação da Equipe de Saúde da Família em Município do Sul do Brasil', *Revista Brasileira de Epidemiologia*, 14, 253–63.

Weyland, K. (1993) 'The Rise and Fall of President Collor and Its Impact on Brazilian Democracy', *Journal of Interamerican Studies and World Affairs*, 35(1), 1–37.

World Bank (2009) *Brazil at a Glance. Development Economics LDB Database* (Washington, DC: World Bank).

Yee, A. and J. Leahy (2008) 'Shock in India over Ranbaxy Sale', *Financial Times*, 11 June.

3
Pharmaceuticals, Health Policy and Intellectual Property Rights in China

Chee-Ruey Hsieh

In 1978 the Chinese government began a series of reforms to restructure its economy away from central planning towards a market system, including an open door policy to encourage foreign trade and investment. Since then the Chinese economy has experienced very rapid growth, which has significantly increased domestic per capita income as well as China's importance in the global economy. As its share of the world economy continues to grow, China faces a series of major challenges in seeking to balance domestic and global rules, including its stance on the protection of intellectual property rights (IPR).

Prior to the open door policy Chinese IPR law was relatively undeveloped, providing only limited patent protection. In 1984, however, China began to enact a patent law that provided for protection of IPR but excluded pharmaceutical products. As a result of trade negotiations with the US, China amended its patent law in 1992 to include patent protection for pharmaceutical products. In order to conform to the provisions of the Trade Related Aspects of Intellectual Property Rights (TRIPS) Agreement, China further amended its patent law in 2000 (Hason and Shimotake, 2006). As a condition of World Trade Organization (WTO) accession, TRIPS-compliant IPR legislation officially came into force in China at the end of 2002.

Since patent protection has important implications for the pharmaceutical sector—including innovation of new products and access to existing products—this chapter focuses on the effect of TRIPS compliance on the pharmaceutical sector in China. The chapter investigates the impact of TRIPS compliance on both demand (and thus the link between patent protection and access to generics and brand-name medicines) and supply (production, competition, international trade and innovation) for both domestic and foreign firms. Legislation and enforcement of pharmaceutical patents in China since the open door policy are traced, as is the evolution of institutional arrangements affecting the pharmaceutical sector. Empirical evidence pertaining to demand for pharmaceutical products in China is then examined in relation to its association with TRIPS compliance. The chapter proceeds to analyse the consequences of changes in the production of generic drugs for the availability, supply and prices of essential medicines, illuminating the effect of TRIPS compliance on competition between domestic and foreign firms in the production and innovation of pharmaceutical products.

Adoption of TRIPS

Although modern patent law in China can be traced back to the 1950s, protection of patents for pharmaceutical products was not included in patent law until 1992 (Hason and Shimotake, 2006). As a result of bilateral trade negotiations and WTO accession, China has now enacted regulations extending all patents to 20 years, with data exclusivity for six years.

During the last two decades three major amendments to China's national intellectual property (IP) legislation have made its patent law more compatible internationally. The first amendment, in 1992, introduced protection for product patents in all industry sectors and increased the terms of patents for inventions (applicable from the application date) from 15 to 20 years (Hason and Shimotake, 2006).

As stated earlier, in order for China to become a member of the WTO another amendment, the 2000 Patent Law, was enacted and came into effect in 2002. Compliance with TRIPS necessitated changes to the law concerning infringements of process patents, resulting in the burden of proof being shifted to the alleged infringer. The most recent amendments, referred to as the 2008 Patent Law, came into effect on 1 October 2009. Three major changes were particularly relevant to the pharmaceutical industry. First, the scope of compulsory licences was expanded so that, for public health purposes, the State Intellectual Property Office (SIPO) could grant a compulsory licence for the manufacture and export of patented pharmaceuticals to countries or regions covered by the international treaties to which China is a signatory. Second, parallel imports of patented products were allowed. Third, an infringement exemption was provided for activities related to obtaining information required for submissions to regulatory authorities for drugs approvals, enabling manufacturers of generics to produce medicines more quickly once the relevant patents have expired.

Although China has substantially revised its patent law to comply with TRIPS, there are many challenges in implementing these amendments. Two of the most important of these are how to deal with counterfeit drugs, and the process for resolving disputes over patents. The production, manufacture and sale of counterfeit medications not only deprives brand-name pharmaceutical firms of sales and revenue, but also threatens to undermine global public health (Hason and Shimotake, 2006; Santoro and Liu, 2009).

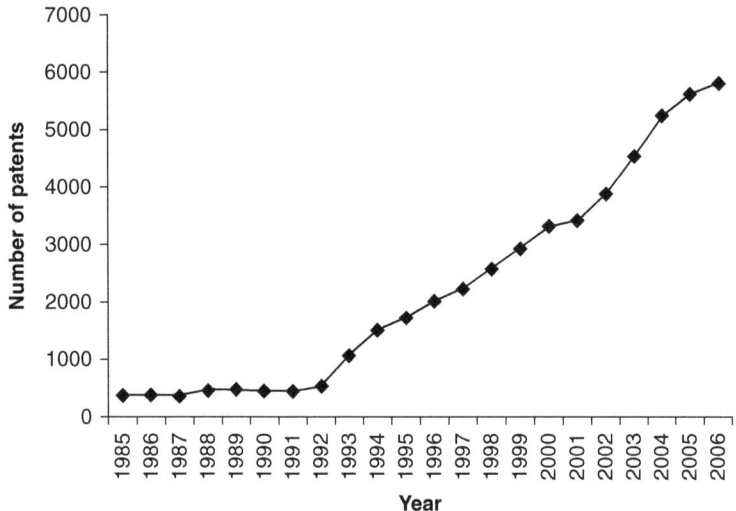

Figure 3.1 Number of foreign pharmaceutical patents in China, 1985–2006
Source: Li et al. (2010, Figure 1).

China has also established a system of judicial protection against infringements of patents. According to data obtained from IPR judgements and decisions, there were 123 pharmaceutical patents cases between 2002 and 2010 (Geng et al., 2011). Two trends were apparent. The annual figure for disputes over patents increased steadily over time, indicating that enforcement was credible, while most of the disputed cases were filed by foreign firms seeking redress from domestic firms over patent infringements. However, there was also an increase in the number of disputed cases in which domestic firms sued foreign firms for patent infringements, which suggests that the enforcement of pharmaceutical patents in China has been used by both domestic and foreign firms.

Figure 3.1 provides evidence in support of the argument that enforcement of patent law in China has been credible. Prior to the first amendment to the Patent Law in 1992, the number of patent applications by foreign companies had been consistently low—ranging from 369 in 1985 to 535 in 1992 (Li et al., 2010). Following the amendment they rose rapidly—from 1068 in 1993 to 3418 in 2002. Patenting increased even more rapidly after the second amendment in 2002—from 3875 in 2003 to 5810 in 2006. This trend suggests that TRIPS compliance has encouraged a rush towards patenting in China by foreign multinational pharmaceutical companies.

Following the adoption of TRIPS, several concurrent trends also influenced the development of the pharmaceutical sector, including overall economic growth, reform of the healthcare sector and reform of the pharmaceutical sector.

Economic growth and healthcare reform

As shown in Table 3.1, real gross domestic product (GDP) per capita in China has increased rapidly during the past three decades, from 1991 yuan (in 2008 RMB) in 1978 to 23,708 yuan in 2008, indicating that the mean annual growth rate was 8.61 per cent. According to the health economics literature, economic prosperity—as measured by income growth—leads to a more than proportional increase in the expansion of the health sector, as measured by the growth of health expenditure (Gerdtham and Jonsson, 2000; Newhouse, 1992). That is, the income elasticity of health expenditure is greater than 1, indicating that the growth rate of health expenditure exceeds

Table 3.1 Health and economic indicators in China, 1978–2008

	1978	1988	1998	2008	Mean annual growth rate 1978–2008 (%)
Economy					
GDP per capita (constant 2008 RMB, CN¥)	1991	4006	8103	23,708	8.61
Population					
Total population (million)	962.59	1110.26	1247.61	1328.02	1.08
Percentage of population aged 65 and over	4.58	5.36	6.47	7.94	1.85
Health service					
Health expenditure per capita (constant 2008 RMB, CN¥)	57	129	352	1095	10.35
Percentage of GDP spent on healthcare (%)	3.00	3.22	4.34	4.62	1.45
Share of public financing (%)	79.57	68.72	45.15	59.58	−0.96
Health					
Life expectancy at birth (years)	65.49	67.53	70.63	73.12	0.37
Infant mortality rate (‰)	6.25	6.64	6.50	7.06	0.41

Note: RMB denotes Renminbi, the official currency of the People's Republic of China. 1 RMB = USD 0.16 in 2012 prices.
Source: Data for life expectancy at birth and percentage of population aged 65 and over are from World Bank Development Indicators 2010; the other data are from the *China Health Statistics Yearbook* (2010). The mean annual growth rates were calculated by the author.

that of income. Between 1978 and 2008 the mean annual growth rate of real per capita health expenditure was 10.35 per cent, which was greater than the mean annual growth rate of per capita income during the same period (see Table 3.1). As a result, the share of GDP expended on healthcare increased over time, from 3 per cent in 1978 to 4.62 per cent in 2008.

Although rapid economic growth has led to a sharp rise in health expenditure, this is not fully reflected in many of the indicators of population health. Between 1978 and 2008 life expectancy increased from 65.49 years to 73.12 years, a longevity gain of 7.63 years over a period of 30 years. This gain was much smaller than that obtained between 1958 and 1978, as well as smaller than the longevity gains of the so-called Four Little Dragons (Hong Kong, Singapore, South Korea and Taiwan) during the period of their economic growth (between 1960 and 1980). In addition, the infant mortality rate in China increased from 6.25 per 1000 babies in 1978 to 7.06 per 1000 in 2008, which suggests that the health sector has not efficiently transformed increased expenditure into improved health outcomes.

There are at least three plausible reasons for this. First, the major force behind the rapid growth in health expenditure between 1978 and 2008 was the increase in the price of healthcare as opposed to the increase in the quantity of healthcare provided per capita (Chow, 2010). An obvious piece of evidence supporting this argument is that there was no significant increase in labour and capital inputs for healthcare, such as the number of medical doctors or beds per 1000 persons. Second, during this period China also experienced rapid change in its demographic structure. For example, the percentage of its population aged 65 and over increased from 4.58 per cent to 7.94 per cent, suggesting increased demand for healthcare services. Finally, low productivity growth in the health sector has constrained the expansion of healthcare services (Yip and Hsiao, 2008). The Chinese government was therefore under considerable pressure to reform the health sector.

Prior to the economic reforms of 1978, China had a public health system, including a rural Cooperative Medical Scheme (CMS) and two urban public health insurance programmes. Healthcare was directly provided through public clinics and hospitals, with the public sector accounting for more than 80 per cent of healthcare funding. Market-oriented reforms resulted in substantially reduced funding for personal healthcare services, the CMS collapsed and, as a result of cutbacks in public financing, coverage of the two public health insurance programmes in urban areas declined. As shown in Figure 3.2, the share of public financing of the Chinese health sector decreased significantly, from nearly 80 per cent in 1978 to 40 per cent in 2001. As a result of the decline, households had increasingly to rely on out-of-pocket payments to finance their healthcare. The share of private financing (in terms of out-of-pocket payments) in total health expenditure increased from 20.4 per cent in 1978 to about 60 per cent in 2001.

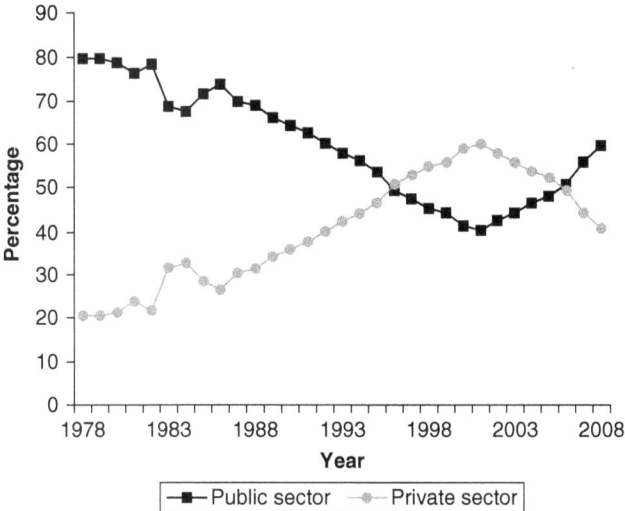

Figure 3.2 Sources of healthcare financing in China, 1978–2008
Source: China Health Statistics Yearbook (2010).

The transition from a public system to one where most healthcare financing relied on out-of-pocket payments created inequalities in health and healthcare utilization (Wagstaff et al., 2009). In response, in 2003 the government launched healthcare reform plans that allocated more public funds to the health sector in order to expand insurance coverage, with a goal of achieving universal coverage by 2011. As shown in Figure 3.2, the share of public financing then increased from 40 per cent to 60 per cent, while the share of private financing gradually decreased, from 60 per cent in 2001 to 40 per cent in 2008. An expected impact on the pharmaceutical sector of increased public health insurance coverage was that demand for prescription drugs would increase (Danzon and Pauly, 2002).

As in other East Asian countries such as Japan, Chinese physicians both prescribe and dispense prescription drugs. The government regulates retail prices of pharmaceutical products, which enables medical providers (including physician clinics and hospitals) to earn the mark-up between the retail and wholesale price. This is currently set at a 15 per cent profit margin on prescription drugs (Yu et al., 2010).

As noted by Iizuka (2007) and Liu et al. (2009), the existence of profit margins for pharmaceuticals distorts the relative prices of prescription drugs and other healthcare services. Compared with prescription drugs, other healthcare services, such as the production of diagnostic information and surgical treatment, are very labour intensive and, as there is no wholesale market for services, medical providers cannot profit from the margin between retail and wholesale prices. Providers, therefore, have a financial incentive to substitute prescription drugs for other inputs, which in turn leads to overprescribing; evidence suggests that overprescription is common in almost every healthcare facility (Sun et al., 2009).

TRIPS compliance and the demand for prescription drugs

Given that the integration of prescribing and dispensing in China provides physicians with a financial incentive to overprescribe, prescription drugs account for a very high share of China's national health expenditure. As noted in Huang and Yang (2009), pharmaceutical spending as a percentage of total health expenditure in China was nearly 50 per cent in the early 1990s and 44 per cent in 2005, still a relatively high level compared with neighbouring countries like Taiwan and Japan, which have many of the same institutional features (Hsieh, 2009; Iizuka, 2007).

One study has evidence supporting the argument that Chinese physicians are likely to overprescribe. Sun et al. (2009) conducted a field survey comparing the prescribing behaviour of village doctors in several counties (in Shandong Province) with different health insurance coverage. The research indicated that overprescribing is common in villages, and this situation worsened when local government introduced a new, community-based rural health insurance programme, known as the New Cooperative Medical Scheme (NCMS). The research found that physicians in counties with the NCMS prescribed an average of 4.6 drugs per patient visit, and 72.4 per cent of their prescriptions included antibiotics. By contrast, physicians in counties that had not implemented the NCMS prescribed an average number of 3.1 drugs per patient visit, and 59.3 per cent of their prescriptions included antibiotics. A plausible explanation for this is that health insurance has increased the demand for healthcare in general and for prescription drugs in particular, which in turn has increased the bargaining power of medical providers in negotiating profit margins with suppliers of pharmaceutical products. A higher profit margin has provided a financial incentive for overprescribing.

If the financial incentives generated by profit margins on prescription drugs were the driving force behind physician overprescribing, gauging the effect of TRIPS compliance on demand for pharmaceutical products depends on how the adoption of TRIPS has influenced profit margins. As noted by Ellison and Snyder (2010), the profit margin on pharmaceuticals is affected by the 'countervailing power' of larger buyers (for example, hospitals) to extract discounts from suppliers. Competition among suppliers is a necessary condition for significant buyer discounts, and providers of medical services are more likely to earn a higher profit margin as the number of competing products increases. A potential effect of TRIPS was that enforcement of IP protection would drive many generics firms out of the

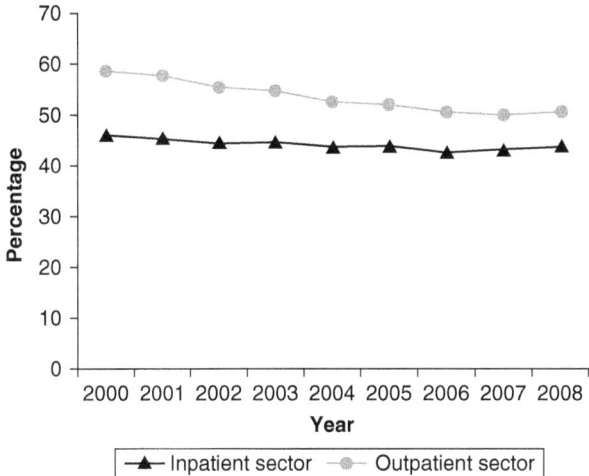

Figure 3.3 Percentage of health expenditure spent on pharmaceuticals
Source: China Health Statistics Yearbook (2010).

market, in turn increasing the bargaining power of the remaining suppliers and thus lowering profit margins and reducing physicians' incentives to overprescribe.

The share of pharmaceutical expenditure according to the different types of healthcare services, as depicted in Figure 3.3, supports the argument that implementation of TRIPS in China may have helped to reduce the incentive to overprescribe. In the case of outpatient services, prescription drugs accounted for nearly 60 per cent of total healthcare costs in 2000, but fell to 50 per cent in 2008. In the case of inpatient services, for 2000–2008 the share of pharmaceutical spending in total healthcare costs ranged between 43 per cent and 46 per cent. Physicians are more likely to overprescribe in an outpatient setting, but this propensity has gradually declined, in part due to the implementation of TRIPS after 2003, although other factors also affected the number of competing products, such as enforcement in recent years of Good Manufacturing Practice in the pharmaceutical sector.

Another likely effect of TRIPS compliance on demand was that it altered the market share of high-quality global products as compared with lower-quality local products. As noted by Wang (2006), generics sold in China, which are mainly produced by local firms, are not bioequivalent and are deemed to be of lower quality than global products developed and produced by multinational firms. In general, the Chinese tend to value foreign goods more highly than domestically produced goods. Wang (2006) has provided evidence in support of the argument that the market is segmented between local generics products deemed to be of low quality and high-quality global brand-name products. His empirical study shows that the number of generics competitors significantly affected the prices of local products, lowering them significantly, but had no effect on the prices of global products. Similarly, a higher number of global therapeutic competitors had the effect of lowering global product prices, but the number of local therapeutic competitors did not significantly affect local product prices. This suggests that local generics are not good substitutes for global brand-name drugs.

As the Chinese economy has grown rapidly, so, too, has the size of the pharmaceutical market. Figure 3.4 shows that pharmaceutical spending as a percentage of healthcare expenditure decreased over time, while healthcare expenditure as a percentage of GDP increased over time. As a result, pharmaceutical expenditure as a percentage of GDP remained relatively constant over time, in the range of 2 per cent. China has become the third largest pharmaceutical market in the world, and the absolute size of GDP has exceeded that of Japan and has become very close to that of the US. The rapid growth in per capita income and the expansion of public insurance coverage are major driving forces accounting for the rapid increase in the market size of the pharmaceutical sector. So, too, is its ageing population, since the majority of pharmaceutical expenditure is allocated to treatment of chronic diseases.

Given the evidence that local and global products are two segmented markets in China, a predictable consequence of rising per capita income for the pharmaceutical market is that demand for high-quality global products will increase while demand for low-quality local products will decrease. Economic theory suggests that demand for high-quality goods increases with income, while demand for low-quality goods decreases as income increases, mainly because wealthier people attach a higher value to quality. As I discuss in more detail below, the implementation of TRIPS provides the infrastructure that global firms need to be able to launch their products in China's market. An increase in the supply of high-quality global products in turn meets rising demand for such products.

This claim is supported by trends in the market share of different versions of drugs. Table 3.2 categorizes pharmaceutical products into three groups: traditional Chinese medicine (TCM), generic drugs and brand-name drugs. The last group is further divided into off-patent and on-patent drugs. As shown in Table 3.2, there are three important time trends in the market share of different versions of drugs between 2005 and 2009. First, as predicted, the market share of generic drugs decreased over time, from 65.8 per cent in 2005 to 61.4 per cent in 2009. Second, although the market share of brand-name drugs remained relatively constant over time, the composition of brand-name drugs changed: the share of on-patent drugs increased from 3.2 per cent in 2005 to 5.6 per cent in 2009, while the share of off-patent drugs declined from 22.1 per cent in 2005 to 19.9 per cent in 2009. This suggests that the availability of patent protection since 2003 has encouraged firms to launch more new drugs into China's market to

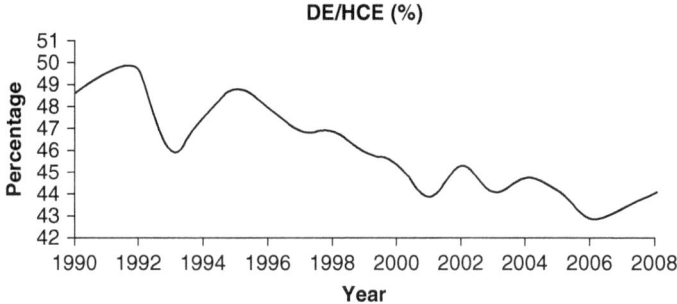
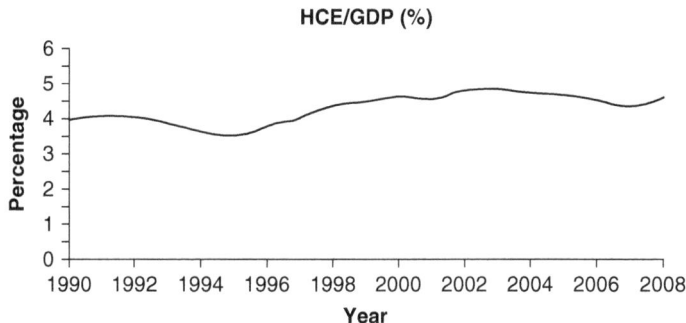
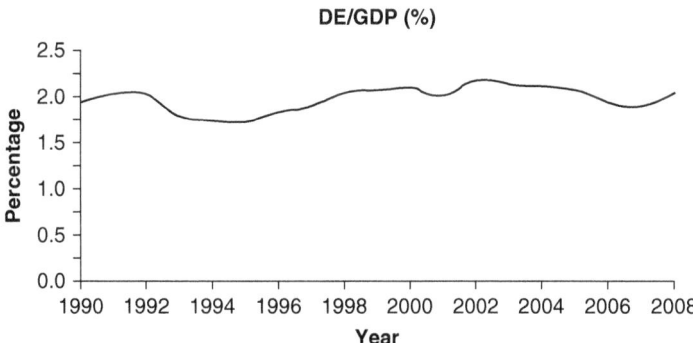

Figure 3.4 Drug expenditure as a percentage of GDP in China, 1990–2008
Note: DE/GDP = (DE/HCE) × (HCE/GDP), where DE represents drug expenditure and HCE represents healthcare expenditure.

meet increased demand for higher-quality products arising from increased per capita income and the expansion of insurance coverage. Third, market share of TCMs also increased over time, from 8.9 per cent in 2005 to 13.0 per cent in 2009. A plausible explanation for this is that after implementing

Table 3.2 Market share of different drug types in China

Year	Traditional Chinese Medicine (TCM)	Generics	Brand-name drugs		
			Off-patent	On-patent	Subtotal
2005	8.9	65.8	22.1	3.2	25.3
2006	10.1	63.8	22.2	3.9	26.1
2007	11.6	61.3	22.1	5.0	27.1
2008	12.5	61.5	20.7	5.3	26.0
2009	13.0	61.4	19.9	5.6	25.5

Source: IMS Health (2010).

TRIPS China selected TCM as a strategic industry to compete with global firms. The quality of TCMs, therefore, increased over time.

Concern has been expressed that compliance with TRIPS would result in rising prices for pharmaceutical products, which might adversely affect access to essential drugs in low- and middle-income countries (t'Hoen, 2009). Direct evidence regarding the relationship between TRIPS compliance and pharmaceutical prices is lacking, but the argument of this chapter is that there has been no significant adverse effect on access to essential drugs in China.

First, compared to other developing countries, such as India, China has devoted a much greater share of public funds to its healthcare sector (Yip and Mahal, 2008). The expansion of public insurance coverage for prescription drugs has partially, if not completely, offset the impact of rising pharmaceutical prices (if, indeed, this has been the case) resulting from TRIPS compliance.

Second, as already mentioned, the Chinese pharmaceutical market contains two segmented markets—one for local generics products and the other for global brand-name products. Wang (2006) has documented that the number of local therapeutic competitors does not have a significant impact on the prices of either local or global products. Thus, overall, withdrawal of selected generic products due to TRIPS compliance would not have a significant effect on pharmaceutical prices.

Third, in 2009 China also began to establish a national list of essential drugs, which, in combination with the expansion of insurance coverage for prescription drugs, provides a safety net against any adverse effect of TRIPS compliance on access to essential drugs. The list of essential drugs consists of two parts: the first made up of chemical drugs and biologics and including 205 products; the second related to TCM, with 102 products (Liu, 2010). The government adopted two strategies to protect essential drugs: in every public medical institution it imposed a regulation of zero profit margins for essential drugs; while all essential drugs were included in the national drug formulary of the public insurance programmes. Given that implementation of the essential drugs measures is so recent, the true effect of this policy in terms of increasing access to drugs remains to be established.

TRIPS compliance and the supply of pharmaceutical products

An analysis of the supply side of the pharmaceutical market requires consideration of the impact of TRIPS compliance on domestic and multinational firms in relation to production and investment in research and development (R&D), as well as on international trade. As mentioned above, the Chinese pharmaceutical market consists of two major segments: products produced by domestic firms, deemed to be of lower quality, and high-quality products produced by multinational firms.

Although the Chinese domestic market is the third largest in the world, the pharmaceutical industry is incredibly fragmented, in the sense that there are thousands of manufacturers and distributors, none of which has a sizeable market share. China currently has more than 5000 pharmaceutical manufacturing firms (Yu et al., 2010). Local pharmaceutical firms are characteristically small-scale, have a low rate of profit and are largely unable to invest in R&D.

These small-scale firms function in a highly competitive environment in which each firm only accounts for a tiny share of the market. For example, in 1997 the largest firm only accounted for 2.61 per cent of total domestic pharmaceutical sales (see Table 3.3). Total sales of the largest firm constituted only 2.5 per cent of global sales made by leading global multinational firms,

Table 3.3 Concentration indices of the pharmaceutical market in China

Index	1997	2005
C1	2.61	2.51
C4	8.10	7.69
C10	15.52	13.3
C20	22.45	–
HHI	622.81	–

Note: Ci ($i = 1, 4, 10, 20$) represents the concentration index for the top ith ($i = 1, 4, 10, 20$) firms, which is defined as the sales of the top ith firms as a percentage of the total sales in the industry as a whole. HHI refers to the Herfindahl-Hirschman Index, which is defined as the summation of the square of the market share among the top 20 firms in the pharmaceutical industry.
Source: Data for 1997 are from Yeung (2002), Table 1; Data for 2005 are from Liu G. (2010, Table 6.9).

such as Merck (Yeung, 2002). The top four largest firms (C4 in Table 3.3) only accounted for 8.1 per cent of total sales in this market. The concentration index for the top ten firms (C10 in Table 3.3) and top 20 firms (C20 in Table 3.3) was 15.52 per cent and 22.45 per cent, respectively. The Herfindahl-Hirschman Index (HHI) for the top 20 firms (in terms of sales) in this industry was only 622.81. These indicators suggest that the market concentration of the pharmaceutical industry in China is extremely low and is close to a perfectly competitive market, in the sense that no single firm possesses a significant degree of market power in determining price and quantity. Data reported in 2005 indicate that the concentration index was similar to that reported in 1997, suggesting that TRIPS compliance has not yet significantly altered the market structure of domestic pharmaceutical firms. Over a longer time period, however, there may well be a trend for small pharmaceutical firms to withdraw from the market.

The mean profit rate (profit as a percentage of sales) in the Chinese pharmaceutical industry is lower than that of global pharmaceutical firms. As shown in Table 3.4, the mean profit rate of all pharmaceutical firms in China was around 6 per cent in 1997, which was significantly lower than the typical profit rate earned by multinational firms. For example, the profit rate of Tianjin Smithkline, a joint venture firm in China, was close to 64 per cent in 1997 (Yeung, 2002). The relatively lower profit rate was a consequence of local pharmaceutical firms not having enough power in the market to enable them to earn 'excess' profit.

With a mean profit rate of around 6 per cent, these firms are unable to afford to invest in R&D for new products and, therefore, they mainly

Table 3.4 Selected indicators of the Chinese pharmaceutical industry by sector, 1997

Items	Western medicines (chemical pharmaceuticals)	Traditional Chinese medicines (TCM)	Pharmaceutical industrial as a whole
Sales value (in millions of RMB)	73,200	25,279	116,619
Value-added (in millions of RMB)	22,307	12,370	40,783
Net profits (in millions of RMB)	3323	2672	7037
Fixed assets (in millions of RMB)	53,671	14,465	78,708
Profits/sales (%)	4.54	10.57	6.03
Profits/fixed assets (%)	6.19	18.47	8.94

Source: Yeung (2002, Table 2).

Table 3.5 Comparisons of R&D capability in China, US and Europe

R&D indicators	China	US	Europe
The number of R&D employees	25,000	124,000	102,000
R&D expenditure per R&D employee (unit: thousands of US dollars)	27	480	291
Share of R&D employees in total employees (%)	3.3	30.6	15.9

Source: Liu, G. (2010, pp. 32–4).

produce generics. Most multinational firms regularly spend more than 6 per cent of their sales on R&D. For example, based on data obtained from 13 large research-based US pharmaceutical companies, it was found that global pharmaceutical firms typically spend about 14 per cent of their sales on R&D (Reinhardt, 2007). Table 3.5 shows that in China the total number of employees, or share of total employees engaged in R&D, is extremely low compared with the US and Europe. In 2010, R&D expenditure per R&D employee in China was only US$27,000, while the US spent US$480,000 and Europe US$291,000. This suggests that local firms are well behind the global pharmaceutical giants in terms of production and R&D capability.

Putting these characteristics together, it is evident that the small scale of operations, lower profit rates and low investment in R&D have created a 'vicious circle' for the pharmaceutical industry, largely arising from its dependent status within the Chinese healthcare system. This system allows the cross-subsidization of intangible professional services (for example, diagnosis and surgical treatment) within the hospital sector and tangible goods (for example, pharmaceutical products) in the pharmaceutical sector. Medical providers, especially the large public hospitals, are engaged in rent-seeking behaviour, earning profits directly from prescription drugs to compensate for government underfunding of and underinvestment in the hospital sector. In 2006, for example, governmental fiscal subsidies only accounted for 6.39 per cent of the total revenue in general public hospitals. By contrast, drug-dispensing revenue in the same year accounted for more than 40 per cent of hospital revenue (Huang and Yang, 2009). This suggests that the pharmaceutical sector serves as a principal source of revenue to support the delivery of professional healthcare services in the hospital sector. Here local pharmaceutical firms' excess profits are being 'captured' by hospital industries, in effect restricting their ability to invest in R&D and placing them in a weak position when competing with multinationals. Yeung (2002), therefore, likens the position of these firms to that of David meeting Goliath.

It is expected that competition between local and global firms will drive many local firms out of the market. The question to be explored now is which local firms are likely to survive and prosper after TRIPS has been fully implemented. Local Chinese pharmaceutical firms can be divided into three sectors: chemical pharmaceuticals, TCM and biologics. Table 3.4 indicates that the TCM sector in China has a relatively high profit rate of 10.57 per cent, compared with the chemical pharmaceuticals sector's 4.54 per cent. Local TCM firms are, therefore, better able to invest in R&D than local firms producing generics, and are also likely to be in a stronger position to compete with global firms. Local TCM firms have two advantages over chemical pharmaceuticals when competing with global firms: the costs of R&D investment in the discovery and development of new products are lower for TCMs, and there is less protection for patents in relation to herbal medicines. Local TCM firms, therefore, are less likely than their counterparts making Western medicines to be adversely affected by the enforcement of TRIPS. All these factors suggest that TCM firms in China have some competitive advantages over multinational firms. Such advantages may not last, however, given that multinational pharmaceutical firms can easily enter the TCM market because the hurdles presented by patent protection for existing products, or for R&D costs for new products in the TCM industry, are lower than those for the Western pharmaceutical sector.

Biological drugs are important new healthcare technologies that are defined as medicines whose active substance is made from, or produced by, a living organism. Compared with chemically synthesized drugs, manufacturing biologics is much more complex (Baumann, 2006; Lacanà et al., 2007). Moreover, biologics have, until recently, usually targeted small patient populations. Given these characteristics of the manufacturing and marketing of biologics, China is in a stronger position to compete with global firms in developing biological products and is in a process of rapidly catching up with US competition (Hu et al., 2006). As shown in Table 3.6, the importance of biologics in the Chinese pharmaceutical industry has increased rapidly, although chemical drugs still account for the largest share of the industry

Table 3.6 Total production value of the Chinese pharmaceutical industry by type of products (in billions of RMB)

Type of products	2000	2006	Mean annual growth rate 2000–2006 (%)
Chemical drugs	107.8 (62)	272.1 (62)	16.69
TCM	53.3 (30)	123.5 (28)	15.03
Biologics	13.6 (8)	43.9 (10)	21.57

Note: numbers in parentheses denote the share of product value in the industry as a whole.
Source: Liu, G. (2010, p. 81).

in terms of total output value. Between 2000 and 2006, the mean annual growth rate of product value for biologics was significantly higher than for chemical drugs and TCM. As a result, the market share of biologics (in terms of product value) increased from 8 per cent in 2000 to 10 per cent in 2006.

Entry of foreign multinational firms

The most significant effect of TRIPS compliance on the pharmaceutical market is that enforcement of IP protection helps multinational firms reap a higher return on their R&D investment, which provides added incentive for them to enter the Chinese market. In general, global firms enter this market by selling imported patented products or patented products produced in China through foreign direct investment (FDI), or a mixture of these strategies.

In decisions by multinational companies to enter a market, the availability of IPR is often secondary to the expected revenues that can be captured, notwithstanding the effects of patents on price (Danzon et al., 2005). Foreign firms also base their decisions regarding market entry on the size of the market, generally preferring to enter larger markets (Iizuka, 2009). This suggests that several competing factors influence the entry of multinationals into China's market and the marketing of patented products, and not just the presence of TRIPS-compliant patent standards.

On the one hand, the Chinese government is likely to continue imposing price regulation on pharmaceutical products, given that an increasing share of pharmaceutical expenditure is paid by the public sector. Looked upon unfavourably by foreign firms, price regulation has become a disincentive to such firms wanting to introduce their products onto the Chinese market. As shown in Figure 3.5, the pharmaceutical price index rose by about 80 per cent between 1990 and 2000, but this trend has now reversed following several rounds of pharmaceutical price adjustments by government (Huang and Yang, 2009). Between 1990 and 2005, however, the consumer price index in China was higher than the pharmaceutical price index, so the real pharmaceutical price index (after accounting for price inflation) decreased by more than 20 per cent during this period.

On the other hand, as China continues to extend health insurance coverage—aimed to achieve universal coverage for its citizens by 2011 (which that country largely succeeded in doing)—the size of the market for patented global products is increasing, in turn providing greater incentive for multinational firms to enter the market.

This analysis suggests that the market for high-quality global products in China can be characterized by lower prices (than would apply in the hypothetical circumstances of a 'free market') but with higher volumes. Whether the benefits of higher volume override concerns over lower prices (a negative incentive for entry) is a matter of profit margin or marginal profit. Although

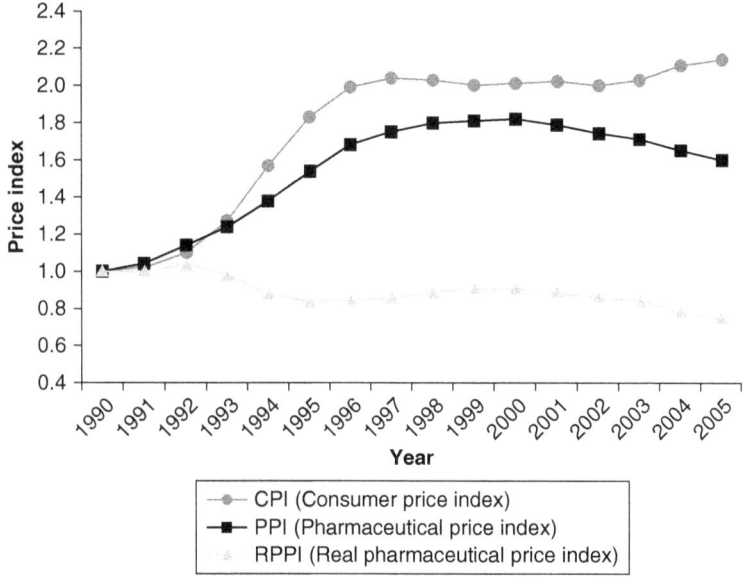

Figure 3.5 Pharmaceutical price index, 1990–2005
Source: PPI from Lui, G. (2010, p. 146); CPI is from China Statistical Yearbook (2010); RPPI = (PPI/CPI) × 100.

such evidence is yet to be collected, the time trend of the aggregate market share, as shown in Table 3.2, seems to indicate that positive incentives created by higher volume have dominance over the disincentives generated by regulated lower prices. As explored further below, imports of chemical drugs and biologics have increased rapidly in recent years, providing additional evidence demonstrating that TRIPS compliance has led to an increase in imports of patented global products as well as the sheer size and value of the Chinese market.

With regard to direct foreign investment, the effect of TRIPS compliance is more obvious. As China has begun to apply internationally recognized practice in respect of IPR for pharmaceutical products, more and more multinational firms have entered the Chinese market in the form of joint venture companies. Of the biggest 25 global giants, at least 20 of these firms have set up joint ventures in China (Yeung, 2002).

The entry of foreign firms has significantly altered the structure of ownership in China's pharmaceutical industry. As shown in Table 3.7, in 2000 state enterprises accounted for more than 60 per cent of asset value and nearly half of production value and profit, while joint venture companies only accounted for about 20 per cent, in terms of asset value, production value and profit. By 2006, however, the importance of state enterprises had

Table 3.7 Ownership structure in China's pharmaceutical industry

Indicators	State enterprises	Joint ventures and FDI	Private and collective enterprises	Others
Share of asset value (%)				
2000	60.83	18.93	5.82	14.42
2006	29.47	22.04	15.13	33.36
Share of production value (%)				
2000	49.6	22.7	27.7	
2006	19.9	25.3	23.0	31.8
Share of profit (%)				
2000	49.66	21.25	29.09	
2006	24.06	31.62	44.32	

Source: Liu, G. (2010, pp. 41, 53, 80).

declined sharply. In terms of production value they only accounted for about 20 per cent of the industry. In 2006, joint venture companies' share of profits was more than 30 per cent, although their asset values only accounted for about 22 per cent of total assets in the pharmaceutical industry. This trend suggests that TRIPS compliance has provided a key incentive for foreign firms to gain market share in China's pharmaceutical industry. Given the evidence that foreign firms are more productive in terms of earning profits per dollar of assets, this trend also suggests that TRIPS compliance has increased the profitability of China's pharmaceutical industry, which in turn increases the capacity for R&D investment in the pharmaceutical industry as a whole.

Table 3.8 reports the pattern of international trade in the Chinese pharmaceutical sector between 2007 and 2009. As already mentioned, China's major output is low-quality generics that are not competitive in the international market. Thus, chemical drugs account for only 5 per cent of the total value of exports in the Chinese pharmaceutical sector. By contrast, China imports patented drugs from developed countries. Thus, chemical drugs account for a relatively larger share of the value of imports than of the value of exports. Between 2007 and 2009, the share of chemical drugs in the total value of imports increased from 30 per cent to 36 per cent, providing support for the previous argument that TRIPS compliance increases incentives for multinational firms to market their patented products in China.

By contrast, most of the international trade is in active pharmaceutical ingredients (APIs). In 2007, APIs accounted for more than 90 per cent of the value of exports and 60 per cent of the value of imports. However, the importance of APIs in international trade has declined over time, indicating that

Table 3.8 Pattern of trade in the Chinese pharmaceutical sector (in billions of US$)

Items	2007	2009	Mean annual growth rate 2007–2009 (%)
Exports			
APIs	13.56	16.55	10.48
	(90.46)	(86.20)	
Chemical drugs	0.78	1.20	24.03
	(5.20)	(6.25)	
Biologics	0.65	1.45	49.36
	(4.34)	(7.55)	
Total	14.99	19.20	13.17
	(100.00)	(100.00)	
Imports			
APIs	5.99	7.71	13.45
	(63.93)	(56.73)	
Chemical drugs	2.84	4.86	30.82
	(30.31)	(35.76)	
Biologics	0.54	1.02	37.44
	(5.76)	(7.51)	
Total	9.37	13.59	20.43
	(100.00)	(100.00)	

Notes: 1. API is the abbreviation for active pharmaceutical ingredients.
2. Numbers in parentheses represent the shares of total exports or imports.
Source: Liu, G. (2010, pp. 85–8).

the trade has shifted in importance from ingredients to final products. Given that TRIPS compliance mainly affects the market for final products, this shift in trade pattern provides additional evidence to support the argument that TRIPS compliance increases incentives for multinational firms to launch their patented products onto the Chinese market.

Conclusion and policy implications

While China began its market-oriented reforms in 1978, reforms in its social sector are well behind those in the economic sector. As a result of bilateral trade negotiations and its accession to the WTO, since 1993 China has implemented reforms to make its IPR legislation consistent with TRIPS. This chapter has focused on the effect of TRIPS compliance on the pharmaceutical sector. Available evidence only permits an evaluation over a relatively short period, and allowance must be made for several concurrent trends—in particular, rapid economic growth and reform of the health sector—which may confound tracing the direct effects of TRIPS compliance on China. In the absence of recent empirical data, this chapter has used deductive reasoning together with aggregate time trend calculations.

To summarize, TRIPS compliance has reinforced incentives for multinational firms to enter the Chinese market, which implies direct competition between low-quality local generics products and patented global products. As a result, some local generics firms will be driven out of the market, which will reduce the number of competing firms. The reduction in the number of local firms will lead to a decrease in the relative bargaining power of the hospital sector when negotiating profit margins with suppliers of pharmaceutical products, in turn reducing the financial incentives for medical providers to overprescribe. Although direct evidence is lacking, the aggregate time series trend in pharmaceutical expenditure as a percentage of total health expenditure is consistent with this argument.

There is no clear evidence that TRIPS compliance has led to an increase in the price of pharmaceutical products in China. Indeed, actual pharmaceutical prices have declined over time. Together with the expansion of public insurance, this suggests that TRIPS compliance in China has not created an access barrier for pharmaceutical products. Meanwhile, the rapid growth in per capita income, combined with healthcare reforms focused on extending health insurance coverage, also raises demand for patented global products. It is expected, therefore, that the market share of global products will increase and the market share of low-quality local products will decline in the post-TRIPS period.

Compared with chemical pharmaceuticals, the TCM industry in China has several advantages over global firms, at least in the short run, and it is expected that local firms specializing in TCM will not lose their market share as a result of TRIPS. The time series data in relation to the aggregate market share of the TCM sector support this claim.

An important implication of this study is that consumers in China receive significant benefits from the adoption of TRIPS in the pharmaceutical sector, including an increased supply of patented global products and a reduction in pharmaceutical expenditure through a reduction in overprescribing. Global concern that Chinese consumers may need to pay higher prices for generics, therefore reducing their access to essential drugs in the post-TRIPS period, may not be a significant issue because recent health reforms have increased the share of public financing of healthcare.

On the supply side, some local generics firms may become the losers in the short term. In the long term, however, full enforcement of TRIPS is likely to result in increased market concentration in the local generics sector, which may enable surviving firms to increase their R&D investment. This may be an opportunity for some local companies to build the capacity to compete with the foreign multinationals, or to become cooperative partners of multinational firms. Moreover, the entry of foreign firms has also helped the Chinese pharmaceutical industry increase its profitability, in turn improving its capacity to engage in R&D. The important exception here is the burgeoning field of biologics and regenerative medicines. Overall, however, TRIPS compliance has benefitted pharmaceutical firms in China by increasing their incentives and ability to engage in R&D investment.

References

Baumann, A. (2006) 'Early Development of Therapeutic Biologics—Pharmacokinetics', *Current Drug Metabolism*, 7, 15–21.
Chow, G. C. (2010) *Interpreting China's Economy* (Singapore: World Scientific).
Danzon, P. M. and M. V. Pauly (2002) 'Health Insurance and the Growth in Pharmaceutical Expenditures', *Journal of Law and Economics*, 45, 587–614.
Danzon, P. M., Y. R. Wang and L. Wang (2005) 'The Impact of Price Regulation on the Launch Delay of New Drugs: Evidence from 25 Markets in the 1990s', *Health Economics*, 14, 269–92.
Ellison, S. F. and C. M. Snyder (2010) 'Countervailing Power in Wholesale Pharmaceuticals', *Journal of Industrial Economics*, 57, 32–53.
Geng, L., J. Ding, R. Shao and M. He (2011) 'An Overall Analysis of Judicial Protection for Drug Patents in China', *China Health Law*, 19, 23–6 (in Chinese).
Gerdtham, U. and B. Jonsson (2000) 'International Comparisons on Health Expenditure: Theory, Data and Econometric Analysis' in A. J. Culyer and J. P. Newhouse (eds) *Handbook of Health Economics* (North Holland: Elsevier Science).
Hason, A. K. and J. E. Shimotake (2006) 'Recent Developments in Patent Rights for Pharmaceuticals in China and India', *Pace International Law Review*, 18, 303–15.
Hsieh, C. R. (2009) 'Pharmaceutical Policy in Taiwan' in K. Eggleston (ed.) *Prescribing Cultures and Pharmaceutical Policy in the Asia-Pacific* (Baltimore, MD: The Brookings Institution Press).
Hu, X., Q. Ma and S. Zhang (2006) 'Biopharmaceuticals in China', *Biotechnology Journal*, 1, 1215–24.
Huang, Y. and Y. Yang (2009) 'Pharmaceutical Pricing in China' in K. Eggleston (ed.) *Prescribing Cultures and Pharmaceutical Policy in the Asia-Pacific* (Baltimore, MD: The Brookings Institution Press).
Iizuka, T. (2007) 'Experts' Agency Problems: Evidence from the Prescription Drug Market in Japan', *RAND Journal of Economics*, 38, 844–62.
Iizuka, T. (2009) 'Generic Entry in a Regulated Pharmaceutical Market', *Japanese Economic Review*, 60, 63–81.
IMS Health (2010) *IMS Market Prognosis, Asia 2005–2009* (London: IMS Health).
Lacanà, E., S. Amur, P. Mummanneni, H. Zhao and F. W. Frueh (2007) 'The Emerging Role of Pharmacogenomics in Biologics', *Clinical Pharmacology & Therapeutics*, 82, 466–71.
Li, Y., X. Sun and H. Chi (2010) 'Analysis on Domestic Foreign Patent in Pharmacy Domain', *China Medical Herald*, 7, 2–4 (in Chinese).
Liu, G. (2010) *China Pharmaceutical Industry Report* (Beijing: Scientific Publishing) (in Chinese).
Liu, Y. M., Y. H. Kao Yang and C. R. Hsieh (2009) 'Financial Incentives and Physicians' Prescription Decisions on the Choice between Brand-name and Generic Drugs: Evidence from Taiwan', *Journal of Health Economics*, 28, 341–9.
Ministry of Health of the People's Republic of China (2010) *China Health Statistics Yearbook* (Beijing: Peking Union Medical College Press) (in Chinese).
National Bureau of Statistics of China (2010) *China Statistical Yearbook* (Beijing: China Statistics Press).

Newhouse, J. P. (1992) 'Medical Care Costs: How Much Welfare Loss?', *Journal of Economic Perspectives*, 16, 3–21.

Reinhardt, U. (2007) 'The Pharmaceutical Sector in Health Care' in F. A. Sloan and C.-R. Hsieh (eds) *Pharmaceutical Innovation: Incentives, Competition, and Cost-Benefit Analysis in International Perspective* (New York: Cambridge University Press).

Santoro, M. A. and C. M. Liu (2009) 'China's Underdeveloped Drug Regulation Regime: A Threat to Global Safety?' in K. Eggleston (ed.) *Prescribing Cultures and Pharmaceutical Policy in the Asia-Pacific* (Baltimore, MD: The Brookings Institution Press).

Sun, X., S. Jackson, G. A. Carmichael and A. C. Sleigh (2009) 'Prescribing Behavior of Village Doctors Under China's New Cooperative Medical Scheme', *Social Science & Medicine*, 68, 1775–9.

t'Hoen, E. (2009) *The Global Politics of Pharmaceutical Monopoly Power: Drug Patents, Access, Innovation and the Application of the WTO Doha Declaration on TRIPS and Public Health* (Diemen: AMB Publishers).

Wagstaff, A., W. Yip and M. Lindelow (2009) 'China's Health System and Its Reform: A Review of Recent Studies', *Health Economics*, 18, S7–23.

Wang, R. Y. (2006) 'Price Competition in the Chinese Pharmaceutical Market', *International Journal of Health Care Finance and Economics*, 6, 119–29.

The World Bank Group (2010). *World Development Indicators* (Washington: the World Bank).

Yeung, G. (2002) 'The Implications of WTO Accession on the Pharmaceutical Industry in China', *Journal of Contemporary China*, 11, 473–94.

Yip, W. and W. C. Hsiao (2008) 'The Chinese Health System at a Crossroads', *Health Affairs*, 27, 460–8.

Yip, W. and A. Mahal (2008) 'The Health Care Systems of China and India: Performance and Future Challenges', *Health Affairs*, 27, 921–32.

Yu, X., C. Li, Y. Shi and M. Yu (2010) 'Pharmaceutical Supply Chain in China: Current Issues and Implications for Health System Reform', *Health Policy*, 97, 8–15.

4
Immunity to TRIPS? Vaccine Production and the Biotechnology Industry in Cuba

Jens Plahte and Simon Reid-Henry

'We don't like patents, remember?' Castro said. The stage was the largest laboratory in Cuba—the Centre for Genetic Engineering and Biotechnology—the time was probably around 1990, and Fidel Castro had just entered a room where some senior scientists were discussing the need for patents to protect their growing market. Just a few years before, in 1986, Cuba had voiced strong opposition to the new global intellectual property rights (IPR) regime in the Uruguay Round of General Agreement on Tariffs and Trade (GATT). But about five years after Castro's 'reminder', in 1995, Cuba signed up to the Trade Related Aspects of Intellectual Property Rights (TRIPS) Agreement and was seeking to bring its domestic biotechnology industry into line—or 'harmonize'—with global IPR standards. Presumably, then, things had changed fundamentally in the intervening years. Or had they? Because, as closer inspection reveals, there are many features of the Cubans' 'older' approach to biotechnology that have not been abandoned. All, therefore, may not be quite as it seems when it comes to the 'rolling out' of global norms, standards and laws in local settings, and our aim in this chapter is to explore why. We do so by delving into the relationship between TRIPS, generics, the availability of essential medicines and the Cuban biotechnology sector.

We explore this through three primary arguments. First, through offering an overview of the development of Cuban biotechnology in the 1980s and into the 2000s, we show that Cuba only acceded to the TRIPS Agreement at a point when Cuban biotechnology had already developed research and development (R&D) capabilities on an innovative level, and, furthermore, had developed a distinctive scientific and technical approach to biotechnology. Second, we show that, although the Cubans may initially have been against TRIPS for ideological reasons, the actual impact of TRIPS in Cuba was limited, due in part to the nature of Cuba's locally developed IPR regime, but also to the unintended side-effects of the US embargo. Third, we show that when it comes to certain areas of scientific research, such as biologicals, patents are relatively less important barriers to entry into global markets than is the case for chemical drugs. Regarding vaccines in particular, we show that there is no such thing as a 'generic' in terms of drug regulation anyway, and that this seems to be the case for other biopharmaceuticals also.

Having set out these main points, we then try to elaborate our findings through two case studies. The first of these is the example of the pentavalent DTP-hepB-HiB vaccine, an essential childhood vaccine; the second is the development of a therapeutic cancer vaccine by the *Centro de Immunología Molecular* (CIM).

These case studies reveal that Cuba has enjoyed particular success in its vaccine development both because of the inherent 'immunity' of the vaccine sector to TRIPS and because Cuba was able to overcome the more important barriers to entry into the vaccine field (such as scale-up and the conduct and cost of clinical trials) on the back of its particular, earlier approach to science. We conclude, however, by suggesting that, even though TRIPS itself may be resisted in certain ways by countries like Cuba (albeit also at a certain cost to them), the more general assimilation of Western practices that have been rolled out alongside TRIPS (for example, the International Standards Organization norms) often present somewhat 'stickier' barriers to entry to developing countries wishing to pursue less marketized approaches to the production of pharmaceuticals.

The Cuban pharmaceutical sector

The Cuban pharmaceutical sector consists of two separate industries—the biotechnology industry and the chemical drugs industry. In Cuba these two industries are organizationally and institutionally separate and work according to fundamentally different principles. The biotechnology industry, which is the focus of our investigations, was until recently run directly by the State Council, and has received highly preferential treatment from the country's top political leadership. The chemical drugs industry, on the other hand, has been run by the Ministry of Public Health and the Ministry of Basic Industries, on terms very similar to other industrial sectors in that country. For the sake of brevity we will not go into further detail about the Cuban chemical pharmaceutical industry, because it is Cuba's biotechnology industry that offers a more unique and compelling case of a low-income country establishing an innovation-based high-tech industry from scratch.

It is worth mentioning, nonetheless, that in 2005 Cuba's chemical drugs industry was reported to have supplied some 80 per cent of the total national consumption of medicines. The country imports raw materials and active pharmaceutical ingredients (APIs) for this, and China is an important supplier (Kaplan and Laing, 2005). Of course, such figures do not give a complete picture of the Cuban drugs supply, particularly since the Cuban population is severely undersupplied with even basic drugs like antibiotics and painkillers, due to the precarious foreign currency situation that has persisted for the past 20 or so years and the impact of the US embargo of the island. For these reasons it is impossible to estimate what would have been the domestic share of national drugs supply in a 'normal' drugs supply situation—whatever that would be in Cuba. Somewhat easier to estimate is what the Cuban chemical drugs industry exports, which in 2007 amounted to about US$12 million in total (One, 2008). In any case, the total revenues for the three major biotechnology centres (the Centre for Genetic Engineering and Biotechnology, Finlay Institute and CIM) amounted to about US$150 million in 2008 (Plahte, 2010c), which, together with Cuban overseas sales of medical services (such as revenues to the state from Cuban health missions abroad), dwarf pharmaceutical exports. So, while the contributions of the chemical drugs industry are far from irrelevant, it is the biotechnology industry in Cuba that holds the most interest for us here.

The Cuban biotechnology sector: Technological maturity prior to TRIPS

Cuba's biotechnology programme was set in motion following a visit to Cuba in 1978 by the US cancer specialist R. Lee Clark. After hearing from Clark of the medical and economic potential of the then rapidly developing biotechnology sector in Western economies, President Castro decided to initiate a domestic pilot project in interferon production. The project was assisted by a high-level consultative body—the Biological Front—and in less than two years the Cubans were producing recombinant interferon for use in clinical trials. From 1981, based upon the success of this initial work, a series of major research and production centres were already under construction, in what must be one of the most ambitious programmes for public sector biotechnology development yet to be seen anywhere in the world (Reid-Henry, 2007a, 2007b). Large-scale investments—with a commonly cited figure being US$1 billion—were reportedly then ploughed back into the sector until the mid-1990s to consolidate this initial success and momentum.[1]

Today this sector is national in scope and scale, although the most important institutes, research and production centres are located predominantly in the capital city, in an industrial district in one of Havana's western suburbs (the Western Havana Scientific Pole).[2] Here more than 60 organizations, employing approximately 14,000 workers, are working in fields that, one way or another, are related to biotechnology. These facilities also include some specialized hospitals, a consulting company, the national drug regulatory agency (CECMED) and a couple of faculties at the University of Havana. This clustering of biotechnology-related institutes can in some respects be likened to the industrial and knowledge-intensive geographical concentrations of Western science parks, at least in its agglomeration of organizations involved in cognate research topics, and in terms of its similarity with the 'learning region' approach to industrial and product development (CubaCiencia, 2003; Dearing, 1995). Much of the focus in Cuba is related to the health applications of biotechnology, although there is substantial work on agricultural applications as well (which have perhaps received less attention in the literature). Nonetheless, from an historical perspective the biotechnology sector—and the Western Havana Scientific Pole in particular—may be seen as the practical amalgamation and manifestation of the Cuban government's long-term strategic priorities of education, health and science.

Within the Western Havana Scientific Pole, the vaccine industry is not a delimited or discrete entity but, rather, an integral part of the overall biotechnology sector. However, the core of the Cuban biotechnology sector, a handful of closely interconnected research and production centres, is in the main involved in vaccine production. These centres include the Centre for Genetic Engineering and Biotechnology (CIGB), Finlay Institute, CIM and the Centre for Biomolecular Chemistry (CQB). The CIGB, founded in 1986, is the flagship of the Cuban biotechnology sector and by far the biggest institute. Its main focus is on recombinant technologies based on single cell organisms (for instance, yeast), and it produces vaccines as well as other medical, industrial and agricultural biotech products. CIM, by contrast, epitomizes the priority granted to investments in the biotechnology sector from the mid-1990s onwards, and focuses on cancer research, including cutting-edge recombinant therapeutic cancer vaccines produced in mammalian cell lines. The third of the trinity of major biotechnology organizations in Cuba is Finlay Institute, which emerged entirely out of a 1980s vaccine development project (through which the Cubans successfully combated a meningitis epidemic by distributing an indigenously developed meningococcal group B vaccine). Finlay's product portfolio remains dominated by vaccines based mainly on 'traditional' bacterial fermentation technologies. Finally, founded in 2008, there is the most recent institute, CQB, the result of a merging of the Centre for Pharmaceutical Chemistry with the Laboratory for Synthetic Antigens at the University of Havana. The Centre for Chemical Biology was developed to support the work of the other centres, and will work on chemical processes related to biological production, like the development of synthetic antigens and conjugation technologies for vaccines.

What makes Cuba distinctive?

As outlined earlier, what really marks the Cuban biotechnology sector out as distinct is not simply the individual contribution of these centres or their particular expertise, but the way in which they are collectively organized and integrated, and the way in which a relatively distinct epistemic, juridical and technological milieu was developed from the mid-1980s. There are numerous factors involved in this development, including the manner in which biotechnology as a sector was intended to be a focal point to and conduit for the emergence of a wider series of political aspirations in the Cuba of the late 1980s and early 1990s. These aims were innately bound up in the government's 'revolutionary' commitments to health and education and the wider discursive framing of these commitments as constitutive of the nation's identity. They were also part and parcel of the political and legal consequences of being an island nation under embargo by the very country that dominated the international biotechnology agenda.

Since the 1981 Cuban interferon pilot project, investments have not only been channelled into founding new biotechnology centres. In parallel, a supporting legal framework has been developed, most specifically a drug regulatory agency, which has been given increasing independence over the same period (Ratanawijitrasin and Wondemagegnehu, 2002). This means that Cuba has implemented internationally accepted regulations and norms, such as ISO-9000 norms, as well as Good Manufacturing Practice, Good Laboratory Practice and Good Clinical Practice norms. Another of the distinctive features of Cuban biotechnology lies in what the Cubans characterize as the 'full-cycle' nature of their biotechnology centres, referring to the manner in which each centre is responsible for the entire innovation process, starting from directed basic science and moving on through applied science, product development, industrial scale-up, IPR management, clinical testing, registration, marketing and sales (Lage, 2006a, 2006b). The logic here was that, by factoring in the needs of the national public health system at the beginning of the cycle, essential products from the sector would be more likely to spill out at its endpoint. Hence, the first three of the four main biotechnology organizations briefly described above perform, to a great extent, full-cycle operations—from research to production—within the confines of their particular technology platforms.

Finally, and perhaps most importantly, the biotechnology sector is entirely state-operated. Up to 2009, the core centres were managed directly by the State Council—one of the top political bodies of the Cuban state. Such central state control has, on the one hand, allowed a prioritized flow of scarce capital and resources into the sector over many years (in which respect Cuban biotechnology development mirrors socialist experience elsewhere in the world). On the other hand, there is always a risk that overt state controls over scientific research agendas, practices and outputs may hinder scientific originality, and blunt creativity.

Notwithstanding this question of the impact of state control, in relative terms the Cuban biotechnology sector has displayed a superior performance, as indicated in Quach and colleagues' (2006) comparative analysis of biotechnology patenting in seven selected developing or emerging economies,[3] in which a ratio of health biotechnology papers to health biotechnology patents of 9:1 was reported. South Korea (with a ratio of 12:1) was second, while Brazil and Egypt were at the lower end of the sample, with 70:1 and 80:1 ratios, respectively. In other words, it appears that in Cuba a comparatively high proportion of scientific results are translated into patentable technology. Pure patenting does not, of course, either indicate or represent the full range of intellectual property strategies that state or commercial entities may explore. Decisions over when, what and how to patent also come into the equation, and patenting strategies are often highly nuanced. In the case of Cuba the intellectual property strategy reflects a deliberate focus on applied research that may not be sustainable outside the island's particular 'mission' approach to science. A full assessment of the success or otherwise of such approaches in Cuba is somewhat beyond the scope of this chapter, although for two early treatments see Tim Beardsley (1986) and Julie M. Feinsilver (1993); for a Cuban analysis from the 1990s, see E. M. Bravo (1998); and for more recent overviews, Jens Plahte (2010a, b, c) and Simon Reid-Henry (2010). Nonetheless, these figures give us an idea of the obvious determination of a socialist state enterprise to take Western patenting and wider regulatory norms seriously.

Our point here is not merely to provide an overview of the distinctive nature of the Cuban biotechnology sector, but, more importantly, to highlight the fact that substantial technological capacity was in place before Cuba acceded to TRIPS. Indeed, by the early 1990s, the main investments had already been made and several innovative products were already well advanced along various pipelines. From the Cuban perspective, the presence of TRIPS was thus treated as a question of how to integrate an already mature and distinctive 'experimental milieu' (Reid-Henry, 2007b) into the more internationally orthodox and universalizing global regulatory landscape that TRIPS was intended to establish. Indeed, the impact of TRIPS in Cuba—along with other forms of international regulation—can only be understood against this background. Thus, as we will argue, rather than seeing the Cubans as being forced by TRIPS to innovate to avoid any potential negative consequences of that new regime, it was more the case that the economic necessities of the crisis that set in after the fall of the Soviet bloc at the start of the 1990s drove Cuba to reorient its biotechnology exports towards Western markets, where strict patenting was and is the norm.

Local and non-local forms of resistance to TRIPS

As is discussed above, and to the surprise of many observers, in 1995 socialist Cuba initiated the transition to full accordance with TRIPS and applied its norms and standards of protection to the fields of pharmaceuticals and agricultural chemicals alike (Hernández, 2001; Quach et al., 2006). Perhaps it simply had no choice in the face of the global trend of the time. But in

1996 Cuba went even further by signing up to the Patent Cooperation Treaty (PCT),[4] with the highest levels of government acknowledging the need (or benefits to Cuba) to fall into line with the international IPR norms of a regulated 'multilateral' world economy (Cuba, Decree Law N. 160, *Consejo de Estado*). However, to the knowledge of the authors, very few of the IPR held in Cuban biotechnology are shared with foreign individuals or organizations. The only exception to this rule known to us is the synthetic HiB vaccine, the patent of which is co-held by René Roy at the University of Ottawa (Pérez and Núñez, 2009). In their comparative study of patenting, Quach and colleagues (2006) found that 95 per cent of biotechnological patents in Cuba were granted to Cuban assignees. This is not a surprising outcome for two basic reasons, which we explore here. The first concerns the way that the Cubans had not only developed their own technological capability but had also established a local IPR regime, which, although in some ways antagonistic to the norms underpinning TRIPS, would nonetheless prove fungible within that broader system. The second concerns the unintended consequences of the US embargo of Cuba. We turn to these variables in order.

Localized IPR regimes

Despite its apparently enthusiastic take-up of TRIPS in 1995, Cuba had, as might have been expected, tried earlier to prevent the roll-out of the proposed GATT-governed IPR regime when it was first tabled during the Uruguay Round of GATT in 1986. Cuba was then a member of the 'Group of Twelve' developing countries (alongside Argentina, Brazil, Chile, China, Colombia, Cuba, Egypt, India, Nigeria, Peru, Tanzania and Uruguay), later joined by Pakistan and Zimbabwe. Together these countries were particularly active in tabling alternative proposals to those forwarded by industry groups, the US and other developed states (see Annex 1 GATT. Doc. MTN/GNG/NG 11/W71 of 14 May 1990).

Such resistance was entirely in keeping with the development of Cuban IPR up to that point. Like many developing countries, Cuba had developed its own IPR laws relatively late. Those intellectual property laws that did exist at the time of the revolutionary takeover in 1959 were largely inherited from the US, and hence were abolished in the 1960s.[5] It was not until the 1970s that a more comprehensive set of intellectual property laws was put into place as part of the more general retreat from the hardline state socialism of the early years of the revolution. This resulted in the formation of a National Office of Inventions and Trademarks (ONIITEM) in 1973. This organization replaced the pre-revolutionary Register of Industrial Property, which dated from 1936 (Cuban government, 1973). The stated intention was that of overcoming 'the exploitation of our economic resources by foreign monopolies' (Cuban government, 1973; ONIITEM, 1982, p. 27). ONIITEM was itself later replaced by the Cuban Office for Industrial Property (OCPI). The Cuban IPR environment that existed at the time of its transition to TRIPS in 1995 was thus a system that sought to facilitate (indeed prioritize) local invention and innovation, but also one framed and guided by a strongly anti-colonial ethic.

In many respects, accession to TRIPS in 1995 did little to alter this quintessentially Cuban approach to IPR. In fact, until very recently Cuba continued to pursue its own variant of the transition period model that the TRIPS Agreement afforded developing countries, ostensibly so as to give them time to develop their IPR systems to a level commensurate with international standards. Under this transitional system, and prior to changes made in 2009, Cuban patents were awarded in just the same way as they had been under the system introduced by ONIITEM, and then developed by the OCPI in the 1980s and early 1990s: namely, as a dual attribute. In this approach patents are issued to organizations, while individual scientists—the actual inventors—are awarded the so-called 'authorship' of the patent. For instance, the OCPI issued a *Certificado de Autor de Invención* (certificate of authorship of invention) for the production method of the meningococcal vaccine in 1987. Thus, Cuban legislation grants the industrial and intellectual property rights to the biologicals manufacturing company (in this case BioCEN), while simultaneously acknowledging the inventor's authorship of the invention (Sierra et al., 1997). This is, of course, effectively the same approach that has long been practised in universities and research institutions in the Global North, where the institution retains the marketing right to the patents. What marks out the Cuban approach as distinct is its scale, or breadth, and the manner in which it is not institutions but, in reality, the state to which the marketing rights are ceded.

As the Quach and colleagues' 2006 study confirms, almost 100 per cent of all biotechnology patents held by Cuban assignees after TRIPS were held by research organizations, all of which were, in turn, state-operated. Unlike in the Global North, therefore, the Cuban 'institutional' approach to patenting meant that growth in the use of patents (which in the West is often held up as an example of the way in which scientific innovation is being marketized) was in actual fact merely 'hardwiring' (McAfee, 2003, p. 215) Cuba's innovation system back into the state. Signing up to international patent laws was in this sense no particular challenge to Cuba's socialist-oriented biotechnology industry.

Today the 'authorship' side of this arrangement is in the process of being phased out by the Cubans. But for many years it allowed a continuation of the older socialist form of intellectual property attribution established during the 1980s to be 'merged' with the international requirements of TRIPS: Cuba could show that it supported a patenting system because it knew that, in effect, the state would retain all effective rights over what to do with its innovations. Thus, the Cuban state could demonstrate compliance with international law at the same time as retaining effective control over who was granted use of Cuban patents or which parties could claim exceptions to those patents rights (which was certainly the sort of regime that TRIPS was intending to promote).

Non-localized processes

The Cuban achievement of global integration without compromise, however, has not been entirely a product of its own policies. Other factors have also helped ensure that TRIPS did not negatively impact on the development, global market entry or ownership of Cuban biotechnology, as has arguably been the case in other developing countries with nascent pharmaceutical innovation capacity or generics sectors. And perhaps the most important of these crucial enabling factors is also the least expected, namely, the US embargo of Cuba.

The embargo was first imposed by President Kennedy in 1962 and tightened greatly under the Clinton administration of the 1990s, particularly through the Helms-Burton and Torricelli amendments. These latter amendments, by seeking to legislate against third party countries who might wish to trade independently with Cuba, are widely understood to have constituted a case of extra-territorial legislation (Kaplowitz, 1998), the effect of which has been to allow the US to control, to some extent, what trade Cuba engages in and with whom. And companies who may have wished to purchase Cuban biotechnology products or supply them with materials have been a target of this legislation. This has probably limited Cuban market opportunities and increased development and manufacturing costs in Cuba. Even the publishing of Cuban scientific articles themselves has been deemed (by the US Treasury) to be in contravention of the embargo, a move resisted by major scientific journals, such as *Nature* and *Science* (Pages, 2004).

At around the time that Cuba was beginning to accede to TRIPS, its entire biotechnology sector thereby became part of a wider, persistent struggle over Cuban sovereignty and that country's ability to trade with other countries in the global economy. While the embargo has been an overriding factor that has had negative impacts on the Cubans' ability both to source reagents and equipment from abroad and to market their biotechnological products outside Cuba, it has also produced an unexpected, positive impact on the country's biotechnology industry. This is because the existence of the US embargo means that America's bilateral regulatory purchase on Cuba is in some ways limited. While other developing country counterparts have often been subjected to the threat of US trade sanctions (under Super 301 powers, for example) for apparent failures to comply with US pharmaceutical patents standards (or, indeed, other areas of IPR), or because of their use of licences or generic versions of US-held pharmaceutical patents, no such lever was available in the case of Cuba because market access to the US or US company trade with Cuba was not an important factor. Neither has Cuba been subjected to bilateral trade negotiations, in which access to the large US market is often used as the 'carrot' to encourage TRIPS-plus standards of IPR (Sell, 2007). It seems to us that biotechnological patenting in Cuba has benefitted from the legal and political space afforded by this localized lack of purchase that the US has over Cuba.

We recognize, of course, that TRIPS is not just about the need for countries to fall into line with technical norms or standards; it is also about enabling a greater flow of trade between countries and, as many scholars would argue, opening up emerging markets to Western-patented goods with minimum threat to exporters' monopolization of knowledge (Cheek, 2001; Coombe, 1995). But this wider political-economic regulatory function of TRIPS (as opposed to its narrow technical and legal function) is also severely limited by the embargo on Cuba, because such patented goods from other countries themselves have difficulty penetrating the Cuban market. European manufacturers of a recombinant vaccine that might compete with one developed in Cuba, or who might want to outsource production to Cuba, are discouraged from doing so through the third party clauses of the embargo. Likewise, Cuba has less reason to be concerned if some of the components of a product it wishes to market are patented in the US, since it cannot access that market anyway (although there have been, as we shall see, exceptions to this). Indeed, since 1995 Cuba's trade in biotechnological goods has largely continued with countries that the US, for one, considers as having low levels of intellectual property protection.

The important point here, then, is that the decision by the Cuban authorities to continue with the dual system of IPR described above (a decision that enabled them to embrace quite fully international intellectual property norms as embodied in TRIPS) was itself made possible by the playing out of the politically driven issue of the embargo. To put it most simply, there are strong grounds for asserting that Cuba was able to sign up to TRIPS because, on top of its already developed technological capabilities, as discussed above, its existing patents framework proved compatible and adaptable, while the additional regulatory burdens of signing up to TRIPS or other free trade agreements (or those stemming from increased trade in knowledge-intensive goods) were limited for Cuba as a result of the externality effects of the US embargo.

Biologicals: Epistemic and material limitations of TRIPS

Notwithstanding the three forces that have allowed Cuba to limit the impact of TRIPS on its biotechnology sector, the Cuban case also reveals that there may be inherent limits to the utility and application of IPR in the particular area of biopharmaceuticals. It may be useful, therefore, to consider how biopharmaceuticals are in a sense 'immune' to the sort of regulation that patenting and TRIPS seek to exert. Biotechnology, by definition, employs live organisms of some sort in production processes, be it in traditional cell culture-based processes or modern recombinant techniques. The point we wish to make is that the use of live organisms infers a necessarily different relationship between intellectual property and the regulation of biopharmaceuticals (like vaccines) than it has with the regulation of chemical-based pharmaceuticals, which are based on chemical reactions between 'dead' substances whose characteristics are predictable and describable.

There are three key issues at play here. First, in terms of drug regulation and patents, there is no such thing as a 'generic' vaccine. A generic pharmaceutical product is, by definition, a product that has been proven to be identical (or within an acceptable bioequivalent range) to the brand-name counterpart with respect to their pharmacokinetic and pharmacodynamic properties, and registration is granted on the basis of that identity. Virtually all biological substances being used in vaccines are so complex, however, that a precise chemical characterization is not possible (Milstien and Kaddar, 2006), so evidently it is not possible to prove a unique chemical identity either. Consequently, all vaccines have to undergo clinical trials of some sort, and the entire production process, including the manufacturing facility itself, has to be documented and validated. Clinical trials and validation processes are costly, and may constitute substantial barriers to entry even for manufacturing of off-patent vaccines.

Second, since the biological substances that are used as antigens in vaccines are both impossible to fully characterize and, as natural substances, not invented by man, IPR for vaccines are most commonly based on process patents rather than product patents (Milstien and Kaddar, 2006). This is not to say that patents are unimportant in the vaccine field. There can be product patents on adjuvants and other non-biological vaccine components, for instance; and process patents are granted on expression systems, conjugation technologies and other production processes. It is difficult, however, to obtain a patent on a vaccine that would block development of other vaccines against the same disease. In most cases it will always be possible to 'invent around' patents on production processes for any specific vaccine. This means that the barriers of entry are different in vaccine markets as compared with chemical drugs markets, as barriers to entry associated with patents are relatively less important (Milstien and Kaddar, 2006). Rather, it is the costs associated with drug regulation, requirements for clinical trials, production facility construction and maintenance, and production process and quality control validation that are all relatively more important as barriers. In order to run clinical trials that will be accepted internationally, an independent National Drug Regulatory Authority has to be in operation. Furthermore, later stage (Phase III and IV) clinical trials also require an operational national epidemiological surveillance system; such systems are difficult to set up and expensive to maintain, and, in order to be operated according to generally accepted best practice, the requirements are demanding. So, in short, the particular technological properties of biological products have consequences both for the drug regulatory regime necessary for their production, acceptability and quality and for the relevance of patents to their regulation.

Finally, a biosimilar product is not generic, and therefore has to undergo clinical trials, either all the way through Phases I to IV or, as is the case for vaccines, at least in Phase I, to demonstrate induction of antibodies above a previously identified protective level. And, since vaccines are often not product patented, compliance with TRIPS requirements (or, indeed, any other similar regime) does not prevent several biosimilar vaccine products, even though the 'original' may be partly protected by different process patents, being simultaneously available on the same markets. In this sense, vaccine production and development activities, particularly in Cuba, are, at least in part, immune to influence by TRIPS.

So how did this relative immunity of vaccine production, along with the localized idiosyncrasies of the Cuban situation, shape actual product development? Two case studies serve to illustrate the situation.

Case studies

What we have described so far represents how TRIPS has been locally reshaped by the interaction of one particular national (state-socialist) system and political economy with the wider global system of geopolitics, political economy and governance. To better understand how this particular national niche developed and operates, we will consider the development of two actual products. These examples are 'lenses' for viewing the broader dynamics associated with Cuban biotechnology and vaccines. The first is the Cuban pentavalent vaccine, the second the Cuban CIMAVax-EGF cancer vaccine. The two case study vaccines are quite distinct, the former being an essential (low-value/high-volume) childhood vaccine with a broad global market, the latter being a therapeutic vaccine of interest to high-price Western niche markets.

The pentavalent DTP-hepB-HiB vaccine illustrates how a vaccine product may be a combination of off-patent products, indigenously developed biosimilar patented products and a product that has been patented by Cubans in collaboration with a foreign university. The pentavalent vaccine contains antigens against five different childhood diseases: diphtheria, tetanus, whooping cough (pertussis), hepatitis B and haemophilus B, commonly abbreviated as DTP-hepB-HiB. The purpose of such a combination is to reduce the number of injections needed to complete the immunization schedule of national immunization programmes, thereby giving rise to savings in terms of cold chain capacity, on disposables like needles and syringes, and on the number of injections required for each child. Several vaccine manufacturers already have this vaccine on the market, but the Cubans decided to develop and manufacture their own, both as an import substitution measure and as a foreign currency earner. Cuban pentavalent vaccines are used globally in national immunization programmes in both developed and developing countries.

In terms of its intellectual property make-up, the pentavalent DTP-hepB-HiB vaccine is a combination of a traditional off-patent product (the DTP vaccine), a reverse-engineered recombinant product (the hepB component), and a truly novel product based on chemical synthesis (the HiB component). Like other international manufacturers, the Cubans have marketed each of these components as independent products (for example, the DTwP-vaccine, Heberbiovac, and Quimi-HiB; see Table 4.1). In relation to IPR, the DTP vaccine manufactured by Finlay Institute has been in the public domain since the mid-twentieth century. The production processes are based on cultivation of the bacteria and purification and modification of the antigenic substances.

CIGB's Heberbiovac HB, by contrast, is based on modern genetic engineering but is largely a reverse-engineered product, very similar to Merck's and SmithKline Beecham's original designs (Milstien and Kaddar, 2006). The gene coding for the surface protein is inserted into the genome of baker's yeast, the yeast is cultivated and the protein purified. Also marketed and used as a single entity, this vaccine has subsequently become one of CIGB's

Table 4.1 Vaccines marketed by Cuban manufacturers

Trademark	Disease
Finlay Vaccines, S.A.:	
vax-TyVi ®	Typhoid fever
VA-MENGOC-BC ®	Meningococcal disease, serogroup B and C
vax-SPIRAL ®	Leptospirosis
DTwP-vaccine	Diphtheria, tetanus, pertussis
VA-DIFTET ®	Diphtheria, tetanus
vax-TET ®	Tetanus
Heber Biotec, S.A.:[1]	
Heberbiovac HB	Hepatitis B
Quimi-HiB	Haemophilus influenzae B
Trivac HB ®	Diphtheria, pertussis, hepatitis B
Heberpenta ®	Diphtheria, tetanus, pertussis, hepatitis B, haemophilus B
CIMAB, S.A.:[2]	
CIMAVax-EGF	Lung cancer (non-small cells)

[1] Heber Biotec is the commercializing branch of CIGB.
[2] CIMAB is the commercializing branch of CIM.
Source: Plahte 2010c, Reid-Henry 2010. http://v3.espacenet.com/publicationDetails/biblio?DB=EPODOC&at=19&locale=en_EP&FT=D&CC=EP&NR=0864649A2&KC=A2.

major foreign revenue generators. Accordingly, it has been patented internationally (albeit less widely than the Cuban HiB vaccine), with patents issued in Europe, Japan and Australia (European Patent Office, 2012a).

The third element of the pentavalent, the Cuban HiB vaccine Quimi-HiB, is a truly novel product, being the world's first vaccine ever to be based on a chemically synthesized antigen. Synthetic production of the HiB polysaccharide is not a Cuban invention, but the development of the industrial-scale manufacturing process was achieved by the Laboratory for Synthetic Antigens (LAS) at the University of Havana in collaboration with a laboratory at the University of Ottawa, Canada, which co-authored the patent. A conjugation technology was then developed by the LAS, with the CIGB assisting in running the clinical trials (Kaiser, 2004; Verez, undated; Verez, 2009). The synthetic HiB vaccine component that resulted from this work has been patented in many countries apart from Cuba, including Canada, Australia, Europe, Japan, Brazil, Slovenia, Ukraine, China and even the US (European Patent Office, 2012b). In most countries the patents were filed for in 2000, with immunization starting in Cuba in 2004.

Looking to the future, the uniqueness of this product is not something that is likely to be easily protected. There seems to be no patent on the composition of the combined DTP-HepB-HiB product itself: the diphtheria, tetanus and pertussis components of the pentavalent vaccine have been in the public domain for several decades, and the patent on the hepatitis B component is about to expire. It is only the HiB component that will have patent protection for the foreseeable future, but even this does not give the Cubans any kind of monopoly. Indeed, the HiB vaccine patent covers only the synthetically manufactured antigen developed at the University of Havana; even the production process of natural HiB antigen is now in the public domain. Finally, there are already four World Health Organization pre-qualified manufacturers of pentavalent vaccines on the global market. Again we are reminded that patent protection of vaccines (and biologicals) may be a less important barrier to entry than it is for chemical drugs.

More important to the main argument of this chapter, however, are the following facts. Cuba manufactured public domain DTP vaccines as early as the 1970s, while in the 1980s Cuban scientists developed the reverse engineered still patentable hepatitis B vaccine, doing so before accession to TRIPS. Furthermore, the genuinely novel synthetic HiB vaccine was developed in the 1990s and 2000s, mainly after the implementation of TRIPS. In other words, by the time TRIPS was implemented Cuba had already developed the industrial and scientific capabilities necessary for overseas patenting of truly novel biopharmaceutical inventions, as well as having achieved immunity or independence from foreign patents and firms. Cuba had also already overcome several important barriers to entry other than that of being capable of innovative patenting; for example, achieving compliance with the International Standardization Organization (ISO), Good Laboratory

Practice, Good Manufacturing Practice and Good Clinical Practice standards (GLP/GMP/GCP), or the necessary, ongoing capital investment and human capital required to develop and apply the technologies.

Our second case study reveals that more recent challenges are associated with the development of Cuban vaccine products in the post-TRIPS period. By 2005 the CIM was working on a suite of 22 different projects, with vaccines such as the EGF-r anti-cancer vaccine featuring strongly among them. The EGF-r anti-cancer vaccine was developed for use in non-small cell lung cancer and works by getting the body to make antibodies against epidermal growth factor (EGF), an important element in cancer growth. The vaccine was thus part of what became a more popular approach to cancer treatments in the 1990s, namely, immunotherapy. It is worth noting that this (re)turn to immunotherapeutic approaches was taken early in Cuba relative to other places, and is an area of research in which the Cubans have continued to seek to innovate, as evidenced by a series of recent articles by CIM General Director Agustin Lage (Lage, 2006a, 2006b; see also Lage et al., 2005). In a development that shows some similarities with the pentavalent vaccine described above, different components of the vaccines were provided by different research institutes in Cuba. As an adjuvant, for example, the vaccine uses a carrier protein (P64K) that was developed at the CIGB, and, according to the Cuban press, batches of the vaccine for clinical trials testing have been manufactured there as well (Riera, 2004).

> Having thus been developed in early phase clinical trials (I and II) in Cuba and, in order to pursue the increasingly costly development further, the EGF-r vaccine was then licensed for foreign development with a Canadian venture capital firm, YMBiosciences, which—in the 1990s—had an extensive collaboration with the CIM. This was very much a part of a deliberate Cuban 'mid-stream' marketing process. According to a Cuban paper on this experience, the strategy behind this consisted of licensing the project for its joint development with other countries, which means that the foreign counterparts covered the expenses of regulatory actions and clinical trials in their territories. As a result of these negotiations, Cuba received payments for milestones.
>
> (Gonzalez et al., 2009, p. 347)

YMBiosciences was ultimately unable to make much progress in taking the drugs through the process of securing regulatory and market approval outside Cuba because, so its chairman David Allan has suggested, the embargo simply made too many people wary about coming on board. While retaining the full rights to some of Cuba's products, from around 2002, YMBiosciences therefore refocused its efforts elsewhere. This enabled a Californian-based firm, CancerVax, to pick up the rights to the EGF-r vaccine.

In contrast to YMBiosciences, CancerVax were able to get approval to license the drug in the US. To do this the lobby machine was put to work to 'drive a wedge in the Helms Burton Act', as YMBiosciences President, David Allan, put it (Zehr, 2004). But there were other obstacles that would ultimately prevent the vaccine's development and marketing in the US. When the exception to the embargo was finally secured in 2004, it was stipulated under the terms of the exception that the US$6 million fee that was then due to the Cubans had to be paid in kind—in the form of food and medicines—not cash. This would perhaps ultimately not have proven an insurmountable barrier to the product's development. But, in a turn of events that even these political concessions were unable to remedy, in 2005 CancerVax was taken over by a German firm in a reverse merger, following the collapse of their own original (and separate) cancer product that was in clinical trials in the US. This effectively stalled efforts to further develop the Cuban product in the US, and there are at present no trials of the vaccine taking place there. As a result, the Cubans have been forced to change their strategy, continuing to push the product through later stage clinical trials in Cuba itself to at least secure its registration and use domestically (it is likely that the milestone payments received in previous years have been used to finance this). Over 800 Cubans have now been treated with the vaccine across 20 hospitals, and clinical trials are once again taking place outside Cuba (in Canada, the UK and Malaysia).

Both the pentavalent vaccine and the anti-cancer vaccine reveal the extent of integration between Cuba's biotechnology and vaccine production centres. They are also examples of innovative work that was either undertaken before TRIPS came into force or carried out largely unimpeded by it, and both demonstrate the increasingly commercial orientation of Cuban vaccine production, with all the possibilities and pitfalls that entails. It is difficult to assess the motivation for developing such a complex product as the pentavalent vaccine, and such a high-risk product as the EGF-r, although we believe it was most likely a combination of needing to meet domestic needs, developing strategic technologies and generating export earnings. What emerges from these case studies, however, is that patents and the regulation of patenting systems under TRIPS have played a shaping, but not determining, role in the Cuban case. Although the Cubans collaborated with a foreign entity in developing one component of the pentavalent vaccine, it is fair to say that the Cubans have retained full control over this product and can market it by their own means. On the other hand, the Cubans have clearly relied on foreign companies for later stage development and marketing of the EGF-r vaccine. While they have been able to develop and use these for specific indications within Cuba, and have shown that they can establish and retain intellectual property relating to various components or processes associated with these products, they are unable to support wider scale development and marketing alone. But, despite their as yet limited success in this regard, it is their interest in such development that is most revealing. Both case studies thus show, above all else, that what prompted Cuba's greater interest in proprietary drugs was not driven by the structuring role of TRIPS and patents rights, but, rather, a desire to reconnect their own system to a global pharmaceutical industry and to make it as competitive as possible. The case studies point also to the value of the extra room for manoeuvre that Cubans have been able to fall back upon—the result of their biotechnology industry's early and unique development and the geopolitical peculiarities of Cuba's position vis-à-vis the US.

Conclusion

As we hope to have shown in this chapter, the Cuban case reveals much about the way in which international regulatory regimes such as TRIPS may be taken up, and modified, in the global periphery. That it may, in the case of Cuba, be true to say that TRIPS has had rather less of a direct impact than might have been expected, in no way suggests that such wider (and often Western) regulatory frameworks do not have a powerful influence on the political economies and scientific practices of poor nations. It does, however, ask us to think carefully about how they do so, and with what effects. When Cuba implemented TRIPS, as we showed at the beginning of this chapter and in the case study of the pentavalent vaccine, the national biotechnology sector had already reached a level of maturity that enabled it to develop patentable technologies. Signing on to TRIPS was thus never going to prevent Cuba from reaching a mature and innovative phase of scientific research; rather, it posed the challenge of *how* Cuba should integrate an already innovative framework into this broader international context.

Even relatively isolated countries like Cuba do not operate in a vacuum, however, and we also sought to illustrate how Cuba has responded to this challenge institutionally, legally and practically and in terms of its characteristic approach to the scientific and industrial bases of production. The relative immunity of the sector to TRIPS has also been shaped by wider processes and factors, including the US embargo and the inherent resilience of some areas of scientific research, such as biologicals, to the sorts of regulatory requirements and strictures that TRIPS implies for chemical pharmaceutical production. For these complex reasons, our two examples are representative of how the vaccine industry in Cuba has been able to develop both a product portfolio of essential childhood vaccines that responds to the needs of the national public health system and an innovative niche product for cancer that targets Western markets, including (thus far without success) the US. With Cuba as exemplar, it could, therefore, be argued that emergent innovation and global market entry of developing countries can spring up precisely in those places where global regulatory structures have been resisted and then later reworked. In order for this to be the case, however, the necessary resources and political will must be present.

Cuban history leaves us with a further lesson. As mentioned above, the external 'challenge' of TRIPS was not itself a particular threat to Cuba's biotechnological development, nor was state-based control over its ultimate course. In the post-TRIPS era, however, there have been adjustments that are the result of yet other extra-territorial forces, particularly those associated with Cuba seeking to fall into line with a much more diffuse array of norms and regulations than IPR (thereby overcoming some of the non-TRIPS-related barriers to entry into global pharmaceutical markets), including the WHO vaccine pre-qualification requirements and GLP, GMP and GCP standards, as well as accepted Western models of accounting and rationalization. While these considerations are not detailed here, the Cuban case serves as a reminder that TRIPS is not the sole problem for developing-country economies seeking to develop their own viable domestic drug production industries.

Notes

1. The figure of US$1 billion circulates through much of the literature on Cuban biotechnology and is often used by spokespersons for the industry in Cuba. We have not been able to trace the initial source of this figure.
2. The Western Havana Scientific Pole is not the only (though it is the most important) science pole in Cuba. As of 1997 there were 15 scientific poles altogether (CITMA, 1997).
3. Quach et al.'s (2006) is a result of the same research project as that presented in Thorsteinsdóttir et al. (2004, 2005, 2006). The group made a comparative study of the biotechnology sectors of Brazil, China, Cuba, Egypt, India, South Africa and South Korea.
4. Resolución no. 66/96 de 15 Julio de 1996 de la Ministra de Ciencia, Tecnología y Medio Ambiente de la República de Cuba, 'Normas para la aplicación del tratado de cooperacion en materia de patentes (PCT) en la República de Cuba'. Cuba was a signatory to the Paris Agreement (joined in 1904), World Intellectual Property Organization (1975), the Patent Cooperation Treaty (joined in 1996) and the Treaty of Budapest (1994). By the late 1990s it was a member of 17 international IPR treaties in total.
5. Beginning with the promulgation of Law 618 (1959), which established a system of compulsory licensing by which the state could take charge of any applications then filed at the Office of Industrial Property.

References

Beardsley, T. (1986) 'Cuban Biotechnology: Progress Despite Isolation', *Nature*, 320(6057), 8.
Bravo, E. M. (1998) *Development within Underdevelopment: New Trends in Cuban Medicine* (Havana: Editorial José Martí/Elfos Scientiae).

Cheek, M. L. (2001) 'The Limits of Informal Regulatory Cooperation in International Affairs: A Review of the Global Intellectual Property Regime', *George Washington International Law Review*, 33, 277–323.

CITMA (1997) *Polos scientifico-productivos* (Havana: Ministerio de Ciencia, Tecnologia y Medio Ambiente, Agencia de Ciencia y Tecnologia).

Coombe, M. (1995) 'The Cultural Life of Things: Anthropological Approaches to Law and Society in Conditions of Globalization', *American University Journal of International Law & Policy*, 10, 791–836.

CubaCiencia (2003) 'Improvement of the Science and Technology System of Cuba', http://www.idict.cu/, accessed 29 April 2013 (IDICT: Instituto de Informacion Cientifica y Tecnologica).

Cuban Government (1973) Resolution 28, 10 September, 1973 'Dictada por el Dr. Carlos Rafael Rodríguez, Vicepresidente del Consejo de Ministros'.

Dearing, J. (1995) *Growing a Japanese Science City: Communication in Scientific Research* (London: Routledge).

European Patent Office (2012a) 'Method for Obtaining Recombinant Surface Antigen of Hepatitis B Virus (HEP B) of Higher Immunogenic Capacity and Use Thereof in a Vaccine Preparation', http://v3.espacenet.com/publicationDetails/biblio?Db=Epodoc&at=19&locale=en_Ep&Ft=D&CC=Ep&Nr=0864649A2&KC=A2, date accessed 7 March 2012.

European Patent Office (2012b) 'Oligosaccharides Derived from Ribose-ribitol-phosphate, and Vaccines Containing Them', http://v3.espacenet.com/publicationDetails/biblio?DB=EPODOC&at=24&locale=en_EP&FT=D&CC=BR&NR=0013686A&KC=A, date accessed 7 March 2012.

Feinsilver, J. M. (1993) *Healing the Masses. Cuban Health Politics at Home and Abroad* (Berkeley: University of California Press).

González, G., A. Lage, T. Crombet, G. Rodríguez, B. García, A. Cuevas, L. Viña, N. Arteaga and E. Neninge (2009) 'CIMAvax-EGF: A Novel Therapeutic Vaccine for Advanced Lung Cancer', *Biotecnología Aplicada*, 26, 345–8.

Hernández, A. I., Patent Examiner, Oficina Cubana de la Propiedad industrial, Personal communication, 24 May 2001.

Kaiser, J. (2004) 'Glycobiology: Synthetic Vaccine is a Sweet Victory for Cuban Science', *Science*, 305(5683), 460.

Kaplan, W. and R. Laing (2005) 'Local Production of Pharmaceuticals: Industrial Policy and Access to Medicines. An Overview of Key Concepts, Issues and Opportunities for Future Research', HNP Discussion Paper (Washington, DC: World Bank).

Kaplowitz, D. R. (1998) *Anatomy of a Failed Embargo: U.S. Sanctions Against Cuba* (London: Lynne Rienner Publishers).

Lage, A. (2006a) 'Socialism and the Knowledge Economy: Cuban Biotechnology', *Monthly Review*, 58(7), http://monthlyreview.org/2006/12/01/socialism-and-the-knowledge-economy-cuban-biotechnology, date accessed 7 February 2012.

Lage, A. (2006b) 'On the Cross-Fertilization Between Biotechnology and Immunology: Current Situation in Cuba', *Vaccine*, 12(24), Suppl 2:S2–6.

Lage, A., R. Perez and L. E. Fernandez (2005) 'Therapeutic Cancer Vaccines: At Midway between Immunology and Pharmacology', *Current Cancer Drug Targets*, 5, 611–27.

McAfee, K. (2003), 'Neoliberalism on the Molecular Scale: Economic and Genetic Reductionism in Biotechnology Battles,' *Geoforum*, 34, 203–19.

Milstien, J. B. and M. Kaddar (2006), 'Managing the Effect of TRIPS on Availability of Priority Vaccines', *Bulletin of the World Health Organization*, 84, 360–5.

National Office of Inventions and Trademarks (1982) 'Objetivos y principales funciones de la ONIITEM', Havana.
ONIITEM see National Office of Inventions and Trademarks.
ONE (2008) *Anuario estadístico de Cuba 2007* (Havana: Oficina Nacional de Estadísticas), http://www.one.cu, accessed November 2008.
Pages, R. (2004) 'Viola primera enmienda constitucional la prohibición de articulos cientificos de Cuba, Irán, Libia y Sudan', *Granma Internacional*, 26 February.
Pérez, I. and J. Núñez (2009) 'Higher Education and Socio-Economic Development in Cuba: High Rewards of a Risky High-tech Strategy', *Science and Public Policy*, 36, 97–101.
Plahte, J. (2010a) 'Development, Organization and Management of Techno-Economic Networks: the Cuban Biotech Sector and Vaccine Industry', Working Papers on Innovation Studies, no. 2010010, Centre for Technology, Innovation and Culture, University of Oslo, http://ideas.repec.org/p/tik/inowpp/20100109.html, date accessed 10 December 2011.
Plahte, J. (2010b) 'Strategic Evaluations and Techno-Economic Networks. Vaccine Innovation in the Cuban Biotech Sector: for Public Health—or for Profits?' Working Papers on Innovation Studies, no. 20100108, Centre for Technology, Innovation and Culture, University of Oslo, http://ideas.repec.org/p/tik/inowpp/20100108.html, date accessed 5 November 2011.
Plahte, J. (2010c) 'Vaccine Innovation for Public Health, or for Profits—or for Both? The Cuban Biotech Sector in a National and Global Context', Centre for Technology, Innovation and Culture, University of Oslo, PhD thesis.
Quach, U., H. Thorsteinsdóttir, J. Renihan, A. Bhatt, Z. C. von Aesch, A. S. Daar and P. A. Singer (2006) 'Biotechnology Patenting Takes Off in Developing Countries', *International Journal of Biotechnology*, 8, 43–59.
Ratanawijitrasin, S. and E. Wondemagegnehu (2002) *Effective Drug Regulation: A Multicountry Study* (Geneva: World Health Organization).
Reid-Henry, S. M. (2007a) 'The Contested Spaces of Cuban Development: Post-Socialism, Post-Colonialism and the Geography of Transition', *Geoforum*, 38, 445–55.
Reid-Henry, S. M. (2007b) 'Scientific Innovation and Non-Western Regional Economies: Cuban Biotechnology's "Experimental Milieu"', *Environment and Planning*, 40, 1966–86.
Reid-Henry, S. M. (2010) *The Cuban Cure: Reason and Resistance in Global Science* (Chicago: Chicago University Press).
Riera, L. (2004) 'Cuban Vaccine Against Lung Cancer: US Clinical Trial to Begin in 2005', *Granma Internacional*, 12 December.
Sell, S. (2007) 'TRIPS-Plus Free Trade Agreements and Access to Medicines', *Liverpool Law Review*, 28, 41–75.
Sierra, G., M. D. C. Sampedro Herrera, C. Campa Huergo, M. M. Gutiérez, G. Bisset, D. d. I. C. Puentes, F. Sotolongo, E. X. L. Reverend and M. A. Galguera (1997) *Método para obtención de una vacuna de amplio expectro protector contra la neisseria meningitidis del grupo B y la vacuna resultante* (Havana: Oficina Cubana de la Propiedad Industrial).
Thorsteinsdóttir, H., T. W. Saenz, U. Quach, A. S. Daar and P. A. Singer (2004) 'Cuba—Innovation Through Synergy', *Nature Biotechnology*, 22, DC19–24.
Thorsteinsdóttir, H., T. W. Sáenz, A. S. Daar and P. A. Singer (2005) 'Different Rhythms of Health Biotechnology Development in Brazil and Cuba', *Journal of Business Chemistry*, 2, 99–106.

Thorsteinsdóttir, H., A. S. Daar, P. A. Singer, E. Archambault and S. Arunachalam (2006) 'Health Biotechnology Publishing Takes Off in Developing Countries', *International Journal of Biotechnology*, 8, 23–42.

Verez, V., Director of CQB, personal communication, 4 February 2009.

Verez, V. (undated) 'Ciencia y compromiso social', Havana: Centro de Estudios de Antígenos Sintéticos, Facultad de Química, Universidad de la Habana.

Zehr, L. (2004) 'Cuban Drug to Make Debut in US market', *Globe and Mail*, 7 September.

5
TRIPS and Access to Medicines in Egypt

Dina Iskander

Egypt became fully Trade Related Aspects of Intellectual Property Rights (TRIPS)-compliant in January 2005, when legislation enacted in 2002 came into effect. An adverse impact of TRIPS compliance on the generics drug industry in Egypt was anticipated (EIPR, 2005), but no careful analysis has been undertaken of the effects of changes in intellectual property rights (IPR) legislation. Generics producers, the patent office, the IP Office affiliated with the Ministry of Health (MOH), and experts on pharmaceutical research and development (R&D), however, appear to agree that TRIPS compliance has so far had a negligible impact on domestic generics manufacturers. This is largely the result of the good use made of the transitional period between 1995 and 2005, when drugs registered in this period were exempted from patent protection. There is, to date, little therapeutic demand for drugs newer than those already registered by the MOH. According to the *Business Monitor International*, 'a maximum of 16 percent of the medicines available on the Egyptian market are patented' (*BMI*, 2009, p. 15). This figure contrasts with other sources that suggest that no more than 5 per cent of drugs are patented (ADE/DOL, 2004, p. 99). But Egypt has been less successful in building R&D capacity in the pharmaceutical sector in preparation for the likely medium- and long-term impacts of TRIPS.

Should Egypt fail to foster R&D capacities in the local pharmaceutical sector, its generics industry will indeed be negatively affected in the long run, and the result will ultimately be lack of accessibility and affordability of essential medicines. This looming crisis will, however, not solely be caused by restrictive IPR. Rather, and more brutally, in view of the evolving biotechnologies in the area of pharmaceuticals, it is lack of know-how and R&D capability that will render the local industry unable to keep up with international scientific and technological advances, and increasingly make the health sector dependent on expensive medicines supplied by multinational companies.

Egypt's pharmaceutical sector: Background

The Egyptian pharmaceutical industry is one of the oldest industries in the country, dating back to 1939 when the firm Misr for Pharmaceutical Industries was established. With the emergence of other companies, including Misr for Chemical Productions, which specialized in active pharmaceutical ingredient (API) production, the industry continued to grow slowly. By the early 1960s, only 10 per cent of the market was supplied by local firms (Dessouki, 2008, p. 66).

Recognizing the strategic importance of the pharmaceutical industry, in 1962 the Egyptian government created an independent institution mandated to reorganize the sector and merge small- and medium-sized companies. Domestic production in this period was significantly encouraged and controlled by the state, which pursued a policy of industrialization through import substitution. Affordability of medicines was a high priority for the government (Dessouki, 2008, pp. 67–9). Government policy, in conjunction with the market entrance of Hoechst, Pfizer and Swiss Pharma and joint ventures with those foreign companies, resulted in domestic production supplying 84 per cent of the consumption of medicines by 1975 (Hamed, 1997, p. 10).

The relative success of the pharmaceutical sector proved to be short-lived. According to a leading Egyptian expert, the decline started in 1974, when the state shifted to an open door policy. For the first time, pharmaceutical production by a fully foreign owned entity, the US company Squibb, was approved (Hamed, 1997, p. 10). The market share of imported drugs then significantly increased, and there was greater incentive for local manufacturers to produce drugs on licence from multinational firms, rather than generics. In the absence of a vision for the pharmaceutical sector, state control of the industry 'disappeared' (Dessouki, 2008, pp. 68–9).

The government has continued to give approvals to multinationals to establish manufacturing sites, and local companies have continued manufacturing products under licence. Around 1990, Egyptian companies were inlicensing from 177 foreign firms. Since the early 1990s, between 86 per cent (Abdel Fadil, 2003, p. 34) and 95 per cent (Dessouki, 2008, p. 69) of the market has been supplied through manufacturing in Egypt by local firms and plants operated by multinationals. The value added in terms of technological capacity building is less evident. It has been reported that multinational manufacturing and local production under licence have mainly resulted in improvements in assembling and packaging (Dessouki, 2008, p. 71). The impact of these two factors on know-how and technology transfer is relatively marginal. Indeed, pharmaceutical production in Egypt continues to rely heavily on imported material and technologies. According to Fayyad (2002, p. 242), the local value added in drugs manufactured by either multinationals or local private–public producers does not exceed

35 per cent. The remaining 65 per cent of inputs into medicine production are imported.

Since the open door policy was implemented, dependence on multinationals has increased dramatically while the role of the public sector has steadily decreased. The state has ceased to protect and develop the local industry; instead, access to affordable medicines is pursued through bargaining over prices with multinational corporations. This is in contrast to India, for instance, where government-adopted strategies in the form of trade protection and investment incentives, together with a large domestic market, enabled the development of a strong domestic industry that was later in a position to benefit from TRIPS (Eren-Vural, 2007).

Accessibility and availability of medicines

The pricing system

Through a compulsory pricing system, Egypt has managed to keep drug prices low compared with neighbouring countries. As part of the drug registration process, prices must be determined by a pricing committee appointed by the Minister of Health. This committee is mandated by the Ministry to rationalize the drug pricing system for the purpose of ensuring the availability of safe and effective drugs at the lowest possible price (MOH, 2004). In theory the committee uses the 'cost-plus' system, as per Ministerial Decree 314/1991, in which the retail price of a drug is calculated on the basis of its manufacturing expenses, to which are added profit margins for the manufacturer, distributor and pharmacist (WHO/HAI, 2007). Practically, however, the scenario works differently.

A regulatory affairs specialist, responsible for the registration of drugs in a local pharmaceutical company, explained that 'during the registration process, the company and the MOH engage in informal bargaining until an agreement is reached on the final retail price of the medicine... The absence or non-implementation of a coherent and transparent pricing policy often leads to pricing decisions based solely on the discretion of the Pricing Committee.' In addition, 'when a product is therapeutically distinct there is greater price discretion...' Firms negotiating over therapeutically distinct drugs typically manage to reach a price that offers substantial profits (Bahgat and Wright, 2010, p. 63).

While price controls apply to products supplied by both multinationals and local manufacturers, the bargaining power of local firms is weak, except when they introduce the first generic version of an important brand-name product.

The Egyptian pharmaceutical market

There are four sources of supply to the Egyptian market: local public sector companies, local private sector firms, multinational firms manufacturing in

Egypt, and imported medicines supplied by one of the above or by scientific offices operating in Egypt.

According to a 2004 Industrial Modernization Centre-commissioned report on the pharmaceutical sector in Egypt, imported medicines in terms of value made up 20 per cent of the market, and domestic production the remaining 80 per cent. Multinational corporations operating in Egypt had a market share of 48 per cent, domestic private sector companies 31.6 per cent, and public sector firms 10 per cent (ADE/DOL, 2004, pp. 100–1). This contrasts with 1980, when public sector companies had a market share of 71.9 per cent. This figure decreased to 52.9 per cent in 1990–1991, 43.8 per cent in 1993–1994, and then 10 per cent in 2004 (Hamed, 1997, p. 12).

In terms of volume, however, public sector companies, combined with local private firms, supplied more than 70 per cent of the market (Dessouki, 2008, p. 278). Yet, a large proportion of local private sector output was licensed from multinational firms, rendering them 'responsible for 65 per cent of the country's total output, with some 30 per cent of the figure achieved through direct production and the remainder through sublicensing' (*BMI*, 2009, p. 29).

In 2006 it was estimated that 'Egypt's retail drug prices are among the lowest in the Middle East' (AmCham, 2006, p. 23). An MOH-commissioned study by the World Health Organization (WHO) and Health Action International (HAI) found public sector procurement prices to be relatively low compared with an international reference price formulated by the WHO–HAI. Despite governmental efforts, however, expenditure on medicines consumed around 11 per cent of the total yearly income of underprivileged Egyptians (Fayyad, 2007, p. 71).

Spending on pharmaceuticals as a proportion of total health costs is huge. According to the 2008–2009 National Health Accounts (NHA), 34 per cent of total health expenditure was for medicines. This is particularly alarming considering that out-of-pocket spending on healthcare is in the order of 72 per cent of the total cost, up from 60 per cent in 2007–2008, and 51 per cent in 1994–1995 (MOH, 2011, p. 4). A partial explanation for this huge burden on Egyptian patients is that public health insurance, through the Health Insurance Organization (HIO), covers only 55 per cent of the population (MOH, 2011, p. 6). Those covered by health insurance live mainly in the urban areas and work in the formal sector. Moreover, the service provided in the public sector is of poor quality (Bahgat and Wright, 2010, p. 58), which forces many public insurance beneficiaries to seek services elsewhere. According to an MOH spokesperson, 'Sixty per cent of those who are insured are not satisfied with current healthcare services'. He describes the HIO system as 'inefficient' and 'in dire need for a new and more competent alternative system' (Leila, 2007).

Pharmaceutical patents granted post-TRIPS

Since the introduction of TRIPS-compliant IPR legislation on 1 January 2005, only 161 patents have been granted in the pharmaceutical sector. It is interesting to compare this figure with other developing countries. According to a South Centre study, 'In Argentina, 951 pharmaceutical patents were granted in 2000–2007; in Brazil, 278 patents were granted in 2003–2008; in Colombia 439 in 2004–2008; in India 2347 in 2005–2008; and in South Africa, 2442 patents were registered in 2008' (Correa, 2011, p. 16). Reasons for the low number of patents in Egypt are discussed below.

Abstracts for granted pharmaceutical patents in Egypt were obtained by the author. These were analysed with the help of a team of lawyers and scientists from Initiative for Medicines, Access, and Knowledge (i-MAK), a group that monitors the patent system in the interest of access to affordable medicines. Since the complete patent document for each granted patent is not publicly available, analysis relied solely on the patent abstracts. Granted patent numbers were searched in US, European and international patent databases. In this way i-MAK was able to establish whether any of the patents granted in Egypt relate to patents listed in the US Food and Drug Administration (FDA)'s Orange Book, that is, pharmaceutical products approved for marketing in the US (Amin, 2011, p. 3).

Of the 161 patents registered in Egypt, only 33 corresponded with US patents for originator branded medicines listed in the Orange Book. i-MAK was able to establish international non-proprietary names (INN) only for products related to these 33 patents, and in this way determined what medicines and therapeutic areas they related to. Since proprietary names are not required for listing of process patents in the Orange Book, it is possible that some patents, other than the 33, correspond to patents listed in the Orange Book. Of the 33 patented products analysed, 23 are not registered with the MOH, meaning that they are not marketed in Egypt, although generics of at least one of them are registered with the MOH and marketed in Egypt. Interestingly, generic versions of five of the patented products are available on the market. Only five patented products out of the 33 are in fact registered with the MOH, with no generic versions registered.

Generic versions of almost all patented drugs of significance to Egypt's burden of diseases are registered. The registrations date from either before January 2005 or after that date, but before the relevant patent was granted. This is gratifying from a public health perspective. Generic alternatives are available for two of three patented diabetes products. High blood glucose level is ranked nine out of the ten leading causes of death for adults in Egypt, according to the National Burden of Disease Study conducted in 1999–2000. While liver cirrhosis and fibrosis rank number one out of the ten leading causes of death, and while peg-interferon, indicated for liver patients infected by hepatitis C (HCV), is indeed patented, a biosimilar product is available. Finally, many generic alternatives to Plavix, indicated for heart disease, are also available. Note that hypertension, atherosclerosis and acute myocardial infarction are ranked number two, five and six, respectively, out of the ten leading causes of death in Egypt (WHO, 2010, p. 15).

Respiratory failure ranks fourth. Yet no generic alternatives are available for two patented products indicated for patients with chronic obstructive pulmonary diseases. Other patents relate to HIV/AIDS, cancer and psychotherapy medicines. Significantly, the HIV/AIDS patents are for medicines that are not part of the WHO recommended regimen, and the medicines they relate to are quite possibly substitutable. While these last three disease categories are not listed as leading causes of death, the financial burden for patients dependent on patented drugs warrants further research. The high cost of patented cancer medicines is of particular concern.

Impact of TRIPS on generics producers

IPR-related cases before 1 January 2005

No IPR infringement cases in the area of pharmaceuticals have been brought to Egyptian courts since TRIPS compliance came into effect. The courts have been asked to rule on only four cases, and these occurred before 1 January 2005. Notably, they were decided in favour of the generics manufacturers.

The first case was brought in 2001 by the generics company Apex against the Minister of Health in relation to the registration of olapex, a generic version of Eli Lilly's Zyprexa (olanzapine). In this case, the court dealt with whether TRIPS should be self-executed, or whether a special domestic law should be promulgated first before TRIPS could actually be enforced. The case was brought to court before the promulgation of the 82/2002 Law (see below). The case was decided on appeal to the Supreme Administrative Court (SAC) in favour of the generics company (SAC, 2004).

The second case was a court motion, filed by Eli Lilly, requesting that the implementation of the 2004 SAC ruling in relation to olanzapine generic medicine be suspended. At the same time Eli Lilly wrote to the MOH requesting that marketing approval given to Apex for this product be revoked 'pending the outcome of the new court motion' (Bahgat and Wright, 2010, p. 68). When the MOH declined the request, Eli Lilly in 2006:

> filed a new court case before the Court of Administrative Justice against the Minister of Health, the Prime Minister, the Chair of ASRT and *Apex Pharma* arguing that it was unlawful to proceed with the marketing of Olapex pending the outcome of Eli Lilly's motion filed against the 2004 SAC decision (no. 22218/60). The suit requested that the generic Olapex be immediately withdrawn from the market, as well as financial

compensation of LE 5 million (US$900,000) to be paid jointly by MOH and Apex.

Bahgat and Wright (2010, p. 68)

In December 2008 the Court of Administrative Justice decided that olapex was registered at a time when Eli Lilly had no rights related to the drug and declined the claim for compensation.

The third case was brought in 2002 by Pfizer against the Egyptian International Pharmaceutical Industries Company (EIPICO), a leading generics producer, in relation to ator, a generic version of Pfizer's Lipitor, 'often referred to as the world's best-selling drug, used to lower cholesterol' (Bahgat and Wright, 2010, p. 69). In this case Pfizer aimed to establish the TRIPS-plus provision of data exclusivity, claiming that, for the purpose of its registration approval, ator relied on confidential clinical data submitted by Pfizer to the MOH (Pfizer, 2003). At the time the Lipitor patent application was still in the 'mailbox', the concept used to describe the mechanism that allowed inventors to file patent applications as of 1 January 1995 although they could only be examined on TRIPS coming into force (WTO, 1994, Art. 70.8, TRIPS Agreement).

Pfizer requested the immediate cessation of the manufacture, distribution and advertising of ator, in addition to LE 6 million (US$1 million) in civil remedies to compensate for lost sales (Pfizer, 2003). In view of the novelty, the specificity and the complexity of the matter, the court mandated the Chair of the National Research Centre in Cairo to appoint a three person expert commission to study the matter and advise the court accordingly. The committee submitted a thoroughly researched document, concluding that 'there was no violation of any laws in the practice of EIPICO'. Satisfied with the outcome of the report, on 30 April 2005 the court found against Pfizer (Bahgat and Wright, 2010, p. 72).

With the motion against EIPICO still pending, in 2004 Pfizer challenged two other generics companies, Delta and Memphis. These firms had jointly developed atorstat, another generic version of Lipitor. In its motion before the Court of Provisional Matters, Pfizer requested 'an immediate and temporary injunction to halt all production, marketing, sales and distribution of atorstat and any other generic version of Lipitor within Egypt. The motion further asked the court to include in the injunction a provision banning the exportation or importation of any drug based upon Atorvastatin.' The court denied the request in May 2004 and Pfizer's appeal to the Court of First Instance was also unsuccessful (Bahgat and Wright, 2010, p. 73).

In these four cases multinationals were trying to push for more rights than they were entitled to under the applicable legislation. According to Judge Badrawi, Assistant Minister of Justice for Parliamentary Affairs, 'Foreign companies knew perfectly well when they filed these court cases that the law was not on their side, but they were betting that judges don't know, don't understand. They were surprised to see how our judges were aware of the subject' (Hassan Badrawi, interview, 2009). It is possible that the multinationals ceased to engage in legal action on IPR-related matters after promulgation of Law N. 82 of 2002 on the Protection of Intellectual Property Rights, which did not encompass TRIPS-plus provisions in the area of health.

Law N. 82, 2002, on the protection of intellectual property rights

In the negotiations preceding the TRIPS Agreement, Egypt, together with other developing countries, played a vital role in pushing for safeguards and flexibilities on the grounds of public health. Egypt adopted its IPR Law in 2002 after lengthy discussions in the People's Assembly, which had been ongoing since the early 1990s. Ahmed Abdel Latif, a former Egyptian diplomat, writes:

> Discussions on the draft law were controversial in Parliament, particularly in relation to the issue of TRIPS and public health. Egyptian policy-makers were particularly concerned with the effects of the introduction of patent protection on pharmaceutical products, in view of the country's sizeable generic industry, mostly state-owned, and that public health was a sensitive issue among Egyptian public opinion.
> Abdel Latif (2010, pp. 38–9)

Law N. 82 of 2002 on the Protection of Intellectual Property Rights (Law 82/2002) integrated many of the public health-related flexibilities of TRIPS, including exclusions from patentability (Article 2), compulsory licensing (Articles 23 and 24), parallel importation and international exhaustion of rights (Article 10). It is worth noting that Article 17 obliges the patent office, after completing its examination of applications, to notify the Ministry of Health of patent applications in the area of health. The Minister may oppose publication of the patent acceptance within 90 days. Should acceptance of the application be made public, the Minister still has another 90 days to oppose the granting of the patent, 'if it appears that the application relates to health significance. Opposition in the aforementioned cases shall stop the procedure of granting the patent' (Article 17). According to the Egyptian Patent Office, while the Minister of Health has used this entitlement only once between 2005 and the end of 2010 (Mona Farag, interview, 2010), this provision is likely to deter applications for patents by multinationals.

Registration of drugs during the transitional phase

With enforcement of TRIPS-compliant IPR legislation, Egypt faces two main problems. First, the generics industry may be threatened, since production of generic versions of originator brand drugs will be hampered should these be protected by the Egyptian Patent Office. Second, legislation will impede importation of generic versions of originator brand drugs produced in other developing countries under compulsory licence, even if the drug is not under patent in Egypt. Ultimately, unless Egypt has its own strong, innovative industry, Egyptian patients will suffer from a lack of affordable necessary drugs. Egypt has mainly focused on protection against the first threat, which is why key stakeholders agree that TRIPS compliance is yet to have a significant impact on the local pharmaceutical sector.

Egypt has certainly been successful in registering as many drugs as it possibly could during the transitional phase between 1995 and 2005. Amoun, ranked third among Egyptian medicines manufacturers, registered more than 90 drugs in this period (Hala Adly, interview, 2010). According to its public relations manager, 'Amoun has 260 drugs registered in the MOH; hence, so far, it does not see the need to introduce new drugs' (Hala Adly, interview, 2010).

EIPICO, ranked first among Egyptian manufacturers, and fourth in terms of market share (AmCham, 2006, p. 11) after GlaxoSmithKline, Novartis and Sanofi-Aventis, has not been negatively affected by TRIPS compliance. Omar el Ahmady, EIPICO's head of R&D, affirms that 'From 2005 up until today, there was no drug that we sought to register and could not for IPR reasons' (Omar el Ahmady, interview, 2010).

Makram Mehanny, head of the Chamber of Trade for Pharmaceutical Producers, agrees, suggesting that the multinationals have been reluctant to apply for patents in Egypt. He recalled several instances since 2005 of drug registrations being refused by the MOH for IPR reasons, asserting that 'multinationals calculate it' and often consider it not worth applying for patents in Egypt (Makram Mehanny, interview, 2011). This view is shared by Tahir Amin, i-MAK's co-founder and director of intellectual property: 'It could be that patent holders do not see Egypt as a key country in terms of its patent filing strategy, many companies do not file in all countries—they pick countries where competition from generic companies is likely to arise' (Tahir Amin, email, 10 January 2012). Tahir Amin does not anticipate that TRIPS will change the face of the local industry, even in coming years.

Although the generics industry has not yet felt the impact of TRIPS compliance, contrary to Mehanny, sections of the industry do realize that it is just a matter of time before negative effects will become apparent. Osama Rostom, EIPICO's vice president, notes that 'we still have not yet felt the impact of TRIPS; the drugs that the consumers have been using before TRIPS are still those drugs that they are using today. The introduction of new medicines has still not changed the market needs drastically' (Osama Rostom, interview, 2010). Hala Adly, Amoun's public relations manager, similarly asserts that 'Possibly, later on, we will face problems, (Hala Adly, interview, 2010). New drugs constitute only 3 per cent to 4 per cent of the drug market, which indicates a low level of innovation in the Egyptian pharmaceutical sector (ADE/DOL, 2004, p. 102). A significant reason for the limited impact of the TRIPS-compliant 82/2002 IPR Law is that drug innovation increasingly takes place in the area of biologics. With few exceptions, Egyptian local manufacturers have not yet entered this field.

Multinationals using the back door

Egypt has curtailed damage to its domestic generic production and access to affordable medicines more successfully than some countries, but the multinationals are using back door tactics to ensure maximum profits.

Making drugs unavailable to push prices up

Over the period November 2003–February 2006 the Information and Decision Support Centre (IDSC) conducted four surveys of pharmacists to assess drug availability and price stability in Egypt. Four hundred and forty pharmacies were visited in eight governorates. A shortage of drugs for chronic diseases was reported consistently, including a shortage of medicines for cardiovascular diseases, hypertension and diabetes. According to pharmacists, lack of availability could be mostly attributed to companies' pressure to increase prices. The same survey found that it was exactly the prices of those unavailable medicines that had increased between November 2003 and February 2006 (Mahmoud and Mohamed, 2006, p. 4). The main scarcity was of imported drugs. Most of the surveyed pharmacists agreed that the major problem was the unavailability of therapeutically important medicines rather than their cost (Mahmoud and Mohamed, 2006, p. 21).

Attack through counter-propaganda

In 2004 Reiferon Retard, a biosimilar to Roche's Pegasys and Schering Plough's PegIntron, was introduced by the Egyptian company Minapharm. PegIntron is the only treatment available for patients with HCV. The prevalence of HCV infection is estimated at 14.7 per cent of the Egyptian population (El-Zanaty and Way, 2009, p. 244). Introduction of Reiferon Retard has helped health authorities bargain for a decrease in the public sector price of Roche's PegIntron from 1400 Egyptian pounds US$250 in 2012 prices) in 2003 to 250 Egyptian pounds in 2011 (circa US$40).

Reiferon Retard was used in the private sector, while the MOH and the HIO dispensed only the PegIntron supplied by Roche and Schering-Plough (since acquired by Merck). It was only in 2009 that the then President of the HIO and the then Minister of Health decided to dispense Reiferon Retard in some HIO centres, as later confirmed by the MOH's submission to the Administrative Court (CAJ decision, 2011, p. 2). This decision triggered a huge media campaign, led by specialist physicians, 'accus[ing] health authorities of dispensing a medicine not fit for the treatment of liver patients...They argue that this decision therefore exposes this category of patients to risk' (EIPR, 2011). The specialists drew on a study conducted by liver specialist Gamal Shiha, who claimed that the rate of sustained virological response among patients treated with Reiferon Retard did not exceed 20.5 per cent (Al-Hofi, 2011), compared with 67 per cent (Roulot et al., 2007) for patients treated with the PegIntron of Roche and MSD. But, according to Wafik Berdissi, Chief Executive Officer of Minapharm, 'We [Minapharm] have a document from Dr Gamal Shiha, with the results of his study on the patients confirming that the RR [Reiferon Retard] is of equal efficacy as that of the multinationals. However, this guy came back to change his mind and started spreading rumours that our product is of less efficacy' (Wafik Berdissi, interview, 2010).

Criticism of the biosimilar Reiferon Retard was endorsed by a patient group, which challenged the MOH and HIO decisions in the Administrative Court. The court's ruling, in May 2011, supported the decision of the administrative authorities, confirming that Reiferon Retard met registration requirements (CAJ, decision, 2011). Yet the publicity favouring the original multinational corporation version has resulted in continuing doubts among HCV patients about the quality, safety and efficacy of Reiferon Retard. According to Berdissi, multinational interests are behind this media campaign (Wafik Berdissi, interview, 2010). In September 2010 the Minister of Health appointed an independent expert committee to examine Reiferon Retard's quality, safety and efficacy. According to a committee member (who wishes to remain anonymous) the report was submitted to the MOH in November 2011, but to date its findings have not been made public. The HIO is, however, still dispensing the biosimilar in its facilities.

There may be legitimate questions about whether the biosimilar is as effective as the originators' PegIntron. But the attacks on the Reiferon Retard are consistent with multinationals' criticism of generics producers and their products in general. Parallels can be drawn between this incident and the role of the International Federation of Pharmaceutical Manufacturers and Associations (IFPMA) in advocating strengthened IPR protection under the umbrella of the International Medical Product Anti-Counterfeit Taskforce (IMPACT) (EATG, 2010), which was established at an international conference organized by the WHO in 2006 (known as the Declaration of Rome), with the mandate of combating counterfeit medicines (WHO, 2006). In practice its activities were premised on an antagonistic approach to generic medicines, deliberately mixing public health issues with IPR (EIPR, 2010). In response to civil society lobbying against IMPACT, only in May 2010 was a decision reached at the World Health Assembly to transfer responsibility for combating counterfeit medicines from a public health perspective to a new working group, composed of governments, and not linked to groups with an interest in strengthening IPR (Mara, 2010).

Non-IPR factors impeding access to essential medicines

As yet, IPRs, in and of themselves, are not a major obstacle to access to medicines in Egypt. But, notwithstanding the registration of generic versions of most essential medicines, the problem of affordable access remains. There has been little research to assess the extent of this problem, which is not, of course, exclusive to Egypt. A working paper published by the Indian Council for Research on International Economic Relations asserts 'that access to older, patent expired essential drugs remains poor and is a very serious threat to public health—yet this situation appears not to be on the road to making substantial progress' (Bale, 2001, p. 4). This suggests that the supposition that availability of generics will automatically make medicines more accessible may not necessarily hold. The HIV/AIDS activist Gregg Gonsalves, in a presentation to the Green Light Committee Initiative (GLI) on accessibility of TB drugs, showed that the price of amikacin increased by 991 per cent from 2001 to 2010 (A2M, 2011), bearing in mind that this chemical compound was initially introduced onto the market in 1972 (Frymark et al., 2010, p. 1). The GLC is a WHO co-founded programme that 'support[s]...countries to manage multidrug-resistant tuberculosis' (WHO, 2011a).

The Non-Communicable Disease Alliance (NCD), a global network of 2000 organizations, reports on other barriers. According to NCD, 'Recent surveys in over 40 countries showed that in the public and private sector, generic medicines for the treatment of chronic diseases were between 11 and 20 per cent LESS available than were acute disease medicines' (NCD, 2011, p. 1). Clearly, there are significant barriers to access for reasons other than IPR. These require addressing 'spending priorities, inadequate infrastructure, lack of needed external financing and insufficient political commitment to providing access to quality health care' (Bale, 2001, p. 5).

The future of pharmaceutical production in Egypt

New technologies threatening local pharmaceutical production

The question of whether biosimilar drugs infringe on patented biologic drugs is still unresolved, with only a few countries having a regulatory process for the registration of biosimilars (EIPR, 2011). In Egypt, as previously noted, Reiferon Retard is a case in point. While Roche used bacteria to pegylate the interferon, Minapharm used yeast (Wafik Berdissi, interview, 2010); Roche never sought to claim an IPR over Reiferon Retard. It is possible, however, that the patent-related debate in the area of biologics could be settled in such a way as to favour multinational corporations, unless developing and least developed countries build their own biotechnological capabilities.

The 2004 Egyptian Industrial Modernisation Centre report argued that Egypt had adopted defensive economic policies for too long (IMC, 2004). The most significant of these were measures to keep prices as low as possible while seeking to maximize local production for domestic consumption. As a result, by the late 1990s, local manufacturers had low profitability, inadequate investment in upgrading their facilities, and a business model completely orientated towards the domestic market—supplying a wide range of products, rather than building specialized capabilities and exports (ADE/DOL, 2004, pp. 27–8).

The TRIPS Agreement allows the granting of compulsory licences for public health purposes, but Article 31(f) requires that 'any such use shall be authorized predominantly for the supply of the domestic market of the member authorizing such use', which would seem to make exports of a drug produced under compulsory licence illegal. Ultimately, 'if one country wishes to benefit from compulsory licens[ing], its national pharmaceutical manufacturing capacities become a precondition' (Peng, 2009, p. 34).

Recognizing that this requirement cannot be met by countries with no manufacturing capacity, in August 2003 the TRIPS Council decided that less developed countries and countries with insufficient manufacturing capability may qualify as importers of generics manufactured under compulsory licence (Decision, 2003). The scope of diseases to which these provisions apply, however, remains ambiguous and it is unclear how countries may qualify as having insufficient manufacturing capabilities. According to the IDSC, Egypt would not be included in this group (Abdel Fadil et al., 2003, p. 41). In the absence of a local industry capable of keeping up with international developments, especially in respect of biotechnology, Egypt's generics industry is under long-term threat, and so are the lives and health conditions of patients. It is for this reason that reliance on strong 'defensive economic policies' was deemed 'redundant' (ADE/DOL, 2004, p. 29).

Research and development in Egypt

The World Bank's Human Development Network is sceptical about the concept of 'self-sufficiency' (Kaplan and Laing, 2005, p. 22). According to this analysis, 'Jordan, the Philippines, Pakistan, Egypt, Brazil and certain EU/OECD countries supply more than 85 per cent of their total market through "local production".' In terms of volume, the pharmaceutical sector in these countries grew at an estimated 30 per cent annually in the 1990s, but this was not accompanied by enhanced R&D activities or production of APIs (Abdel Fadil et al., 2003, p. 34). Egypt is, therefore, not an exception among developing countries in this regard. According to a World Bank Health, Nutrition and Population Partnership (HNP) discussion paper, local production for most, if not all, developing countries implies 'secondary manufacture and finishing of bulk active [ingredients] sourced from global suppliers' (Kaplan and Laing, 2005, p. 22).

Many observers agree that Egypt does not have 'a real pharmaceutical industry', but, rather, an industry of assemblage of imported chemical compounds (cited in Dessouki, 2008, p. 73). At least 85 per cent of raw material, including APIs, is imported (AmCham, 2006, p. 22). Imports and local production by multinationals in Egypt have a market share of less than

30 per cent, but cater for more than 50 per cent of newly introduced drugs—usually the top-of-the-line, most expensive drugs, which are also likely to be patented (ADE/DOL, 2004, p. 102).

Major pharma multinationals claim R&D expenditure of around 15 per cent of sales value, but they undertake very little research in Egypt (Mahfouz Kassem, interview, 2011). This hampers the transfer of technology and exchange of know-how that the local pharmaceutical sector relied on in earlier periods. A survey of 20 multinational firms operating in several sectors in Egypt confirmed that their local R&D was mostly adaptive rather than inventive (Kadah, 2003, p. 9).

In the public sector, R&D as a share of pharmaceutical company expenditure has been estimated at only 1.3 per cent (Dessouki, 2008, p. 119; ADE/DOL, 2004, p. 22) and in the private sector, including the subsidiaries of multinationals, at no more than 3 per cent. R&D spending was mainly directed at enhancing the efficacy of particular products, prolonging stability, and enhancing packaging, storage and distribution (Dessouki, 2008, p. 141). While R&D spending is indeed small, it is interesting to note that Indian pharmaceutical firms spend less than 2 per cent of total sales value on R&D (UNCTAD, 2003, p. 14).

Technology transfer and consolidated policy framework: The way forward

According to the World Bank's HNP discussion paper, 'the debate on science and technology policies in Egypt is highly focused on strengthening the role the local R&D community plays in the productive sector' (Kadah, 2003, p. 4). It suggests that there should be more emphasis on international technology transfer. The study asserts that

> Actual technological spillovers from FDI [Foreign Direct Investment] only take place when linkages with local firms involve a degree of quality improvement, trained personnel of MNCs [multinational corporations] move to local firms, or when demonstration effects take a technological competition approach. Notably, there is a general lack of these actual spillovers in developing economies.
>
> (Kadah, 2003, p. 4)

Minapharm's experience during development of Reiferon Retard, referred to above, exemplifies one form of international technology transfer, whereby Minapharm established a subsidiary company, Rhein Minapharm, as a joint venture with Rhein Biotech Germany, 'devoted to the development, manufacturing and commercialization of biopharmaceutical immune modulators and cytokines'. A separate building was constructed for this purpose in 2003, meeting the requirements of Good Manufacturing Practice, the WHO and the FDA (Minapharm website). According to Minapharm's Chief Executive Officer, 'in the absence of a research culture in Egypt we have "imported" researchers' (Wafik Berdissi, interview, 2010). This type of technology transfer may well be successful in economic and industrial terms, but not necessarily those of public health. Medicinal products that make maximum profits are not necessarily those that people need most. Meeting therapeutic needs requires clear vision, political commitment and coordination between Egypt's health policy and its research and corporate sectors—this is not the case at present.

Also, R&D efforts and technology transfer need to go hand in hand with a more comprehensive vision for the health sector. A joint paper by the WHO, the United Nations Conference on Trade and Development, and the International Centre for Trade and Sustainable Development underscores the importance of a consolidated policy framework for local production in developing countries to improve access to medicines (WHO, 2011b). The authors argue that 'Governments in developing countries have often supported pharmaceutical production from an industrial development perspective...without recognizing its special importance as a source of commodities that directly affects the health of the people' (WHO, 2011b, p. 38).

In Egypt, linkages between pharmaceutical companies and university and other research centres remain weak (Hala Adly, interview, 2010; Mahfouz Kassem, interview, 2011). The research centres are well resourced, but they play an insignificant role in the development of the pharmaceutical sector (Dessouki, 2008, p. 96–7). In the absence of external linkages, companies rely solely on internal capacities in advancing their R&D, which has been described as follows:

> There are individual efforts from some companies being carried out, there are some efforts from research centers; and all these are but individual efforts that have not yet caused a real change in the pharmaceutical research in Egypt.
> Tageldin and Hamed (2003, p. 43)

Studies of successful industrial sectors in several developing countries show that a common factor is coordination between stakeholders around a common goal. In the automobile industry in South Africa, for example, 'collaboration between motor assembly firms and the South African Bureau of Standards, as well as the engineering faculties of some of the leading universities', played a vital role (UNCTAD, 2003, p. 16). Similarly, interaction between firms and other social organizations and institutions has been considered a 'key element of industrial change' in the success of the Indian pharmaceutical industry (Chataway et al., 2007, p. 560).

The Egyptian pharmaceutical industry's legal framework is not generally supportive of invention. According to a 2009 ministerial decree (Minister of Health, 2009), each product must have reference to a product registered abroad for it to merit registration in the Egyptian MOH. In other words, no Egyptian company is—even theoretically—entitled to invent a new product and have this registered and eventually marketed in Egypt (Mahfouz Kassem, interview, 2011). This decree goes hand in hand with a legal vacuum regarding scientific research (Makram Mehanny, interview, 2011). In effect, there are no laws or policies that companies or research entities must follow for the purpose of discovery research. It is, therefore, understandable that the MOH takes a precautionary approach, protecting patients from products whose origins are unknown.

Ultimately, a joint effort between the MOH, industry and the research sector, coupled with the political will to design a favourable legal framework, is what Egypt's pharmaceutical sector requires to move forward. A health-driven policy framework is required that draws on lessons from success stories in other developing countries. Such a policy will need to focus on building linkages between stakeholders and recognize the importance of technology transfer.

Conclusion

The TRIPS-compliant IPR legislation introduced in 2002, which came into force in 2005, has not yet significantly affected generics manufacturers in Egypt. Due to technological developments in the pharmaceutical sector, reverse engineering of chemical compounds is expected to gradually disappear. The real challenge is in producing compounds that are biosimilar to biotechnology-based medicines. In that regard, IPR may possibly develop into a factor impeding access to medicines in Egypt. But the problem is principally one of weak know-how and training facilities, which renders local firms incapable of developing biosimilars and new medicinal products. It is vital that greater attention be focused within international legal and political fora on forms of international technology transfer to developing countries.

Egypt is not in a unique position in these respects. Els Torrelee notes that, in her meeting with access to medicines activists in Africa, there was a shared view that IPR is currently not the main barrier to access to medicines in Africa, but that this may become a more significant issue in years to come (A2M, 2011). Human rights activism in this field commenced in response to the issue of access to anti-retroviral medicines in South Africa (George, 2011). It is the success of this movement that civil society is today trying to replicate it in other therapeutic areas. The core issues may, however, now be different. As demonstrated in this chapter, access problems arise for many reasons other than IPR. Prices of some off-patent medicines are now increasing rather than decreasing. Issues related to international technology transfer, pricing and procurement warrant equal, if not more, research and activism. The access to medicines movement has so far mainly been led by

IPR activists. Greater participation by public health experts, health policy advisers, physicians, pharmacists and pharmaceutical researchers is needed to address other issues relating to access to medicines.

References

A2M (2011) Open Society Foundations Public Health Program Seminar Series, Civil Society Strategy Meeting on the Future of Access to Medicines, Bangkok, 13–15 December.

Abdel Fadil, M. (2003) 'The Current Crisis of the Pharmaceutical Market in Egypt,' *el azma el rahina le souq el dawaa fi misr*, Information and Decision Making Support Centre, Council of Ministers Egypt, Cairo, September.

Abdel Fadil, M., N. El Zeini, S. Younis and M. Fadel (2003) *Impact of the Implementation of the TRIPS Agreement on the Pharmaceutical Industry in Egypt, athar tatbeeq etefaqeyet trips* (Cairo: Information and Decision Making Support Centre, Council of Ministers Egypt).

Abdel Latif, A. (2010) 'Egypt's Role in the A2K Movement: An Analysis of Positions and Policies' in N. Rizk and L. Shaver (eds) *Access to Knowledge in Egypt: New Research on Intellectual Property, Innovation and Development* (London: Bloomsbury Academic).

ADE/DOL (2004) *Egypt's Pharmaceutical Sector Survival and Development Strategy Report Incorporating Results and Conclusions of Review Activity* (Egypt: Development Options Limited, Industrial Modernization Centre).

Adly, H. (2010) Public Relations Manager of Amoun, interview, December.

al-Hofi, N. (2011) 'The Battle of Egyptian Interferon Rages...and the Ministry of Health is Absent', *Al-Masry al-Youm*, newspaper, 21 April 2011.

AmCham, *see* American Chamber of Commerce in Egypt.

American Chamber of Commerce in Egypt (2006) *Pharmaceutical Sector Developments in Egypt* (Egypt: AmCham Egypt Business Studies and Analysis Centre).

Amin, T. (2011) 'Granted Pharmaceutical Patents in Egypt', Initiative for Medicines, Access and Knowledge (i-Mak), http://www.i-mak.org/i-mak-blog-updates/2011/12/8/granted-pharmaceutical-patents-in-egypt.html, date accessed 29 March 2012.

Amin, T. (2012) Initiative for Medicines, Access and Knowledge (i-Mak), Co-founder and Director of Intellectual Property, email interview, 10 January.

Badrawi, H. (2009) Judge and Assistant Minister of Justice for Parliamentary Affairs, interview, May.

Bahgat, H. and R. Wright (2010) 'Access to Medicines in Egypt: A Human Rights Approach to IP, Trade and Health' in N. Rizk and L. Shaver (eds) *Access to Knowledge in Egypt: New Research on Intellectual Property, Innovation and Development* (London: Bloomsbury Academic).

Bale, H. E. (2001) 'Consumption and Trade in Off-Patented Medicines', Working Paper No. 65, Commission on Macroeconomics and Health Working Paper Series, Paper No. WG 4: 3, Indian Council for Research on International Economic Relations, http://apps.who.int/medicinedocs/en/m/abstract/Js18254en/, date accessed February 2012.

Berdissi, W. (2010) Chief Executive Director of Minapharm, interview, October.

BMI, see Business Monitor International.

Business Monitor International (2009) 'Egypt Pharmaceuticals and Healthcare Report', quarterly report Q4, 29.

CAJ, *see* Court of Administrative Justice.

Chataway, J., D. Kale and D. Wield (2007) 'The Indian Pharmaceutical Industry Before and After TRIPS', *Technology Analysis and Strategic Management* 19, 559–63.

Correa, C. M. (2011) 'Pharmaceutical Innovation, Incremental Patenting and Compulsory Licensing', Research Paper 41, South Centre, September, http://www.thaidrugwatch.org/download/rp_41_pharm_complice_ccorrea.pdf, date accessed February 2012.

Court of Administrative Justice (2008) Decision on case no. 22218/60, Eli Lilly vs. the Legal Representative of Apex Pharma, the President of Academy of Science and Technology, Minister of Health and Population and the Prime Minister, 20 December.

Court of Administrative Justice (2011) Decision on case no. 5792 for the 65th Judicial Year, Department of Economic Disputes and Investment, 7th District, Cairo, 14 May 2011.

Dessouki, A. (2008) 'Analyzing the Public Pharmaceutical Policies in Egypt', PhD Thesis, Department of Economics and Political Science, Cairo University.

EATG, *see* European AIDS Treatment Group.

Egyptian Initiative for Personal Rights (2005) 'New Study Urges Egyptian Government to Use TRIPS Flexibilities to Protect People's Right to Health', http://eipr.org/en/pressrelease/2005/01/11/247, date accessed 29 March 2012.

Egyptian Initiative for Personal Rights (2010) 'The International Medical Products Anti-Counterfeiting Taskforce (IMPACT)', Briefing note, blog, *waraqa taerifeyya— magmou'et el 'amal el dawleya le mokafa'et ghesh wa taqleed el montagat el tebeyya*, http://eipr.org/report/2010/08/15/948, date accessed 14 February 2012.

Egyptian Initiative for Personal Rights (2011) 'The Egyptian Interferon: A Scientific Debate and Necessary Regulations that Need to be Issued', Briefing note, blog, August 2011, http://eipr.org/en/report/2011/08/21/1258, date accessed 14 February 2012.

EIPR, *see* Egyptian Initiative for Personal Rights.

El Ahmady, O. (2010) Head of R&D Department in the Egyptian International Pharmaceutical Industries Company (EIPICO) and former Vice Dean of the Faculty of Pharmacy Ain Shams University, interview, December.

El-Zanaty, F. and A. Way (2009) *Egypt Demographic and Health Survey* (Cairo: Ministry of Health), http://www.measuredhs.com/pubs/pdf/FR220/FR220.pdf, date accessed 14 February 2012.

Eren-Vural, I. (2007) 'Domestic Contours of Global Regulation: Understanding the Policy Changes on Pharmaceutical Patents in India and Turkey', *Review of International Political Economy* 14, 105–42.

European Aids Treatment Group (2010) 'NGOs Concerned over WHO's Role in "Counterfeit" Drugs, IMPACT', 15 May, http://www.eatg.org/eatg/Global-HIV-News/Access-to-treatment/NGOs-concerned-over-WHO-s-role-in-counterfeit-drugs-IMPACT, date accessed February 2012.

Farag, M. (2010) General Director, Pharmaceutical Compositions, Egyptian Patent Office, interview, November.

Fayyad, S. (2002) 'Health in Egypt: Current Status and Future Scenarios till the Year 2020', Third World Forum, Middle East Office, Cairo.

Fayyad, S. (2007) Unpublished policy paper on Health Sector Reform in Egypt, January.

Frymark, T., H. Leech, R. Mullen, T. Schooling, R. Venediktov and B. Wang (2010) 'Evidence-Based Systematic Review: Drug-Induced Hearing Loss— Amikacin', National Center for Evidence-Based Practice in Communication Disorders, American Speech-Language-Hearing Association, http://www.asha.org/uploadedFiles/EBSRAmikacin.pdf, date accessed 29 March 2012.

George, E. (2011) 'The Human Right to Health and HIV/AIDS: South Africa and South–South Cooperation to Reframe Global Intellectual Property Principles and Promote Access to Essential Medicines', *Indiana Journal of Global Legal Studies* 18 167–97.

Hamed, M. R. (1997) 'Future of the Pharmaceutical Sector in Egypt', *Mustaqbal sena'aet el dawa'a fi masr wa el manteqa el arabeya*.

Industrial Modernisation Centre (2004) 'Egypt's Pharmaceutical Sector. Survival and Development. Strategy Report Incorporating Results and Conclusions of Review Activity'. http://www.imc-egypt.org/studies/FullReport/Pharmaceutical%20Development%20Strategy_EN.pdf. date accessed 29 March 2012.

Kadah, M. (2003) 'Foreign Direct Investment and International Technology Transfer to Egypt', Economic Research Forum Working Paper Series, Working Paper 317, http://econpapers.repec.org/paper/ergwpaper/0317.htm, date accessed 29 March 2012.

Mara, K. (2010) 'New Resolution Gives Governments Control of WHO Work on False Medicines', *Intellectual Property Watch*, 21 May, http://www.ip-watch.org/2010/05/21/new-resolution-gives-governments-control-of-who-work-on-false-medicines/, date accessed 29 March 2012.

Kaplan, W. and R. Laing (2005) 'Local Production of Pharmaceuticals: Industrial Policy and Access to Medicines. An Overview of Key Concepts, Issues and Opportunities for Future Research', *Health, Nutrition, and Population*, World Bank Human Development Network, January 2005.

Kassem, M. (2011) Research and Development Consultant, Medical Union Pharmaceuticals, interview, January 2011.

Law No. 82 of 2002 on the Protection of Intellectual Property Rights, http://www.wipo.int/clea/en/details.jsp?id=1301, date accessed 27 February 2012.

Leila, R. (2007) 'Ensuring Health Insurance', *Al Ahram Weekly Online* no. 854, 19–25 July, http://weekly.ahram.org.eg/2007/854/eg8.htm, date accessed 13 February 2012.

Mahmoud, I. E. and S. K. Mohamed (2006) Survey of Pharmacists' Opinions on the Availability and Price Stability of Drugs in Egypt (Egypt: Information and Decision Making Support Centre, Council of Ministers).

Mehanny, M. (2011) Head of the Chamber of Trade for Pharmaceutical Producers and President of the Egyptian Global Napi, interview, June 2011.

Minister of Health (1991) Ministerial Decree on Pricing of Medicines 314/1991.

Minister of Health (2009) Decree on the Reorganization of the Rules and Procedures for the Registration of Human Pharmaceutical Preparation 296/2009, issued 28 June.

Ministry of Health (2004) *National Drug Policy 2004–05* (Egypt: Ministry of Health).

Ministry of Health (2011) *National Health Accounts 2008–2009 Summary of Key Findings* (Egypt: USAID and the Ministry of Health).

MOH, *see* Ministry of Health.

NCD, *see* Non-Communicable Diseases Alliance.

Non-Communicable Diseases Alliance (2011) 'Access to Essential Medicines and Technologies for NCDs', briefing paper, http://www.ncdalliance.org/node/3485, date accessed 14 February 2012.

Peng, Xiao (2009) 'TRIPS Agreement and Public Health Crisis in Developing Countries: Problems and Solutions', *US–China Law Review*, Serial No. 51, 6(2).

Pfizer (2003) Submission by the Legal Representative of Pfizer Inc. and Pfizer Egypt to the Sixth Civil Circuit of the Zagazig Court of First Instance in case no. 1855/2003, Pfizer vs. Egyptian International Company for Pharmaceutical Production (EIPICO), submitted 18 June.

Rostom, O. (2010) Vice President of the Egyptian International Pharmaceutical Industries Company (EIPICO), interview, November.

Roulot, D., V. Bourcier, V. Grando, P. Deny, Y. Baazia, et al. (2007) 'Epidemiological Characteristics and Response to Peg Interferon plus Ribavirin Treatment of Hepatitis C Virus Genotype 4 Infection', *Journal of Viral Hepatitis*, 14, 460–7, http://www.ncbi. nlm.nih.gov/pubmed/17576387, date accessed 14 February 2012.
SAC, *see* Supreme Administrative Court.
Supreme Administrative Court (2004) Decision of the Supreme Administrative Court, First Circuit, appeal no. 6965/49, Apex Pharma vs. President of Academy of Science and Technology, Minister of Health and Population, the Prime Minister and the Legal Representative of the Company Eli Lilly, issued 25 December.
Tageldin, M. A. and M. R. Hamed (2003) 'Pharmaceutical Policies in Egypt: Situation, Problems and Future', *Public Policy Forum Papers*, 16, Public Administration Research and Consultation Centre, School of Economics and Political Science, Cairo University, http://www.parcegypt.org/english/link.php?cat_id=32andId=408andsearch_word=2003, date accessed 14 February 2012.
UNCTAD, *see* United Nations Conference on Trade and Development.
United Nations Conference on Trade and Development (2003) *Transfer of Technology for Successful Integration into the Global Economy*, UNCTAD/ITE/IPC/2003/6 (New York and Geneva: United Nations).
WHO, *see* World Health Organization.
World Health Organization (2006) 'Conclusions and Recommendations of the World Health Organization Conference on Counterfeit Medicines: Declaration of Rome', 18 February 2006, http://www.who.int/medicines/services/counterfeit/RomeDeclaration.pdf, date accessed February 2012.
World Health Organization (2010) *Country Cooperation Strategy for WHO and Egypt: 2010–2014*, EM/ARD/037/E (Cairo: WHO Regional Office for the Eastern Mediterranean).
World Health Organization (2011a) 'The New Global Framework to Support expansion of MDR-TB services and care', the Green Light Committee Initiative Website, http://www.who.int/tb/challenges/mdr/greenlightcommittee/en/, date accessed 14 February 2012.
World Health Organization (2011b) *Local Production for Access to Medical Products: Developing a Framework to Improve Public Health* (Geneva: World Health Organization).
World Health Organization and Health Action International (2007) 'Medicine Prices in Egypt', unpublished report presented at the WHO and Health Action International Post-Medicine Price Survey Workshop, Cairo, January.
WTO, *see* World Trade Organization.
World Trade Organization (1994) *Agreement on Trade-Related Aspects of Intellectual Property Rights* (TRIPS), Annex 1C, Marrakesh Agreement Establishing the World Trade Organization, 15 April, http://www.wto.org/english/docs_e/legal_e/legal_e.htm#TRIPs, date accessed February 2012.

6
The Pharmaceutical Industry in India after TRIPS

Sudip Chaudhuri

The Indian pharmaceutical industry occupies a special position among developing countries.[1] It has demonstrated strong innovation capabilities, tremendous strength in developing cost-efficient processes and significant capacity in setting up manufacturing plants for drugs satisfying international quality norms. India supplies medicines not only to other developing countries but also to developed countries such as the US. One of the most important factors contributing to this remarkable development was the abolition of product patent protection for pharmaceuticals in 1972. After independence, wanting to develop a pharmaceutical industry, India had invited multinational corporations (MNCs) to help develop the industry. Before 1972, although not keen to manufacture pharmaceuticals in India, they had used their patent rights to prevent Indian companies from doing so. As a result, in this period the industry remained underdeveloped, while at the same time multinationals' monopolies led to high prices. The abolition of product patents eliminated the multinationals' monopoly power, and the cost-efficient processes developed by the indigenous sector—often in collaboration with government laboratories—were then used for manufacturing the latest drugs. These cost a fraction of international prices, dislodging the multinationals from their position of dominance in the domestic market.[2]

From 1 January 2005, however, drug product patent protection was reintroduced, to comply with the requirements of the Agreement on Trade Related Aspects of Intellectual Property Rights (TRIPS). A key question is how multinational pharmaceutical companies and Indian generics companies are responding to the new policy environment. It might be assumed that, as in the pre-1972 situation, India is experiencing monopolization of the industry and high prices. It has, however, also been argued that strong patent protection will be beneficial for India. The TRIPS negotiations were driven by specific claims that TRIPS-compliant patent protection would prompt companies in developing countries to conduct more research and development (R&D) for new drugs more suited to local needs. Are Indian generics companies mature enough to take advantage of stronger patent protection? Might India's experience suggest a rethinking of the relationship between patents, R&D and innovation in developing countries? In this chapter I examine these questions to gauge the impact of TRIPS on India's pharmaceutical industry.

Rising dominance of the multinationals

India's generics companies are no longer permitted to manufacture new patented drugs. They can only be manufactured by the patentees and their licences. Thus, depending on the rate of introduction of these drugs, multinationals' market share is expected to increase.

But multinational firms are not interested only in markets for patented drugs. They are also seeking to grow, and to do so aggressively, in the generics segments of the industry. Traditionally, multinationals relied for growth on patented drugs and focused mainly on markets in developed countries. The high monopoly prices of patented drugs yielded high returns. But recent years have witnessed a sharp fall in the number of new drugs introduced onto the market. Multinational corporations are increasingly finding it difficult to fill the product gap, as patents on their blockbuster drugs are expiring and they are facing constraints on further profitable growth in markets in developed countries. Pfizer, for example, is set to lose a US$10 billion a year revenue stream when the patent on its blockbuster drug Lipitor expires. Desperate attempts by Pfizer to find a replacement have not yielded results (Wilson, 2011). Overall, the net profit of the top 15 multinationals declined sharply, by 20.1 per cent in 2010, with major setbacks for companies like Merck, Bristol Myers Squibb and GlaxoSmithKline (Pingle, 2011). On the other hand, some markets in developing countries are experiencing rapid growth. The seven emerging markets of China, Brazil, India, Russia, South Korea, Mexico and Turkey contributed more than half the growth of the global pharmaceutical market in 2009, compared with only 16 per cent by North American, Western European and Japanese markets. The figures were, respectively, 7 per cent and 79 per cent in 2001 (Tempest, 2011). Not unexpectedly, multinational firms are targeting the generics industry in these emerging markets as well.

The involvement of multinationals in the generics market is not new in India. When product patents were abolished in India in 1972, they did not stop operating in India. All the major multinationals decided to stay. GlaxoSmithKline (GSK; earlier known as Glaxo) in fact remained the largest seller in the domestic formulations market until quite recently. But in general MNCs maintained a low profile. They were hesitant to introduce their latest products. Some of them continued to compete, but created new local brands rather than use their international brands. Others stopped selling products they thought were priced too low (Chaudhuri, 2005, Chapter 4).

What is new in the post-TRIPS situation is the vigour with which MNCs are trying to expand not only into the patented drugs markets but also into generics markets. Pfizer, GSK and Merck had opted at an earlier time not to introduce some of their blockbuster drugs into India. These are now being introduced. Examples include Azithromycin and Quinapril by Pfizer, Simvastatin by Merck and Carvedilol by GSK. In fact, the multinationals are not hesitating to market products developed by other multinationals. Pfizer, for example, is marketing telmisartan, originally developed by Boehringer Ingelheim (Idfc-Sski, 2010, p. 16).

In India's case the most obvious reflection of such changes in strategy is the takeover of Indian companies by multinationals and strategic alliances between multinationals and Indian companies (see Table 6.1).

Table 6.1 M&As and tie-ups in Indian pharmaceutical industry, 2006–2010

Indian company	Foreign company	Date	Type	Comments
Aurobindo	AstraZeneca	September 2010	Tie-up	Licensing and supply agreements for several solid dosage and sterile products for emerging markets across anti-infectives, cardiovascular system (CVS) and central nervous system (CNS) segments.
Primal Healthcare	Abbott	May 2010	M&A	Abbott acquires the domestic formulation business of Piramal for US$3.7 billion.
Cadila	Abbott	May 2010	Tie-up	Abbott licenses 24 Cadila products in 15 high-growth emerging markets, holds option for more than 40 additional products
Orchid Chemicals	Alvogen	May 2010	Tie-up	Alvogen to have marketing rights for eight oral generic formulations for US in the area of CNS and osteoporosis. The product to be sourced exclusively from Orchid.
Indoco	Aspen	March 2010	Tie-up	Generic supply deal for ophthalmic products across 30 countries in emerging markets. Aspen will have market authorization over these products.

Table 6.1 (Continued)

Indian company	Foreign company	Date	Type	Comments
Torrent	AstraZeneca	March 2010	Tie-up	Generic supply deal for 18 products across nine countries. Further flexibility to add more products and new countries.
Strides	Pfizer	January 2010	Tie-up	Generic supply of off-patent sterile injectable and oral products. Expects supplies of 40 off-patent products in oncology therapeutics.
Orchid Chemicals	Hospira	December 2009	M&A	Hospira acquires generic injectable business for US$400 million.
Shantha Biotech	Sanofi-Aventis	2009 July	M&A	Sanofi-Aventis acquires Shantha for US$ 783 million.
Dr Reddy's	GSK	June 2009	Tie-up	GSK will gain exclusive access to Dr Reddy's rich and diverse portfolio and future pipeline. Dr Reddy's to manufacture but will be licensed and supplied by GSK in Latin American markets, with the exception of co-marketing in certain markets.
Aurobindo	Pfizer	May 2009	Tie-up	Licensing and supply agreements for several solid dosage and sterile products for emerging markets. Offers rights to Pfizer for 55 solid and five sterile products in Latin American markets covering anti-infective, CVS and CNS.
Claris Lifescience	Pfizer	May 2009	Tie-up	The deal offers Pfizer marketing rights for 15 injectable products in areas of anti-infectives and pain management for regulated markets.
Ranbaxy	Daiichi-Sankyo	June 2008	M&A	Daiichi-Sankyo acquires Ranbaxy for US$4.6 billion.
DaburPharma	Fresenius Kabi	April 2008	M&A	Fresenius Kabi of Singapore acquires Dabur for US$219 million.
Matrix Laboratories	Mylan	August 2006	M&A	The US generics company Mylan acquires Matrix for US$736 million.

Sources: SBICAP (2010); Government of India (2010).

Indian companies like Dr Reddy's, Aurobindo, Cadila Healthcare and Torrent have entered into supply agreements with GSK, AstraZeneca and Abbot. Dr Reddy's, for example, will supply about 100 branded formulations to GSK for marketing in different emerging markets across Latin America, Africa, the Middle East and the Asia Pacific region, excluding India. Dr Reddy's will get a predetermined share of the revenue earned by GSK for these products. In some markets where Dr Reddy's has a presence formulations will be marketed jointly. Another example is the Aurobindo–Pfizer deal. Aurobindo will supply more than 100 formulations to Pfizer for the regulated markets of the US and EU, and more than 50 products for about 70 non-US/EU markets. It has been reported that, apart from revenue sharing, the deal involves payment of upfront licence fees by Pfizer to Aurobindo. Such deals enable multinationals to get access to low-cost reliable products without having to engage in the lengthy process of regulatory approval in different markets or incurring capital expenditure setting up manufacturing plants. In this way Indian companies gain by having access to the formidable marketing resources of the multinational firm they work with. Experience suggests that it is not easy for Indian companies to enter simultaneously into different markets on their own. Efforts by some to enter and expand into foreign markets with their own marketing infrastructure have not always led to the desired results. Indian companies hope to better realize their manufacturing capacities and capabilities through such alliances (Idfc-Sski 2009, 2010).

More significant than these alliances is the takeover of Indian companies by multinationals. Multinational corporations' share of the domestic formulations market has dramatically increased, from less than 20 per cent in March 2008 to 28 per cent in December 2010, with the takeover of Ranbaxy by Daiichi Sankyo in June 2008; Dabur Pharma by Fresenius Kabi Oncology in August 2008; Shantha Biotechs by Sanofi-Aventis in July 2009; and the domestic formulations business Piramal Healthcare by Abbott in May 2010. In March 2008 there was only one multinational (GSK) among the top ten companies in India. By December 2010 the number of multinationals in the top ten had increased to three (GSK, Ranbaxy and the Abbott group). The Abbott group, comprising Abbott, Piramal Healthcare and Solvay Pharma, is now the largest company in India, with a market share of 6.2 per cent, ahead of the second largest, Cipla, at 5.7 per cent. Abbott was the thirtieth largest company in the domestic formulations market in March 2008, with a market share of only 1.1 per cent.[3]

Thus, the declining trend in the aggregate market share of multinationals that started in the 1970s has been reversed. Now they are recovering lost ground. The post-TRIPS environment and the strategy being adopted by them suggest that they are on the way to dominating the industry again. First, in a reversal of attitude from the earlier period, multinationals are now aggressively pursuing growth in generics. Second, they will enjoy monopoly power in the patented drugs market. Third, they have the financial capacity to take over still more Indian companies. If just a few other major Indian companies—for instance, Cipla (5.7 per cent market share in 2010), Sun (4.3 per cent), Cadila Healthcare (3.9 per cent), Mankind (3.2 per cent), Alkem (3 per cent), Lupin (2.9 per cent)—were taken over, the multinational share would exceed 50 per cent immediately.

Market structure and prices of patented products

Considering the role abolition of product patent protection played in the pharmaceutical industry in India, reintroduction of product patent protection since 2005 has crucial significance. The basic concern is whether India will go back to the pre-1972 situation of multinationals' monopoly and high prices. Although product patents were introduced on 1 January 2005, from 1 January 1995 a mailbox facility was in place to receive and hold product patent applications.[4] As per the TRIPS agreement, these applications have been processed since 1 January 2005 for grant of patents. Thus, to understand the impact on market structure and prices, we need to consider the period since 1995.

Indian generics companies are no longer permitted to manufacture and market new drugs for which patents have been granted in India. But not all new drugs are patentable in India. Under Article 70(3) of TRIPS, a World Trade Organization (WTO) member country has no obligation to provide patent protection for any subject matter that has fallen into the 'public domain' before the WTO came into being, that is, before 1 January 1995. Thus, any drug product patented abroad before 1995 could continue to be manufactured and sold in India after 1995 even though it might have been under patent protection in another country.

Drugs patented after 1 January 1995 can be classified as:

- those involving new chemical entities (NCEs) (also known as new molecular entities or NMEs); and new biological entities (NBEs) patented after 1995, and
- those involving NCEs/NBEs developed before 1995 but with patents after 1995 for
    - new formulations and compositions
    - new combinations
    - new chemical derivatives (salts, esters and so on).

According to TRIPS Article 27(1), it is required to provide patents for inventions that are 'new, involve an inventive step and are capable of industrial application'. The Agreement, however, does not define these terms. This provides some flexibility. India has taken advantage of this flexibility by enacting Section 3(d) in its amended Patents Act and restricting product patents to some extent. Under Section 3(d) India is not obliged to provide protection to any secondary patents (of new formulations, combinations or chemical derivatives) after 1995 involving NCEs developed before 1995 'unless they differ significantly in properties with regard to efficacy'.

Further, in cases where Indian companies were already producing and marketing before 1 January 2005—the products for which patent applications were made via the mailbox—they need not suspend production even if multinationals secure the patents. Under Section 11A(7) they can continue to produce on payment of a 'reasonable royalty'.

As Table 6.2 shows, 180 new drugs have been marketed in India since 1995 (at least until 2010). These accounted for about 9.1 per cent of the total pharmaceutical market in India in 2010. These 180 drugs are further classified into:

- 62 drugs for which patents have expired in the US (3.8 per cent of the Indian market)
- 67 drugs for which patents were granted in the US before 1995 and hence are not patentable in India in accordance with TRIPS (4.2 per cent)
- 51 drugs for which patents were granted in the US after 1995 and hence are patentable in India, subject to Section 3(d) provisions (1.2 per cent).

Thus, the market share of patentable new drugs market in India is still very small. It would, however, not be correct to infer from this that patented drugs are not a problem in India. As we will see below, for life-threatening diseases such as cancer, exorbitant prices are being charged for new patented drugs. Patients who cannot afford the high cost of drugs are simply not receiving proper treatment. Moreover, it is just a few years since product patent protection was introduced. The time lag between the patenting of an NCE or NBE and final approval for marketing means that no post-1995 NCE or NBE is yet available. Some multinationals, for example GSK, have revealed

Table 6.2 Patent status of new drugs marketed in India, 1995–2010

	No.	Sales 2010 Rs million	Sales 2010 (%)	MNC share 2010
New drugs	180	47,266.63	9.1	10.9
Patented post-1995	51	5999.51	1.2	25.2
Patented pre-1995	67	21,732.00	4.2	5.5
Patent expired	62	19,535.12	3.8	12.6
Total pharmaceutical market		520,525.60	100.0	19.1

Sources: http://www.fda.gov/Drugs/DevelopmentApprovalProcess/HowDrugsareDevelopedand Approved/DrugandBiologicApprovalReports/ucm121136.htm; http://cdsco.nic.in/listofdrug approvedmain.html; date accessed 8 August 2011. Gopakumar (2010, Table F).[5]

Table 6.3 Market structure of new drugs, 2010

	Total no. of molecules	No. of molecules with five or more sellers	No. of molecules with two to four sellers	No. of molecules with one seller
Patented post-1995				
No. of molecules	51	19	6	26
Sales 2010 (Rs million)	5999.51	4626.68	155.94	1216.89
No. of molecules (%)	100.0	37.3	11.8	51.0
Sales 2010 (%)	100.0	77.1	2.6	20.3
Patented pre-1995				
No. of molecules	67	46	11	10
Sales 2010 (Rs million)	21,732.00	21,153.82	309.21	268.97
No. of molecules (%)	100.0	68.7	16.4	14.9
Sales 2010 (%)	100.0	97.3	1.4	1.2
Patent expired				
No. of molecules	62	43	11	8
Sales 2010 (Rs million)	19,535.12	19,125.04	256.65	153.43
No. of molecules (%)	100.0	69.4	17.7	12.9
Sales 2010 (%)	100.0	97.9	1.3	0.8

Sources: http://www.fda.gov/Drugs/DevelopmentApprovalProcess/HowDrugsareDevelopedand Approved/DrugandBiologicApprovalReports/ucm121136.htm; http://cdsco.nic.in/listofdrug approvedmain.html; Gopakumar (2010, Table F).

ambitious plans to launch a basket of patented products. They are expanding their marketing infrastructure in anticipation of the future patented market.

Table 6.3 indicates the competition in these three categories of new drugs. In respect of the first two categories, for which patent barriers do not exist in India, markets are much more competitive than for the third category. For patent-expired molecules there are five or more sellers for 43 products, accounting for 97.9 per cent of this market segment. For pre-1995 molecules the figures are 46 products and 97.3 per cent, respectively. Monopolies exist in only 1 per cent of the market. Thus, these market segments are essentially competitive.

But for the third category of post-1995 drugs there are monopolies in 51 per cent of products, accounting for 20 per cent of this market segment. Surprisingly, even for post-1995 products, for about three-quarters of the market the number of sellers is five or more. Two TRIPS flexibilities may explain this. Under Section 11A(7), Indian generics companies that commenced manufacturing before 2005 are not required to suspend production if patents are granted.

More important is the flexibility provided under Section 3(d). Consider, for example, two post-1995 products: Novartis' anti-cancer drug imatinib mesylate and Gilead's anti-HIV/AIDS drug tenofovir disoproxil fumarate. Product patents are in force in the US for these products. But in the case of both these products the original compounds—imatinib and tenofovir—were disclosed before 1995. What actually have been patented are a particular beta crystalline form (mesylate) and a particular salt (disoproxil fumarate). Hence, these are not patentable in India subject to the enhanced efficacy clause of Section 3(d). The Patent Office and states' High Courts have rejected these patent applications. The matter is currently with India's Supreme Court (see Park, 2010). In the absence of any legal barrier to entering these markets, a number of Indian generics companies are manufacturing and selling these products on the market. There are 14 companies selling imatinib mesylate and six selling tenofovir disoproxil fumarate. Another product whose product patent has been contested is the anti-cancer drug erlotinib (trade name Tarceva). This is manufactured by six Indian companies.

In a product patent regime the main interest centres on the action of MNCs. Multinationals are involved in marketing 92 out of the 180 new drugs in India. As Table 6.4 shows, they have monopolies in 33 products, accounting for 31 per cent of their sales of Rs 5171.42 million (US$1.104 million) of these 92 products.[6] In fact, in 59 products they have a market share of 50 per cent or more, accounting for more than three-quarters of their sales. It is interesting to note that, out of these 33 products, patents have expired or are, in the case of eight products, pre-1995 molecules, for example, anidulafungin, caspofungin, micafungin and pegaptanib. This suggests that there are entry barriers other than patent barriers, for example, a complex manufacturing process.[7]

Table 6.4 New drugs marketed by MNCs, 2010

	No. of molecules	MNC sales 2010 Rs million	MNC sales (%)
Marketed by MNCs	92	5171.42	100.0
MNC monopoly	33	1601.87	31.0
Patented	25	1214.00	23.5
Patent expired	2	120.99	2.3
Pre-1995	6	266.88	5.2
MNC share: 50–100%	8	910.19	17.6
MNC share: 25–50%	12	1376.49	26.6
MNC share: 10–25%	7	566.98	11.0
MNC share: 5–10%	9	531.87	10.3
MNC share: 1–5%	12	165.92	3.2
MNC share: <1%	11	18.10	0.3

Sources: http://www.fda.gov/Drugs/DevelopmentApprovalProcess/HowDrugsareDevelopedandApproved/DrugandBiologicApprovalReports/ucm121136.htm; http://cdsco.nic.in/listofdrugapprovedmain.html; Gopakumar (2010, Table F).

Table 6.5 provides an indication of the pricing policies adopted by MNCs for these 33 monopoly products. A 50 ml injection of Roche's anti-cancer drug Herceptin (generic name trastumuzab) costs Rs 135,200 (circa US$2400). Among the other high-priced drugs are Merck's Erbitux (cetuximab): Rs 87,920 (circa US$1500); Bristol Myers Squibb's Ixempra (ixabepilone): Rs 66,430 (circa US$1200); Pfizer's Macugen (pegaptanib): Rs 45,350 (US$830); Sanofi-Aventis' Fasturtec (rasburicase): Rs 45,000 (US$825); and Roche's Avastin (bevicizumab): Rs 37,180 (US$790). There are six products that cost between Rs 10,000 and Rs 45,000 (for example, Wyeth's Enbrel (etanercept): Rs 15,761 or US$285); eight products between Rs 1000 and Rs 10,000 (for example, GSK's Tykerb (lapatinib): Rs 4468 or US$80); another six products between Rs 100 and Rs 1000 (for example, Bayer's Xarelto (rivaroxaban): Rs 480 or US$9); and only eight products with prices below Rs 100 (for example, MSD's Januvia (sitagliptin): Rs 43 or US$0.7).

It is important to note that the prices mentioned in Table 6.5 are for a single injection or tablet. The cost of treatment per person per year would be much higher. Consider, for example, Dasatinib, used for the treatment of chronic myeloid leukaemia. The price of a 70 mg Dasatinib tablet is Rs 3905 (US$71). Assuming a treatment regimen of 100 mg per day, the cost of treatment per person per year exceeds Rs 2 million (US$31,000). The corresponding cost in the UK is GBP 30,477 (or US$49,000), suggesting that the company (Bristol Myers Squibb) is essentially charging the same price, or even more, and not using differential pricing (NIHCE, 2011).[8]

All the drugs listed in Table 6.5 are monopoly drugs, in the sense that there is only one seller of the molecule concerned. Effective competition in pharmaceuticals takes place within therapeutic categories, for example, cardiac or anti-diabetic, where different molecules may compete against one another. It is important to note that in therapeutic categories like these, where different molecules are available in the market, the prices of the monopoly molecules are relatively low, for example, for cerivastatin, dronedarone, saxagliptin and sitagliptin. But, in the case of life-threatening diseases such as cancer, essential drugs without effective substitutes are priced exorbitantly, for example, trastumuzab, cetuximab and ixabepilone. Similarly, the prices of vital drugs—like Wyeth's Enbrel (etanercept) (Rs 15,761 or US$284 per injection) used for rheumatoid arthritis, which can incapacitate people; Pfizer's Macugen (pegaptanib) (Rs 45,350 or US$600 per 90 ml per injection) used for preventing loss of vision in the case of age-related macular degeneration; Sanofi-Aventis' Fasturtec (rasburicase) (Rs 45,000 or US$595 per injection) used to treat the side-effects of chemotherapy for leukaemia and lymphoma—are very high.

Table 6.5 does not cover all the patented and monopoly drugs marketed in India. The focus is on products for which multinationals have a monopoly. There are also products for which MNCs do not have a monopoly but are charging very high prices pending settlement of patent disputes. This

Table 6.5 Prices of MNC monopoly drugs

Molecule name	Brand name	MNC	MRP[1] in Rs	Therapeutic group
Trastuzumab	Herceptin injection 50 ml	Roche	135,200	anti-cancer
Cetuximab	Erbitux 700 mg injection 50 ml	Merck	87,920	anti-cancer
Ixabepilone	Ixempra 45 mg injection	Bristol Myers Squibb	66,430	anti-cancer
Pegaptanib	Macugen 0.3 mg injection 90 ml	Pfizer	45,350	ophthalmic/otologicals
Rasburicase	Fasturtec 1.5 mg injection	Sanofi-Aventis	45,000	cancer-related
Infliximab	Remicade 100 mg injection	Fulford	41,039	pain/analgesics
Tocilizumab	Actemra 400 mg injection	Roche	40,545	anti-cancer
Bevacizumab[2]	Avastin 100 mg injection		37,180	
Abatacept	Orencia 250 mg Injection	Bristol Myers Squibb	31,851	pain/analgesics
Daclizumab	Zenapax 25 mg Injection 5 ml	Roche	28,875	anti-cancer
Etanercept	Enbrel 50 mg injection	Wyeth	15,761	pain/analgesics
Caspofungin	Cancidas 70 mg injection 10 ml	MSD	12,500	anti-infectives
Anidulafungin	Eraxis 100 mg injection	Pfizer	9107	anti-infectives
Sunitinib	Sutent 50 mg capsule	Pfizer	8715	anti-cancer
Micafungin	Mycamine 50 mg injection	GlaxoSmithKline	6250	anti-infectives
Lenograstim	Granocyte 34 mg injection	Sanofi Aventis	5720	anti-cancer
Daptomycin	Cubicin 350 mg injection	Novartis	5051	anti-infectives
Lapatinib	Tykerb 250 mg tablet	GlaxoSmithKline	4468	anti-cancer
Liraglutide	Victoza 6 mg injection 3 ml	Abbott	4315	anti-diabetic
Dasatinib	Sprycel 70 mg tablet	Bristol Myers Squibb	3905	anti-cancer
Fondaparinux	Arixtra 2.5 mg injection 0.5 ml	GlaxoSmithKline	620	cardiac
Reviparin	Clivarine PFS SC 4200 IU injection 0.6 ml	Abbott	482	cardiac
Rivaroxaban	Xarelto 10 mg tablet	Bayer	480	cardiac
Ceftibuten	Procadax 90 mg syrup 30 ml	Fulford	384	anti-infectives

Table 6.5 (Continued)

Molecule name	Brand name	MNC	MRP[1] in Rs	Therapeutic group
Zuclopenthixol	Clopixol Depot 200 mg injection	Lundbeck	247	neuro/CNS
Certoparin	Troparin 3000 IU injection 0.3 ml	Novartis	235	cardiac
Dronedarone	Multaq 400 mg tablet	Sanofi Aventis	84	cardiac
Varenicline	Champix 1 mg tablet	Pfizer	59	neuro/CNS
Aliskiren	Rasilez 300 mg tablet	Novartis	58	cardiac
Sitagliptin	Januvia 100 mg tablet	MSD	43	anti-diabetic
Saxagliptin	Onglyza 5 mg tablet	Bristol Myers Squibb	38	anti-diabetic
Cerivastatin	Lipobay 0.3 mg tablet	Bayer	32	cardiac
Piribedil	Trivastal L.A 50 mg tablet	Serdia	20	neuro/CNS
Mianserin	Depnon 30 mg Tablet	Organon	12	neuro/CNS

[1] Maximum retail price.
[2] Roche holds 96 per cent of the market for this drug.
Source: MNC monopoly products are derived from the same sources as used in Table 2. Price data are from AIOCD Pharmasofttech AWACS's sales audit data. For the selected molecules, we sought prices from two large retail outlets in Kolkata, Calcutta Chemist Corner and AMRI Hospitals.

chapter does not present a systematic study of these products. But an example can be given. The price of pegylated interferon beta (Roche's Pegasys) is between Rs 14,000 and Rs 18,000 (circa US$300) per dose. It is used for hepatitis co-infected with HIV. Roche patented the product in India. But, as a result of patent disputes, some Indian generic companies are also manufacturing and marketing it (ITCP, 2011).

Table 6.5 lists the monopoly products directly marketed by multinationals. But, as mentioned above, multinationals not operating in India are using the marketing infrastructure of Indian companies to import and sell their products. It is not possible here to outline the prices of these imported products. But the example of poractant alfa shows that these prices, too, can be very high. Imported by Piramal (see CDSCO, 2009) as the sole seller, it costs Rs 17,957.8 (US$325) per 80 mg injection at 3 ml per vial.

Although it was not possible to list all highly priced products in Table 6.5, it is clear from the table that the days of monopolies and high drug prices are back, particularly for drugs without close substitutes.

In the product patent regime, the prices of new drugs will depend on:

- what prices multinational firms holding patents charge
- what steps are taken to regulate prices, including price control and price negotiation
- what steps are taken to stimulate competition from generics producers.

If the multinationals charge affordable prices for patented drugs in developing countries, access may not be adversely affected. Some are selling drugs at a discount compared with prices in developed countries. GSK, for example, has adopted a policy of selling drugs in India at a discount compared with prices in the US. But even with a discount the cost of treatment with Tykerb is about Rs 0.6 million (circa US$11,000) per person per year (*Hindu Business Line*, 2011). If, on the other hand, multinationals were to give voluntary licences to generics companies to manufacture patented drugs, the consequent competition could make drugs more affordable. Voluntary licences have mainly been given for products that have very little patent life left, however, and have rarely been given voluntarily. Usually such actions follow public pressure or legal action, and sometimes have been used as a strategy to thwart opposition by generics companies (Amin, 2007).

Price control is not forbidden under TRIPS or any other agreement of the WTO. The 'Draft National Pharmaceuticals Policy, 2006' recommended mandatory price negotiations for patented drugs before granting marketing approval and stressed the importance of studying the experiences of Canada, Australia, France and other countries believed to have good systems (Department of Chemicals and Petrochemicals, 2005, p. 15). In fact, the Committee on Price Negotiations on Patented Drugs has been set up in the Indian Department of Pharmaceuticals. This is an important initiative, and action should now be expedited to initiate measures to control the price of patented drugs. One important difference between direct price control measures and efforts to enhance generics competition to keep prices directly under control may be noted. The former, if properly implemented, makes drugs more affordable but does not provide any room for generics companies. The latter not only makes prices more affordable through competition; it also ensures generics companies have some breathing space, which is vital for their long-term growth and viability.

The importance of competition in generics is clear from Section 3(d) cases. Like dasatinib, imatinib mesylate is indicated for chronic myeloid leukaemia. But, unlike dasatinib, there are about 14 Indian generic companies manufacturing imatinib mesylate. As a result, the cost of treatment has decreased sharply compared with Novartis' equivalent product. Sun, the market leader, charges Rs 203 (US$3.7) for a 400 mg tablet. Similarly, there are six manufacturers of tenofovir. Cipla, the market leader, charges Rs 150 (or US$2.7) per 30 mg tablet. Again for erlotinib, compared with Roche's Tarceva's price of Rs 4200 (or US$74 for a 150mg tablet), Cipla's Erlocip costs Rs 1530 (US$27).

While Section 3(d) has played quite a useful role in India in recent years, the much more potent and sustainable policy option is compulsory licensing. Compulsory licensing is permission given by government to a non-patentee to manufacture a drug without (or even against) a patentee's consent. As is widely recognized, compulsory licensing is one of the ways in which TRIPS attempts to strike a balance between promoting access to existing drugs and promoting R&D of new drugs. If generics companies get licences to produce a patented drug on payment of royalties, then competition among manufacturers drives down prices, but royalties paid to the innovators continue to provide funds and the incentive for R&D.

The exorbitant prices MNCs charge for some products provides a very good rationale for compulsory licensing intervention. In March 2012 a compulsory licence was granted by the Controller of Patents in India to a generics company, Natco Pharma, to manufacture the anti-cancer medicine, sorafanib, patented by Bayer (and marketed as Nexavar). The very high price charged by Bayer was cited as one of the major reasons for the issuing of the licence. This is the first compulsory licence to be issued in India in the post-TRIPS environment. If this ushers in a user-friendly compulsory licensing system, it will provide commercial opportunities for Indian firms and be of great relief to the users of patented medicines (Controller of Patents, 2012).

R&D strategies

Before 1972, in the context of an underdeveloped Indian pharmaceutical industry, the capacity to conduct R&D was limited. Has the situation changed so much following the rapid growth of the industry since the 1970s as to now justify stronger patent protection? Might product patent protection have an adverse impact on access, making prices higher, or might it nevertheless be good for the R&D-based pharmaceutical industry? What has been the nature of R&D activities and innovation in the Indian pharmaceutical industry? Does India's experience support the claims of multinational firms and their supporters that strong patent protection is needed in India for R&D and innovation?

Traditionally the Indian pharmaceutical industry spent very little on R&D. In the early 1990s its R&D expenditure amounted to around 1.5 per cent of sales (Grace, 2004, p. 37). Even larger companies like Ranbaxy and Dr Reddy's Laboratories spent only 2–3 per cent of their sales on R&D in 1992–1993.[9] Since then, however, and particularly since the early 2000s, there has been a substantial increase in research spending in at least one segment of the industry. While most Indian companies continue to be minor R&D spenders, for the 38 companies with R&D expenditure of more than Rs 100 million in 2010–2011, R&D expenditure increased steadily from 1.7 per cent of sales in 1992–1993 to 4.3 per cent in 2001–2002, and then sharply to 8.1 per cent in 2004–2005, and 9.1 per cent in 2005–2006. Thereafter, however, there was a decline to 7.2 in 2010–2011. This area affords a focus on a more dynamic segment of the Indian industry, for which R&D expenditures have substantially increased.

The objectives of R&D conducted by Indian companies can be broadly classified into the following:

- development of NCEs
- modification of existing chemical entities to develop new formulations, compositions, combinations (also known as incrementally modified drugs)
- development of generics, that is, development of processes for manufacturing active pharmaceutical ingredients (APIs) and development of formulations to satisfy quality and regulatory requirements for marketing patent-expired drugs.

The development of NCEs is not yet a significant part of Indian R&D activities, constituting less than a quarter of the total R&D expenditure of the major companies (Chaudhuri, 2010, p. 47). Nor are all the large R&D spenders involved in NCE development. Cipla, for example, is the third largest spender on R&D but has no NCE portfolio.

The Indian pharmaceutical industry is now highly export-oriented. Growth in exports has been one of its most outstanding features. Exports were negligible in the product patent regime before the 1970s but began to increase in the 1970s after the amendment of the Patents Act. Initially growth was modest, accelerating in the 1980s. Growth has been particularly rapid since the mid-1990s, with exports increasing annually at more than 20 per cent in most recent years. The export market is larger than the domestic market not only for large companies, such as Ranbaxy (63 per cent of net sales in 2010–2011), Dr Reddy's (65.1 per cent) and Cipla (53.2 per cent), but also for smaller companies like Granules (77.8 per cent), Shilpa Medicare (76.7 per cent) and Kopran (58.6 per cent).[10]

Significant R&D efforts are directed towards developing processes and products to obtain regulatory approval for entry and growth in patent-expired generics markets in developed countries. The development of processes for manufacturing APIs and product development of formulations, process validation, bioequivalence testing and generation of other data required for obtaining international regulatory approval are specifically highlighted as areas where R&D is being undertaken by companies active in regulated markets (see, for example, Dr Reddy's Laboratories, 2006, p. 85; Ranbaxy, 2005, p. 46). Thus, a good deal of R&D by Indian pharmaceutical companies has nothing to do with TRIPS. It is the result of the increasing export orientation of Indian pharmaceutical companies and diversification to regulated markets, particularly the US.

R&D for new chemical entities

A remarkable feature of pharmaceutical R&D in India is that, although relatively small, the Indian private sector has started investing in R&D for new chemical entities. This began around the time TRIPS came into effect in the mid-1990s.[11] R&D investments were initiated by Dr Reddy's Laboratories, followed by Ranbaxy Laboratories. Since then 11 other companies—Sun, Cadila Healthcare, Lupin, Nicholas Piramal, Dabur Pharma, Torrent, Wockhardt, Orchid, Glenmark, Biocon and Seven Lifesciences—have joined in. These companies are among the major pharmaceutical R&D spenders. Together they invested Rs 26,032.5 million (US$578.2 million) (9.4 per cent of net sales) on R&D in 2010–2011.

It is important to note that none of these companies is engaged in the entire process of drug development. The reason is simple: Indian pharmaceutical companies are not yet ready for a start-to-finish model in NCE research because of a lack of the skills and funds necessary to develop a drug and put it onto the market (see Chaudhuri, 2005, Chapter 5). While the 13 Indian companies together spent US$578.2 million in 2010–2011, Pfizer, the largest multinational, alone spent US$7.8 billion in 2009 (Clinton and Mozeson, 2010). The model that Indian companies have adopted, rather, is to develop new molecules up to a certain stage and then license them out to partners from developed countries, primarily to multinationals. Here we see a marriage of interests. The development of biotechnology companies encouraged specialization according to stages of the drug development process. MNCs seek and contract out specific activities. Ever since their NCE pipeline started drying up they have intensified efforts to license promising compounds developed by others, and most major MNCs have opened compound acquisition departments. There are also specialized companies that keep track of and catalogue promising compounds and offer them for sale to prospective clients.

Even at the pre-clinical stage Indian companies are not engaged with all the elements of the R&D process. For example, they are not involved in basic research around target identification for new drugs. They rely on the basic research of others, adopting an approach called 'analogue research'. This entails working on certain pre-identified targets for specific diseases to develop molecules that alter the target's mechanism in the diseased person (Glenmark Pharmaceuticals, 2004). But even this requires medicinal chemistry and biology skills that are still scarce in India. In the pre-TRIPS era Indian scientists primarily acquired and developed the organic chemistry skills needed for process development. Indian companies are now filling this gap, primarily by hiring Indian scientists who have worked in multinationals' laboratories in India and abroad, and in India's public sector laboratories.[12]

The entry of Indian companies into new drug R&D was associated with tremendous optimism. The licensing deals of Dr Reddy's, Ranbaxy and others were major news, arousing the expectation that Indian companies would be recognized not only as successful manufacturers but also as successful innovators of new drugs. About 30 NCEs developed by Indian companies are in various stages of clinical trials. But drug development did not progress as anticipated, and the prospect of huge licensing revenue through milestone and other payments has failed to materialize.[13] Indian companies, particularly Ranbaxy and Dr Reddy's, the two companies that have invested most heavily and served as prime advocates for new drug R&D in India, have each suffered several setbacks. MNCs like Novo Nordisk and Novartis discontinued further development of compounds inlicensed from them.

Indian companies initially did not understand that, while their objectives were to earn licence fees and royalties from successful commercialization, multinationals do not necessarily aim to develop inlicensed compounds for commercialization. In fact, where compounds compete with a multinational's existing or planned products, the company's objective may actually be to 'kill' the compound.

Indian companies are now aware of this potential conflict. In some cases they are attempting to develop drugs further despite the lack of interest of the company that initially licensed them. Torrent, for example, entered into an agreement with Novartis in 2002 for the development of an Advanced Glycation Endproduct or AGE breaker compound for the treatment of heart disease and diabetes. In 2004 the compound was outlicensed to Novartis. The agreement was terminated in 2005 when Novartis decided not to proceed further with the compound. Torrent is now trying to develop it independently and explore other options. Torrent received only US$0.5 million initially, and then US$3 million, from Novartis (Torrent Pharmaceuticals, 2002, 2004).This was too small an amount for a large multinational like Novartis to have any stake in the project. Dr Reddy's has experienced similar setbacks.

The later the stage at which a compound is licensed out, the higher will be the licence revenues. The licensor is also in a better position to select a licensee who is actually interested in developing the drug for commercialization and may therefore provide a genuine possibility of earning royalties. But Indian companies face the predicament that the unilateral development of a drug to a later stage entails considerable cost and risk.

Rising R&D expenditure combined with poor returns has put strains on the profitability of these companies. Several companies—Ranbaxy, Dr Reddy's, Sun Pharmaceuticals, Piramal Healthcare—cut their R&D budgets around 2005–2006/2006–2007. Ranbaxy, Sun and Piramal have de-merged their NCE business. Such de-risking and reduction of R&D expenditure admits indirectly that NCE R&D has not been working as expected. Significantly, Ranbaxy and the domestic formulations business of Piramal have been taken over by multinationals, as noted above. Dr Reddy's has also changed its R&D strategy. It is experimenting with alternative business models, including setting up a separate drug development company to reduce risk and dependence on MNCs.

No NCE developed by an Indian company has yet been approved for marketing in any country. As noted, 30 NCEs developed by Indian companies are at various stages of clinical trialling. Dr Reddy's and Ranbaxy, which have been very active in NCE R&D and are the largest R&D spenders, have only two NCEs each undergoing clinical trials. Some smaller companies have a larger NCE pipeline. Glenmark and Cadila Healthcare, for example, have five molecules under clinical trial, followed by Lupin and Piramal Healthcare, each of which has four. The NCEs being developed by Indian companies are related primarily to 'global diseases' like diabetes, cancer, heart diseases, asthma and obesity—the diseases that offer much larger and more lucrative markets in developed countries (although they are also prevalent in developing countries). The 'neglected diseases' that primarily or exclusively affect developing countries and promise much more meagre financial returns are absent from the list, except for malaria and TB. In these cases public sector or philanthropic funding is involved. Ranbaxy is participating in an international project sponsored and funded by the Medicines for Malaria Venture (MMV), a public–private partnership developing a synthetic anti-malarial drug. Lupin is involved in developing an anti-TB drug in partnership with some publicly funded research institutions in India.

Conclusions

This study shows that little has changed to dispute the conventional wisdom that developing countries should not grant product patent protection.

They are already paying the cost of high prices for patent protected products, while the technological benefits claimed are yet to be seen.

The days of product monopolies and high prices are back. MNCs have started marketing new patented drugs at exorbitant prices, particularly for life-threatening diseases like cancer. Manufacturing and importing behaviour since the 1990s bears a close resemblance to that of the pre-1970s era. Imports of highly priced finished formulations are expanding rapidly, with manufacturing investments lagging far behind. Multinationals are also expanding vigorously in the generics segments. They are trying to grow not only organically but through mergers and acquisitions, and strategic alliances with Indian generics companies. The aggregate market share in the formulations market has gone up dramatically, with the takeover of some Indian companies by multinationals: they are on the way to dominating the industry again.

While R&D activities have diversified, Indian pharmaceutical firms are yet to prove their competence in innovating new products. No NCE has yet been developed for marketing. There have been several setbacks, and the partnership model has not always worked well. What Indian companies have really demonstrated is the ability to develop generics—an ability they acquired and improved in the pre-TRIPS period. Contrary to what was claimed during TRIPS negotiations, the product patent regime has not prompted Indian companies to devote more resources to developing drugs for neglected diseases that exclusively or predominantly affect developing countries. The large Indian pharmaceutical companies, which are the major R&D spenders in the country, have focused on the larger and more lucrative markets of the developed world, particularly the US. In that regard, the primary incentive to invest in R&D, whether for NCEs, for modifications, or for the development of generics, has not been the new TRIPS-compliant product patent regime in India but the product patent regime in developed countries, which was in place well before TRIPS. TRIPS may have accelerated the trend towards such R&D because of the anticipated shrinkage of domestic opportunities. But in the absence of TRIPS such R&D activities would still have been undertaken. With larger domestic operations, Indian companies, in fact, would have had access to greater resources and been better placed to undertake such R&D.

Notes

1. In this chapter I draw liberally from some of my other work, particularly Chaudhuri 2010, 2011 and 2012.
2. See Chaudhuri (2005, Chapter 2) for an account of the rise and growth of the Indian pharmaceutical industry.
3. For annual sales and market share figures I have used the sales audit data of AIOCD Pharmasofttech AWACS (AIOCD-AWACS). AIOCD-AWACS is a pharmaceutical market research company formed by All Indian Origin Chemists & Distributors Ltd (AIOCD Ltd) in a joint venture with Trikaal Mediinfotech Pvt.

Ltd. AIOCD Ltd is a corporate pharmaceutical retail chain set up by 550,000 members of the All India Organization of Chemists and Druggists.
4. Under TRIPS Articles 65.2 and 64.4 India had until 1 January 2005 to introduce product patent protection for pharmaceuticals. But Articles 70.8 and 70.9 put a limitation on the transition period allowed under Article 65. India was required to introduce 'mail box' and 'exclusive marketing rights' from 1 January 1995.
5. The list of NCEs and NBEs since 1995 was obtained from the US Food and Drug Administration (FDA) website. Marketing status in India was ascertained from the Central Drugs Standard Control Organization website. For the period 1999–2010 ready lists are available from the USFDA and CDSCO websites, respectively:

http://www.fda.gov/Drugs/DevelopmentApprovalProcess/HowDrugsareDevelopedandApproved/DrugandBiologicApprovalReports/ucm121136.htm and http://cdsco.nic.in/listofdrugapprovedmain.html. Information for the period 1995–1998 is taken from Gopakumar (2010, Table F). This table covers only NMEs. Hence, NBEs approved in the US between 1995 and 1998 are not included. Products approved in the US before 1995 but introduced in India after 1995 are also not included. Another limitation is that products not in use in the US (and hence not approved by USFDA) but in use in India are not covered. But the table also includes the following 12 molecules marketed in India for which MNCs are the sole sellers. This, to an extent, may take care of the limitations of the methodology associated with the fact that NMEs and NBEs approved during 1995–2010 may not have been included initially. The 12 molecules are: certoparin, daclizumab, etanercept, infliximab, lenograstim, mianserin, piribedil, rasburicase, reviparin, tocilizunab, trastuzumab, zuclopenthixol.

The numbers of sellers and sales figures were obtained from the sales audit data of AIOCD Pharmasofttech AWACS Pvt. Ltd (AIOCD-AWACS). Only single-ingredient formulations were considered, except in the cases of emtricitabine with tenofovir, ethinylestradiol with drospirenone, and artemether with lumefantrine. The simplified names of molecules as given in AIOCD-AWACS, for example tenofovir rather than tenofovir disoproxil fumarate, are used.

For the patent status I have used the electronic *Orange Book: Approved Drug Products with Therapeutic Equivalence Evaluations*. The *Orange Book* also lists the patents with expiry dates relating to those NMEs covered by it. Typically several patents—not only the patent on the NME but also secondary patents, for example, formulation patents—are listed, with different expiry dates. The patent with the earliest expiry date is considered the NME patent, since this is usually the first patent applied for. The patent term is 20 years. Hence, any patent with an expiry date before 31 December 2014 is considered to be a drug for which the patent was granted before 1 January 1995. These drugs are considered to be 'pre-1995' molecules, for example, pegaptanib. The expiry date of the earliest patent is 27 October 2013. Hence, it is considered to be a drug with an NME patent granted in 1993. Where the earliest expiry date is after 31 December 2014, the drug is considered to be patented, for example, lapatinib. The earliest expiry date is 11 July 2017. Hence, it is considered to be a drug patented in 1997 ('patented 1997').
When the *Orange Book* says that there are 'no unexpired patents for this product', the drug is considered to be 'patent expired', for example, tamsulosin. The *Orange Book* lists generics manufacturers such as Wockhardt and Sun. Where information on patent status is not available from the *Orange Book*, as, for example, in the

case of NBEs, the drug is understood as patented if a multinational is the sole seller in India. The drug is treated as patent expired where there are multiple sellers. It is important to point out that use of the *Orange Book* is not a foolproof way of establishing patent status. One of the major limitations is that patents on NBEs are not required to be listed there. The *Orange Book* is relied upon here in the absence of any systematic information on pharmaceutical product patents granted in India.
6. All prices are converted on December 2012 rates.
7. Or else the use of the USFDA Orange Book did not correctly reveal patent status. As explained in the notes accompanying Table 2, the patent with the earliest expiry date is taken to be the NME patent. The earliest patents for these four products, for example, expire during 2011–2013 and hence they have been treated as pre-1995 molecules. But there are also other patents listed that expire after 2014, and, if any of these are relevant product patents, then these are actually post-1995 products.
8. Foreign exchange rates fluctuate. Assuming a rate of Rs 70 per GBP, the cost of treatment is the same.
9. Information in this section has been calculated using the CMIE Prowess database.
10. Export shares have been calculated using CMIE India Trades database.
11. In the Indian private sector, Sarabhai Research Centre was the first to be set up, in the 1960s, for developing new drugs. But it was wound up in the 1980s.
12. In the pre-TRIPS regime, too, some R&D for new drug development was undertaken in India, primarily by the Central Drug Research Institute (CDRI) (public sector), and Ciba Geigy, Hoechst and Boots (all multinationals). Not many drugs have come onto the market as a result of these efforts, but it generated specialized skills. See Chaudhuri (2005).
13. There are exceptions: Glenmark earned a total of $117 million in licensing revenue over 2004–2007. But Glenmark, too, has been facing problems (corporate presentation, August 2009, http//: www.glenmarkpharma.com).

References

Amin, T. (2007) 'Voluntary Licensing Practices in the Pharmaceutical Sector: An Acceptable Solution to Improving Access to Affordable Medicines?', Oxfam, http://www.i-mak.org/storage/Oxfam%20-%20Voluntary%20Licensing%20Research%20IMAK%20Website.pdf, date accessed 19 March 2012.
Business Monitor International (2011) 'India: Pharmaceuticals and Healthcare Report', *Business Monitor International*, June.
CDSCO, *see* Central Drugs Standard Control Organization.
Central Drugs Standard Control Organization (2009) List of Finished Formulations Registered from 2003 to 2009, http://cdsco.nic.in/LIST%20OF%20FF%20REGISTERED%20FROM%202003-2009.doc, date accessed 13 March 2011.
Chaudhuri, S. (2005) *The WTO and India's Pharmaceuticals Industry: Patent Protection TRIPS and Developing Countries* (New Delhi: Oxford University Press).
Chaudhuri, S. (2010) 'The Industry Response' in S. Chaudhuri, C. Park and K. M. Gopakumar (eds) *Five Years into the Product Patent Regime: India's Response* (New York: United Nations Development Programme).
Chaudhuri, S. (2012) 'Multinationals and Monopolies: Pharmaceutical Industry in India after TRIPS', *Economic and Political Weekly*, 47, 46–54.

Chaudhuri, S., C. Park and K. M. Gopakumar (eds) (2010) *Five Years into the Product Patent Regime: India's Response* (New York: United Nations Development Programme).
CIPIH, *see* Commission on Intellectual Property Rights, Innovation and Public Health.
Clinton, P. and M. Mozeson (2010) 'The 2010 Pharm Exec 50', http://www.pharmexec.com/pharmexec/data/articlestandard//pharmexec/222010/671415/article.pdf, date accessed 21 March 2012.
Commission on Intellectual Property Rights, Innovation and Public Health (2006), *Public Health Innovation and Intellectual Property Rights*, Report of the Commission on Intellectual Property Rights, Innovation and Public Health.
Controller of Patents (2012) Application for compulsory licence under Section 84(1) of the Patents Act, 1970 in respect of Patent no. 215758, http://www.ipindia.nic.in/ipoNew/compulsory_License_12032012.pdf, date accessed 26 March 2012.
Department of Chemicals and Petrochemicals (2005) Draft National Pharmaceuticals Policy, Government of India, http://www.drugscontrol.org/draftNPP2006.pdf, date accessed 19 March 2012.
Dr Reddy's Laboratories (2006) *Annual Report, 2005–06*, http://www.drreddys.com/, date accessed 19 March 2012.
Glenmark Pharmaceuticals (2004) *Annual Report, 2003–04*, http://www.glenmarkpharma.com/GLN_NWS/homepage.aspx?res=P_GLN, date accessed 19 March 2012.
Gopakumar, K. M. (2010) 'Landscape of Pharmaceutical Patent Applications in India: Implications for Access to Medicines' in S. Chaudhuri, C. Park and K. M. Gopakumar (eds) *Five Years into the Product Patent Regime: India's Response* (New York: United Nations Development Programme).
Government of India (2010) *Discussion Paper: Compulsory Licensing* (New Delhi: Department of Industrial Promotion and Policy).
Grace, C. (2004) *The Effect of Changing Intellectual Property on Pharmaceutical Industry Prospects in India and China Considerations for Access to Medicines* (London: DFID Health Systems Resource Centre).
Hindu Business Line (2011) 'GlaxoSmithKline launches two cancer drugs at reduced prices', *Hindu Business Line*, 22 July, http://www.thehindubusinessline.com/companies/article2285697.ece, date accessed 19 March 2012.
Idfc-Sski (2009) 'Recent MMNC Alliances: Signalling Paradigm Shift?', IDFC-SSKI Securities Ltd, June.
Idfc-Sski (2010) 'MNCPharma: New Avatar?', IDFC-SSKI Securities Ltd, March.
International Treatment Preparedness Coalition India (2011) 'Hepatitis C Virus—Prevention and Treatment', media release, 21 October.
ITCP, *see* International Treatment Preparedness Coalition.
National Institute for Health and Clinical Excellence (2011) *Leukaemia (chronic myeloid)—Dasatinib, High Dose Imatinib and Nilotinib (Review): Appraisal Consultation Document*, http://guidance.nice.org.uk/TA/WaveR/99/Consultation/DraftGuidance, date accessed 19 March 2012.
NIHCE, *see* National Institute for Health and Clinical Excellence.
Park, C. (2010) 'Implementation of India's Patent Law: A Review of Patents Granted by the Indian Patent Office' in S. Chaudhuri, C. Park and K. M. Gopakumar (eds) *Five Years into the Product Patent Regime: India's Response* (New York: United Nations Development Programme).
Pingle, S. (2011) 'Leading 15 Global Pharma Majors Suffer Setback in 2010, Net Falls by over 20%', http://pharmabiz.com/, date accessed 25 August 2011.

Ranbaxy (2005) *Annual Report, 2005*, http://www.wto.org/english/tratop_e/trips_e/implem_para6_e.htm, date accessed 17 February 2009.

SBICAP (2010) *India Equity: Pharma* (Mumbai: SBICAP Securities Ltd).

Tempest, B. (2011) 'Structural Changes in the Global Pharmaceutical Marketplace and their Possible Implications for Intellectual Property', UNCTAD-ICTSD Project on IPRs and Sustainable Development, Policy Brief no. 10, July, http://ictsd.org/i/publications/111430/, date accessed 4 August 2011.

Torrent Pharmaceuticals (2002) 'Novartis Acquires Rights in Torrent's AGE Compound', media release, 31 October 2002, http://www.torrentpharma.com/, date accessed 28 February 2007.

Torrent Pharmaceuticals (2004) 'Torrent Licenses AGE Compound to Novartis', media release, 29 July 2004, http://www.torrentpharma.com/, date accessed 28 February 2007.

US Food and Drug Administration, *Orange Book: Approved Drug Products with Therapeutic Equivalence Evaluations*, http://www.accessdata.fda.gov/scripts/cder/ob/default.cfm, date accessed 19 March 2012.

Wilson, D. (2011) 'Drug Firms Face Billions in Losses as Patents End', *Business Standard*, 3 August.

7
The Healthcare System and the Pharmaceutical Industry in Indonesia

Richard Husada and Raymond R. Tjandrawinata

Indonesia has experienced rapid economic and political change in the past decade. Its democratic transformation is of particular significance. Many analysts see Indonesia as the new BRIC (Brazil, Russia, India, China and South Africa) on the block. With a gross domestic product (GDP) growth rate of around 6.5 per cent in 2011, Indonesia is outstripping many other emerging markets (*Economist*, 2011). The majority of the population of around 238 million live in rural areas, with income dependent upon agriculture. In 2010 per capita income was estimated at US$4300. Both economic statistics and health indicators underscore how the country has surpassed the expectations of many development specialists (Bloom et al., 2011). While little is known about Indonesia's healthcare system internationally, it is clear that economic development presents opportunities for better healthcare and growth in the pharmaceutical sector. This chapter provides a perspective on the Indonesian healthcare system and the development of its pharmaceutical industry in the post-Trade Related Aspects of Intellectual Property Rights (TRIPS) era.

The Indonesian healthcare system

Indonesia's health system is characterized by striking regional and social inequalities. Around 55 per cent of the population live in rural areas, spread across some 6000 islands. Healthcare is most developed on the main island of Java, which is home to around 51 per cent of the population. In an effort to address the uneven availability of health services, the government has established a decentralized network of public health centres (or *puskesmas*) in the rural areas. Each provincial and district government operates its own health centres. In 2007 there were more than 8100 primary health centres, as well as an additional 28,000 mobile and auxiliary centres. There were almost 1300 general hospitals, split evenly between the public and private sectors (DepKes, 2008a). The number has risen significantly in recent years. The government is also actively promoting the growth of private healthcare, particularly at secondary and tertiary levels, with the aim of compensating for the shortcomings of the public system (DepKes, 2011). The growing role of the private sector in healthcare raises questions about access to health services in general, although private facilities are required to provide subsidized services to the poor. At the same time, Indonesia is coming under increasing international pressure to open up its healthcare services to international competition (International Trade Centre of UNCTAD/WTO, 2005).

The general decentralization process that has defined many areas of Indonesian government policy was initiated in 2001, and has had an important impact on the health system, even though it was not designed specifically with the health sector in mind. Health financing, health information systems, human resources for health, and service provision have all been affected. Again, under the decentralization programme, responsibility for healthcare provision rests largely with the regional governments. With a GDP of around Indonesian rupiah (IDR) 3943 billion, healthcare spending in Indonesia is low by regional standards, accounting for only 2.7 per cent of GDP in 2008 (Sampurno, 2009). This compares, for example, with 3.5 per cent in Thailand and 3.2 per cent in the Philippines (WHO, 2011). Indonesian healthcare expenditure per head was around US$60 in 2009.

Pharmaceuticals are expensive relative to average incomes (International Trade Centre of UNCTAD/WTO, 2005). The market for traditional medicines, however, which are cheaper and readily available, is thriving. At the same time, demands on the state healthcare system are rising. Demographic trends show an ageing population and growing migration to the cities. Indonesia's elderly population does not constitute the same potential strain on public resources as the 'silver tsunami' phenomenon in other parts of Asia. People aged 65 or over accounted for just 5.8 per cent of the population in 2008, and will make up only 6.3 per cent in 2013. Nevertheless, the rise in average life expectancy from 62.8 years in 1990 to nearly 71 years in 2008 has led to an increase in the prevalence of degenerative diseases (WHO, 2011).

There are major deficiencies in human resources in the healthcare sector, in terms of both numbers and quality of the healthcare workforce. Decentralization is one of many factors exacerbating long-standing problems with uneven distribution of health workers, with the workforce biased towards urban areas (Akita and Pirmansah, 2011). These factors have obvious impacts on the quality, efficiency and equity of healthcare provision. In 2007 the ratio of general practitioners to population was 19.9 per 100,000 population (although in 2008 the number improved modestly to 30 per 100,000 population), while the ratio of midwives per 100,000 population was 35.4 (DepKes, 2008a). Most general practitioners and midwives work in urban areas, and only a limited number in remote areas.

In 2001 the Ministry of Health (MOH) reorganized its human resource functions by establishing a new body—the Institute for Empowerment and Development of Health Manpower. This was explicitly set up to link and coordinate previously separate centres in the development of an overall integrated strategic plan for health workforce development, including a corresponding integrated information system. The number of hospital beds is similarly inadequate, at just 0.6 per 1000 people, with this resource skewed in favour of cities, especially Jakarta. According to the MOH, around 53 per cent of beds were in the public sector in 2006, down sharply from the 1990s, when close to 70 per cent of hospital beds were in the public sector (DepKes, 2008a). The situation has been improving, however, with many hospitals recently receiving international accreditations for being able to provide care at international standards.

There are several ways to measure the health status of a country's population. One proxy measure is the infant mortality rate (IMR) as an inexpensive indicator of population health (Reidpath and Allotey, 2003). In 2009 the IMR in Indonesia was reported as 34 cases in 1000 births, a figure down by roughly half of that of 1991, when the IMR was 64 per 1000 births (DepKes, 2009). The figure for deaths of children below 5 years was 44 cases per 1000 population in 2009, down from 97 per 1000 population in 1991 (MOH, 2009). The figures of deaths for mothers after giving birth were reported as 228 out of 100,000 successful births in 2009. In 1991 the figure was 390 cases out of 100,000 successful births (DepKes, 2008a). Furthermore, life expectancy at birth was measured at around 67 years in 2006 (Meads, 2006), but recent data from the World Bank showed an increase to an age of 71 in 2009 (World Bank, 2011). These figures strongly suggest that the need for quality medical and healthcare services is still compelling, and also provide a rationale for increased pharmaceutical spending.

To complicate the interpretation of these indicators, the MOH only registers cases from government hospitals throughout the country. As there are no aggregated published data emerging from private hospitals and clinics, government figures can be used only as proxy measures of Indonesia's disease pattern. Reports from government hospitals for ambulatory patients in 2009 showed 488,794 cases with upper respiratory tract infection, 275,254 cases with unknown diseases with fever, and 172,013 cases of skin diseases. The pattern for in-patients was different: 143,696 cases of diarrhoea and gastroenteritis; 121,334 cases of dengue haemorrhagic fever; 80,850 cases of typhoid and paratyphoid (DepKes, 2011). Figures for 2009 related to morbidity showed the highest case fatality rate of 11.06 per cent (23,163 patients) for diseases related to circulation disorders; followed by 9.74 per cent for certain prenatal conditions, and 6.73 per cent for metabolic diseases. Other diseases causing morbidity are neoplasm, with a rate of 4.73 per cent, while 3.99 per cent of deaths were due to respiratory diseases and 3.56 per cent to urinary tract or sexually transmitted diseases (DepKes, 2011).

Indonesia has recently faced outbreaks of polio and measles among children, and is battling an increase in the incidence of HIV/AIDS, as well as malnutrition in some parts of the country. In 2010 Indonesia also recorded 115 human deaths from avian influenza (bird flu), representing 44 per cent of the global total. Other diseases, such as chikungunya, an insect-borne virus, also pose challenges. Lifestyle and cardiovascular diseases associated with rising incomes and a more affluent urban population, which are becoming more prevalent in other parts of Asia, remain a secondary concern. Smoking-related diseases are a problem, as an estimated 30 per cent of the adult population are habitual smokers, according to WHO data for 2005 (WHO, 2008). As pharmaceuticals and vaccines can alleviate the disease burden, it is readily apparent that they will be increasingly needed and used in the future.

Notwithstanding significant progress in health outcomes over recent decades, there are many challenges in the administration of health services throughout Indonesia. For example, as disease patterns have become more complex, current decentralized services provided by local provincial and regional governments have proven to be inadequate for improving priority health outcomes and in terms of the efficiency of the whole health system (World Bank, 2004). In fact, a recent study on decentralization of health service administration suggests that there has been little improvement in the performance of the health system since decentralization occurred in 2001, even though there have been significant increases in public funding for health overall (Heywood and Choi, 2010).

The Indonesian healthcare system and medicines

With regard to the distribution of medicines, it has been the government's ambition to provide cheaper alternative unbranded generic drugs instead of patented branded products, which command premium prices (World Bank, 2009). Unbranded generic medicines, known in Indonesia as *Obat Generik Berlogo* (OGB), were once predominantly produced by state-owned enterprises, but are currently also produced by several private sector manufacturers. Government hospitals and local clinics provide OGB drugs to patients according to the National List of Essential Medicine (NELM), which is formulated by the *Daftar Obat Esensial National* (DOEN) (DepKes, 2008c). The NELM is a list of selected medicines that satisfy the priority healthcare needs of the population and are intended to be available within the context of a functioning healthcare system (DepKes, 2008c).In addition, government employees and some segments of the population working for the private sector receive drug coverage via the National Health Insurance scheme, called *Askes* (*Asuransi Kesehatan*). Askes is developing its own formulary, based on the DOEN but also including products with lower prices from different companies. This formulary is known as *Daftar Plafon Harga Obat* (DPHO, Lowest

Level Price List) and the medicines list is published nearly every year (PT Askes (Persero), 2011). Askes has only 16.3 million eligible members, and there are, additionally, 678,000 private members of its subsidiary PT *Asuransi Jiwa Inhealth Indonesia* (ASJII) (PT Askes (Persero), 2009). The MOH started to provide free medication for the lowest-income groups in 2005 through Askes, under a scheme named *Askeskin* (*Asuransi Kesehatan bagi para miskin*). This scheme provided mainly unbranded generic medicines, for all therapeutic areas, from acute to chronic diseases, with prices controlled by the government. This initiative was, however, transformed in 2008 to a social health security network called *Jamkesmas* (*Jaminan Kesehatan Masyarakat*). The change of management under the new name provides a better description of its operations, as these services have nothing to do with health insurance. Jamkesmas registered 73.4 million members for the provision of free medical services through the puskesmas (health centres). The rest of the population is accessing puskesmas on an out-of-pocket basis, or making other individual arrangements for which there are no statistics.

The various government institutions are using unbranded generic medicines, which are prescribed by primary care physicians working in health centres. The new, amended Indonesian Constitution (Sekretaris Negara RI, 2002), however, stipulates the right of each citizen to receive adequate health services. Under this broad obligation the state is required to develop a system of social security for the whole population to empower the underprivileged sections of society in accordance with the basic requirements for human dignity. As a consequence, the Indonesia Legislative Assembly has recently passed the National Social Security System (SJSN) Law (Sekretaris Negara RI, 2004), mandating the government to provide universal health coverage (via national health insurance) under the SJSN. It is expected that the scheme will give preference to the use of unbranded generic drugs, unless foreign brand firms (which now sell mainly into the private sector) can demonstrate the benefits of their more expensive products and have them adopted under the reformed health insurance scheme.

The geographical spread and scale of Indonesia is a major challenge for the government's management of its own pharmaceutical supply chain (Husada, 2008). The location of puskesmas and other health centres is guided by population density. Puskesmas are, therefore, located much more densely in urban areas than in rural Indonesia. In most cities puskesmas are invariably within 500 metres apart (compared with km). Most poor people in rural areas have greater difficulty accessing health centres, with distances between centres as great as 15 km or more. While private suppliers focus on customers in urban areas, it is the responsibility of the government (via puskesmas) to supply medical products to patients also in the peripheral areas (Arya, 2009). In odd cases doctors in private practice in rural areas are permitted to dispense medicines, but the normal route is via pharmacies. Most of the pharmacies are also located in urban areas or other major population centres.

The government's efforts to improve the supply of medicines to more than 7000 health centres have progressed, despite an absentee rate for doctors of some 40 per cent in these centres (Wanandi, 2009). The supply chains also cover the supply of generic products for poorer patients under the national health insurance and Jamkesmas schemes.

Regulation of drug registration and approval

Under government law the *Badan Pengawas Obat dan Makanan* (BPOM) or National Agency of Food and Drug Control (NAFDC) is responsible for the pre-market evaluation of safety and marketing of all medicines. Its functions also include regulation, standardization and Good Manufacturing Practice (GMP) certification of medical and food producers. Manufacturers can produce and market medicines only after clearance by NAFDC, following a registration process with strict criteria drawn from the Swedish regulatory model (DepKes, 2008b). Manufacturing can only start if firms hold a GMP certificate, which forms the initial requirement for drug registration. The GMP certificate specifies the dosage form of the product for manufacturing. Other data on efficacy, safety (with toxicology studies), manufacturing processes with specifications about brand name, packaging and so on are included in the documentation necessary for obtaining regulatory approval. For new products, such approval and fulfilment of all registration requirements should by rights take no more than one year. In practice, it takes approximately three years for new product approvals post first registration submission. After NAFDC registration approval, promotional and marketing material should comply with claims approved in the regulatory application (Badan Pom, 2002). Promotion material for both prescription and over-the-counter (OTC) products requires preliminary approval by NAFDC of all written material, and rough sketches of pictures or video material have to be submitted. This clearance also takes time, so applicants must have a good understanding of all rules and regulations to manage the launch of new products.

As a member of Association of Southeast Asian Nations (ASEAN), Indonesia is working with other members for the realization of regional free trade (ASEAN, 2009a), as a follow-up of formerly agreed activities (ASEAN, 2007). Recently, NAFDC and its respective partner food and drugs authorities from other ASEAN countries have conducted a number of meetings to discuss the format and content of the harmonized ASEAN Common Technical Dossiers (ACTD) for prescription (generics and patented products) as well as OTC drug applications. ACTD is actually a guideline for an agreed common format for the preparation of Common Technical Dossier applications to ASEAN regulatory authorities for the registration of pharmaceuticals for human use (ASEAN, 2009b). ACTDs require a complete record of all the active pharmaceutical products and their excipients (the inactive compounds used as carriers or media for active ingredient delivery) used in a particular drug, as well as details of labelling and quality and (non-)clinical data. NAFDC has implemented the ACTD format for drugs submitted since 2009, resulting in a decline of new drug approvals, for both drugs encompassing new chemical entities and generic drugs. NAFDC's 2008 application for membership of the Pharmaceutical Inspection Convention and the Pharmaceutical Inspection Co-operation Scheme (PIC/S) is currently in the evaluation process. PIC/S are two international instruments that have been agreed among countries and pharmaceutical inspection authorities that provide active cooperation in the field of GMP.

The purpose of PIC/S is to take a lead in the international development, implementation and maintenance of harmonized GMP standards and quality systems of inspectorates in the field of medicinal products (Pic/S, 2011). This is to be achieved by developing and promoting harmonized GMP standards and guidance documents; by training competent authorities (in particular inspectors); through assessing (and reassessing) inspectorates; and by facilitating the cooperation and networking of competent authorities and international organizations (Pic/S, 2008). Indonesia was expected to become a full member of PIC/S in 2012, following in the footsteps of its neighbouring countries, Singapore (2000) and Malaysia (2002) (Pic/S, 2011). In becoming a PIC/S member, NAFDC is expected to step up its quality inspection of manufacturing facilities, leading to an overall improvement in the quality of medicines.

The pharmaceutical industry

The pharmaceutical industry in Indonesia began during the Dutch colonial period. In 1958 the post-colonial Indonesian government merged several independent pharmaceutical companies founded by the Dutch into one company—called PNF Bineka Kimia Farma, or Kimia Farma (for short). Kimia Farma is therefore regarded as the progenitor of the Indonesian pharmaceutical industry. In 1971 Kimia Farma's status was changed to a limited liability company, and in 2001 it was offered publicly as a listed company. Nevertheless, Kimia Farma remains one of four state-owned pharmaceutical enterprises. The others are Indo Farma, Phapros and Biofarma.

The pharmaceutical industry has seen major growth, particularly since 1967, when the government opened the door to foreign investment through a series of new investment regulations (Dep Hukum dan Ham, 1967, 1968). At the beginning of President Suharto period in office, an era of free-market liberalization, incentives were given to foreign investors, as formalized in the Foreign Investment Law No. 1/1967. As the economy strengthened, in 1970 the government adopted a free-floating foreign exchange system. By the early 1970s approximately 30 international pharmaceutical companies had invested and established operations in Indonesia, and previously imported medicines began to be replaced in the market by products manufactured locally. The enactment of investment laws for domestic as well as foreign companies has, in a period of economic growth, resulted in an investment boom in the Indonesian pharmaceutical industry.

Active Pharmaceutical Ingredients (APIs) required by domestic Indonesian firms continue to be largely imported from India and China. International pharmaceutical companies import materials largely through their own supply chains. Foreign and domestically owned manufacturing plants process the APIs into finished products, including both patented and generic drugs, for distribution throughout the country via some 2560 distributors (Panjaitan, 2009) to more than 10,000 pharmacies and other retailers (Wanandi, 2009). Distributors in Indonesia are specialized logistics firms, sometimes owned by local pharmaceutical companies, and distribute pharmaceutical products to retail and hospital outlets. Often regional distributors are only active locally. These regional distributors do not service pharmacies, which is the reason for the high number of distributors relative to the number of pharmacies. As detailed above, pharmacies are primarily located in urban areas, as market size and purchasing capacity in rural areas offer insufficient incentive for their operation (Sanusi, 2009). In areas where pharmacies are not present, local health centres and puskesmas provide drugs for the poor through their drug dispensing system.

As of 2011, the Indonesian total market for pharmaceuticals was estimated at IDR 33.97 trillion, about US$3.6 billion. Prescription drugs had a market share of 57 per cent and OTCs 43 per cent. Generics represented less than 10 per cent of the total market in value terms (Data Compilation, 2011). These figures equate to a per capita consumption of medicines in the vicinity of US$15.30 per person per year.

Unbranded generic medicines

As noted, many unbranded generic medicines are manufactured and marketed by state-owned enterprises. Since the late 1980s, however, private companies, such as Dexa Medica, Hexpharm and others, have also produced and marketed generics. But the four state-owned companies in this market segment together command a higher market share than their private counterparts. Price levels of unbranded generics are regulated and not left to market forces, as is the case in some countries. The MOH determines the price level for generic products, and the maximum price ratio for branded generics is three times the price for unbranded generics for supply to governmental premises. The intention of the government to reduce the price of generics was demonstrated in the 2004–2007 period, when eight regulations on generics prices were introduced (DepKes, 2007). Although the prices of unbranded generics have long been regulated and tend to be lower than in other categories, their usage is very low, at around 10 per cent of total drug expenditure during the last decade (Data Compilation, 2011). When the national social security system is implemented in 2014, however, it is expected that the use of unbranded generics will increase.

The state-owned companies, which are the biggest suppliers of generics, have had difficulties in meeting profit targets laid down by the Ministry of State Owned Enterprises. As noted, branded generics companies can price their products maximally three times above the prices of non-branded generics, and have to print the price level (for better transparency) on the original boxes (DepKes, 2006b, 2007). Despite previous instructions from the MOH, the Minister in 2010 again had to urge doctors to prescribe unbranded generics, as their low market share continued to prevail (Bland, 2009). Opportunities to extend their market share (as is the case in many countries) may well be achieved through a focus on better supply chains and incentives for retailers by allowing higher margins (Babar et al., 2007; Narciso, 2005). It also seems that Indonesian regulators could do more to achieve greater accessibility to generics, but further changes seem necessary to match countries like China (Chui, 2009). The difference between China and Indonesia is largely a consequence of the greater availability in China of health insurance, which has not yet been developed in Indonesia. Similarly, in Japan, government support is expected to enable generics to reach 30 per cent of market share in 2013, and lessons for the Indonesian government in generics promotion are readily available from many other countries, including the mature generics markets in Europe (Simoens, 2009).

In Indonesia, as noted, the market share of generic products is still very low. During the period 2005–2009 the market share for generics decreased from 10 per cent to 7.2 per cent of the total market, or from IDR 2.5 trillion to IDR 2.4 trillion of a total market of IDR 23.5 trillion to IDR 32.9 trillion (Ditjen Binfar dan Alkes: Informasi Program and Kegiatan, 2010). For this market segment to gain ground would need better regulatory support and better promotion to resistant consumers to correct information asymmetries. Ahlquist et al. (2010), for example, argue that consumers need to be educated effectively about the value and costs of their drug purchasing decisions. In modifying purchasing behaviour, carrots (incentives and transparent information) often work better than sticks (restrictions and fines). Despite this, to date few such programmes have been undertaken in Indonesia to educate patients or improve health literacy measures, which would allow patients to understand more about healthy living and drug use in general, and the use of generics specifically. One programme being enacted by the MOH, however, is the promotion of self-medication of some medicines for common indications. These medicines are offered in packs of limited quantities and priced cheaply, at around ten US cents per pack (Ananto, 2007).

As already noted, prices of pharmaceutical products are regulated. During registration, companies must supply the prices of their own and competing products. The aim is that patients should benefit not only from better efficacy offered by a new product, but also financially. The Association of Pharmaceutical Enterprises of Indonesia was successful in introducing a price calculation that considered a ratio between the factory gate and margins for the distributor, and other ratios for the mark-ups of distributors and pharmacists. Margins for pharmacies are commercially viable, as long as the price level is high. There is also a regulation pertaining to clear printing of prices on packages to provide transparency for the consumer (DepKes, 2006b). Because the government reduced the price level of generics on eight occasions between 2004 and 2007, however, official prices are now so low as to leave insufficient margins in real terms for pharmacies. This is not the situation in many other countries with price controls, where such calculations allow reasonable pharmacy margins (Babar et al., 2007). It is, therefore, not surprising that many Indonesian pharmacists are reluctant to handle generic products as compared with higher-priced branded generics.

In the context of health insurance, the state insurance body Askes has introduced a system of price standardization of products after a stringent process of screening for the drug formulary in the so-called List and Ceiling of Drug Prices (DPHO) (PT Askes (Persero), 2005). As detailed above, however, people covered by Askes make up a small percentage of the Indonesian population. Most people not covered by any insurance scheme pay for medicines from their own pockets and usually do so at the 10,000 pharmacies and 7000 plus health centres.

Intellectual property rights

Notionally, Indonesia has had a system of intellectual property rights (IPR) since 1844, when the Netherland East Indies was included in the Dutch legislation. But the very idea of IPR was in conflict with traditional culture and the civil laws applicable to native Indonesians. There was, in fact, no serious consideration given to enforcement of IPRs until the United States and the European Union commenced applying pressures on Indonesia in the 1980s. These pressures provided the context for the Patents Act 1989, which came into effect in 1991, the first legislation in independent Indonesia which provided unambiguously for patent protection (Antons, 2009, p. 90; President of Republic of Indonesia, 1989).

The 1989 Act was followed by ratification of TRIPS in 1994. The Act was further amended for TRIPS compliance in 1997 and 2001. The Indonesian government in this period also ratified several other IPR conventions, including the Patent Cooperation Treaty in 1997 (President of Republic of Indonesia, 1997). But enforcement remained weak and continues to be relatively ineffective. Indicative of the ongoing concern of the multinational pharma companies and the government of the United States is the inclusion of Indonesia in 2012 on the US Trade Representative Priority Watch List. As Kusumadara (2009) sees it, ratification of the TRIPS Agreement did not mean that the government seriously intended to enforce IPR. Rather, legislation for TRIPS compliance was a concession to external pressures. The principal policy orientation continued to be encouragement of local pharmaceutical production and related technology transfer (UNCTAD, 2011a). With respect to medicines, the situation before 2001 was chaotic, with many companies copying patented products, sometimes even prior to the originator launching its product (Deere, 2007).

The patent law of 2001 consolidated into a single text all previous IPR legislation. In 1997, legislation was enacted to extend the term of patent protection from 14 to 20 years. Provisions were also introduced for a two-year patent extension period, which is not required under TRIPS. Around 5000 patents are now issued annually, and, as in other developing countries, these are issued mostly to foreign applicants (UNCTAD, 2011b, p. 182). The 2001 legislation also allowed the patenting of plants and animals. Several aspects of the legislation remain controversial, and there is no clarity over whether new uses of known substances can qualify for patent protection.

The Doha Declaration of 2001 confirmed the legality under TRIPS for governments to issue compulsory licences, and several other so-called flexibilities (Germano, 2007). According to UNCTAD (2011a), Indonesia has not taken advantage of TRIPS flexibilities to the extent necessary to meet the need for essential, affordable medicines. For example, compulsory licences can be issued under TRIPS on several grounds not recognized in current legislation, such as anti-competitive behaviour (UNCTAD, 2011a, p. 44). Indonesia has also not incorporated into legislation the so-called Paragraph 6 system, which would allow exports to countries lacking manufacturing capacity (such as neighbouring Pacific island states). As a consequence of not making effective use of available TRIPS flexibilities, 'generics generally come on the market later than they would otherwise' (UNCTAD, 2011b, p. 182).

Yet, in October 2004, Indonesia was only the second country in Asia to issue a government-use licence (essentially a compulsory licence), through a Presidential Decree, for the production of two anti-retroviral drugs (ARVs)— lamivudine and nevirapine—by the state-owned enterprise Kimia Farma (DepKes, 2006a). 'In issuing the decree, the Government cited the price differential between the patented drug and the cost of producing a generic equivalent as the rationale for issuing the government-use licence. Compensation to the patent holders was established under the Decree at 0.5% of the generic net sales value' (UNCTAD 2011a, p. 6). In March 2007, the decree was renewed to cover another ARV drug, efavirenz, which replaced nevirapine as the first-line drug treatment. Indonesia uses lamivudine, efavirenz and zidovudine as the three first-line ARVs for its HIV/AIDS patients. The country did not impose a compulsory licence on zidovudine as its patent had already expired. These three drugs are now produced locally by Kimia Farma (Tunsarawuth, 2007). But the legislative provisions for compulsory licensing are, as noted, unnecessarily constricted. UNCTAD (2011a, p. 2) recommends that Indonesia should 'consider expanding the grounds for issuing a CL beyond non-working to at least encompass national emergencies (which could include pandemics)'.

The Indonesian virus case

Indonesia has recently proven a vocal and critical voice in challenging both a key element of the global health governance architecture and the inequities in access to medicines that characterize the basic global political economy of pharmaceutical markets. In 2006, amidst growing fears over the potential for a full-blown avian influenza pandemic, the then Indonesian Minister of Health announced that her country would withhold viral samples of H5N1 from (or cease to share them with) the WHO-managed Global Influenza Surveillance Network (GISN). The GISN was a decades-old model wherein regional centres were used to collect influenza virus samples in order for pharmaceutical firms to produce annual seasonal flu anti-viral medicines. The H5N1 crisis had put elements of that system under severe strain, and it was in this context that Indonesia (a primary source of new influenza viral samples) threatened collapse of the system by withdrawing.

The case revolved around a number of issues. Indonesia expressed anger that its viral samples were being passed on to firms and being patented and sold at prices which meant that it could not benefit from anti-virals. In the context of huge global demand for anti-virals as a pandemic threat loomed large, Indonesia had found itself unable to secure oseltamivir, produced by Roche and marketed by that company as Tamiflu, as production capacity for the drug was effectively being swallowed up by Northern governments. The decision to withdraw from the GISN also reflected two basic 'structural hurdles' facing low and medium-income countries (LMICs) vis-à-vis access to medicines more widely, problems made more acute in the face of a pandemic (Kamradt-Scott and Lee, 2011). First, the Tamiflu supply crisis made obvious the fact that the health needs of LMICs (in this case a particularly pressing need, given the propensity of new influenza viruses to emerge in Southern Asia) were in many cases dependent on access to pharmaceuticals imported from developed countries. The lack of technical and manufacturing capacities is, therefore, a basic structural reason why LMIC countries cannot meet demand for medicines. Second (and irrespective of the presence of patents), the global pharmaceutical market is subject to the laws of supply and demand, and the Tamiflu episode starkly displays how firms can command higher medicine prices globally when demand is inelastic and the source of supply monopolistic.

The Indonesian episode also polarized debate in the global health community. Indonesia was roundly condemned by many parties (especially in the US) for threatening the international surveillance system and global health security (see, for example, Holbrooke and Garrett, 2008). However, in contrast, many other LMICs and commentators on the wider issue of access to medicines supported Indonesia's move (Bedford, 2008), with other countries also concerned about the anti-viral supply crisis. The viral sharing system was seen to mainly benefit developed countries (Elbe, 2010). Other LMICs did not withdraw from the GISN system, but Indonesia acting alone was sufficient to punch a major hole in the viability and integrity of the system.

To resolve the conflict, in 2007 WHO initiated a concerted attempt to bring the parties together and negotiate. The negotiations (which ended in 2011) concentrated on two basic issues: attempting to address the inequitable access to influenza vaccines, and the benefits derived from medicines developed from donated viral samples (WHO, 2007). The negotiations were split in North–South terms. Issues of manufacturing capacity and the need for the funding and technology transfer to Southern states became key. In terms of extant anti-viral manufacturing, it has been noted that production facilities are located in just nine developed country markets (Kieny et al., 2006), and in the case of the looming H5N1 pandemic supplies had been tied up by a series of advanced purchase agreements with the major manufacturers (Elbe, 2010). Capacity and access thus became locked together, with Indonesia using its 'viral sovereignty' as a major bargaining chip to secure positive gains under a new Pandemic Influenza Preparedness Network. However, as Elbe suggests, the real gains appear to be fairly token. There is, for example, a commitment for firms to provide some 10 per cent of medicines and diagnostics to developing countries at more affordable prices (Karmadt-Scott and Lee, 2011, p. 839). Technology transfer and technical assistance are likewise promised, and this will involve sustained financing if the scheme is to generate anti-viral manufacturing capacities in Indonesia or any other country.

The virus sharing case reveals something fundamental about Indonesia's emerging role in global health and access to medicines. It is certain that Indonesia, alongside China, Brazil and India (see the introductory chapter of this volume), feels capable of flexing its muscles and challenging the existing political economy of pharmaceuticals, and is prepared to destabilize a vital international health surveillance system to secure its goals. The case also reveals that Indonesia and the LMICs that supported its actions are perfectly aware of how health governance interacts with a skewed global pharmaceutical market to generate inequalities of access. The fact that pharmaceutical firms are based in Northern countries, and have close collaborative association with governments (and multilateral fora such as the WHO), is also now at the forefront of increasingly assertive strategies of resistance by LMICs, in areas not simply linked to IPRs. Indonesia and other LMIC states seem also to be aware that indigenous drug manufacturing capacity is the key to overcoming dependence on the current political economy of pharmaceuticals under which, in various areas such as R&D and production for neglected and other diseases, their health needs are not being catered for adequately.

If Indonesia can translate the rhetoric of inequality that it employed in the WHO negotiations into concrete support for its own generic sector, then the political economy of pharmaceuticals in that country might well change. If this is a pattern echoed in other key LMICs, especially in China and India, then real alternatives to current LMIC dependency will be possible.

Conclusion

Indonesia, with a growing population of some 240 million people, has enormous market potential for pharmaceuticals. Government efforts to achieve better distribution of healthcare, and better access to unbranded generic medicines, will potentially enhance the health condition and increase the economic productivity of the population. Bloom et al. (2003) have suggested that a one-year improvement in a population's life expectancy contributes to an increase of 4 per cent in output and economic growth. Guidelines on how to motivate medical doctors, pharmacists and patients to use more generic medicines (Simoens and De Coster, 2006) are needed to increase the use of generics. Healthcare services in rural Indonesian areas need more attention, together with the provision of reasonable margins for pharmacies, as is shown in the case of Malaysia (Babar et al., 2007). This is also true for manufacturers and distributors, who will lose motivation following extreme price reductions coerced by government. Pharmacists will support the use of generics if provided with adequate commercial incentives (Al-Gedadi and Hassali, 2008).

While Indonesia's economy is being developed, the health of Indonesian people is improving only slowly. Despite high penetration of health centres, the accessibility of medicines, as part of the fulfilment of the right to the highest attainable standard of health, is not well understood. While ensuring quality, safety and efficacy, regulatory procedures can pose difficulties for the availability of medicines as approval requirements become more stringent. Nevertheless, such challenges must be overcome for Indonesian pharmaceutical companies to survive in the event of AFTA (Asian Free Trade Area) implementation. More efforts are needed to comply with international standards if the Indonesian pharmaceutical industry is to gain the respect of its ASEAN peers, and counterparts elsewhere. Knowing the real picture of health service delivery to the lower quintile of the income pyramid would provide a better basis than we have at present for devising strategies to improve accessibility in rural areas. Better accessibility to healthcare will also result in higher market growth for medicines and allow more companies to perform effective research and development.

References

Ahlquist, G., M. Javanmardian and A. Kaura (2010) 'The Pharmacy Solution', *Strategy + Business* 58, 1–5.

Akita, T. and A. Pirmansah (2011) 'Urban Inequality in Indonesia', Working Paper, *Economics and Management Series*, International University of Japan, 4, http://www.iuj.ac.jp/research/workingpapers/ems_2011_04.pdf, date accessed 29 March 2012.

Al-Gedadi, N. A. and M. A. Hassali (2008) 'Pharmacists' Views on Generic Medicines: A Review of the Literature', *Journal of Generic Medicines* 5, 209–18.

Ananto, E. (2007) 'Menyebarlah! Obat Murah Serba Seribu', *Pharma Magazine* 6, 20–2.

Antons, C. (2009) 'Indonesia' in P. Goldstein and J. Straus (eds) *Intellectual Property in Asia* (Berlin: Springer).

Arya, E. K. (2009) 'Pharmaceutical Activities in a Puskesmas: An Interview', *Surabaya* 30 July.

ASEAN (2007) The Implementation of Item 2.7.2(F) of the Hanoi Plan of Action Checklist on the Implementation of the TRIPS Agreement, http://www.docstoc.com/docs/22275818/THE-IMPLEMENTATION-OF-ITEM-272(F)-OF-THE-HANOI-PLAN, date accessed 27 April 2011.

ASEAN (2009a) ASEAN Trade in Goods Agreement, Cha-am, Thailand.

ASEAN (2009b) *The ASEAN Common Technical Dossier (ACTD) for the Registration of Pharmaceuticals for Human Use: Organization of the Dossier* (Jakarta: ASEAN).

Babar, Z.-U.-D., M. I. M. Ibrahim, H. Singh, N. I. Bukahri and A. Creese (2007) 'Evaluating Drug Prices, Availability, Affordability, and Price Components: Implications for Access to Drugs in Malaysia', *PLoS Medicine* 4, 466–75.

Badan Pom (2002) Keputusan Kepala Badan POM Nomor HK 00.05.3.02706 Tahun, Tentang Promosi Obat.

Bedford, A. (2008) 'Indonesia's Bird Flu Warrior Takes on the World' *Macau Daily Times*, 8 December, http://www.intelasia.net/indonesias-bird-flu-warrior-takes-on-the-world-88640, date accessed 7 October 2012.

Bland, B. (2009) 'Indonesian Doctors Told to Prescribe more Generics', *E-Drug*.

Bloom, D. E., D. Canning and J. Sevilla (2003) 'The Effect of Health on Economic Growth: A Production Function Approach', *World Development* 32, 1–13.

Bloom, D. E., E. T. Cafiero, E. Jané-Llopis, S. Abrahams-Gessel, L. R. Bloom, S. Fathima, A. Feigl et al. (2011) *The Global Economic Burden of Noncommunicable Diseases* (Geneva: World Economic Forum).

Chui, M. (2009) 'Despite Global Downturn, Generics Makers Stand to Reap Great Rewards in China's Evolving Pharmaceutical Market', *Journal of Generic Medicines* 6, 230–6.

Data Compilation (2011) Data compiled by the authors through interviews at different organizations, Melbourne and Jakarta.

De Carolis, D. M. and D. L. Deeds (1999) 'The Impact of Stocks and Flows of Organizational Knowledge on Firm Performance: An Empirical Investigation of the Biotechnology Industry', *Strategic Management Journal* 20, 953–68.

Deere, C. D. (2007) The Implementation Game: Developing Countries, the TRIPS Agreement and the Global Politics of Intellectual Property, presented at the Global Economic Governance Programme, University College, Oxford, http://papers.ssrn.com/sol3/Papers.cfm?abstract_id=1405224, date accessed 27 April 2011.

Dep Hukum dan Ham (1967) Undang-Undang Nomor 1 Tahun 1967 tentang Penanaman Modal Asing.

Dep Hukum dan Ham (1968) Undang-Undang Nomor 6 Tahun 1968 tentang Penanaman Modal Dalam Negeri.

DepKes (2006a) Pemerintah Berharap Tambah Stok Tamiflu Dalam Waktu Tiga Bulan (Jakarta: Departemen Kesehatan RI).

DepKes (2006b) Keputusan Menteri Kesehatan Nomor 069/Menkes/SK/II/2006 tentang Pedoman Pencantuman Harga Obat Pada Label Obat (Jakarta: Departemen Kesehatan RI).
DepKes (2007) Peraturan Menteri Kesehatan Republik Indonesia Nomor 696/MenKes/Per/VI/2007 Tentang Harga Obat Generik Bernama Dagang pada Sarana Pelayanan Kesehatan Pemerintah, p. 4.
DepKes (2008a) Profil Kesehatan Nasional 2007 (Indonesian Health Profile 2007) (Jakarta: Departemen Kesehatan RI).
DepKes (2008b) Peraturan Menteri Kesehatan Republik Indonesia Nomor 1010/MenKes/Per/XI/2008 Tentang Registrasi Obat, p. 10 (Jakarta: Departemen Kesehatan RI).
DepKes (2008c) Daftar Obat Esensial Nasional (*National Essential Drug List*) (Jakarta: Departemen Kesehatan RI).
DepKes (2009) *ProfilKesehatan Indonesia 2008* (Jakarta: Departemen Kesehatan RI).
DepKes (2011) Profil Kesehatan Indonesia 2010 (Jakarta: Departemen Kesehatan RI).
Ditjen Binfar dan Alkes: Informasi Program dan Kegiatan (2010) Pemerintah Lakukan Revitalisasi Penggunaan Obat Generik (Government revitalized use of generics) January 12 (Jakarta: Departemen Kesehatan RI).
Economist (2011) 'Missing BRIC in the Wall', *The Economist* 21 July, http://www.economist.com/node/18989153, date accessed 19 March 2011.
Elbe, S. (2010) 'Haggling over Viruses: The Downside Risks of Securitizing Infectious Disease', *Health Policy and Planning* 25, 476–85.
Germano, S. (2007) 'Compulsory Licensing of Pharmaceuticals in Southeast Asia: Paving the Way for Greater Use of the TRIPS Flexibility in Low- and Middle-Income Countries', *UMKC Law Review* 76, 273–94.
Heywood, P. F. and Y. Choi (2010) 'Health System Performance at the District Level in Indonesia after Decentralization', *BMC International Health and Human Rights* 10, 1–12.
Holbrooke, R. and L. Garrett (2008) ' "Sovereignty" that Risks Global Health' *Washington Post* 10 August, http://www.cfr.org/public-health-threats/sovereignty-risks-global-health/p16927, date accessed 8 October 2012.
Husada, R. (2008) 'The Role of Customers as Resource: A 10-Year Case Study of Business Strategy Diversity of Pharmaceutical Companies in Indonesia' (PhD), Institute Business and Informatics Indonesia, Jakarta.
International Trade Centre of UNCTAD/WTO(2005) Indonesia, Supply and Demand Survey on Pharmaceuticals and Natural Products, http://apps.who.int/medicinedocs/documents/s18012en/s18012en.pdf, date accessed 26 April 2011.
Kamradt-Scott, A. and K. Lee (2011) 'The 2011 Pandemic Influenza Preparedness Framework: Global Health Secured or a Missed Opportunity?', *Political Studies* 59, 831–47.
Kieny, M. P., A. Costa, J. Hombach, P. Carrasco and Y. Pervikov (2006) 'A Global Pandemic Influenza Vaccine Action Plan', *Vaccine* 24, 6367–70.
Kusumadara, A. (2009) *Problems of Enforcing Intellectual Property Laws in Indonesia* (Malang: Brawijaya University).
Meads, G. (2006) *Primary Care in Twentieth Century: An International Perspective* (Seattle: Radcliff Publishing).
Narciso, S. (2005) 'Retailing Policies for Generic Medicines', *International Journal of Health Care Finance and Economics* 5, 165–90.

Panjaitan, R. (2009) Prospek Dunia Farmasi Indonesia 2020, in B. D. Wanandi *Pemikiran dan Pandangan bagi Kemajuan Farmasi: Pergumulan Kompleks bagi Kesehatan Rakyat* (Jakarta: PT Combiphar).
Pic/S (2008) PIC/S Committee Meeting Geneva, Switzerland, media release, http://www.picscheme.org/publication.php?id=7, date accessed 19 March 2011.
Pic/S (2011) 'Introduction', website, http://www.picscheme.org/pics.php, date accessed 23 February 2011.
President of Republic of Indonesia (1989) Undang-Undang Republik Indonesia Nomor 6 Tahun 1989 Tentang Paten (Patent Law, 1989) (Jakarta: Secretary of State RI).
President of Republic of Indonesia (1997) Undang-Undang Republik Indonesia Nomor 13 Tahun 1997 Tentang Perubahan atas Undang-Undang Nomor 6 Tahun 1989 Tentang Paten (Law Nr 13/1997 Complementing Patent Law 1989) (Jakarta: Secretary of State RI).
Pt Askes (Persero) (2005) *Daftar dan Plafon Harga Obat* (Price List and Ceiling Price of Medicines) Ed. XXIV2005 (XXIV) (Jakarta: PT Askes).
Pt Askes (Persero) (2009) *Annual Report 2009* (Jakarta: PT Askes).
Pt Askes (Persero) (2011) *Daftar dan Plafon Harga Obat* (Jakarta: PT Askes).
Reidpath, D. D. and J. Allotey (2003) 'Infant Mortality as an Indicator of Population Health', *Journal of Epidemiology & Community Health* 57, 344–6.
Sampurno, H. D. (2009) Industri Farmasi: Tantangan, Dinamika Persaingan dan Peluang, in B. D. Wanandi *Pemikiran dan Pandangan bagi Kemajuan Farmasi: Pergumulan Kompleks bagi Kesehatan Rakyat* (Jakarta: PT Combiphar).
Sanusi, D. (2009) Kompetensi Sumber Daya Manusia Farmasi, in B.D. Wanandi *Pemikiran dan Pandangan bagi Kemajuan Farmasi: Pergumulan Kompleks bagi Kesehatan Rakyat* (386) (Jakarta: PT Combiphar).
Sekretaris Negara Ri (2002) UUD 1945 Amandemen IV2002 (Jakarta: Sekretaris Negara RI).
Sekretaris Negara Ri (2004) UU RI Nomor 40 tentang Sistem Jaminan Nasional (Jakarta: Sekretaris Negara RI).
Simoens, S. (2009) 'Developing the Japanese Generic Medicines Market: What can We Learn from Europe?', *Journal of Generic Medicines* 6, 129–35.
Simoens, S. and S. De Coster (2006) 'Sustaining Generic Medicines Markets in Europe', *Journal of Generic Medicines* 3, 257–68.
Tunsarawuth, S. (2007) 'Indonesia Mulls Compulsory Licences on Three More HIV/AIDS Drugs', http://www.ip-watch.org/2007/11/26/indonesia-mulls-compulsory-licences-on-three-more-hivaids-drugs/, date accessed 23 February 2011.
UNCTAD (2011a) 'Development Dimensions of Intellectual Property in Indonesia: Access to Medicines, Transfer of Technology and Competition' (Vol. UNCTAD/DIAE/PCB/2011/6) (New York: United Nations Conference on Trade and Development).
UNCTAD (2011b) 'Local Production of Pharmaceuticals and Related Technology Transfer in Developing Countries: A Series of Case Studies by the UNCTAD Secretariat' (New York: United Nations).
Wanandi, B. D. (2009) 'Pemikiran dan Harapan untuk Pengembangan Industri Farmasi dalam Rangka Meningkatkan Derajat Kesehatan', in B. D. Wanandi, *Pemikiran dan Pandangan bagi Kemajuan Farmasi: Pergumulan Kompleks bagi Kesehatan Rakyat* (Jakarta: PT Combiphar).
WHO (2007) 'WHA 60.28 Pandemic Influenza Preparedness: sharing of influenza virus and access to vaccines and other benefits'. Available at: http://www.apps.who.int/gb/ebwha/pdf_files/WHASSA_WHA60-Rec1/E/reso-60-en.pdf.

WHO (2008) 'Core Health Indicators', WHO Statistic Information System, http://www.apeiresearch.net/document_file/news_20070705110028-1.pdf, date accessed 10 February 2009.
WHO (2011) World Health Statistics 2011, http://www.who.int/whosis/whostat/2011/en/index.html, date accessed 26 September 2011.
World Bank (2004) 'Improving Indonesia's Health Outcome', http://siteresources.worldbank.org/INTEAPREGTOPHEANUT/Resources/health.pdf, date accessed 26 April 2011.
World Bank (2009) 'Indonesia Health Care Sector Review, Pharmaceuticals: Why Reform Is Needed', http://siteresources.worldbank.org/HEALTHNUTRITIONANDPOPULATION/Resources/281627-1292531888900/INSPolicyNote Pharmaceutical.pdf, date accessed 26 April 2011.
World Bank (2011) 'Indonesia at a Glance', http://devdata.worldbank.org/AAG/idn_aag.pdf, date accessed 26 April 2011.

8
TRIPS, Free Trade Agreements and the Pharmaceutical Industry in Malaysia

Mohamed Azmi Hassali, Jayabalan Thambyappa, Shankaran Nambiar, Asrul Akmal Shafie and Hans Löfgren

Malaysia has a relatively well-functioning healthcare system that, with small and limited resources, ensures access to services for the vast majority of the population, including the poor. Between 1990 and 2009 life expectancy at birth increased significantly (from 69.0 to 71.5 years for men, and from 73.5 to 76.3 years for women); the infant mortality rate fell (from 13.5 to 6.2 per 1000 live births); while the maternal mortality rate held steady (at 29 per 100,000 live births) (MOH, 2010). Malaysia has a dual system of public and private health services. The main public healthcare provider is the Malaysian Ministry of Health (MOH), which operates primary care, secondary care and tertiary care facilities across the country through general hospitals, district hospitals and health clinics. In 2010 there were 2833 health clinics, 131 MOH hospitals (with 33,211 beds), and six special medical institutions (with 4582 beds), for a population of 28.3 million (MOH, 2010).

The health system, however, is under threat as a result of increased pharmaceutical and healthcare costs. The World Trade Organization's (WTO) Agreement on Trade Related Aspects of Intellectual Property Rights (TRIPS) and several bilateral and regional free trade agreements (FTAs) (already signed or under negotiation) threaten access to a sound healthcare delivery system. The implementation of stricter intellectual property rights (IPR) protection is affecting the cost of medicines, while these several agreements can also be expected to have a negative impact on the viability of the domestic pharmaceutical industry.

In this chapter we explain Malaysia's healthcare system and its financing and provide an overview of the country's pharmaceutical industry. We discuss the possible impact on the industry of tightened intellectual property standards contained in the TRIPS Agreement and FTAs. We move on to discuss compulsory licensing and examine TRIPS and generic drugs in relation to domestic suppliers. Following an analysis of the role of government regulation, the question of pricing and distribution of essential medicines is addressed. Finally, the issues confronting domestic generics suppliers are examined, followed by our concluding remarks.

Financing the healthcare system

Healthcare in Malaysia is funded through general taxation, social and private insurance and out-of-pocket payments. It has been reported that total expenditure on health for 2009 was RM33.7 billion, amounting to 4.96 per cent of gross domestic product (GDP) (World Bank, 2011). The government funds public health services through a consolidated revenue fund under the Ministry of Finance; other services are paid for through consumer contributions. Primary care services at public health clinics are delivered almost free of charge. Patients pay a nominal fee of RM1 (equivalent to US$0.31 in 2010) for each outpatient visit. Government employees, numbering 1.4 million, and their family members are also the beneficiaries of this system, even after retirement. The Ministry of Defence has its own healthcare unit for the health needs of its personnel. Secondary and tertiary care provided at public hospital facilities is highly subsidized by the government. A total of RM13.7 billion (US$4.4 billion) was allocated to the MOH for funding public health services in 2009 (MOH, 2010). Fees collected by the MOH constitute only about 2 per cent of the MOH budget, which means that about 98 per cent of the cost of MOH health services was funded directly by government (Yu et al., 2008).

Social insurance is provided through the Social Security Organization, established in 1971. This programme essentially covers local private sector workers, excluding the unemployed and self-employed (Yu et al., 2008). There is also an income cap for enrolment in this scheme and contributions are compulsory. Healthcare coverage is restricted to private primary care doctors, and private or public hospitals willing to work on a fixed fee schedule. Workplace accidents and work-related illnesses are also covered, with compensation being paid for both temporary and permanent lay-off. Migrant workers, numbering more than 2 million, are supported through a workers' compensation insurance scheme (Yu et al., 2008). The central Employees' Provident Fund also apportions an amount for healthcare.

The middle class use private healthcare services and pay high user fees, or co-payments if covered by private insurance. A 2006 World Health Organization (WHO) report found that the majority of private health finance was accounted for by out-of-pocket payments (73.8 per cent), with private insurance a minor component (13.7 per cent) (WHO, 2006). Private providers mainly focus on curative services through general practitioner clinics, medical centres and private hospitals. Hospitals in the private sector function as business entities, and medical practitioners are paid lucrative remuneration packages. But the vast majority of people, estimated at 60–70 per cent of the population, including the poor and disadvantaged, rely on government-provided public hospitals and healthcare centres (Ding, 2010). Of Malaysia's total health expenditure, government funding amounts to about 58 per cent, with private expenditure accounting for the remaining 42 per cent (Tarn et al., 2008).

Health is a federal responsibility (the state governments have little influence), and, while there is no single, comprehensive health policy, elements of such a policy are in place. A medicines policy was developed and endorsed by the Malaysian Cabinet in 2006, covering the areas of licensing, product safety, quality control, research and development (R&D) and rational use of medicines. This policy does not employ direct price controls. Instead, the government seeks to contain prices by fostering competition in the private market (Pharmaceutical Services Division, 2007).

The Malaysian pharmaceutical industry

Pharmaceutical industry activities in Malaysia can be divided into manufacturing, importation and distribution (MOPI, 2010). Manufacturing commenced in 1958 when Glaxo Wellcome (now GlaxoSmithKline, GSK) established a production plant in the state of Selangor (Zaman, 2001). In 1981, with an increase in the number of manufacturers, eight local, foreign and joint venture companies came together to establish the Malaysian Organisation of Pharmaceutical Industries (MOPI) (MOPI, 2010).

The Malaysian government considers pharmaceuticals a strategic industry with strong growth prospects (Economic Planning Unit, 2010). In 2009 the pharmaceutical market was valued at around RM4.29 billion (US$1.22 billion). A *Business Monitor International* report estimates that its value will reach RM6.29 billion (US$1.81 billion) by 2014 (*BMI*, 2010). The same report estimated the value of the generics market at RM1.11 billion (US$316 million) in 2009.

Domestically owned companies are important market players as producers of generic drugs. Well-established local companies include Pharmaniaga, CCM Pharmaceuticals, Hovid, Kotra Pharma and Xepa Soul Pattinson. They also export drug products to more than 30 countries. Multinational pharmaceutical firms in Malaysia are mainly engaged in the marketing of imported products. They rely on local firms for logistics, inventory control, warehousing, order processing and distribution (Azmi and Alavi, 2001).

Prescription drugs represent approximately 70 per cent of the pharmaceutical market and this predominance is likely to prevail into the future. There are three categories of prescription drugs: imported patented drugs, generics manufactured locally by Malaysian companies, and imported generics. Patented drugs have the largest market value. It is reported that imported patented products, mainly from Germany, France and the UK, represent 65–80 per cent of the value of the pharmaceutical market. This category includes new generation antibiotics and cholesterol-lowering, anti-diabetic, cardiovascular and anti-cancer drugs (MITI, 2007). In 1994 the government spent about RM300 million (US$85.7 million) to procure medicines. By 2005 this figure had increased to more than RM1 billion (US$285.7 million) (Lek, 2005). Total expenditure for the top 150 prescription medicines was estimated at RM2.176 billion (US$723 million) in 2007, with nearly equal expenditures between the public and private sectors (Faridah et al., 2010).

Expenditure by the public sector refers to drugs dispensed through the public health system at little or no direct cost to patients. The government is committed to making essential drugs available through a large-scale public procurement system. Pharmaceutical and medical products were distributed to MOH hospitals and medical institutions through the Government Medical Store until 1994, when this service was outsourced under the national privatization policy. The tender was awarded directly to Pharmaniaga without a transparent tender process. Pharmaniaga (formerly known as Remedi Pharmaceutical) is the country's largest integrated pharmaceutical firm. When it was established under this name in 1994, the majority of shares (86 per cent) were owned by the government investment company Khazanah Holdings. The latter is a government-linked company operating as a corporate business. In June 2010 Khazanah sold all of its shares to a Malaysian private conglomerate, Boustead Holdings Bhd, and Pharmaniaga became a fully private entity (Paul-Raj, 2010).

It cannot be ascertained whether public expenditure on prescription medicines is being managed appropriately and efficiently. A more transparent system of public procurement would be needed for such an assessment. The lack of transparency can be attributed to a structure of crony capitalism whereby privileges are awarded to firms close to the government. This system of public procurement was a bone of contention during negotiations with the US on an FTA. The US Trade Representative pressed for foreign firms to be able to participate in bidding for tenders and insisted on transparency in the evaluation and awarding of tenders. The US also opposed restrictions based on ethnic grounds arising from preferential treatment of *bumiputera* or native Malay firms (a policy under the New Economic Policy of 1971) intended to increase the participation of Malays in the national economy.

The Drug Control Authority, under the purview of the MOH, is responsible for the regulation of pharmaceuticals. The legal framework underpinning the Authority's operations provides for proper regulation and enforcement of safety and quality. Regulations for this purpose were put in place as early as the 1950s, prior to Malaysia's independence. Pharmaceutical products, traditional medicines and cosmetics must be registered, and manufacturers, importers, wholesalers and retailers licensed. Licences must be renewed annually and production plants are subject to annual site inspections by the regulatory authorities.

At the end of 2009 there were a total of 248 firms in Malaysia licensed by the Drug Control Authority to manufacture pharmaceutical products. Of these, 73 were licensed to produce prescription products and over-the-counter pharmaceuticals and 175 were licensed to manufacture traditional medicines (National Pharmaceutical Control Bureau, 2009). Local manufacturers are largely engaged in production of less sophisticated drugs, including antibiotics, antacids, anti-fungals, health supplements and drugs for coughs and colds. The large number of local manufacturers is, therefore, no indication of capacity to supply a comprehensive range of drugs. Despite their numbers, local manufacturers have limited R&D capabilities in new product formulation and have not demonstrated capabilities in the production of active pharmaceutical ingredients (APIs) or in reverse engineering.

Intellectual property rights, TRIPS and free trade agreements

Malaysia first introduced a patent registration system through the Patents Act 1983, since amended several times. This Act provides for the granting of patents for all products, including pharmaceuticals. A patent office was established prior to 1983. It was initially placed under the Ministry of Trade and Industry but shifted to the Ministry of Domestic Trade and Consumer Affairs in 1990. The Patents (Amendment) Act 2000 provides for full compliance with the requirements of the TRIPS Agreement. Coming into force on 1 August 2001, it extended the patent term from 15 to 20 years from date of filing (Azmi and Alavi, 2001).

While continuing to give priority to the multilateral trading system under the WTO, Malaysia has also been pursuing bilateral and regional FTAs (Rasiah, 2005). Their remit includes investment, trade facilitation and IPR, as well as economic cooperation in a wide variety of areas. Malaysia has concluded, signed or implemented bilateral FTAs with Japan, Pakistan, New Zealand and Chile. At the regional level, Malaysia and fellow member states of ASEAN (the Association of South-East Asian Nations) have established the ASEAN Free Trade Area. ASEAN has also concluded FTAs with China, Japan, Korea and India, as well as Australia and New Zealand. Free trade agreements still under negotiation at the time of writing include those between Malaysia and Turkey, Malaysia and Australia, the Trade Preferential System and the Organization of Islamic Conference, the Developing-Eight, the Preferential Tariff Agreement and the Trans-Pacific Partnership Agreement (TPP) (Ministry of International Trade and Industry, 2010).

Many of these FTAs extend the scope of IPR protection beyond what is required under TRIPS through so-called TRIPS-plus provisions. These provisions make it more difficult for developing countries like Malaysia to supply their population with essential medicines and for local generics firms to prosper. In particular, extended IPR protection through TRIPS-plus provisions enables patent-owning multinationals to enjoy monopoly pricing for a longer period, to the detriment of the availability of affordable drugs and the cost of healthcare. Extension of the period of monopoly supply delays the market entry of generics and discourages small- and medium-sized enterprises from producing generic drugs (Smith et al., 2009). Developing countries generate little intellectual property of their own, and so stronger patents rights result in an increase in the outflow of royalties. The net outflow of royalties for Malaysia in 2005 was estimated to be US$1.7 billion (Smith, 2008).

The FTAs Malaysia has signed with Pakistan and India do not seem to jeopardize the local pharmaceutical industry or supply of affordable drugs. The TPP—a proposed regional trade pact involving Australia, Brunei Darussalam, Chile, Malaysia, New Zealand, Peru, Singapore, Vietnam and the US—and the possible EU–Malaysia FTA, however, would have serious consequences for consumers of medicines in Malaysia. Both agreements are considered significant FTAs from the perspective of the EU and the US, in the sense that they include stringent requirements with respect to government procurement and extended intellectual property protection. If implemented, these FTAs will have a serious impact on the local drug industry and healthcare costs.

Ongoing TPP talks appear to have superseded earlier negotiations on a bilateral US–Malaysia FTA. The American Malaysian Chamber of Commerce, which includes multinational companies with drug patents in Malaysia, had claimed that the proposed USMFTA would not affect pricing of medicines or the generics industry (AMCHAM, 2006). But this contention has been challenged by the Malaysian generics manufacturers represented by MOPI. It will take at least 15 years for the full impact of a US–Malaysia FTA, with its stronger IPR protection, to take effect, because extended patents would only apply to new medicines. Under the US–Malaysia FTA—and, by extension, the TPP—local generics manufacturers will struggle to compete with multinational firms and, consequently, Malaysians are likely to continue to pay higher prices for medicines (Third World Network, 2008).

We have already noted Malaysia's keenness to engage in FTAs. Through FTAs, bilateral investment treaties and other agreements, however, partner countries are being compelled by the US and EU to adopt US and European standards of IPR protection and enforcement. An example of the impact of such IPR protection is Malaysia's use of pharmacists to curtail the volume of generics coming from elsewhere (especially from India and Europe) and supplied to primary healthcare practitioners and private hospitals. This trade was affecting proprietary drug distributors' sales, and one way of stemming it was to allow only a limited quantity to be brought in on a prescription-only basis (pharmacists ensure that the drugs match the prescription).

In 2010, following complaints from US companies that unauthorized copies of pharmaceutical products were being granted marketing approval, Malaysia was placed on the US Trade Representative's 'Special 301 Watch List' (Flynn, 2010). This resulted in mounting pressure to adopt more stringent IPR standards. In March 2011 the Malaysian government responded by introducing rules covering data exclusivity under the Control of Drugs and Cosmetics Regulations. The Director of Pharmaceutical Services introduced data exclusivity of five years for new products containing a new chemical entity and three for second indications of a registered drug product (National Pharmaceutical Control Bureau, 2011).

Data exclusivity is not a requirement under TRIPS, yet the Malaysian government has yielded to pressure from foreign drug companies seeking to protect their investments, thereby further delaying the appearance of generics in the market. Data protection is provided only for data that has been obtained through 'a considerable effort', but it is investment that is being protected rather than new medicines. It must also be remembered that under the TRIPS Agreement only new chemical entities require protection, while new dosage types or new uses of a known product do not. The US Trade Representative's arm-twisting tactics, evident in the use of the Special 301 programme, limit access to medicines and are in violation of international human rights and the right to health. It would be fair to say that, if Malaysia concludes the FTAs with the US (under the TPP) and the EU, data exclusivity will continue to be highly contentious. In fact, the EU FTA might require data exclusivity for up to 11 years (Flynn, 2010).

Compulsory licensing

Despite pressure for further tightening of intellectual property standards, existing provisions in the TRIPS Agreement do allow countries flexibility to override IPR under certain circumstances. Following adoption of the WTO's Doha Declaration on the TRIPS Agreement and Public Health in 2001, Malaysia became the first Asian country to issue a government-use licence. This is the only instance of the government taking advantage of TRIPS flexibilities. Initiated by the MOH, the licence was issued by the Ministry of Domestic Trade and Consumer Affairs for a period of two years, commencing 1 November 2003, for importation of generic versions of patented anti-retrovirals, namely didanosine (ddI) 100 mg tablet (patent holder, Bristol Myers Squibb); didanosine 25 mg tablet (Bristol Myers Squibb); zidovudine (AZT) 100 mg capsule (GSK); and lamivudine 150 mg + zidovudine 300 mg tablet (GSK). These drugs were sourced from the Indian company Cipla to treat AIDS patients in government hospitals and clinics (Khor, 2009). These imported generic medicines have been prescribed and distributed through government hospitals since June 2004 (Khor, 2009). According to former Health Minister Dr Chua Soi Lek, the monthly cost of treating a patient was thereby reduced from RM1200 to RM200–220. Thus '[w]ith the cheaper cost, we can treat at least 4000 HIV patients compared to the present 1500'

(Foong, 2004). Another consequence of the government-use authorization was that patent holders reduced their own prices, resulting in a considerable reduction in the cost of treatments (Khor, 2009).

Domestic pharmaceutical production and government regulation

Government regulation of the pharmaceutical sector encompasses licensing, regular inspection of manufacturing premises and registration of drug products for the purpose of ensuring drug quality and safety (Kudrin, 2009). More broadly, government policies and regulations shape the business environment for local pharmaceutical production. Until 1994 the government extensively subsidized the cost of drugs distributed by the Government Medical Store to public sector health services. The supply of drugs to government health facilities, as previously noted, was then outsourced to Pharmaniaga under the government's general privatization policy, which aimed to reduce the financial and administrative burden on government (Merican and Yon, 2002; Naidu, 1999). While patients were still supplied with medicines and devices listed on its formulary, an element of co-payment was introduced for other medicines. In short, privatization meant some healthcare subsidies were removed.

Following the East Asian financial and economic crisis of 1998, the government sought to reduce its expenditure on health and implemented measures to address the rising cost of medicines, including attempts to extend the use of locally produced generics (Razak, 1998). Although Malaysian generics manufacturers work closely with the MOH to enhance the uptake of locally manufactured medicines, an effective generics substitution policy is yet to be implemented in either the public or private sector. Educating consumers on the use of generic medicines has been ineffective, and there is no policy requiring dispensing clinics and pharmacies to stock the full range of generic medicines (Al-Gedadi et al., 2008). In 2010, generics were estimated to account for only 26.40 per cent of total sales (BMI, 2011).

A low entry barrier to the Malaysian pharmaceutical market, courtesy of ASEAN's harmonization policy, has led to increased competition (Hassali et al., 2009). For generics companies to continue to prosper, it will be necessary to change the perception of most physicians and the general public that locally manufactured generics are ineffective and of low quality. An increased market share for locally manufactured generics would also have broader community benefits (Hassali et al., 2009).

Pricing and distribution of essential medicines

Malaysia's National Essential Drugs List (NEDL) includes all those medicines that are necessary to meet the healthcare needs of the majority of the population. Such lists are the cornerstone of public health policy in most developing countries. By rights, all listed drugs should be available, accessible and affordable at all times. The NEDL was launched in 2000 for use by public healthcare providers. It consists of a primary list, containing preparations needed for primary, secondary and tertiary healthcare, and a supplementary list, containing preparations for specialist treatments. The list was revised in 2008 and currently consists of 605 preparations on the primary list and 391 preparations on the supplementary list (Pharmaceutical Services Division, 2011).

The prices of drugs on the NEDL are not regulated, as Malaysians only pay a fixed fee for treatment in public health facilities, irrespective of the number or type of drugs prescribed. Any increase in drug procurement prices is absorbed by the government (which subsidizes drug costs by as much as 99 per cent). With drug prices increasing year by year, this has been expensive for the government. Between 2001 and 2003, for example, public sector procurement costs increased by around 80 per cent (Babar et al., 2005). In 2007 the sale price increase for generic drugs was higher than for innovator brand medicines, although innovator brands were still 27–90 per cent more expensive at nominal value (Pharmaceutical Services Division, 2008; Shafie and Hassali, 2008).

In the private sector, the prices of innovator and generic brand medicines have been shown to be, respectively, 16 and 6.6 times higher than the International Reference Price (Babar et al., 2007). The International Reference Price is the median of recent procurement prices offered by international suppliers to developing countries for multi-source, generically equivalent products. For the lowest-paid government worker, the cost of a month's medicine for treatment of a peptic ulcer is equal to a week's salary. Drug prices are significantly affected by mark-ups applied by healthcare providers, ranging from 25 per cent to 140 per cent of the manufacturer's price (Babar et al., 2007). Higher mark-ups apply on medications dispensed by doctors in the private market (as compared with retail pharmacies) and on generic medicines.

The domestic generics industry

In recent years the domestic generics industry has enhanced its ability to produce for both the domestic and export markets. Increasing healthcare spending, the need to contain rising healthcare costs, and increased demand for pharmaceuticals from an ageing population are major factors explaining this growth. Healthcare spending is growing at about 13 per cent a year (Hassali et al., 2009). It is estimated that local firms produce 30–40 per cent of the domestic drug demand by volume (MOPI, 2010). Besides providing high-quality and affordable pharmaceuticals, domestic firms have significantly contributed to export revenue.

The government has also helped to propel the growth of the pharmaceutical sector through industry policy initiatives like the granting of 'Bionexus' status to recognized biotechnology companies, provision of grants to small- and medium-sized enterprises, and tax incentives and financing schemes for R&D designed to nurture the pharmaceutical industry. Malaysia's membership of the Pharmaceutical Inspection Co-operation Scheme has helped to improve the standard and quality of the local industry. In turn, this has facilitated the export of pharmaceutical products to over 30 countries, including those in ASEAN, Africa, the Middle East and Central America. It has also enabled access to fellow members in the scheme, like the EU, Australia and Canada (Hassali et al., 2009). There is no certainty, however, that this positive trend will continue. As the technological capabilities and production capacity of local firms increase, there is a risk that such firms will be acquired by multinationals.

A further boost for the local industry came in 2010 when the government launched the 12 National Key Economic Areas (NKEAs) as part of the agenda for Malaysia's Economic Transformation Programme, its key goal being to become a high-income nation by 2020 (Economic Transformation Programme, 2010). An NKEA is defined as a driver of economic activity with the potential to directly and materially contribute to economic growth. Healthcare has been designated as one of the NKEAs, with three priority sub-sectors: pharmaceuticals, health travel medical tourism, and medical technology products. With the launching of the healthcare NKEA, many local generics companies have been encouraged to play a greater role in capturing both overseas and local markets using innovative production technologies.

With patents expiring on many key pharmaceutical products, and pressures to control ever-rising healthcare costs, the rationale for using lower-priced generics will only become stronger. Given this, there is great interest among multinationals in venturing into the generics market (Chandler and Samaroo, 2010; Seiter, 2007). In Malaysia, multinationals like GSK and Novartis have started to gain a market niche with their own generics (*BMI*, 2011). Novartis, through its subsidiary Sandoz, has been aggressively marketing generics in the local market, while GSK has launched five branded generics in the cardiovascular therapeutics category (*BMI*, 2011). The availability of products supplied by multinationals puts pressure on industry players in Malaysia to compete in terms of pricing, thereby potentially affecting the viability of local firms.

Stringent controls are imposed on drug products submitted for registration. Good Manufacturing Practice, stability and bioequivalence requirements, guidelines for pharmaceutical development, and the Common Technical Document for regulatory submission have been adopted from regulatory agencies in the EU, the US and the International Conference on Harmonization. In turn, this has increased the quality of generics and made it easier for locally manufactured generics to compete in international markets. Escalating healthcare costs brought about by patented prescription drugs are a major concern in all countries and, in this regard, the Malaysian government should be more proactive in encouraging the use of generic medicines, which would also provide opportunities for local generics firms to increase their market share.

Generics from India are also an important factor in efforts to contain healthcare costs. In 2009 alone 635 prescription product items were imported from India, the major source of imported prescription products (National Pharmaceutical Control Bureau, 2009). But the Indian Patents (Amendment) Act 2005, and the acquisition of Indian pharmaceutical companies by foreign multinationals, may weaken India's role as a source of low-cost essential medicines (Chaudhuri, 2011). It is significant that in June 2008 Daiichi Sankyo, a Japanese multinational, acquired Ranbaxy, one of India's largest drug companies and a source of cheap generics in Malaysia (Padma, 2011). It is believed that the purpose of the takeover was to acquire Ranbaxy's well-established marketing network and that Daiichi Sankyo will use it to distribute its own highly priced patented products rather than continue Ranbaxy's business model of producing and selling cheap generics (Gopakumar, 2010).

Conclusion

In this chapter we have examined key features of Malaysia's healthcare system. We have discussed the system of healthcare financing and the dual framework of a public health system for the majority alongside private hospitals and other private health services for the wealthy. It must be acknowledged that there is substantial dependence on the public system, and there would be even greater reliance on it if not for problems of poor delivery. Since the role of the pharmaceutical industry cannot be divorced from the healthcare system, the status of the industry in Malaysia has been analyzed.

The TRIPS Agreement, as implemented through Malaysian IPR legislation, has had and will continue to have an impact both on the industry and on the cost of drugs and, by extension, the cost of healthcare. Malaysia is in the process of negotiating several FTAs, which, if concluded, will have serious impacts on the nature and cost of healthcare. Domestic pharmaceutical firms forced to comply with TRIPS-plus provisions under various FTAs will be constrained in their production of generic drugs, resulting in reduced supply of low-cost generics.

Malaysia's local pharmaceutical industry, however, has some potential for expansion, although it must contend with increasing competition from multinationals and growing regulatory demands. Local firms manufacture relatively unsophisticated drugs and do not produce APIs or have R&D capabilities. These companies, however, are to some extent able to satisfy domestic demand for basic drug formulations, and they are also exporting their products. The conclusion of negotiations of some of the FTAs noted above could stifle their activities. The Malaysian government also has to grapple with the complex demands of TRIPS. To date it has only once taken advantage of the flexibilities in the Agreement. A crucial challenge for the government will be balancing TRIPS compliance with maintaining an accessible, affordable healthcare system for the public as a whole.

References

Al-Gedadi, N. A., M. A. Hassali and A. A. Shafie (2008) 'A Pilot Survey on Perceptions and Knowledge of Generic Medicines Among Consumers in Penang, Malaysia', *Pharmacy Practice* 6, 93–7.
AMCHAM see American Malaysian Chamber of Commerce.
American Malaysian Chamber of Commerce (2006) 'Public Submission for the Proposed US–Malaysia Free Trade Agreement', http://www.ftamalaysia.org/file_dir/189810006944cdb0c12ad9b.pdf, date accessed 12 April 2011.
Azmi, I. M. and R. Alavi (2001) 'TRIPS, Patents, Technology Transfer, Foreign Direct Investment and the Pharmaceutical Industry in Malaysia', *The Journal of World Intellectual Property* 4, 947–76.
Babar, Z. D., M. I. M. Ibrahim and N. I. Bukahri (2005) 'A Pricing Analysis of Cardiovascular and Blood Products after Privatization of Drug Distribution System in Malaysia', *Journal of Pharmaceutical Finance, Economics & Policy* 14, 3–25.
Babar, Z. U. D., M. I. M. Ibrahim, H. Singh, N. I. Bukahri and A. Creese (2007) 'Evaluating Drug Prices, Availability, Affordability, and Price Components: Implications for Access to Drugs in Malaysia', *PLoS Medicine* 4, e82.
BMI, see Business Monitor International Business Monitor International (2010) *Malaysia Pharmaceuticals & Healthcare Report* (London: Business Monitor International), http://xa.yimg.com/kq/groups/18751725/281346239/name/Malaysian+pharmaceutical+and+Healthcare+report+Q4+2010.pdf, date accessed 12 December 2010.
Business Monitor International (2011) *Malaysia Pharmaceuticals & Healthcare Report* (London: Business Monitor International), http://www.businessmonitor.com/pharma/malaysia.html, date accessed 12 December 2012.
Chandler, L. L. and H. D. Samaroo (2010) 'Pfizer and the Greenstone Brand: A Sustainable Competitive Advantage & Quest', *Journal of Medical Marketing* 10, 155–64.
Chaudhuri, S. (2011) 'Multinationals and Monopolies: Pharmaceutical Industry in India after TRIPS', http://apps.who.int/medicinedocs/documents/s19026en/s19026en.pdf, date accessed 3 January 2012.
Ding, J. A. (2010) 'Private Healthcare: Too Expensive?' *The Nut Graph*, 6 July, http://www.thenutgraph.com/private-healthcare-too-expensive/, date accessed 12 April 2011.
Economic Planning Unit (2010) *Tenth Malaysia Plan (2011–2015)*, Prime Minister's Department, Putrajaya, http://www.epu.gov.my/html/themes/epu/html/RMKE10/img/pdf/en/foreword.pdf, date accessed 10 August 2011.

Economic Transformation Programme (2010) *Economic Transformation Programme*, Putrajaya, http://etp.pemandu.gov.my/Overview_of_NKEAs_-@-Overview_of_NKEAs.aspx, date accessed 10 December 2010.

Faridah, A. Y., O. Nourhanah, A. R. Fatimah, M. G. Nadia and A. Goh (2010) 'Expenditure on Medicines in Malaysia' in *Malaysian Statistics on Medicines 2007* (Ministry of Health: Kuala Lumpur), https://www.macr.org.my/nhsi/document/publication/MalaysianStatisticsOnMedicine2007.pdf, date accessed 4 December 2010.

Flynn, S. M. (2010) 'Special 301 of the Trade Act of 1974 and Global Access to Medicines', *Journal of Generic Medicines* 7, 309–33.

Foong, P. Y. (2004) 'Cheaper 3-in-1 HIV Treatment', *The Star*, 7 June, http://thestar.com.my/news/story.asp?file=/2004/6/7/nation/8153623&sec=nation, date accessed 14 December 2010.

Gopakumar, K. M. (2010) 'Foreign Acquisition and Access to Medicines: Case of India', *Trade Insight* 6(3–4), 52–3.

Hassali, M. A., K. H. Yuen, M. I. Ibrahim, J. W. Wong, B. H. Ng and H. S. David (2009) 'Malaysian Pharmaceutical Industry: Opportunities and Challenges', *Journal of Generic Medicines* 6, 246–52.

Khor, M. (2009) 'Patents, Compulsory Licences and Access to Medicines: Some Recent Experiences', *Intellectual Property and Access to Medicines: Papers and Perspectives*, http://www.twnside.org.sg/title2/IPR/pdf/ipr10.pdf, date accessed 6 December 2010.

Kudrin, A. (2009) 'Challenges in the Clinical Development Requirements for the Marketing Authorization of New Medicines in Southeast Asia', *The Journal of Clinical Pharmacology* 49, 268–80.

Lek, C. S. (2005) 'Health Plan to be Modelled after Socso', *The Star*, 14 December, http://thestar.com.my/news/story.asp?file=/2005/12/14/nation/12859112&sec=nation, date accessed 2 December 2010.

Malaysian Organization of Pharmaceutical Industries (2010) 'The Malaysian Pharmaceutical Industry', http://www.mopi.org.my, date accessed 10 December 2010.

Merican, I. and R. Yon (2002) 'Health Care Reform and Changes: The Malaysian Experience', *Asia-Pacific Journal of Public Health* 14, 17–22.

Ministry of Health (2008) *Malaysia's Health. Chapter 3-Health System Management*, pg 162–165 available at http://www.moh.gov.my/images/gallery/publications/mh/Malaysia%20Health%202008-2.pdf, date accessed 8th March 2012.

Ministry of Health Malaysia (2010) *Malaysian Health Facts 2010*, http://www.moh.gov.my/v/stats_si, date accessed 4 June 2011.

Ministry of International Trade and Industry (2007) *Industry Profile: Chemical*. Malaysia Trade and Industry Portal, http://www.miti.gov.my/ekpweb/application?origin=publishedcontents.jsp&event=bea.portal.framework.internal.refresh&pageid=miti&subpageid=contentdetails&section=content&global, date accessed 2 December 2010.

Ministry of International Trade and Industry (2010) *Free Trade Agreement*, http://www.miti.gov.my/cms/content.jsp?id=com.tms.cms.section.Section_8ab55693-7f000010-72f772f7-46d4f042, date accessed 3 December 2010.

MITI *see* Ministry of International Trade and Industry.

MOH *see* Ministry of Health Malaysia.

MOPI *see* Malaysian Organization of Pharmaceutical Industries.

Naidu, G. R. (1999) 'Demand/Supply Study for Pharmaceuticals in Malaysia', Report Prepared for the International Trade Centre, http://www.intracen.org/sstp/Survey/pharma00/Malaysia-pharmacafe00-sds.pdf, date accessed 7 December 2010.

National Pharmaceutical Control Bureau (2009) *Annual Report 2009*, http://apps.who.int/medicinedocs/en/m/abstract/Js18585en/, date accessed 6 December 2010.
National Pharmaceutical Control Bureau (2011) *Directive on Data Exclusivity*, http://portal.bpfk.gov.my/index.cfm?menuid=90&parentid=15, date accessed 3 January 2012.
Padma, T. V. (2011) 'Action Urged on Foreign Takeovers of Indian Drug Makers', *Nature Medicine* 17, 141.
Paul-Raj, A. (2010) 'Boustead Takes over Pharmaniaga for RM534m', *New Strait Times*, 15 June, http://www.pharmaniaga.com:8080/pharmaweb/files/news-20100615043757-NST%2012%20June.pdf, date accessed 14 February 2012.
Pharmaceutical Services Division (2007) *National Medicines Policy of Malaysia*, http://www.pharmacy.gov.my/, date accessed 10 January 2011.
Pharmaceutical Services Division (2008) *Medicine Price Monitoring Survey—An Analysis of Price Variation, Trend and Mark-Ups in the Public and Private Sector*, http://www.pharmacy.gov.my/aeimages//File/Bulletin_My.MedPrice_2009.pdf, date accessed 5 December 2010.
Pharmaceutical Services Division (2012) *National Essential Drug List*, http://www.pharmacy.gov.my/v2/sites/default/files/document-upload/nedl-only-list-publish-website.pdf accessed 8th March 2012.
Rasiah, R. (2005) 'Trade-related Investment Liberalization under the WTO: The Malaysian Experience', *Global Economic Review* 34, 453–71.
Razak, A. D. (1998) 'Going Generic and Bringing Health to All', *New Straits Times*, 25 June, http://www.prn.usm.my/old_website/edl/generic.html, date accessed 1 December 2010.
Seiter, A. (2007) 'Access to Medicines and the Innovation Dilemma—Can Pharmaceutical Multinationals Be Good Corporate Citizens?' in G. Hanekamp and F. Wütscher (eds) *Business Ethics of Innovation* (Berlin: Springer).
Shafie, A. A. and M. A. Hassali (2008) 'Price Comparison Between Innovator and Generic Medicines Sold by Community Pharmacies in the State of Penang, Malaysia', *Journal of Generic Medicines* 6, 35–42.
Smith, R. D., C. Correa and C. Oh (2009) 'Trade, TRIPS, and Pharmaceuticals', *The Lancet* 373, 684–91.
Smith, S. R. (2008) *Intellectual Property in Free Trade Agreements* (Penang: Third World Network), http://www.twnside.org.sg/, date accessed 20 December 2010.
Tarn, Y. H., S. Hu, I. Kamae, B. M. Yang, S. C. Li, V. Tangcharoensathien, Y. Teerawattananon, S. Limwattananon, A. Hameed and S. M. Aljunid (2008) 'Health Care Systems and Pharmacoeconomic Research in Asia Pacific Region', *Value in Health* 11, S137–55.
Third World Network (2008) *Preliminary Analysis of the Likely Impact of a US/EU Free Trade Agreement on Malaysian Small and Medium Enterprises*, http://www.ftamalaysia.org/file_dir/57172350648771a540fb2c.doc, date accessed 4 December 2010.
WHO *see* World Health Organization
World Bank (2011) *Harnessing National Health Accounts to Strengthen Policymaking*, http://siteresources.worldbank.org/INTHSD/Resources/376278-1261143298590/6660179-1321038458305/CaseStudiespub92911web.pdf, date accessed 16 January 2012.
World Health Organization (2006) *The World Health Report 2006: Working Together for Health*, http://www.who.int/whr/2006/en/index.html, date accessed 25 December 2010.

Yu, C. P., D. K. Whynes and T. H. Sach (2008) 'Equity in Health Care Financing: The Case of Malaysia', *International Journal for Equity in Health* 7, 1–15.

Zaman, H. H. (2001) 'The Generic Pharmaceutical Industry in Malaysia', B. Pharm Thesis, Department of Pharmacy, Faculty of Medicine, University of Malaya, Kuala Lumpur, Malaysia.

9
The Pharmaceutical Industry, Intellectual Property Rights and Access to Medicines in Pakistan

Zaheer-Ud-Din Babar, Shazia Qasim Jamshed, Muhammad Ashar Malik, Hans Löfgren and Anwarul-Hassan Gilani

The pharmaceutical industry in Pakistan is worth around US$1.18 billion, with annual growth in 2010 approaching 10 per cent (Khan, 2012). There are more than 650 registered companies, including 31 multinationals, which in 2006 had a market share in value terms of 53.3 per cent, with national firms controlling the remaining 46.7 per cent (IMS Health, 2007). In 2007 medicines worth about US$100 million were exported. Medicines are a vital component of healthcare, and Pakistan spends around three-quarters of its healthcare budget on medicines (WHO, 2004). This chapter provides an overview, from a public health perspective, of the national pharmaceutical market and the development of drug policies and regulation. Pakistan adopted a Trade Related Aspects of Intellectual Property Rights (TRIPS)-compliant patent regime in 2000, and the intersection between patents and public health is a central policy challenge. This chapter highlights key issues related to intellectual property, Free Trade Agreements (FTAs), and production and access to medicines.

The health system

Pakistan has a multicultural and multiethnic, mostly young population of approximately 180 million, which makes it the world's sixth most populous country (Economist Intelligence Unit, 2012). This is projected to increase to 210 million by 2025. The United Nations estimates that Pakistan will be the fourth most populous country by 2050, which will make access to scarce resources and food even more difficult (Ministry of Health, 2009). Pakistan has four provinces: Punjab, Sindh, Khyber Pakhtunkhwa (formerly North Western Frontier Province) and Baluchistan. The federal Ministry of Health is responsible for curative and preventive services, although the role of the provinces in the provision of healthcare services has been enhanced through recent institutional reform (Nishtar, 2010a). But the health sector has not been a priority for successive governments. Nearly one-third of the population lives below the poverty line, and healthcare indicators demonstrate a bleak state of health. According to the Economic Survey of Pakistan, public sector expenditure on health in 2005 was only 0.8 per cent of gross domestic product (GDP) (Government of Pakistan, 2006). Around three-quarters of the population are not covered by either public or private health insurance. This large segment of the population pays the full cost of healthcare through out-of-pocket payments at the point of service delivery (Nishtar, 2010a).

The burden of disease is dominated by communicable diseases. Malnutrition-related conditions and reproductive health account for 50 per cent of the total burden of disease. This is further complicated by the non-communicable disease group dominated by cardiovascular diseases, diabetes, injuries and neuro-psychological diseases (Ministry of Health, 2009). Pakistan is one of four countries where polio is still endemic. In 2008, 118 polio cases were reported (Ministry of Health, 2009). Hepatitis B and C are endemic diseases, with about 10 million carriers. Tuberculosis is responsible for 5.1 per cent of the total national disease burden, and there are about 250,000–300,000 new cases every year. Malaria is endemic, with little change in its incidence over the past five years. Punjab, Khyber Pakhtunkhwa and Sindh have low rates of malaria but Baluchistan and the Federally Administered Tribal Areas (FATA) are seriously affected. An emerging communicable disease challenge is the 'concentrated epidemic' of human immunodeficiency virus (HIV) disease among vulnerable populations, particularly injecting drug users (Ministry of Health, 2009).

Social protection and medical reimbursement

Healthcare is notionally free at all public health facilities, but in reality patients are expected to pay charges at government-funded hospitals. Indeed, most citizens have no or very limited access to health services because of the scarcity of service facilities, lack of resources and poor management.

There has been much debate on options for healthcare funding. Many models have been tried and still there is a need for finding more effective ways of financing public health services. One option that has recently been given a good deal of attention is public health insurance. Since 1967 Pakistan has had an insurance system in the form of its Social Security programme, but this is very limited in terms of the population and services covered (Eastern Mediterranean Regional Office, 2010). Social Security pays for medical services for employees of private sector industries, who are eligible after formal registration and a qualifying period of three months. This system is similar to employment-based health insurance found in many developed and developing countries. Employers pay Social Security contributions and employees incur no co-payments or any other direct costs when accessing health services. Coverage is equal for all insured individuals irrespective of individual health status and expenses. Social Security operates in the Provinces of Punjab, Khyber Pakhtunkhwa and Sindh (Eastern Mediterranean Regional Office, 2010).

State-owned enterprises and autonomous organizations have their own health services, or operate schemes for reimbursement of medical expenses. These include the Water and Power Development Authority and Pakistan International Airlines (Thatte et al., 2009). Public sector employees are entitled to free medical treatment at all public hospitals. They are also eligible for reimbursement of expenditures incurred on medicines. The medical reimbursement available to public sector employees and under social health insurance schemes, however, covers only around 5 per cent of the population. Government-funded services are intertwined with those of *Zakaat*, an Islamic system of charitable contributions. All in all, publicly provided health services and public health insurance are fragmented and still at the infant stage, with problems of eligibility and different benefit entitlements under different schemes. As noted, about three-quarters of the population pay out of pocket for the full cost of healthcare.

National health policy

In 1978 Pakistan endorsed the World Health Organization's (WHO) strategy of 'Health for All (HFA) by the year 2000'. The government declared its first National Health Policy (NHP) in January 1990, which aimed to provide universal health coverage in accordance with the HFA 2000 strategy (Ministry of Health, 1990). In 1997 the NHP was renewed and upgraded in line with modern health standards (Ministry of Health, 1997). In the third version of the NHP, in 2001, the government accepted the need for a more comprehensive policy. In 2008 a Health Policy Task Force (HPTF) was constituted to formulate a new health policy aspiring to universal health coverage along the lines of the National Health Service (NHS) in the UK (Government of Pakistan, 2010a). The draft version of this policy set new targets in terms of financing, planning and delivery. The NHP 2010 proposed universal social health insurance for the small formal sector and encouragement of micro-health insurance plans for the poor (Nishtar, 2010b). Progress on this agenda will require enhanced financial protection against private out-of-pocket expenditure and, in particular, medicine costs, which constitute a major share of private health expenditure.

The WHO in 2006 recommended health expenditures of US$34 per capita in developing countries. In that year, Pakistan spent US$18 per capita, of which the total government contribution was US$4 (Akram and Khan, 2007). Funding from international sources contributed to only about 7 per cent of total health expenditure. The average for low-income countries is above 14 per cent, and for Bangladesh it is more than 22 per cent (Federal Bureau of Statistics, 2009).

The healthcare system comprises a public sector, private for-profit, and private not-for-profit providers, and an informal sector. Some *hakims*—traditional *unani* (Greco-Arab) medical experts and homeopaths—are private practitioners, while others operate within the public sector. Until 2011 the public sector was made up of the national federal Ministry of Health and provincial and district health departments. The federal ministry was responsible for legislation and national health policy, including standards for medical education, medical equipment and manufacturing of pharmaceuticals. Other responsibilities included coordination with international agencies, management of federally run hospitals and planning, and management of national programmes for AIDS, malaria, tuberculosis and family planning (Akram and Khan, 2007; Mezzera, Aftab and Yusuf, 2010). Several federal ministry responsibilities have recently been decentralized. The provinces are now responsible for the delivery of health services, including the provision of resources to the districts for implementation of health programmes and supervision of their performance (Mezzera et al., 2010).

The pharmaceutical industry

At the time of independence, in 1947, there was no pharmaceutical manufacturing in Pakistan and drug needs were met through imports. Manufacturing operations commenced on a small scale after independence, but significant developments came only after 1980. The local industry in Pakistan since the early 1980s has responded to domestic demand, growing to a value in 2007 of about Rs88 billion (US$1.2 billion) with an annual export of around US$100 million (0.22 per cent of the global pharmaceutical market). Between 1980 and 1999 the overall share of world exports of pharmaceuticals from developing countries fell, but Pakistan (together with a small number of other countries, including India and Indonesia) increased its share of global drug exports (WHO, 2004).

Machinery and equipment are mostly imported from China, Taiwan, Korea, India, Germany, the UK, the US and Japan. Active Pharmaceutical Ingredients (APIs) are imported at a cost of nearly US$450 million (Khan, 2012). In value terms the domestic market is divided about equally between local manufacturers and multinationals (Economist Intelligence Unit, 2012). There are 47,000 products registered and produced, as noted already, by 650 companies, including 31 multinationals (Government of Pakistan, 2010a). The industry produces various dosage forms, including tablets, capsules, syrups, suspension drops, creams, gels, ointments, ophthalmic/optic drops, infusions, insulin, suppositories, vaccines, liquid and powder injections, inhalers, vitamin sachets, disposable enemas and modified release dosages (TRTA, 2007). The Pharma Bureau represents the multinationals, while more than 100 local pharmaceutical firms are members of the Pakistan Pharmaceutical Manufacturers Association (PPMA, 2012).

In volume terms, the market is dominated by locally produced pharmaceuticals. These firms, however, rely on imported raw materials and standardized excipients, as there is little local API production. Local production of raw materials is restricted to amoxacillin, ampicillin, aspirin, cefixime, cefadroxil, cephalexin, cefradine, ciprofloxacine, cloxacillin, ephedrine, ephedrine sulphate, flucloxacillin, furazolidone, ibuprofen, magnesium stearate, methyl salicylate, norfloxacillin, sulphamethoxazole and paracetamol. Some of these locally produced APIs do not meet the entire needs of the industry, and a high proportion of special grades are still imported (TRTA, 2007). The companies producing APIs include Army Welfare Pharmaceuticals and Himont Pharmaceuticals. Army Welfare Pharmaceuticals produces APIs for aspirin, paracetamol and methyl salicylate, while ibuprofen and sulphamethoxazole are manufactured by Himont Pharmaceuticals (Himont Group, 2012). That Pakistani pharmaceutical products are of good quality is acknowledged and accepted by many quality certification authorities. For example, quality accreditation has been given by the EU (German Good Management Practice) and the Ministries of Health of Yemen, Uzbekistan, UAE, Turkmenistan, Senegal, Tanzania, Canada, Sudan and Sri Lanka (TRTA, 2007).

Medicines regulation

Medicines regulation in Pakistan is focused on product quality and pricing. The Drug Act 1976 provides the legal basis for the regulation of quality, imports, exports, production, storage, distribution and sale of medicines, as well as price controls (Government of Pakistan, 1976; Nishtar, 2010a). The Drug Control Organization at the Ministry of Health was until recently the main regulatory body responsible for medicines, whether manufactured locally, imported or exported (Drug Control Organization, 2008). Product and quality regulation included registration of medicines, grant of manufacturing and marketing licences, and regulation of retailing. However, under the eighteenth amendment of Pakistan's Constitution in April 2010, responsibility for 'health' was decentralized and assigned to the provinces (Government of Pakistan, 2010b). Hence, Pakistan's central drug control organization, along with its parent Ministry of Health, ceased to exist. The four provinces were expected to develop their individual drug regulatory mechanisms, but were hampered by weak infrastructure and lack of qualified personnel (Ahmed, 2012).

In January 2012 an incident involving serious adverse reactions to a medication occurred in Lahore, where 150 patients died and more than 450 patients were admitted to hospital. An investigation established that an anti-anginal medicine (isosorbide mononitrate) was contaminated with large quantities of pyrimethamine, which resulted in an overdose and bone marrow suppression (British Broadcasting Corporation, 2012; Nishtar, 2012).

It was recognized that this disaster could have resulted from the regulatory vacuum that had opened up as a consequence of the transfer of regulatory responsibility to the provinces (Malik et al., 2012; Nishtar and Mehboob, 2011).

On 6 February 2012, taking note of this tragedy, Pakistan's Supreme Court directed the federal government to establish a central drug regulatory authority. In the same month all four provincial assemblies passed resolutions requesting that the federal government establish an independent drug regulatory authority (Ahmed, 2012). On 17 February 2012 the President of Pakistan ordered that a national drug regulatory authority be established to assume the responsibilities of the previous Drugs Control Organization (Government of Pakistan, 2012).

It should be noted that the government approved the establishment of an independent federal drug regulation authority in 2005, but the Ministry of Health moved slowly because it was reluctant to relinquish its own direct control (Nishtar, 2012). Now the new authority will not only be responsible for issuing production licences but also for the registration and quality of medicines. A drug regulatory authority should be independent and free from the influence of the pharmaceutical industry. This, however, is not consistent with the government mindset and customary relations between regulators and the industry. Rather, the pharmaceutical policy agenda is largely driven by the pharmaceutical industry, and a public health perspective is only weakly represented (Babar et al., 2011).

Medicines pricing

Medicines pricing in Pakistan is controlled by government. This is in contrast to the more market-oriented approach to pricing in, for example, Malaysia, Thailand, the Philippines and Indonesia (Babar et al., 2007). The Price Review Committee, a subcommittee of the Drug Registration Board formed under the Drug Act 1976, until 1993 set the maximum wholesale and retail price for each medicine, with the maximum retail price printed on the medicine package. In that year, the pricing system changed such that all products were divided, for the purpose of pricing, into the categories of controlled or decontrolled drugs, with prices in both categories being regulated by government. About 800 essential medicines were placed on the controlled list. Prices for products on this list were subjected to periodic across the board increases on account of the general rate of inflation and changes in the rupee exchange rate. A more liberal system applies for products in the decontrolled category, with higher price increases allowed at more frequent intervals (Drug Control Organization, 2008; Kiani, 2009).

The maximum retail price is fixed on the basis of manufacturing costs and retail mark-ups. Shipping cost is an additional factor in the case of imported medicines. Prices of equivalent products in the South Asian

Association of Regional Cooperation (SAARC) countries (including India, Bangladesh and Sri Lanka) serve as reference points. In the absence of equivalent SAARC prices, international prices are taken into consideration. Locally manufactured products for export are not subject to the price control mechanism.

Notwithstanding government price controls, regulatory flaws and the absence of transparency present problems. For instance, local manufacturers frequently cite inflated costs of imported raw materials and packaging as a reason for price hikes, but APIs are in many cases exempted from excise duty. Hence, there is always scope for scaling down estimates of product costs by investigating the individual price-related components (Nishtar, 2010a). The price control system is excessively complex, and in reality manufacturers are often able to increase prices unilaterally due to poor enforcement of regulations.

In 2004 a World Health Organization and Health Action International (HAI) pricing survey was conducted in Pakistan. Local prices were compared with international reference prices, and median price ratios were calculated (Kiani, 2009; Network, 2006; WHO/HAI, 2003). Where this ratio was <1 for the public sector (government hospitals, clinics and so on) and <2 for the private sector (private pharmacies, medical stores), prices were considered reasonable (Babar et al., 2007). Public procurement prices were found to be below international reference prices for generics and above them for originator products (Pakistan Pharmaceutical Profile, 2010). Although overall prices were found to be reasonable in the public sector, prices of branded versions of some off-patent drugs, such as ciprofloxacin, atenolol and acyclovir, were very high when compared with the international reference price. Some generic prices, for example for ciprofloxacin, a commonly used antibiotic, were also found to be high. This is of particular concern given that 77 per cent of pharmaceutical expenditures are paid for out of pocket (Kiani, 2009; WHO, 2004).

Moreover, chronic shortages and non-availability of essential medicines are common in government health facilities. This partly explains why an estimated 67 per cent of patients consult private physicians and seek treatment almost three times more often from a private pharmacy than from a basic health unit or rural health centre. Physicians have dispensing rights, and it is common practice for patients to receive medicines from their physician as part of the consultation, instead of filling a prescription at the pharmacy (Kiani, 2009). The physician usually charges a global consultation fee which includes dispensed medications, so that what patients actually pay for medicines is not transparent. As already emphasized, only a small proportion of the population has access to any form of health insurance that covers the cost of medicines. This means that at least 45 million people living below the national poverty line (29 per cent of the population) have no, or very limited, access to basic essential medicines (Kiani, 2009).

Previously, drug inspectors from the Drug Control Organization visited pharmaceutical companies to audit and assure the quality of medicines produced (Drug Control Organization, 2008). They also visited private retail pharmacies to ensure adherence to relevant price regulation controls, but they never had the capacity to effectively monitor adherence to price controls (Network, 2006). Following the problems of decentralization to the provinces, one of the functions of the newly formed independent drug regulatory authority is to control medicine prices throughout the country (Government of Pakistan, 2012).

The local generics pharmaceutical industry

Pakistan was a pioneering nation in introducing a mandatory scheme for use of generic names following the implementation of the Drugs Act 1972 (Generic Names). This legislation prohibited manufacturing, distribution and prescription by brand or proprietary name (Quraeshi et al., 1983). The objective was to make local manufacturers competitive with the multinational companies, which was expected to result in lower medicine prices.

The generics drug policy operated only until 1975, when manufacturing licences for 38 companies were suspended on account of substandard drug manufacture (*Medical Gazette*, 1975). This cancellation had an adverse impact on all local manufacturers, including those producing quality medicines (Quraeshi et al., 1983). At the same time, multinational companies accelerated their efforts to persuade doctors to prescribe under the name of the manufacturer along with the generic name. They also revamped packaging by using exaggerated colours or pictorial representations unique to each company, promoting their brands via mass media campaigns and through discounting and bonuses to retailers. This marketing effort resulted in the multinationals retaining their market share in the presence of generics competition, and the plan to bring down prices eventually failed. In 1976, after scrutiny of this experience, the Director General of Health issued orders that terminated the compulsory requirement of manufacturing and marketing by generic names (Quraeshi et al., 1983).

A study by the WHO/HAI on medicine prices and availability has shown that both consumers and prescribers favour brand products and believe generics to be of lower quality (WHO/HAI, 2003). Only 50 per cent of medicines are prescribed as generics (WHO, 2004). It is noteworthy that there are very few well-established laboratories with the capacity to conduct bioequivalence studies (Ali, 2007). In a country with such a huge and poor population, however, it is imperative that the use of cheaper generics be maximized. There is a clear need to sensitize patients, prescribers and providers to increase the judicious use of generic medicines (Babar and Jamshed, 2008). This requires improvement of the quality of generic medicines and government backing for the promotion of generics to physicians and pharmacists, as well as to patients. Several recent studies recommend educating prescribers and consumers about the quality and efficacy of generic medicines (Jamshed et al., 2011a, 2011b, 2011c).

National drug policy

In 1996 a comprehensive national drug policy was drafted that included the objective of increased local production and procurement of essential medicines (Mirza, 1996). This policy was opposed by the pharmaceutical industry, and the upshot was that the initiative largely failed (Mirza, 1996). In 1997 another drug policy was announced. According to critics, it had an industry bias and was full of ambitious, incoherent and non-committal plans (Tahirkheli, 2006; The Network, 1998). It did not address difficult trade-offs and competing interests, such as reconciling the promotion of exports with the rational use of drugs. There is also little evidence that policy makers have since made any serious attempt—or have the capability—to tackle such issues. The current national drug policy, which claims to be a draft to meet the challenges of the medicines sector, is available on the Ministry of Health website. A more comprehensive drug policy and more effective implementation are clearly required (Tahirkheli, 2006).

The government does support the drug industry, for reasons of economic development. In 2007 the import duty on pharmaceutical products was reduced, but manufacturers did not lower prices in response. Moreover, one of the challenges for pharmaceutical production for exports is the non-availability of a bioequivalence test laboratory (Anon, 2011; Yasir, 2007). Many potential export markets will no longer accept generic medicines that cannot present bioavailability and bioequivalence certificates (TRTA, 2007).

There is tension between support for industry growth and national medicines policies in most countries. In developed countries, however, such issues are widely debated and the trade-offs are well understood. But in Pakistan there is little academic and scholarly research on such problems, and industrial achievements are too often considered a panacea. This approach is evident when the Pakistan government disregards environmental destruction in favour of production as a source of revenue and jobs. Industrial growth is then viewed as a means of generating resources for the health sector. But there is little evidence that financial earnings have been properly used for better healthcare. While the country's GDP has risen, Pakistan in 2010 spent a mere 0.7 per cent of its budget on health (Perera, 2010). The pharmaceutical industry claims to manufacture a wide range of research-based medicines (Mooraj, 2005), but its research capacity is insignificant (Babar et al., 2011). As noted, most raw materials are imported and the industry is mostly producing finished products. Despite the rhetoric, in 2006 the pharmaceutical industry's share of Pakistan's exports was a mere 0.34 per cent (Export Promotion Bureau, 2007).

Developed countries such as Japan, Germany, Switzerland and the UK have created enormous wealth from the pharmaceutical industry through innovation, while maintaining a strong emphasis on access and affordability. In the UK, drug companies have to invest in research and development (R&D) proportionate to their revenues, but in Pakistan there is little regulation or monitoring of how much the industry is spending on drug promotion versus R&D. Another example of the weakness of Pakistan's national medicine policy is the lack of skilled human resources and expertise in the field of health and pharmaceutical policy. For example, the former Pricing Board of the Ministry of Health did not include a health economist (Drug Control Organization, 2008).

Intellectual property rights and medicines

Pakistan is a member of the World Trade Organization (WTO). In 2006 the government established an Intellectual Property Organization (IPO) to ensure that TRIPS-compliant IPR legislation is administered effectively. Its remit is to address institutional inadequacies in the implementation of intellectual property protection. The mission statement of the IPO is to 'integrate and upgrade intellectual property (IP) infrastructure for improved service delivery; increased public awareness and enhanced enforcement coordination for achieving the goal of being an IP based nation' (Intellectual Property Organization, 2007). The intellectual property legislation encompasses the Copyright Amendment Ordinance 2000; the Patents Ordinance 2001, as amended by the Patents (Amendment) Ordinance 2002; the Registration of Layout Designs of Integrated Circuits Ordinance 2000; the Industrial Designs Ordinance 2000; and the Trademarks Ordinance 2000, previously the Trademarks Act 1940 (Asif and Awan, 2006; WTO Cell, 2006).

Patents are registered under the Patents Ordinance 2002 (previously the Patents & Designs Act 1911) and trademarks are registered under the Trademarks Ordinance 2001. The Patents Ordinance 2002 confers on the patentee exclusive privilege for making, selling and using an invention throughout Pakistan and of authorizing others so to do. The primary purpose of this ordinance is to protect new inventions and to encourage industrial growth.

Until 2001 protection for patents was only for processes, and the duration of protection was 16 years. Since 1989 Pakistan has been on the US Trade Representative's 'Special 301' Watch List due to alleged violations of copyrights and patents. In 1996, however, the government expeditiously moved to provide a form of interim protection for certain qualifying pharmaceutical products through a 'mailbox' provision, as per its obligations under TRIPS (Consumer Project on Technology, 1999).

Under the Patents Ordinance 2000 (promulgated in 2001) and as per Article 27 of TRIPS covering patentable subject matter, the duration of patent protection has now been set at 20 years, and the scope of patents has been extended to both products and processes. The government has also provided better protection for IPR by ensuring effective implementation of Patents

Ordinance 2000. Under this law both the patent owner and licensees can file a suit against an infringer. The local industry, however, argues that extension of the patent period will fortify the monopoly of multinational companies. The industry historically has been dependent on manufacturing basic generic medicines, but in the recent past it has started to manufacture some recently off-patented products.

Lamivudine is one such example, for which the patent expired on 30 April 2011. The local company, Biocare, started to manufacture lamivudine, but the process patent was challenged by GlaxoSmithKline (GlaxoSmithKline, 2007). The Additional District Judge granted an *ex parte* interim injunction preventing its manufacture and sale by generics companies. Biocare argued that its manufacturing process for lamivudine was different, and submitted details of that process. It also argued that the basic patent had expired, and that subsequent patents were patents of addition, which had expired at the same time as the basic patent. After a full hearing the application for an injunction was dismissed and the High Court issued interim orders restraining Biocare from manufacturing, selling or supplying lamivudine products. The Supreme Court dismissed Biocare's appeal and held that the order of the High Court was just and proper (Khan, 2008).

In another example, Lilly vs. Werrick (a national company), the Islamabad Additional District Court held that patent infringement had occurred. The court held that by launching and selling the disputed pharmaceutical product the infringer had violated a decree of the trial court. The patent holder then initiated proceedings against the infringer for enforcement and execution of the decree (Khan, 2008). This example again suggests that a strict implementation of IPR and process patents will decrease the options available to domestic firms. This could increase the price of medicines and hence could have implications for access to medicines and public health. For instance, around 5 per cent of Pakistan's population has hepatitis (Agencies, 2011) and the non-availability of locally manufactured lamivudine means that patients have to buy branded lamivudine out of pocket, putting this medicine out of the reach of most patients.

In accordance with the Doha Declaration (WTO, 2001), Pakistan's IPR legislation provides for key flexibilities under TRIPS, including Bolar exceptions and parallel importing provisions. To date, however, no compulsory licences have been issued (Pakistan Pharmaceutical Profile, 2010). Patents are granted irrespective of whether drugs are produced locally or imported. There are no legal provisions for data exclusivity or for patent extension for pharmaceuticals. Also, there is no legal provision for linkage between patent status and marketing authorization (Drug Control Organization, 2008).

Neighbouring countries, such as India and Bangladesh, operate in different patent scenarios. Bangladesh is designated as a Least Developed Country (LDC) and has suspended intellectual property protection until 2016, which allows low drug prices. In India multinational manufacturers campaigned for data protection, and companies like Ranbaxy and Dr Reddy's, which invest in R&D, welcomed better patent protection. The scenario of strategic alliances between multinationals and Indian generics companies, together with an increase in the market share of multinationals in the formulation market, suggests that they may again come to dominate the Indian pharmaceutical industry (Chaudhuri, 2011).

Pakistan, as noted, has carried out a comprehensive overhaul of its intellectual property legislation, which must now be considered adequate and effective from a TRIPS perspective. Critics, however, continue to argue that IPR protection for pharmaceuticals is weak, with Pakistan in 2011 remaining on the US Trade Representative's Watch List (Economist Intelligence Unit, 2012). There have been cases of infringements of patented processes for pharmaceuticals, as well as patented compounds and compositions, by local generics manufacturers. However, with statutory changes now in place, it is up to IPR holders to assert their rights through legal proceedings (Khan, 2008).

As mentioned above, many court cases are won by multinational companies, and the local pharmaceutical industry puts some onus on the Pakistan Patent Office (PPO) for this. According to the industry, the PPO is not fully equipped to cope with the challenges posed by TRIPS and the new domestic IPR regime. The PPO, for example, has begun issuing examination reports in respect of 'black box' applications, and the pharmaceutical sector is concerned that improper, ineffective and non-comprehensive examinations of black box applications will result in a large number of product patents, evergreening of patents and patents that go beyond the stipulated 20 years. In a survey conducted in 2007, the local industry perspective was that of acceptance of the new IPR regime, but it is the view of local companies that legislation should be applied fairly and that misuse or abuse of intellectual property laws by multinationals should be prevented (TRTA, 2007).

Free trade agreements and the pharmaceutical industry

An FTA is a settlement between two or more countries to lower or eliminate tariff and non-tariff barriers for the purpose of enhancing welfare through trade and investment. Free trade negotiations with the US are often criticized for inclusion of TRIPs-plus provisions that, for example, increase the *de facto* patent term beyond 20 years, thus hampering production of and access to generic medicines (Babar et al., 2011).

Pakistan is a signatory to the South Asian Free Trade Agreement (SAFTA, 2012), which is an extension of the South Asian Association of Regional Cooperation (SAARC) Preferential Trading Arrangement into a free trade area among SAARC members (Bangladesh, Bhutan, India, Nepal, Maldives, Pakistan and Sri Lanka). The South Asian Free Trade Area's framework agreement envisages a reduction in tariffs to 0–5 per cent and removing quantitative barriers to trade within ten years by its LDC members—Nepal, Bhutan and Maldives—and between seven to eight years in the case of India, Pakistan, Bangladesh and Sri Lanka. Negotiations are ongoing for signing FTAs with Bangladesh, Turkey and Kenya. In April 2005, during Chinese Premier Wen Jiabao's visit to Pakistan, the two countries announced the launch of negotiations on a free trade area, and a FTA was entered into in November 2006, taking effect in July 2007 (China FTA Network, 2012). The impact of these FTAs on access to medicines, pricing and public health is unknown because research-based studies and empirical evidence are scarce. It is, therefore, vital that in the midst of all the concessions and flexibilities the impact of each FTA on the domestic pharmaceutical industry is carefully analysed.

In 2009 Pakistan's Ministry of Health approved the importation of lifesaving drugs from China and India under respective FTAs, regardless of threats to the development of the domestic drugs market or local production. The Ministry also allowed the importation of finished products, such as anti-cancer vaccines and thalassaemia medicines not manufactured in Pakistan. The government, more recently, has agreed in principle to grant 'most favoured nation' status to India, although there is a need to consider the implications of this for the local pharmaceutical industry (Zaman, 2011).

There are two dimensions to the wave of FTAs and most favoured nation status between neighbouring countries, including China and India. First is the likely effect of these agreements on the pricing of medicines in the local market: drug prices are higher in Pakistan than in India, so importing medicines from India could pose challenges for local manufacturers, who have repeatedly opposed extension of both types of agreements to include pharmaceutical imports. Second, there is the issue of illegal importation of medicines from India: Pakistan shares a long border with India and the Pakistani government has so far been unable to control smuggling of medicine from India. It is likely that, if the government includes medicines in the list of imports from India, prices of locally manufactured generic medicines will significantly decline and illegal imports will be curbed (Government of India, 2011). In addition, this will be a new challenge to the multinational pharmaceutical companies, which are selling similar products at comparatively lower prices in India than in Pakistan (Laskar, 2011).

Concluding remarks

The pharmaceutical industry in Pakistan is a vibrant sector which meets most of the domestic demand for medicines. The industry has the advantage of a big population, with a growing middle class and the availability of a large pool of skilled manpower, including engineers, pharmacists and chemists. This potential, however, has not been fully exploited in terms of innovation and development of new products and processes. Although Pakistani firms export some medicines to African and Central

Asian countries, the industry must increase its capacity in terms of manufacturing raw material, operating new bioavailability laboratories and establishing research links with universities.

The government supports the local pharmaceutical industry, but policy makers should understand that increasing the number of companies and molecules in the market will not guarantee universal access to medicines. To promote access to medicines, the government needs to carefully monitor price control mechanisms and other affordability measures, such as cost sharing schemes and health insurance programmes. Government support for the industry should also not compromise medicines regulation and quality standards. Although many pharmaceutical companies produce medicines of good quality, the industry as a whole has to improve its standards regarding safety, effectiveness and quality.

The new drug regulatory authority faces a huge task in terms of monitoring and regulating prices, production and product quality, distribution and ensuring equitable access to medicines. For evidence-based decision making, the drug regulatory authority should develop linkages with universities to generate research-based evidence on pharmaceutical policy and the drug supply chain. It is also imperative that the newly created drug regulatory authority be free from the influence of the industry and managed professionally.

Pakistan has tightened its IPR legislation, which may increase overseas investment in the pharmaceutical sector, but could also impact negatively on the production and accessibility of medicines. Empirical evidence on these issues remains scarce, and there is a dire need for research to assess the full impact of the new IPR regime on the local medicines situation. With an increasing number of FTAs, it is also imperative that the effects of such agreements on access to medicines be carefully assessed.

References

Agencies (2011) 'Ten Per cent of Pakistan's Population Suffering from Hepatitis', *Dawn*, 20 March, http://dawn.com/2011/03/20/10-per-cent-of-pakistans-population-suffering-from-hepatitis/, date accessed 28 March 2012.

Ahmed, S. I. (2012) 'Drug Regulation Follows Heart Patient Deaths', *Dawn*, 12 March, http://www.dawn.com/2012/03/12/drug-regulation-follows-heart-patient-deaths.html, date accessed 26 March 2012.

Akram, M. and F. J. Khan (2007) 'Health Care Service Delivery and Government Spending in Pakistan', *Pakistan Institute of Development Economics, Working Papers 2007*, http://www.pide.org.pk/pdf/Working%20Paper/WorkingPaper-32.pdf, date accessed 22 March 2012.

Ali, I. (2007) 'Drug Testing Lab Imperative to Check Quality Standards', *The News International*, http://www.translations-news.com/en/news/quality/93127/Drug_testing_lab_imperative_to_check_quality_standards.html, date accessed 6 February 2012.

Anon. (2011) 'Punjab to Establish Drug Testing', *Express Tribune*, 19 April, http://tribune.com.pk/story/152104/punjab-to-establish-drug-testing/, date accessed 5 March 2012.

Asif, M. and M. U. Awan (2006) 'Pakistani Pharmaceutical Industry in WTO Regime—Issues and Prospects', Institute of Quality and Technology Management, University of the Punjab, Lahore, Pakistan, http://pu.edu.pk/images/publication/PPI_in_WTO_%20regime-Issues_and_Prospects.pdf, date accessed 25 March 2012.

Babar, Z.-U.-D. and S. Jamshed (2008) 'Social Pharmacy Strengthening Clinical Pharmacy: Why Pharmaceutical Policy Research is Needed in Pakistan?', *Pharmacy World & Science* 30, 617–19.

Babar, Z.-U.-D., M. I. M. Ibrahim, H. Singh, N. I. Bukahri and A. Creese (2007) 'Evaluating Drug Prices, Availability, Affordability, and Price Components: Implications for Access to Drugs in Malaysia', *PLoS Med* 4, e82.

Babar, Z.-U.-D., M. I. M. Ibrahim and M. A. Hassali (2011) 'Pharmaceutical Industry, Innovation and Challenges for Public Health: Case Studies from Malaysia and Pakistan', *Journal of Pharmaceutical Health Services Research* 2, 193–204.

British Broadcasting Corporation (2012) 'Pakistan Heart Drugs: Lahore Death Toll Reaches 100', http://www.bbc.co.uk/news/world-asia-16742832, date accessed 5 March 2012.

Chaudhuri, S. (2011) 'Multinationals and Monopolies: Pharmaceutical Industry in India after TRIPS', Indian Institute of Management Calcutta, Working Paper 685, http://apps.who.int/medicinedocs/en/m/abstract/Js19026en/, date accessed 22nd March 2012.

China FTA Network (2012) 'The China Pakistan FTA', http://fta.mofcom.gov.cn/topic/enpakistan.shtml, date accessed 5 March 2012.

Consumer Project on Technology (1999) 'Intellectual Property Barriers', http://www.cptech.org/ip/health/phrma/nte-99/pakistan.html, date accessed 24 March 2012.

Drug Control Organization (2008) *Drugs Control Organization* (Islamabad: Ministry of Health).

Drug Control Organization (2009) *Booklet of Drug Control Organization* (Islamabad: Ministry of Health), Eastern Mediterranean Regional Office (2010) 'Health Systems Profile—Pakistan Regional Health Systems Observatory', *EMRO*, Egypt, http://gis.emro.who.int/HealthSystemObservatory/PDF/Pakistan/Exec%20summary.pdf, date accessed 11 March 2012.

Economist Intelligence Unit (2012) 'The Pharmaceutical Market: Pakistan', http://www.espicom.com/prodcat2.nsf/Product_ID_Lookup/00000314?OpenDocument, date accessed 5 March 2012.

European Commission Trade Related Technical Assistance (2007) 'TRTA for Pakistan, European Commission, Trade Related Technical Assistance program for Pakistan, The Pharmaceutical Sector in Pakistan', http://www.tradecapacitypakistan.com/new/pdf/itc/SS2.pdf, date accessed 11 March 2012.

Export Promotion Bureau (2007) *Regional Country Variation Analysis* (Karachi: Export Promotion Bureau, Government of Pakistan).

Federal Bureau of Statistics (2009) 'National Health Accounts 2005–06', Statistics Division, Government of Pakistan.

GlaxoSmithKline (2007) 'Statement on Lamivudine Position', http://www.gsk-china.com/asp/News/client/newconten/515200784150.htm, date accessed 28 March 2012.

Government of India (2011) 'International Trade-Trade Agreements: Ministry of Commerce and Industry', http://commerce.nic.in/trade/international_ta_current_details.asp, date accessed 5 March 2012.

Government of Pakistan (1976) 'Pakistan Drug Act 1976', http://www.wipo.int/wipolex/en/details.jsp?id=8576, date accessed 6 March 2011.

Government of Pakistan (2006) *Economic Survey of Pakistan 2005–06* (Islamabad: Government of Pakistan).

Government of Pakistan (2010a) *National Health Policy Draft Document* (Islamabad: Ministry of Health), http://www.ilo.org/wcmsp5/groups/public/@ed_protect/@protrav/@ilo_aids/documents/legaldocument/wcms_117438.pdf, date accessed 5 March 2012.

Government of Pakistan (2010b) *Constitution (Eighteenth Amendment) Act*, http://www.pakistani.org/pakistan/constitution/amendments/18amendment.html, date accessed 6 March 2012.

Government of Pakistan (2012) *Establishment of Drug Regulatory Agency of Pakistan, Special Order* (Islamabad: Ministry of Law and Justice).

Himont Group (2012) 'Active Pharmaceutical Ingredients', http://www.himont.com/apis.php?id=8, date accessed 21 March 2012.

IMS Health (2007) 'Country Profile', http://www.imshealth.com/, date accessed 5 March 2012.

Intellectual Property Organization (2007) 'Introduction to IPO Pakistan', http://www.ipo.gov.pk/Contents/AboutIPO.aspx, date accessed 14 September 2011.

IPO *see* Intellectual Property Organization.

Jamshed, S., M. A. Hassali, M. I. M. Ibrahim and Z.-U.-D. Babar (2011a) 'Knowledge Attitude and Perception of Dispensing Doctors Regarding Generic Medicines in Karachi, Pakistan: A Qualitative Study', *Journal of Pakistan Medical Association* 61, 80–3.

Jamshed, S., M. I. M. Ibrahim and M. A. Hassali (2011b) 'Generic Medicines in Pakistan: A Questionable Boon', *International Journal of Clinical Pharmacy* 33, 53–4.

Jamshed, S., M. I. M. Ibrahim, A. A. Shafie, M. A. Hassali and Z.-U.-D. Babar (2011c) 'Generic Medicines in Pakistan: A Viable Cost-Effective Option for Consumers', *European Journal of Clinical Pharmacology* 67, 193–201.

Khan, H. I. (2008) 'Recent Trends in Patent Enforcement', United Trademark and Patent Services, http://www.buildingipvalue.com/08_AP/223-225UnitedTrademark.pdf, date accessed 24 March 2012.

Khan, N. (2012) 'Where Does Competitive Edge of Pakistan's Pharmaceutical Industry Lie?', Karachi, http://www.docstoc.com/docs/19713409/Where-does-Competitive-Edge-of-Pakistans-Pharmaceutical-Industry, date accessed 5 March 2012.

Kiani (2009) *Prices, Availability and Affordability of Medicines in Pakistan* (Islamabad: The Network for Consumer Protection), http://www.haiweb.org/medicineprices/surveys/200407PK/survey_report.pdf, date accessed 28 June 2011.

Laskar, R. H. (2011) 'Do Not Open Pharma Sector to Indian Cos: Pakistan Industry to Govt', http://news.in.msn.com/international/article.aspx?cp-documentid=5605900, date accessed 5 March 2012.

Malik, U., M. Khalil, A. Ulikpan and A. M. Ahmad (2012) 'A Tale of Devolution, Abolition, and Performance', *The Lancet* 379(981) 409.

Medical Gazette (1975) 'Licenses of Thirty-Eight Pharma-Firms Cancelled', 15 August.

Mezzera, M., S. Aftab and S. Yusuf (2010) 'Devolution Row: An Assessment of Pakistan's 2001 Local Government Ordinance', http://www.clingendael.nl/publications/2010/20101119_CRU_publicatie_mmezzera.pdf, date accessed 5 March 2012.

Ministry of Health (1990) *National Health Policy* (Islamabad: Government of Pakistan).

Ministry of Health (1997) *National Health Policy* (Islamabad: Government of Pakistan).

Ministry of Health (2009) *Final Draft National Health Policy* (Islamabad: Government of Pakistan), http://www.ilo.org/wcmsp5/groups/public/@ed_protect/@protrav/@

ilo_aids/documents/legaldocument/wcms_117438.pdf, date accessed 5 March 2011.
Mirza, Z. (1996) 'Islamabad Non-Emergence of Pakistan's National Drug Policy', *The Lancet* 348 (9020), 119.
Mooraj, Z. (2005) 'Pharmaceutical Industry', *Dawn* 24 June.
Network (2006) 'Prices, availability and affordability of medicines in Pakistan', *The Network for Consumer Protection*, http//www.haiweb.org/medicineprices/surveys/200407PK/survey_report.pdf, date accessed 8 July 2011.
The Network (1998) 'The Network For Consumer Protection', *Report of the Committee of the Task Force On "Review of Drug Act 1976"*, Islamabad, Pakistan.
Nishtar, S. (2010a) *Choked Pipes: Refining Pakistan's Mixed Health Systems* (Karachi, Sind: Oxford University Press).
Nishtar, S. (2010b) 'National Health Policy 2010', Islamabad, http://www.heartfile.org/pdf/73_National_Health_Policy_2010.pdf, date accessed April 2011.
Nishtar, S. (2012) 'Pakistan's Deadly Cocktail of Substandard Drugs', *The Lancet* 379 (9819), 10 March.
Nishtar, S. and A. B. Mehboob (2011) 'Pakistan Prepares to Abolish Ministry of Health', *The Lancet* 378 (9792), 648–9.
Pakistan Pharmaceutical Manufacturers Association (2012) 'Pakistan Pharmaceutical Industry', http://www.ppma.org.pk/PPMAIndustry.aspx, date accessed 5 March 2012.
Pakistan Pharmaceutical Profile (2010) 'World Health Organization', http://www.who.int/medicines/areas/coordination/pakistan.pdf, date accessed 5 March 2012.
Perera, S. (2010) 'Austerity Measures Unveiled in Pakistan's Budget', http://www.wsws.org/articles/2010/jun2010/paks-j16.shtml, date accessed 5 March 2012.
PPMA *see* Pakistan Pharmaceutical Manufacturers Association.
Quraeshi, Z. A., M. Luqmani and N. Malhotra (1983) 'Brands or Generics: The Dilemma of Pharmaceutical Marketing in a Developing Country', *Journal of Health Care Marketing* 3, 27–37.
SAFTA *see* South Asian Free Trade Area.
South Asian Free Trade Area (2012) 'Agreement on South Asian Free Trade Area', http://www.commerce.nic.in/trade/safta.pdf, date accessed 5 March 2012.
Tahirkheli, M. (2006) 'Critical analysis of Pakistan National Medicines Policy', *The Watch on Medicines*, Islamabad: The Network for Consumer Protection 15(5), 2006.
Thatte, U., S. Hussain, M. D. Rosas-Valera, M. A. Malik (2009) 'Evidence-Based Decision on Medical Technologies in Asia Pacific: Experiences from India, Malaysia, Philippines, and Pakistan', *Value in Health* 12(Suppl 3), S18–25.
TRTA *see* European Commission Trade Related Technical Assistance.
WHO *see* World Health Organization.
WHO/HAI *see* World Health Organization and Health Action International.
World Health Organization (2004) *The World Medicines Situation*, WHO/EDM/PAR/2004.5. (Geneva: World Health Organization), http://apps.who.int/medicinedocs/pdf/s6160e/s6160e.pdf, date accessed 5 February 2011.
World Health Organization and Health Action International (2003) *Medicine Prices: A New Approach to Measurement* (Geneva: World Health Organization).
World Trade Organization (2001) 'Declaration on the TRIPS Agreement and Public Health,' Doha WTO Ministerial 2001: TRIPS WT/MIN(01)/DEC/20 November, http://www.wto.org/english/thewto_e/minist_e/min01_e/mindecl_trips_e.htm, date accessed 5 March 2012.

World Trade Organization Cell (2006) 'Government of the Punjab, Lahore, Pakistan', http://www.wtopunjab.gov.pk/, date accessed 6 March 2012.

WTO *see* World Trade Organization.

WTO Cell *see* World Trade Organization Cell.

Yasir, M. (2007) 'Import Duty Cut to Boost Pharmaceutical Exports', *Daily Times*, 25 September, http://www.dailytimes.com.pk/default.asp?page=2007%5C09%5C25%5Cstory_25-9-2007_pg5_1, date accessed 5 March 2012.

Zaman, Q. (2011) 'Pakistan to Offer India Trade Concessions', *Express Tribune*, 12 October, http://tribune.com.pk/story/272550/pakistan-decides-to-grant-mfn-status-to-india-khar/, date accessed 5 March 2012.

10
TRIPS, Access to Medicines and Local Production in South Africa

Andrew L. Gray and Yousuf A. Vawda

As a leading economy on the African continent, but also the country most affected by HIV/AIDS and a high-burden tuberculosis country, South Africa has often been seen as a particularly important case study for access to medicines issues. The country has both an established generic medicines manufacturing industry and a notable presence of transnational pharmaceutical firms, some of which manufacture locally. South Africa also chose to be compliant with the Trade Related Aspects of Intellectual Property Rights (TRIPS) Agreement before the deadline imposed for developing countries. Nonetheless, intellectual property rights (IPR) concerns have been prominent in the struggle to reform medicines legislation since the change to democratic government in 1994. While South Africa has not taken full advantage of the flexibilities inherent in TRIPS—for instance, as outlined in the Doha Declaration (WTO, 2001)—access to generic anti-retroviral medicines (ARVs) has been a key enabler in allowing the country to place more than 1.2 million patients on life-prolonging treatment. Access to such products has depended on voluntary licences, which are often issued under duress. The legal levers used have included competition (anti-trust) law, but not the specific TRIPS flexibilities. As with many developing countries, however, South Africa faces new challenges in the form of bilateral trade negotiations and agreements, which potentially include strengthened TRIPS-plus IPR protection, specifically in relation to compulsory licensing and data protection (Sell, 2007).

This chapter provides a brief introduction to the organization and financing of the South African healthcare system and the challenges faced in terms of burden of disease. It then outlines the history of IPR protection in South Africa, the changes in domestic legislation necessitated by the TRIPS Agreement, and the degree to which the various flexibilities available under TRIPS are used in South Africa. Examples are provided of specific medicines access issues and how these have been resolved in recent years. The chapter then provides a brief description of the pharmaceutical sector in South Africa and how this sector has responded in the post-TRIPS era.

Access to healthcare in South Africa

South Africa is an upper middle-income country with an estimated population in mid-2010 of just under 50 million, almost 80 per cent of which is Black African. A comprehensive review of health and related indicators for South Africa is published each year in the *South African Health Review*. The data presented below are drawn from the 2010 edition (Day and Gray, 2010). In 2009 just over 41 million South Africans were not beneficiaries of a medical scheme—in other words, they were uninsured and dependent on either the state or out-of-pocket payment for all health services. For those who are uninsured, however, all health services at primary healthcare facilities are provided free of charge, and this includes medicines listed on the Essential Drugs List. In 2009 74.4 per cent of the White population was insured, compared with only 9.0 per cent of the Black African population. Those who are uninsured generally access healthcare services at clinics, community health centres and hospitals operated by the provincial and local authorities, but may also purchase services and products out of pocket in the private sector. Those who are insured generally access healthcare services from private health practitioners, pharmacies and private hospitals. Despite the vast majority of the population being uninsured, most health professionals practise in the for-profit private sector. In 2009 South Africa spent 8.9 per cent of gross domestic product (GDP) on health, with 5.2 per cent of GDP expended in the private sector and 3.7 per cent in the public sector. This disparity was also reflected in per capita expenditure, which was ZAR9605 (approximately US $1372) per medical scheme beneficiary in 2009, compared with ZAR2206 (US $315) per uninsured person in the 2009–2010 public sector fiscal year.

South Africa faces a quadruple burden of disease due to the ravages of HIV and AIDS, other infectious diseases, injuries and non-communicable diseases (Coovadia et al., 2009). As the population ages, the burden of non-communicable disease is expected to increase (Mayosi et al., 2009). However, the health problems that have received the greatest attention, and for which access to affordable quality medicines is an imperative, are the linked epidemics of HIV and tuberculosis (Abdool Karim et al., 2009). South Africa has both the largest number of HIV-infected persons of any country and also the largest number on ARV treatment.

Intellectual property protection in South Africa—the background

South Africa has had patent legislation since at least 1916, with the statute currently in force promulgated in 1978 (Republic of South Africa, 1978; Union of South Africa, 1916). The country undertook to become TRIPS-compliant in 1997 (Republic of South Africa, 1997a) with the passage of the Intellectual Property Laws Amendment Act. South Africa also became bound by the Patent Co-operation Treaty in 1999 (Burrell, 1999). Further amendments to the Patents Act 57 1978 were made in 2002 and 2005 (Republic of South Africa, 2002, 2005). While, on the face of it, agreements such as TRIPS appear to be the rational outcome of a process of international patent harmonization, they can also be viewed as further evidence of the extension of patent monopolies, as they simplify the process of obtaining IPR in developing countries. This was evident from the process and character of the negotiations which have resulted in such agreements and treaties (Drahos and Braithwaite, 2004).

Globally, compliance with the international intellectual property regime has come at great cost. Many developing countries have adopted it against their own best interests and out of fear of inviting trade sanctions. Countries such as South Africa and Brazil attracted the wrath of the US when they adopted legislation that used flexibilities in the TRIPS Agreement more broadly than the US wanted (Abbott, 2002; Bond, 1999). The 1997 amendments to the South African Medicines and Related Substances Control Act No. 101 1965 (Medicines Act) drew not only a legal challenge (Pharmaceutical Manufacturers' Association and Others v President of the Republic of South Africa and Others, case no. 4183/98, High Court of South Africa (Transvaal Provincial Division)), but also saw the US Trade Representative placing South Africa on its 301 Watch List, a precursor to sanctions. At about the same time, the US lodged a complaint with the WTO Dispute Resolution Panel against Brazil regarding its compulsory licensing legislation. The South African case was only withdrawn after intense international scrutiny. The complaint against Brazil was also withdrawn.

Such strong-arm tactics, however, persist to the present day in trade negotiations between the developed and developing countries. South Africa has recently engaged in negotiations on a free trade agreement (FTA) with the US through its participation in the Southern African Customs Union, and, although the formal FTA talks have proved inconclusive, there are ongoing discussions on selected trade topics that have significance for access to medicines and generics production (Anonymous, 2006). As a result, many countries that have negotiated bilateral or regional FTAs have adopted measures in their patents systems which go beyond the requirements of the TRIPS Agreement (hence the moniker of TRIPS-plus). An example of such measures is the heightened level of protection for clinical test data demanded by pharmaceutical manufacturers, which is not mandated by Article 39 of TRIPS, and which the US is routinely demanding be included in bilateral and regional trade negotiations.

South Africa's patent legislation already contains more stringent conditions than are necessary under international law (Republic of South Africa, 1978). Examples include the disclosure standards (Section 32) and the process for compulsory licensing (Section 56). Furthermore, South Africa has not made full use of provisions in its existing medicines law to take measures to improve the accessibility of medicines (such as the provisions to allow parallel importation), nor has it made the necessary legislative amendments consequent to the flexibilities provided in the Doha Declaration and subsequent 30 August 2003 Agreement (WTO, 2001; WTO Council for TRIPS, 2003).

The constitutional framework

The post-apartheid South African Constitution contains several provisions dealing with socio-economic rights in general, and health rights in particular (Republic of South Africa, 1996). These include the right to access healthcare (section 27); bodily and psychological integrity (Section 12(2)); privacy (Section 14(a)); and the right to an environment that is not harmful to health or wellbeing (Section 24(a)). In addition, the state must respect, protect, promote and fulfil the rights in the Bill of Rights (Section 7(2)), including socio-economic rights. These obligations collectively mean that the state is required not only to refrain from the unfair and unreasonable curtailment of a person's rights, but also to take proactive measures to, for example, develop and implement a comprehensive legal framework for the realization of those rights and to create the necessary conditions under which individuals may be enabled to themselves realize those rights. Most importantly, it provides a universal right to access to healthcare services, and requires the state to take reasonable legislative and other measures, within its available resources, to achieve the progressive realization of this right (Sections 27(1) and (2)).

This latter right is, however, subject to two important qualifications, namely, that it must be progressively realized, and that it is subject to available resources. The leading decision on the issue of access to medicines is undoubtedly the Treatment Action Campaign (TAC) case (Minister of Health & Others v Treatment Action Campaign and Others 2002 (5) SA 721 (CC) and Minister of Health and Others v Treatment Action Campaign and Others (no. 2) 2002 (5) SA 717; 2002 (10) BCLR 1033 (CC)). First, the judgement affirmed the centrality of access to medicines in the realization of the right of access to healthcare. Second, it recognized that constraints on the public purse are not necessarily an impediment to the realization of rights. Third, the Court stood firm on the challenge to its authority to make pronouncements on policy matters, in various guises, notably under the separation of powers doctrine. It recognized that disputes over socio-economic rights invariably require the evaluation of state policy and an order for 'appropriate relief' where such policy is inconsistent with the Constitution, which could include mandatory orders and supervisory jurisdiction or structural interdicts. Finally, the decision elaborated the understanding of the concept of 'progressive realization of rights' as not merely signifying 'pious wishes' but entailing a serious commitment to the delivery of healthcare services (Mathipa and Budlender, 2002, p. 29).

The tension between the attainment of human rights (in particular, the right of access to healthcare) and trade and intellectual property rules that impede the realization of those rights will not be resolved if medicines continue to be viewed as private items of consumption. It is increasingly contended that medicines, already subject to a significant degree of regulation, must be construed as public goods because of their critical public health and public interest impacts (Parmet, 2006). In addition to specific IPR law, South Africa also has competition (anti-trust) legislation—the Competition Act No 89 1998 (Competition Act), which permits divestiture as a remedy for anti-competitive practices. Section 15C of the Medicines Act also allows the Minister to enable parallel importation in order to facilitate affordable access to medicines. One may ask: is this interference with the rights of pharmaceutical patent holders constitutionally tenable, or does it violate their protected private property interests? The test of reasonableness entails a balancing of interests and rights, the public interest served by saving lives taking precedence over the private commercial interests of the patent holder. Where there is a conflict between the right to health and private property protection the 'constitutional right will always trump policy' (Davis, 1992, p. 480). This principle has also been tested in law (Ex parte Chairperson of the Constitutional Assembly: In re Certification of the Constitution of the Republic of South Africa 1996 (4) SA 744 (CC)).

Components of South Africa's patent regime

Compliance with the TRIPS Agreement required relatively few, though critical, amendments in 1997. The key relevant features of the patent regime are recounted below.

Patent standards

The Patents Act provides that a patent 'may be granted for any new invention which involves an inventive step and which is capable of being used or applied in trade or industry or agriculture' (Section 25(1)).

Novelty

Novelty requires that the invention be new, namely, that it has not previously been described (usually in writing) or widely used. As regards this requirement, the Act states that 'an invention shall be deemed to be new if it does not form part of the state of the art immediately before the priority date of that invention' (Section 25(5)).

Inventiveness

An invention is deemed to involve an inventive step 'if it is not obvious to a person skilled in the art' having regard to any matter already available to the public (Section 25(10)). In other words, it must be a step beyond routine discovery, or more than the mere adding together of previously known products or processes (for example, Gentiruco AG v Firestone SA (Pty) Ltd 1971 BP 58 (A) 172) and that 'the objection based on a lack of inventiveness is one of long standing in our patent law' (Ensign-Bickford (South Africa) (Pty) Ltd and Others v AECI Explosives and Chemicals Limited 1998 BIP271 (SCA) 281).

New uses of an invention

Having considered the parameters of what is patentable, the question arises: in defining patentability criteria in respect of medicines, should new uses of the invention (other than its originally intended use) or new forms (for example, use in paediatric as opposed to adult therapy) be excluded from patentability? Would such instances constitute novelty and an inventive step? In general, the position South African courts have adopted is that, once a substance forms part of the state of the art, a new or second use thereof will not make it eligible for a new patent (Burrell, 1999). This interpretation is consistent with the relative freedom countries have to opt for higher standards for the requirement of inventiveness (UNCTAD–ICTSD, 2005). India is a good example of how this flexibility (Section 3(d)) can be used to disallow the patenting of a new form of a known substance that does not result in enhanced efficacy, or a new use of a known substance or process (Republic of India, 2005). However, as South Africa does not have an examination system for patent applications, the appropriate standard is not likely to be observed unless subjected to a legal challenge through revocation or infringement proceedings (such as in H Lundbeck A/S & Another v Cipla Medpro (Pty) Ltd 2008 BIP 79).

Industrial applicability

The requirement that the invention must be one 'which is capable of being used or applied in trade or industry or agriculture' (Section 25(1)) resonates with the concept of utility found in many jurisdictions. South African courts have held that 'useful' bears the 'special meaning of effective to produce the result aimed at' or promised (Burrell, 1999, p. 182). In other words, for an invention to be 'useful', any suitably knowledgeable person following the specifications of the patent must be able to make the invention.

Disclosure

The South African equivalent of the disclosure provision spells out the contents of a specification in some detail. It requires an abstract; a sufficient description illustrating or exemplifying the invention and the manner of performance; and the claim(s) defining the invention, which have to be clear and fairly based on the matter disclosed in the specification (Sections 32(3) and 32(4)).

Opposition procedures

South African legislation makes no provision for opposition procedures, limiting the examination of applications and specifications to the Registrar of Patents, who is empowered to grant the application if it complies with the requirements of the Act (Section 34). However, inspection by the public is permitted after the patent has been sealed and granted.

Furthermore, there appears to be a complete lack of transparency in the patent processing process, as the statute merely requires of the registrar a formal tick-box approach to an application (Section 34). Given that patent grants, particularly in the case of essential medicines, have such far-reaching impacts on the broader public, the process ought to accommodate public scrutiny and comment. Perhaps the best method of achieving this participation is through the opportunity to file a pre-grant opposition. Once again, the Indian experience is instructive, where Sections 25(1) and 25(2) of the Indian Patents Amendment Act 15 2005 (Indian Patents Act) provide for both pre- and post-grant opposition (Republic of India, 2005).

Exclusions from patentability

South African legislation covers most of the exclusions envisaged by TRIPS Article 27, namely, inventions that encourage offensive or immoral behaviour (Section 25(4)(a)); any plant or animal variety or any essentially biological process for their production, excluding a microbiological process or its product (Section 25(409b)); as well as any surgical, therapeutic or diagnostic method of treatment of humans or animals (Section 25(11)). Furthermore, the South African Patents Act empowers the Registrar of Patents to refuse any application that is frivolous or whose use encourages illegal, immoral and offensive behaviour, and the prohibition extends to publication or exploitation of the invention as well (Section 36). As the concepts of morality and offensive behaviour are relative, particularly in a diverse and evolving society such as South Africa, it is unclear how this provision is to be applied.

Exceptions

There is no general provision in South African law equivalent to Article 30 of TRIPS, but through its provisions relating to infringement the Patents Act specifies two instances of exceptions: the use of patented inventions aboard convention vessels, aircraft or land vehicles temporarily or accidentally within territorial waters or in the Republic, and the making, use, exercise, disposal, offer to dispose and importing of the patented invention for purposes of obtaining regulatory approval for the manufacture, production, distribution, use or sale of any product (sections 69 and 69A of the Patents Act). The latter, Bolar-type exception allows a generics producer seeking to register a follow-on equivalent of a previously approved or registered medicine to begin product development and compilation of the required registration dossier even before a patent has expired.

South African legislation is, however, lacking to the extent that it makes no provision for educational, experimental and research exceptions, or for the export of an invention manufactured on a non-commercial scale in pursuance of the early working exception.

Compulsory licensing

The Patents Act permits the granting of compulsory licences under two broad categories: for dependent patents (Section 55) and in instances of abuse of patent rights (Section 56). The latter is of more direct significance to access to medicines. It sets out four circumstances under which patent rights are deemed to be abused, namely:

1. If the patented invention is not being worked in the Republic on a commercial scale or to an adequate extent
2. If the demand for the patented article in the Republic is not being met to an adequate extent and on reasonable terms
3. If the refusal of the patentee to grant a licence on reasonable terms prejudices trade, industry or agriculture
4. If the demand in the Republic for the patented article is being met by importation and the price is excessive compared with the price in the country of manufacture.

No compulsory licences have to date been granted on pharmaceutical products in South Africa, although there are a handful of reported decisions on the issue. For example, the Supreme Court of Appeal rejected an application for a compulsory licence on the grounds of abuse of patent being nonworking and failure to license (Syntheta (Pty) Ltd v Janssen Pharmaceutica NV & Another 1999 (1) SA 85 SCA) on the grounds that the applicant had not placed sufficient information before it to establish the abuse alleged.

Finally, on the issue of compulsory licences, South African law has not incorporated the important flexibility contained in the Doha Declaration facilitating such licences for public health emergencies.

Government use

Section 4 of the Patents Act provides that 'a Minister of State may use an invention for public purposes on such conditions as may be agreed upon with the patentee, or in default of agreement on such conditions as are determined by the commissioner on application by or on behalf of such Minister and after hearing the patentee.' Further, section 78 states that 'The Minister may, on behalf of the State, acquire, on such terms and conditions as may be agreed upon, any invention or patent.' Under Section 25(2) of the Constitution the government could also 'take' or expropriate the patent, subject to just compensation.

Voluntary licences

In South African law a voluntary licence is an 'authorisation given by a patentee to another to invade the patent monopoly with impunity' (Burrell, 1999, p. 297). A voluntary licence may take one of three forms: non-exclusive (where the patentee may still grant licences to others); exclusive (all others, including the patentee, are excluded); and sole (all others, with the exception of the patentee, are excluded) (Burrell, 1999).

The best-known cases of voluntary licences in respect of pharmaceuticals are those granted as part of the settlement of the Competition Commission complaint against GlaxoSmithKline and Boehringer Ingelheim in favour of local companies (Hazel Tau & Others v GlaxoSmithKline & Boehringer Ingelheim (Case no. 2002 Sep226)). Although subsequent applications by generics manufacturers for voluntary licences on other ARVs were successful, this has not always been the case (Avafia et al., 2006).

Parallel importation

South African law recognizes the doctrine of exhaustion, although the Patents Act did not make explicit provision for it until recently. It had been left to the judiciary, drawing on the UK and US jurisprudence, to enunciate the rules governing exhaustion (Stauffer Chemical Co v Agricura Ltd 1979 BP 168 (CP)). In 2002, amendments to the Patents Act (Patents Amendment Act No. 58 2002) saw the introduction of a provision permitting parallel importation (Republic of South Africa, 2002).

Furthermore, the 1997 amendments to the Medicines Act expressly introduced a provision authorizing the Minister of Health to remove patent protection on medicines put on the market by the owner or with his consent, effectively permitting parallel importation (Republic of South Africa, 1997b). The question of whether this included the importation of generic medicines legitimately produced under a compulsory licence became the subject of litigation by the pharmaceutical industry against the government. This issue was settled by the promulgation of regulations that specify the conditions under which parallel importation may take place. Another grey area is whether the TRIPS Agreement requires parallel importation to be limited to patented products, and, indeed, Kenya's 'liberal' provisions in this respect appear to have passed muster with the TRIPS Council review for compliance (Lewis-Lettington and Banda, 2004).

Revocation of patent

The issue of revocation has particular currency in the South African context, given that patent applications are not subjected to examination and scrutiny on the basis of their merits. The Patents Act makes provision for patents to be revoked on the grounds of ineligibility of the patentee; a patent granted in fraud of another's rights; non-patentability of the invention; inability of performance of the invention as illustrated in the specification; incompleteness of the method of performance; claims in the specification not being clear or not fairly based on matter disclosed; intentionally false representation in the application; frivolity or offensive or immoral use of the invention or claims of a microbiological process or product as an invention (Section 61(1)); and where a patentee makes a false declaration as to the origin of indigenous biological resources and his or her authority to use them (Republic of South Africa, 2005).

The grounds available are signally ones that relate to fraudulent acts, mistakes or non-disclosure of complete specifications. What is conspicuously lacking is the possibility of revocation in the case of abuse of patent, as provided for in Article 5A of the Paris Convention on Intellectual Property of 1883.

Competition law

The exercise of IPR, to the extent that such rights create monopolies, may give rise to anti-competitive behaviour either by individual companies or through collusive activity. Competition law and policy as a strategy to access medicines is a relatively new development in South Africa. In at least one Competition Commission ruling (the Hazel Tau case detailed above), innovator companies were found to have engaged in anti-competitive conduct, and thereby to have abused their patents, by charging excessive prices and denying a competitor access to an essential facility. In the Hazel Tau case, TAC and others brought a complaint before the Competition Commission that GlaxoSmithKline and Boehringer Ingelheim had violated the Competition Act by (among other things) charging excessive prices for certain ARVs, to the detriment of consumers. In the face of compelling evidence the drug companies settled the case, granting several voluntary licences on favourable terms. Competition law thus provides another effective sanction against abuse of patents in the form of an anti-competitive compulsory licence, which is consistent with Article 31(k) of TRIPS and is, further, not subject to the domestic use and prior negotiations requirements.

Data protection

Protection of clinical trial data in South Africa pre-dates its inclusion in the TRIPS Agreement, which requires that undisclosed clinical trial data be protected against unfair commercial use and disclosure (Article 39). In line with the practice of regulatory authorities worldwide, the Medicines Control Council (MCC) does not publicly disclose or share data submitted for registration purposes. However, when considering an application for the registration of a generic equivalent, the MCC does not require the applicant to furnish any new data on the safety and efficacy of the drug, but merely on the quality of the generic (Gray, 2007). Data presented by previous applicants are not directly accessed or cross-referenced, but exemption from providing such data is allowed. There is no obligation on members to grant exclusive rights over data, as is the case in the US, the EU and other countries (Correa, 2006). The effect of such protection is that generics producers are 'precluded from relying on pre-existing data to establish safety and efficacy even when the producer has evidence that the two drugs are bioequivalent' (Druce et al., 2004, p. 17).

The issue of data protection has gained greater prominence because of its inclusion in FTAs. Many FTAs require the parties to grant data exclusivity rights for a minimum of five years, irrespective of whether a patent is issued or not, or whether the data is undisclosed or not. Following the collapse of the FTA negotiations between the US and the Southern African Customs Union (SACU), the pressure to adopt stringent data exclusivity rules has eased (Vawda, 2007).

In keeping with the imperative to incorporate all available flexibilities in the international intellectual property and regulatory regimes to advance the agenda of universal access to medicines, South Africa should legislate to secure the MCC's right to rely on the innovator's data when considering applications for generic medicines without direct cross-reference to such data. Public health interest demands that data protection be limited strictly to the parameters outlined in Article 39.3 of TRIPS.

Summary

The changes introduced in South African law as a result of TRIPS thus included, in the main, the extension of patent protection for a period of 20 years (previously 16), and the removal, as a ground for compulsory licensing, of the situation in which the commercial working of an invention is hindered by importation of the patented article. Also introduced were provisions for the use of the regulatory early working exception, the deletion of the requirement for disclosure of the best method of performing the invention known to the applicant at the time of lodgement of the application, and the lowering of the disclosure standard further by amending the requirement for the specification to be 'fully' described to 'sufficiently' described. Significantly, a provision has been introduced that effectively permits parallel importation.

Nonetheless, important flexibilities have not been incorporated into the legislation, notably those relating to compulsory licences for public health purposes; stricter rules for patenting standards; provisions for the use of the Paragraph 6 Decision; educational, research and experimental exceptions to patent rights; additional grounds for revocation of patents; and procedures for opposition to patent applications before and after grant. In all these respects the legal framework for intellectual property protection in South Africa could be improved to considerably enhance access to medicines.

While free trade negotiations in which South Africa was a participant have stalled, this particular potential threat to a pro-access intellectual property system still exists. South Africa can expect to come under increasing pressure to provide linkages between patent status and medicines regulatory practice and to increase data protection measures.

The pharmaceutical sector in South Africa

Shape and size

South Africa has a large and highly developed pharmaceutical system, including considerable local production capacity. Local production, however, is almost entirely dependent on imported active pharmaceutical ingredients (APIs). Local API production is poorly developed and restricted to a very narrow range of products. As of October 2009, the South African MCC had licensed 221 entities as manufacturers, importers and exporters of medicines (or in at least one of these categories). Of these, 76 entities were listed as manufacturers of medicines, meaning that some element of local production was involved. Of the total, 45 were locally registered subsidiaries or offices of transnational pharmaceutical concerns, including the major US and European innovators in this field. While most were licensed as importers and exporters, some were licensed to manufacture locally and operated such plants. Of the balance, 13 were locally registered subsidiaries or offices of international generic pharmaceutical manufacturers, including Teva, Sandoz and Ranbaxy. The remainder—163 entities—were locally based firms licensed to manufacture, import or export medicines. This excluded those operating exclusively as wholesalers or distributors of medicines.

The oldest South African generics manufacturers have been operating for over 100 years and are major players in the local market, if not globally. However, a 2005 report on the issue of local production cited the view that the pharmaceutical industry in South Africa was then 'small and not very wealthy', and lacking 'an ability to achieve economies of scale in production' (Kaplan and Laing, 2005, p. 14). This report also claimed that '[m]uch of the equipment has not been replaced or maintained', but still held that 'a key strategic question is whether South Africa can recognise the importance of the generic sector and shift to generic drug manufacture as the primary way of restructuring the pharmaceutical industry' (Kaplan and Laing, 2005, p. 14). It concluded that there were 'areas within the South African manufacturing sector where existing or new producers could be introduced with a reasonable chance of success' (Kaplan and Laing, 2005, p. 14). As would be expected, local research and development has largely been restricted to formulation issues, although a number of public–private partnerships and academic research centres are involved in new drug discovery projects.

Medicines for supply in South Africa have to be registered by the MCC, a statutory regulatory authority located within the national Department of Health (Gray, 2007). The regulatory authority is required to consider only issues of quality, efficacy and safety, and there is no linkage between patent status and regulatory approval. The enabling Act of Parliament (the Medicines and Related Substances Act, 1965 as amended) also provides for a degree of regulation of medicine pricing, but this is exercised by the Minister of Health as informed by a Pricing Committee (Gray, 2009). In brief, annual increases in the single exit price (the price at which medicines are sold in the private sector) are regulated by the Minister, who issues an annual maximum limit for such increases. The dispensing fees charged by pharmacists and other licensed dispensers are also regulated, and adjusted on an annual basis. An international benchmarking system, in which the prices of innovator products will be compared with those in a basket of countries (Australia, Canada, New Zealand, Spain), has been proposed but not yet implemented. In the public sector, medicines are procured by the provinces, and by military and prison authorities in terms of centrally determined competitive tender processes, limited to locally registered products. The 2010–2012 ARV tender, however, also introduced a benchmarking step, in which indicative global best prices will be provided before tenders are accepted. In this way, the public sector has been able to achieve competitive prices for first- and second-line ARVs. However, the prices of newly launched patent protected medicines, generally brought to the market by transnational innovator firms, remain unregulated. Such medicines may not be included easily in the public sector Essential Drugs List, and may be refused reimbursement or attract considerable co-payments in the private sector.

Post-TRIPS prospects

As outlined above, South Africa has comprehensive intellectual property legislation in operation, with some TRIPS-plus elements. Since 1997 South Africa has amended its medicines legislation to promote the use of generics and has incorporated some flexibilities in IPR legislation (such as Bolar provisions), but has not taken concrete steps to incorporate some of the elements that have enabled the Indian pharmaceutical industry to manage the post-TRIPS era (Love, 2011). The process enabling compulsory licensing remains rigid, without the necessary flexibilities allowing government use to meet health emergencies. The provisions of the Medicines Act enabling the parallel importation of medicines have not been used. Where generic versions of patented medicines have become accessible, as has been the case with many first-line ARVs, this has depended on patent holders not exercising their rights (as in the case of stavudine), the issuing of non-exclusive voluntary licences under pressure from activists (as in the case of zidovudine, lamivudine, nevirapine and efavirenz), or the non-patenting of key molecules in South Africa (as in the case of tenofovir). Information about the patent status of medicines in South Africa is not easily accessible, except in the case of the ARVs listed in the Medicines Patent Pool database (Medicines Patent Pool). South Africa has not enabled the type of pre- and post-grant opposition that has been used effectively in India.

Nonetheless, efforts to promote the use of generic medicines in the South African private sector have been successful. South Africa has used a requirement for mandatory offer of generics substitution to promote the use of lower-cost generic medicines since 2003. The trends in private sector medicines sales over time are shown in Figures 10.1 and 10.2. In this categorization, non-generic products are those that are patent protected, original brands sold after patent protection has lapsed, and first-launch products without patent protection. Generic medicines are approaching 50 per cent of private sector market share by volume and 30 per cent by value. In the public sector, the limited Essential Drugs List contains predominantly older, off-patent medicines, and these are procured by tender, making substitution irrelevant.

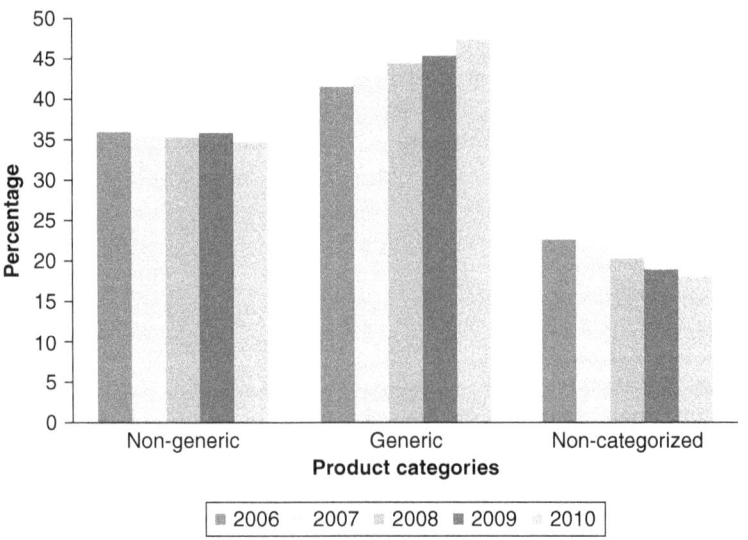

Figure 10.1 Percentage private sector market share by volume (packs), 2006–2010, based on year to September data
Source: IMS Health South Africa.

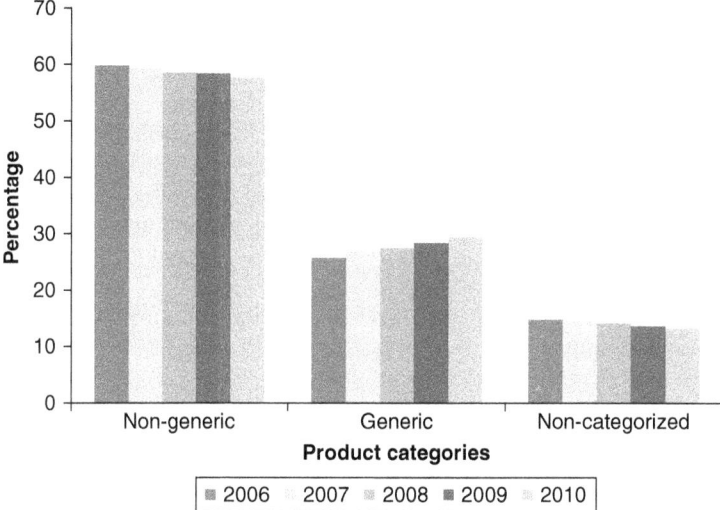

Figure 10.2 Percentage private sector market share by value (single exit price), 2006–2010, based on year to September data
Source: IMS Health South Africa.

The 1996 National Drug Policy for South Africa (Minister of Health, 1996, p. 4) included the following (principally economic) objectives: 'to lower the cost of drugs in both the private and public sectors' and 'to promote the cost-effective and rational use of drugs'. However, it also included an objective characterized as a 'national development objective', namely, 'to support the development of the local pharmaceutical industry and the local production of essential drugs' (Minister of Health, 1996, p. 4). It is difficult to find evidence of a concerted industrial policy in this regard, and this is perhaps reflected in the lack of specific attention to including in South African law the sort of TRIPS flexibilities that might stimulate and support the local production of generic medicines. Since 1997, when both the medicines and IPR legislation was amended, large local generics manufacturers (notably Aspen Pharmacare and Adcock Ingram) have continued to show strong growth. A number of international generics manufacturers have also increased their visibility in the country, either in the form of wholly owned subsidiaries or through joint ventures with local partners. Local firms have also negotiated access to generic medicines manufactured elsewhere, imported in finished form or locally packaged. However, the fundamental shape of the South African generics pharmaceutical industry remains as it was. Local API production has not been stimulated to a significant degree, although there is continuing interest in this issue, at least from the Departments of Science and Technology and of Trade and Industry.

At the April 2011 launch of the newly formed Southern African Generics Medicines Association (SAGMA, bringing together both local and foreign-owned generics firms), Aspen Pharmacare's head of strategic trade was quoted as saying: '[W]e need support from government to reignite industrialisation' (Kahn, 2011). In particular, he criticized donors for an exclusive focus on the price of medicines:

> Well intentioned as their policies are, they have prejudiced local producers, because they look at price (only). South African and African producers don't participate on a level playing field. Often importers enjoy incentives that locals don't [such as] tax breaks or accelerated depreciation schemes. SA hasn't yet got it right.
>
> (Kahn, 2011)

A government official's response was blunt: 'We prefer to give back-end support like tax breaks and creating industrial hubs...to drive down the cost of production' (Kahn, 2011). The SAGMA chairman (deputy CEO of locally owned, but Indian-linked, generics pharmaceutical company Cipla Medpro) expressed the view that a key issue was 'to harmonise the regulatory environment for the region' (Kahn, 2011). In essence, these comments capture the challenge for South Africa: it has the potential to contribute to access to affordable generic medicines through local production, but lacks some of the enabling provisions, in terms of both industrial policy and a supportive IPR policy. Efforts to harmonize the medicines regulatory regime in the region (or more widely across Africa) have faced many challenges but remain on the agenda. However, local efforts to reform the medicines regulatory authority and to extend its remit to include medical devices will, of necessity, restrict the resources available for regional efforts.

Conclusion

The South African case presents both significant challenges and opportunities for access to medicines. On the one hand, South Africa has a progressive constitutional dispensation with strongly enforceable socio-economic rights. On the other hand, while there are reasonable provisions in IPR legislation to facilitate access, there have been numerous shortcomings in their implementation. South Africa has failed to use all available flexibilities, such as compulsory or government-use licences. The inherent weakness of a patent-granting system in which the authority does not conduct an examination as to the merits of the application remains a problem. Overall, there appears to have been a lack of political will to avail ourselves of those measures (such as compulsory licences) which challenge the agendas of developed-country governments and the industrial and commercial interests they represent.

Additionally, there are serious challenges at the level of the capacity of the regulatory system to process applications for medicines registration, as well as a lack of clear policy direction in relation to the development of the local pharmaceutical sector. Each of these tensions contributes to an inability to make optimal use of legal and regulatory mechanisms to enhance access. Civil society has played, and continues to play, a leading role in promoting the access agenda. It is time government displayed stronger leadership regarding its obligations to its citizens in the critical areas identified in this chapter.

References

Abbott, F. (2002) 'The Doha Declaration on the TRIPS Agreement and Public Health: Lighting a Dark Corner at the WTO', *Journal of International Economic Law* 5, 469–505.

Abdool Karim, S. S., G. J. Churchyard, Q. Abdool Karim and S. D. Lawn (2009) 'HIV Infection and Tuberculosis in South Africa: An Urgent Need to Escalate the Public Health Response', *Lancet* 374(9693), 921–33.

Anonymous (2006) 'US Drops FTA with SACU, Starts Trade and Investment Work Programme', *Inside US Trade* 21 April.

Avafia, T., J. Berger and T. Hartzenberg (2006) *The Ability of Select Sub-Saharan African Countries to Utilise TRIPS Flexibilities and Competition Law to Ensure a Sustainable Supply of Essential Medicines: A Study of Producing and Importing Countries*, Tralac Working Paper No. 12 (Stellenbosch: University of Stellenbosch Printers).

Bond, P. (1999) 'Globalization, Pharmaceutical Pricing, and South African Health Policy: Managing Confrontation with U.S. Firms and Politicians', *International Journal of Health Services* 29, 765–92.

Burrel, T. (1999) *Burrell's South African Patent and Design Law* (Durban: Butterworths).

Coovadia, H., E. Jewkes, P. Barron, D. Sanders and D. McIntyre (2009) 'The Health and Health System of South Africa: Historical Roots of Current Public Health Challenges', *Lancet* 374(9692), 817–34.

Correa, C. (2006) 'Protecting Test Data for Pharmaceutical and Agrochemical Products under Free Trade Agreements' in P. Roffe, G. Tansey and D. Vivas-Eugul (eds) *Negotiating Health: Intellectual Property and Access to Medicines* (Sterling, VA: Earthscan Publications).

Davis, D. (1992) 'The Case Against the Inclusion of Socio-Economic Demands in a Bill of Rights Except as Directive Principles', *South African Journal on Human Rights* 8, 475–90.

Day, C. and A. Gray (2010) 'Health and Related Indicators' in S. Fonn and A. Padarath (eds) *South African Health Review 2010* (Durban: Health Systems Trust).

Drahos, P. and J. Braithwaite (2004) 'Who Owns the Knowledge Economy? Political Organising Behind TRIPS', Corner House Briefing (Sturminster Newton: The Corner House).

Druce, N., B. K. Baker, E. Gardiner, C. Grace and S. Hill (2004) *Access to Medicines in Under-served Markets. What are the Implications of Changes in Intellectual Property Rights, Trade and Drug Registration Policy?* (London: DFID Health Systems Resource Centre).

Gray, A. (2007) 'Developing, Registering and Using Medicines' in A. Hassim, M. Heywood and J. Berger (eds) *Health and Democracy: A Guide to Human Rights, Health Law and Policy in Post-Apartheid South Africa* (Cape Town: Siber Ink).

Gray, A. (2009) 'Medicine Pricing Interventions—the South African Experience', *Southern Med Review* 2(2), 15–19.

ICTSD, *see* International Centre for Trade and Sustainable Development.

Kahn, T. (2011) 'Donors Accused of Hurting Africa's Drug Makers', *Business Day* 5 April.

Kaplan, W. and R. Laing (2005) 'Local Production of Pharmaceuticals: Industrial Policy and Access to Medicines. An Overview of Key Concepts, Issues and Opportunities for Future Research' in J. De Beyer (ed.) *Health, Nutrition and Population (HNP) Discussion Paper* (Washington, DC: World Bank).

Lewis-Lettington, R. and C. Banda (2004) *Willingness and Ability to Use TRIPS Flexibilities—Kenya Case Study* (London: DFID Health Systems Resource Centre).

Love, J. (2011) 'The Production of Generic Drugs in India', *British Medical Journal* 342, d1694.

Mathipa, K. and G. Budlender (2002) 'Concluding Observations: Key Themes and Challenges for Government and Civil Society', *ESR Review* 3, 38–40.

Mayosi, B. M., A. J. Flisher, U. G. Lalloo, F. Sitas, F. S. M. Tollman and D. Bradshaw (2009) 'The Burden of Non-Communicable Diseases in South Africa', *Lancet*, 374(9693) 934–47.

Medicines Patent Pool, http://www.medicinespatentpool.org/Licensing/Patent-Status-of-ARVs, date accessed 28 June 2011.

Minister of Health (1996) *National Drug Policy for South Africa* (Pretoria: National Department of Health).

Parmet, W. (2006) 'Pharmaceuticals, Public Health, and the Law: a Public Health Perspective' in J. Cohen, P. Illingworth and U. Schuklenk (eds) *The Power of Pills: Social, Ethical & Legal Issues in Drug Development, Marketing and Pricing* (London: Pluto Press).

Republic of India (2005) Patents (Amendment) Act (Act 15 of 2005).

Republic of South Africa (1978) Patents Act (Act 57 of 1978).

Republic of South Africa (1996) Constitution of the Republic of South Africa (Act 108 of 1996).

Republic of South Africa (1997a) Intellectual Property Laws Amendment Act (Act 38 of 1997).

Republic of South Africa (1997b) Medicines and Related Substances Control Amendment Act (Act 90 of 1997).

Republic of South Africa (2002) Patent Amendment Act (Act 58 of 2002).

Republic of South Africa (2005) Patent Amendment Act (Act 20 of 2005).

Sell, S. K. (2007) 'TRIPS-Plus Free Trade Agreements and Access to Medicines', *Liverpool Law Review* 28, 41–75.

UNCTAD, *see* United Nations Conference on Trade and Development.

Union of South Africa (1916) Patents, Designs, Trademarks and Copyright Act (Act 9 of 1916).

United Nations Conference on Trade and Development–International Centre for Trade and Sustainable Development (2005) *Resource Book on TRIPS and Development: An Authoritative and Practical Guide to the TRIPS Agreement* (New York: Cambridge University Press).

Vawda, Y. (2007) 'Free Trade Agreements with the US: Are They Good for Your Health?', *Journal for Juridical Science* 32, 114–29.

World Trade Organization (2001) WTO Doha Ministerial Declaration on the TRIPS Agreement and Public Health (WT/MIN(01)/DEC/2), http://www.wto.org/english/thewto_e/minist_e/min01_e/mindecl_trips_e.htm, date accessed 3 March 2012.

World Trade Organization Council for Trips (2003) Implementation of Paragraph 6 of the Doha Declaration on the TRIPS Agreement and Public Health (IP/C/W/405), http://www.wto.org/english/tratop_e/trips_e/implem_para6_e.htm, date accessed 3 March 2012.

WTO, *see* World Trade Organization.

11
TRIPS and New Challenges for the Pharmaceutical Sector in South Korea

Bong-min Yang and Hye-young Kwon

The South Korean economy has been growing over the past five decades at an average annual rate of 6.2 per cent. In 2011 gross domestic product (GDP) per capita was US$20,870 (World Bank, 2012). The rapid ageing of South Korea's population, however, has sparked intense debate and recognition of the imperative to shift the focus of growth away from manufacturing to services, including welfare services. South Korea's National Health Insurance (NHI), which covers 97 per cent of the population, and the Long-term Care Insurance System, introduced in 2008, will assist this transition to an ageing society.

The NHI and expansion of social insurance coverage have been beneficial to the pharmaceutical industry. South Korea's pharmaceutical market is ranked among the world's top 15, valued at Korean Won (KRW) 18.2 trillion (US$17.3 billion) in 2009, with a global market share of 1.7 per cent (IMS Health, 2010). Drug expenses in that year totalled KRW11.7 trillion (US$11.1 billion), accounting for 29.6 per cent of the total health expenditure of KRW39.4 trillion (US$37.5 billion). This is significantly greater than the 2009 average among OECD countries of 17.6 per cent of total health spending on drugs (OECD Health Data, 2011).

Local Korean companies usually supply generic (out-of-patent) drugs while global companies supply patented brand-name products. Some domestic companies, however, have demonstrated a capacity to develop new drugs; 18 new chemical entities (NCEs) have been introduced by domestic firms. But these are medicines approved only in Korea, and do not meet the standards required for global marketing. Only one of these 18 NCEs has been approved by the US Food and Drug Administration. In general, Korean domestic firms have weak research and development (R&D) capacity, spending on average about 6.2 per cent of total revenue on R&D (KHIDI, 2010). The market is characterized by low entry barriers, no generics price competition and heated sales promotions by a large number of small-sized drug suppliers, including manufacturers and wholesalers. High generics prices and the absence of price competition, coupled with the Korea Food and Drug Administration's (KFDA) moderately stringent new drug approval process, create an environment that invites newcomers to enter the market as generics producers. This explains the high number of local drug companies—over 580 in 2009 (KHIDI, 2010).

The South Korean government had established a framework for granting drug patents and patent term extensions even before the Trade Related Aspects of Intellectual Property Rights (TRIPS) Agreement came into effect in 1995. The initial framework was created through the Korea–US Trade Agreement in 1986, and was modified following the TRIPS Agreement to extend patent terms from 15 to 20 years. Since then several attempts have been made to extend intellectual property rights (IPR) protection further. For example, in the process of establishing the Korea–US Free Trade Agreement (KOR–US FTA) in 2006, the South Korean government was asked to review its policies on data exclusivity and patent linkage, both of which were included as TRIPS-plus provisions in this Agreement, which was expected to be ratified in 2012.

Extended IPR protection, however, has produced unintended negative consequences. Global companies have repeatedly refused to supply drugs for orphan (rare) disease patients, claiming that prices offered by the Korean health authority are too low. Such incidents give rise to different interpretations of the impact of TRIPS and IPR. In the following discussion we will explore these issues in detail. A feature of the Korean pharmaceutical market, not directly related to IPR, is the ever-growing tension between the NHI system and the pharmaceutical industry. On the one hand, global companies face strict controls on new drug prices through health technology assessments undertaken through the NHI system. On the other hand, domestic companies selling generics face occasional general price cuts, with the most recent price cut taking place in January 2012.

This chapter first introduces South Korea's healthcare system. This is followed by a description of the process of introducing IPR and subsequent legal IPR amendments. We then examine cases of conflict between TRIPS and the public health system around the right of access to medicines, and we demonstrate the rigidity and negative effects of the TRIPS system. We then attempt to assess the potential impact of TRIPS-plus provisions coming into force with the ratification of KOR–US FTA. Finally, we focus on the Korean pharmaceutical sector, which is a product of preceding IPR-related changes and domestic drug policies.

The healthcare system in South Korea

NHI is the central organizing mechanism of the Korean healthcare system through which resources flow between the government, consumers, corporations and service providers. As noted, 96.7 per cent of Koreans (out of a total population of 49 million) are currently beneficiaries of NHI. Healthcare for the remaining 3.3 per cent, the poorest members of Korean society, is covered by the tax-financed Medical Protection Program (NHIC, 2011). The remarkable achievement of extending healthcare coverage to 100 per cent of the population in a relatively short period (1977–1989) was made possible by continuously growing per capita income and political democratization. (During the 1980s civil society groups advocated strongly for expansion of social health insurance coverage for the self-employed, which was finally achieved in 1989.)

Providers are paid on a fee-for-service basis for services covered by insurance. These fees are paid in part by the National Health Insurance Corporation (NHIC), with the remainder paid for by patients out of pocket. The estimated out-of-pocket rate is 37.8 per cent in 2009, which is one of the highest in the OECD. NHI, in turn, is financed by premium contributions paid by consumers and employers, along with a government subsidy from tax revenues. As of 2010, beneficiaries on average pay 5.4 per cent of their income as premium contributions (NHIC, 2011).

Healthcare is provided mainly in the private sector. Private provision of healthcare, which was dominant in Korea before the introduction of the insurance plans, has continued to expand, with increases in per capita income and growth of health insurance coverage.

Korea is among the world's leaders in the adoption of new medical technologies. An OECD report on availability of key equipment per million population in 2009 shows that among all OECD member countries Korea was second in the use of the computer tomography scanner, fourth in magnetic resonance imaging units, and first in mammography (OECD Health Data, 2011).

There were 14,883 items listed on the NHI formulary (its reimbursable drug list) as of January 2010. Of these, 12,938 items (86.9 per cent) were in the category of prescription-only medicines, with the remaining 13.1 per cent in the over-the-counter category. A majority of listed products, 14,463 items (97.2 per cent), are generic drugs. Most of the medicines included in the World Health Organization's (WHO) Essential Drug List are protected under a special government program for drug shortage prevention. Reasonably high prices are guaranteed for these products to dissuade discontinuation by manufacturers. Another category of drug under special protection of supply is that of products with no treatment substitute (for example, Novoseven, Gleevec, Elaprase and Myozyme). There is separate provision under the authority of the Ministry of Health and Welfare to include these 'necessary' drugs on the formulary even in circumstances of a breakdown in price negotiations for these drugs.

Intellectual property protection in South Korea

The first South Korean patent act was enacted in 1946 after liberation from the Japanese occupation. It is viewed as merely a way of abolishing the

Japanese Patent Act, and was heavily influenced by the US Patent Act at that time. In contrast, the Patent Act 1961 may be regarded as the country's first IPR legislation established by its sovereign government (Jung, 2004).

In the 1961 legislation, any substance that could be manufactured by chemical methods, including pharmaceutical products, was deemed non-patentable. Where patents were granted for products other than pharmaceuticals, terms were 12 years from the date of issue. Amendments were enacted on 31 December 1986 to allow patent protection for pharmaceutical and chemical products. In addition, these amendments extended the length of patent terms from 12 to 15 years and allowed five years of additional patent protection for inventions requiring licensing and registration, including pharmaceutical products. These changes were in part attributed to the 'Record of Understanding between the Government of the Republic of Korea and the Government of the United States of America', effective from 28 August 1986. The US Congress had amended US trade laws in 1984 to include intellectual property protection mandated under Article 301, which had a direct impact on South Korea's intellectual property law reforms of 1986 (Nam, 2006).

South Korea became a member of the World Trade Organization (WTO) at its formation in 1995. On 29 December of the same year, Korea's Patent Act was again amended to reflect the TRIPS Agreement. The new amendments included extending duration of patents from 15 to 20 years and restricting non-patentable inventions to 'any inventions that may disturb public order or good tradition, or may harm public health'. It is fair to say that South Korea's patent policy, particularly as it pertains to pharmaceutical products, was more influenced by the Record of Understanding with the US than by the TRIPS Agreement. But legislation to provide for full TRIPS compliance included extending the patent term to 20 years.

Patentability

According to the TRIPS Agreement Article 27 Paragraph 1, patents shall be available for any inventions in all fields of technology provided that they are new, involve an inventive step and are capable of industrial application. Article 29 of South Korea's Patent Act 2011 stipulates patentability criteria consistent with TRIPS. Novelty is defined under the Patent Act Article 29 Paragraph 1 as any invention that is not publicly known or not worked in the Republic of Korea, or any inventions that are not described in domestic publications, prior to the filing of the patent application. Inventiveness is defined under the Patent Act Article 29 Paragraph 2 as any invention that could not easily have been made prior to the filing of the patent application by a person having ordinary skill in the art to which the invention pertains.

The extent of non-patentability has been reduced through successive alterations to the Act over the years. The following product categories have been removed from the list of non-patentable inventions: pharmaceutical or chemical products in the Patent Act Amendments of 1986; food, alcohol and cigarettes in the Amendments of 1990; and any substances produced by nuclear transmutation methods in the Amendments of 1995. In other words, pharmaceuticals and chemical products have been patentable since 1986.

TRIPS Article 30 states that 'members may provide limited exceptions to the exclusive rights conferred by a patent, provided that such exceptions do not unreasonably conflict with a normal exploitation of the patent and do not unreasonably prejudice the legitimate interests of the patent owner, taking account of the legitimate interests of third parties.' This can be interpreted as WTO members being allowed to restrict patent rights only if the legitimate interests of the patent holder or exclusive licensee and normal use of patent rights are not violated. Regulations in relation to Prior User Rights and exceptions to patent protection of pharmaceutical products are included in this agreement (Park, 2007).

A significant exception to patent protection stipulated in Article 96 of the Patent Act is for the working of patented inventions for research or testing purposes, including research or testing for drug approval in accordance with the Pharmaceutical Affairs Law, and for pesticide registration in accordance with the Pesticide Control Act 2011. In addition, compounding acts or compounded products defined by the Pharmaceutical Affairs Law are not protected by patent rights.

Compulsory licensing

Compulsory licensing may be viewed as a restriction of patent rights, but the difference is that TRIPS Article 31 may be implemented without regard to Article 30. Article 31 may be interpreted as allowing compulsory licensing only under the condition that the interests of patent holders and exclusive licensees can be reasonably negotiated. TRIPS Agreement Article 8 Paragraph 1 also states that 'members may, in formulating or amending their laws and regulations, adopt measures necessary to protect public health and nutrition, and to promote the public interest in sectors of vital importance to their socio-economic and technological development.'

Although the term 'compulsory licensing' is not used in the Patent Act, it is implied in Article 106 on expropriation of patent rights, in Article 106–2 on implementing patented inventions by the government or a third party, and in Article 107 on adjudication for the grant of a non-exclusive licence. According to Article 106 and 106–2, the Korean government may expropriate a patent right, implement a patented invention or require a third party to implement a patented invention in situations of national crisis for the purpose of national security or public interest. In other words, it is only in circumstances of national crisis that government or a third party is allowed to implement patented inventions. Some of the amendments introduced on 27 January 2010 mitigated the requirements of compulsory licensing by declaring that 'in cases of national crisis, emergency of highest importance or for the purpose of addressing public interest, government or a third party may implement patented inventions for non-commercial use only,' and by establishing Article 106 Paragraph 2 separately.

Article 107 states that:

> if patented inventions have not been implemented for more than three consecutive years in the Republic of Korea, if the domestic demand for the patented invention has not been satisfied to an appropriate extent and under reasonable conditions, if the implementation of the patented invention is necessary especially for the public interest, if the working of the patented invention is necessary to remedy a practice determined to be unfair after the judicial or administrative process, if there is need to export to a country that intends to import pharmaceutical products to cure diseases threatening the health of the people, or if the patent holder and the exclusive licensee fail to discuss or agree on non-exclusive license, the Commissioner of the Korea Intellectual Property Office (KIPO) may be requested to adjudicate for authorization of non-exclusive license.

In cases of implementing such patented inventions in the public interest for non-commercial use, however, or correcting practices determined to be unfair, requests for adjudication may be made without any prior attempt at consultation.

There have been three cases of compulsory licensing petitions for drugs in South Korea. In all of them the petitions were eventually dismissed. The more recent two, involving Gleevec and Fuzeon, provide a glimpse of the impact of the enforcement of IPR on access to affordable medicines.

Gleevec

On 30 January 2002 Civic Groups for Public Health and the Korea Leukaemia Coalition made a petition for compulsory licensing of imatinib mesylate (marketed by Novartis as Gleevec) for the treatment of chronic myeloid leukaemia. For two years Novartis had been refusing to supply the drug in retaliation for the low price of the product on the South Korean market. As a result a pricing battle had ensued between the company and the government, with the lives of leukaemia patients at stake. In the end the government was forced to raise the price of Gleevec. This case led to the eventual recognition of several problems in the system for the supply of medicines, including the limited insurance benefit package at the time, and individual economic hardship due to high out-of-pocket payments. Novartis did provide Gleevec free of charge during the period of non-supply for a select few leukaemia patients. Members of the Korea Leukaemia Coalition, however, had to import and supply Veenat (a copy of Gleevec manufactured by NATCO Pharma in India) to treat other patients.

In February 2003 the KIPO dismissed this compulsory licensing petition on several grounds: that leukaemia was not an infectious disease that could pose a serious threat on a national or society-wide level; that approval of the petition would undermine the basic purposes of the Korean Patent Act; that co-payments were only ten per cent of the drug price; that drugs were being provided to some patients free of charge; and that imports of similar products were permitted.

Fuzeon

Enfuvirtide, for the treatment of HIV infection, marketed by Roche Pharmaceuticals as Fuzeon, was listed on the NHI formulary in November 2004. Roche never supplied Fuzeon, however, as the price offered by the Korean health authority was considered too low. Patients who needed the drug had to seek the help of foreign aid agencies, which led to the filing of a compulsory licensing petition by the Korean AIDS Coalition and Civic Groups on 23 December 2008. As a direct result of this petition Roche commenced distribution of Fuzeon free of charge through the Korea Orphan Drug Centre (KODC) in February 2009. The decision on the petition was that public interest in a compulsory licence had not been demonstrated. The petition was dismissed on the grounds that Fuzeon was being offered free of charge, domestic production of the drug would be impossible even with a non-exclusive licence, and other alternative drugs were on the horizon.

Tamiflu

Another example is the evaluation by the KFDA of the potential for increased domestic production through compulsory licensing of oseltamivir (marketed by Roche as Tamiflu) in response to the avian influenza (AI) pandemic in October 2005. During the influenza A (H1N1) outbreak in 2009, the need for compulsory licensing of Tamiflu was brought to the attention of various civil society groups, as well as the National Assembly. Domestic companies such as Chong-kun-dang Pharmaceutical Corporation submitted to the KFDA test results on biological equivalents, but the company's application of Tamiflu production was not approved.

Ultimately, the reason for the failure of compulsory licensing in South Korea is that any such measure is likely to lead to trade frictions with other countries, notably the US. However, the recent amendment to the Patent Act (January 2010), which mitigates the requirement for compulsory licensing, may make compulsory licensing more likely in the future.

Parallel importation

There are no obvious regulations in the Korean Patent Act that allow parallel importation. TRIPS Article 6 would seem to exclude parallel importation: 'For the purposes of dispute settlement under this Agreement, subject to the provisions of Articles 3 and 4 nothing in this Agreement shall be used to address the issue of the exhaustion of intellectual property rights.' This may be interpreted as an agreement to allow parallel importation, but, strictly speaking, it is not obvious that parallel importation is implied in that statement. This wording, however, is clearer than that of the Doha Declaration of 2001: 'the effect of the provisions in the TRIPS Agreement that are relevant to the exhaustion of intellectual property rights is to leave each member free to establish its own regime for such exhaustion without challenge, subject to the MFN (Most Favoured Nation) and national treatment provisions of Articles 3 and 4' (Lee, 2007).

With new KFDA regulations for cosmetic products in 1999, the South Korean government permitted parallel importation of such products, but systematic hurdles remain for the expansion of parallel importation of pharmaceuticals. Importers of pharmaceutical products are required to submit to the KFDA the original manufacturer's certificate, as well as data on the safety and efficacy of the product in question, when applying for approval. It is extremely difficult for importers to acquire either the original manufacturer's certificate or the data on safety and efficacy, making parallel importation practically impossible. According to the Pharmaceutical Affairs Law and Regulation on Standards for Reimbursement of the NHI, however, there is a policy that allows the KODC to import and distribute crucial drugs as 'Pharmaceuticals Urgently Required' without prior KFDA market authorization. This process—which makes an exception of the KODC importing and dispensing pharmaceuticals under the NHI's Pharmaceutical Benefit Scheme without KFDA market authorization (Kwon and Yang, 2010)—may be regarded as modified parallel importation.

Anti-trust law

Patent protection is likely to give rise to monopoly pricing. There are no specific anti-trust laws in South Korea to prevent threats to a patient's right to legal access to drugs resulting from the abuse of patents. Even the Antitrust and Fair Trade Act 2011, designed to ensure fair and free competition by limiting monopolies through regulating anti-competitive and unfair trade practices, states (Article 59) that such regulation does not apply in the case of any legal application of IPR, such as copyright law, patent act, utility model law, design protection law or trademark law. Regulations to prevent unfair practices and abuse of monopoly power in the field of pharmaceuticals are, therefore, virtually non-existent.

TRIPS-plus

'TRIPS-plus' refers to measures to extend IPR protection beyond the requirements of TRIPS. Two TRIPS-plus provisions are particularly important in the pharmaceutical area: data exclusivity and patent linkage.

Data exclusivity

According to the TRIPS Agreement, test data are to be protected only against unfair commercial use. Exceptions have been made, however, in bilateral free trade agreements, such as the KOR–US FTA, where such protection is referred to as 'data exclusivity'. In other words, global companies' test data are now strictly protected through free trade agreements against all unlicensed use for a set period.

The Pharmaceutical Affairs Law Article 88 states that the government shall protect any data submitted for registration, re-evaluation or clinical trial approval purposes if the submitter (a global company in most cases) requests that the data be protected from public disclosure, unless such disclosure would benefit the public good. In addition, according to Article 32 any drug subject to authorization for safety and efficacy must undergo re-evaluation by the KFDA after having been available on the market for either four or six years, depending on its status. (For NCEs or new combined preparations containing a new substance as an active ingredient, drugs already licensed but with different dosage strength or a different route of administration, a six-year re-evaluation period is granted. A four-year re-evaluation period is granted for drugs already licensed with a different formulation, with a different indication or with a new salt or isomer.) In this period of either four or six years a generics version may not be approved unless a copy drug producer submits data equivalent to or better than those of the branded product, in accordance with the Regulation on Evaluation of Drug Safety and Efficacy Article 5 Paragraph 9 (No. 2007–20). This regulation was amended in April 2007, mainly for consistency with clauses in the KOR–US FTA of 2006. One Article in the KOR–US FTA states that, when safety and efficacy data are submitted for approval of a NCE, no other approval for the same or similar products may be granted for at least five years for pharmaceutical products, or for at least ten years for agricultural products, without the consent of the original submitter. This amendment confirms strict data exclusivity.

Drugs produced with a salt change used to be considered incrementally modified drugs (IMD) and the main development strategy for local companies. After confirmation of data exclusivity in 2007, however, such products were deemed to be new generics. Thus, approval of a drug with a salt change is no longer possible during the safety and efficacy re-evaluation period of a branded drug. As an example, in 2006 Han-mi Pharmaceutical Company developed sibutramine mesylate (Slimmer) through a salt change to sibutramine hydrochloride monohydrate (Abbott, Reductil). Even before any examination of the issue under the data exclusivity policy of 2007, the KFDA denied its approval. At that time it was customary for a chemical entity with a salt change to be approved even during the period of the re-evaluation. Some believed that the KFDA's denial of Han-mi's sibutramine mesylate went against existing policy, and interpreted its actions as a consequence of trade pressure applied by the US (ultimately linked to FTA-bound data exclusivity within KOR–US FTA). (Sibutramine was withdrawn from the market in 2010 due to its high risk of myocardial infarction and stroke.)

Patent linkage

'Patent linkage' is a term that refers to coordination between the safety and efficacy regulator (KFDA) and the patent office (KIPO) to prevent marketing approval of generic drugs when there is the possibility of a breach of IPR. Under such linkage provisions, the regulator has first to check with the patent office whether the patent covering the drug or its approved use has expired. Patent linkage is a TRIPS-plus provision, that is, it is not mandated under the TRIPS Agreement. Until the end of 2011, KFDA was granting approvals for drugs regardless of whether patents had been issued. KOR–US FTA stipulates, however, that, for any patented pharmaceutical product or for any product with patented usage, KFDA is required to notify the patent holder (a global company in most cases) when an application is submitted for marketing approval.

This often leads to delays in market entry of generic drugs by providing patent holders with an opportunity to build new protective barriers against them. Patent linkage is thought to have negative implications for the domestic pharmaceutical industry, which is mainly engaged in the supply of generics. According to data reported to the National Assembly in 2007, domestic manufacturing of generic drugs is expected to decrease by an annual amount of KRW90 to KRW168 billion over the next ten years due to patent linkage. As a result, despite reductions and elimination of tariffs, consumer benefits are expected to decrease by an annual amount of KRW12.7 to KRW13.64 billion over the same period. On a similar note, according to a report released by the Korea Health Industry Development Institute (2007), additional spending of NHI funds, with delayed entry of generics, is expected to reach KRW16.1 to KRW32.91 billion over the next five years. With the expected ratification of the Korea–US FTA, patent linkage and concerns over its impact on domestic pharmaceutical industry are emerging as hot political issues.

The pharmaceutical sector in South Korea

There is no doubt that the Korean pharmaceutical sector has been shaped extensively by successive changes to IPR legislation influenced by international pressures, including the Report of Understanding between Korea and the US, the TRIPS Agreement and TRIPS-plus measures resulting from FTAs. It is also fair to say that other domestic health policies, such as the Positive List System Policy, through which the NHI selects reimbursable drugs based on manufacturer-submitted pharmaco-economic data, and the Separation of Drug Dispensing from Prescription (SDP) Policy have contributed to shaping the Korean pharmaceutical sector in the last two decades. With the latter policy, separation of drug dispensing (by pharmacists) from prescription (by doctors) became mandatory for all out-patient services (including hospital out-patients). Before the policy came into effect in 2000, both physicians and pharmacists could dispense any drug without prescription in any circumstance. We examine in this section the current situation and changes that are likely to come.

Shape and size

South Korea's pharmaceutical industry has made significant progress over the years. Its total output (including end products, raw materials and herbal medicines) in 2009 was KRW15.8 trillion, a 7.25 per cent increase from 2008. It accounted for 1.49 per cent of GDP and 5.95 per cent of the country's total manufacturing output (see Figure 11.1). South Korea's pharmaceutical market is 1.7 per cent of the world market, which is estimated at US$810 billion.

In January 2006, under the existing Negative List System, 28,374 items were eligible for NHI reimbursement; and 21,740 drug items (77 per cent) were registered in the NHI reimbursement list for insurance benefits. With the introduction of a Positive List System in 2007—a result of government policy to reduce reimbursable drug items—by January 2010 the number of items had decreased to 14,883. But, compared with many other countries, a high proportion of drugs on the market remain eligible for insurance benefits. As of 2009 total drug production was valued at KRW13.176 trillion, and the value of imports reached KRW2.714 trillion, making the total pharmaceutical market worth KRW15.890 trillion. The amount paid in drug expenses by health insurance benefits was KRW11.643 trillion, reaching 73.3 per cent of the total pharmaceutical market in South Korea.

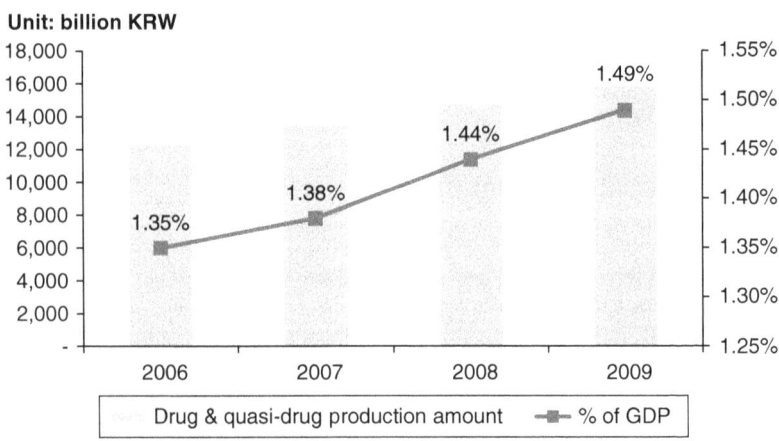

Figure 11.1 South Korea's pharmaceutical industry outputs

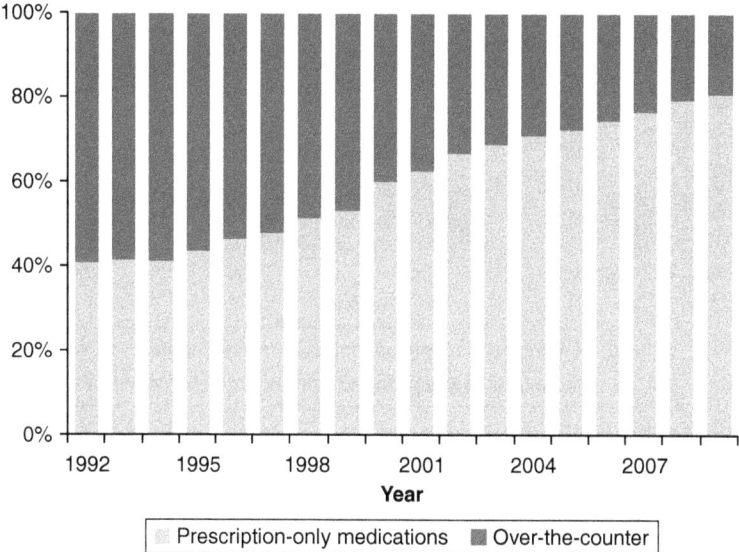

Figure 11.2 Changes in proportions of over-the-counter and prescription-only medications, 1995–2007
Note: Finished pharmaceutical products, excluding narcotics.
Source: KPMA (2010).

It can, therefore, be reasonably assumed that the South Korean pharmaceutical industry is, for the most part, supported and influenced by the NHI reimbursement environment. This assumption is also substantiated by the increasing proportion of prescription-only medications compared with over-the-counter medications. The former have become dominant since the implementation of the SDP Policy in 2000 (see Figure 11.2).

Global firms consider South Korea one of the most attractive markets in the Asia-Pacific region. With a population of about 50 million and an expanding economy, there is a growing demand for health services. Unlike China and India, South Korea is close to providing comprehensive healthcare to all citizens. Unlike in Japan, Korean pharmaceutical companies have a low potential for developing new drugs, making this market more dependent on imports. Administrative barriers to protect domestic companies do not exist in South Korea. Most new drugs are brought to the South Korean market directly by global pharmaceutical companies or by domestic pharmaceutical companies through in licensing.

The strong presence of global pharmaceutical companies is demonstrated in Figure 11.3. In 2005 foreign firms made up only 8.2 per cent of the total number of pharmaceutical companies. They accounted, however, for

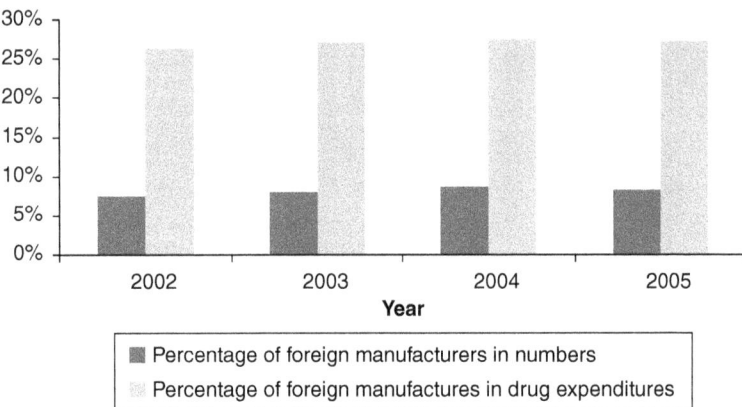

Figure 11.3 Percentage of foreign manufactures in numbers and in drug expenditure, 2002–2005
Source: KHIDI (2008).

27.3 per cent of total drug expenditures. In 2006 only five of the top 20 products in terms of NHI reimbursement cost were produced by domestic companies (KHIDI, 2008).

South Korean domestic companies mostly make their profits from manufacturing generic drugs. In 2009 the majority of the approximately 580 pharmaceutical companies with manufacturing facilities were focused on the marketing of generics, resulting in excessive competition among domestic companies. With government support for bio-industry promotion for the twenty-first century, however, there is a trend away from the manufacture of copy drugs to the expansion of existing technologies through development of IMDs and new drugs.

A significant proportion of drugs registered annually for reimbursement benefits remain generics (see Figure 11.4). However, led by the introduction of amlodipine camsylate (Hanmi, Amodipine) in 2003, an IMD of amlodipine besylate (Pfizer, Novasc), more IMDs are being developed using isomers and salt changes. As a result, a number of Patent Act suits have been brought against these domestic companies. This has been used by other governments to pressure the South Korean government. Of 536 drugs registered for insurance coverage in South Korea from 2001 to 2009, ten were discovered and developed by domestic pharmaceutical companies. As noted above, 18 drugs were developed domestically, but only one of them has acquired US Food and Drug Administration (USFDA) approval (Ministry of Health and Welfare, 2010).

Drugs become available to patients after being approved by the KFDA. With the implementation of the Positive List System in 2007, NHI

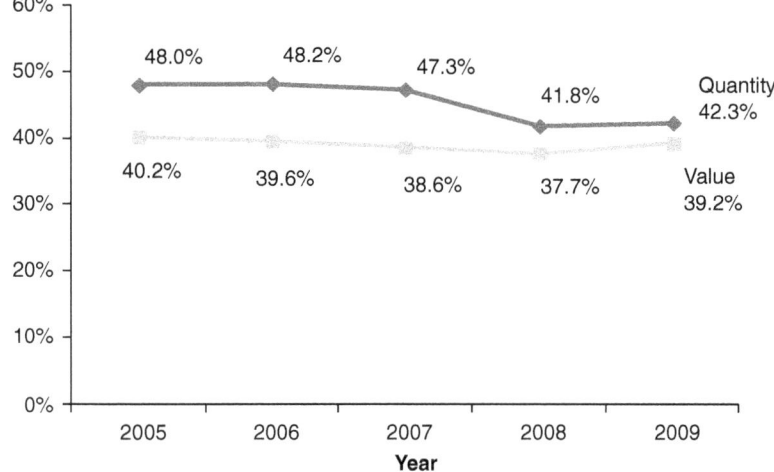

Figure 11.4 Share of generic drugs in pharmaceutical expenditure (quantity, value)
Source: Ministry of Health and Welfare (2010).

reimbursement decisions have been made on the basis of pharmacoeconomic data, with prices determined through negotiations with the NHIC as a single payer. The NHIC is required to negotiate prices in favour of its subscribers, with its bargaining power derived from market monopsony. However, when there are no alternatives to essential drugs, such supply monopoly means it is difficult for governments to enforce regulations effectively.

As noted above, cases of supply monopoly abuse leading to refusal by pharmaceutical companies to supply essential drugs have occurred in respect of numerous drugs, including Gleevec in 2001; Fuzeon in 2004; Prezista (Janssen, darunavir, for HIV/AIDS treatment) in 2008; and Elaprase (Shire, idursulfase, for treatment of mucopolysaccharidosis II), Naglazyme (Genzyme, galsulfase, for treatment of mucopolysaccharidosis IV), Myozyme (Genzyme, alglucosidase alfa, for treatment of Pompe disease) and Novoseven (Novo Nordisk, eptacog alfa for treatment of haemophilia) in 2009. This refusal of supply reached a level that began to threaten the lives of patients. The vast majority of cases were attributed to patent holder dissatisfaction with NHIC drug pricing. Some argue that refusal to supply not only undermines patients' rights to legally supported access to drugs, but may also reflect government failure (Kwon and Yang, 2010). The South Korean government's position on compulsory licensing, which has been proposed as a response, may depend more on economic and diplomatic circumstances, such as trade relations, and concern over reduced foreign investment, than legalities such as guaranteed rights to healthcare.

Post-TRIPS prospects

Intellectual property protection of new drugs has significant implications for public health and politics, as well as for the dynamics of the economy. The South Korean government had already established the foundation for strict IPR prior to TRIPS. Meanwhile, the possibility of abuse of patent rights resulting from strong patent protection continues to grow as data exclusivity and patent linkage are enforced by so-called FTAs. Unfortunately, there are currently no legal means of effectively counteracting such abuse of patent rights.

A major concern, as shown above, is that TRIPS-plus measures such as data exclusivity and patent linkage may create additional hurdles to market entry of generic drugs, leading to a contraction of the domestic pharmaceutical industry and a substantial increase in costs to consumers.

According to the most recent data released by the KFDA (*Health Korea News*, 2010), the current trend is for the pharmaceutical industry to develop combination drugs with more than two active substances, or new formulations, rather than make simple changes to the chemical structure of existing drugs. In today's environment, where there are increasing concerns about strong patent protection and trade pressure, such trends may bring about a more positive outlook for domestic companies, as well as for public health.

Conclusion

With the continuous growth of Korea's economy over the past five decades, as well as expansion of NHI coverage and services, the Korean pharmaceutical sector has grown both in size and in its significance for improving people's health. The market is ranked 12th globally and is worth KRW18.2 trillion (US$17.3 billion), with a global market share in 2009 of 1.7 per cent (IMS Health, 2010). Pharmaceutical expenditure in Korea has tended to grow even more rapidly than other healthcare spending (NHIC, 2011). This is the context of the introduction of cost-containment measures for the purpose of putting pressure on pharmaceutical expenditure to achieve lower pharmaceutical prices.

The growth of the market has been accompanied by international pressures for stricter IPR for pharmaceutical products, particularly through the Record of Understanding between Korea and the US, TRIPS and, more recently, pressures for TRIPs-plus provisions. There is little doubt that the current Korean pharmaceutical sector has been influenced by these successive international IPR schemes. This is of particular significance, as South Korea, like other developing and emerging economies, is heavily dependent on drug imports.

In this chapter we have provided details of IPR developments and their implications for both health policy and South Korea's domestic pharmaceutical industry. We have explained some of the legal and administrative measures that have been taken by the South Korean government as a result of changes in IPR. As emphasized, IPR-related schemes have significantly shaped the South Korean pharmaceutical industry. The industry operates in a bifurcated market—one for branded products supplied by global companies, the other for generics-focused domestic companies.

We have noted that the extension of IPR and insurance arrangements resulted in the phenomenon of pharmaceutical companies refusing to supply certain products. These cases provided valuable insights into how the government views possible economic losses resulting from treading the thin line between enforcing IPR and ensuring patient rights to legal access to drugs, and points up the question of the government's political will to address weaknesses in current drug patent policy.

Both TRIPS and the Doha Declaration make possible a range of measures that provide legal access to affordable medicines, such as compulsory licensing and parallel importation. However, there has been no purposeful reinterpretation of the South Korean understanding of TRIPS to enhance legal access to drugs and rights to healthcare.

The South Korean government is facing increasing pressure to strengthen IPR even further, as agreed to in the KOR–US FTA. And yet it has not been able to prevent the pharmaceutical industry's refusal to supply drugs and has not been able to guarantee rare disease patients legal access to needed drugs. There is increasing concern over how strict enforcement of IPR will impact on government policy making and patients in years to come.

References

Health Korea News (2010) 'There is Something Special About Drugs Developed Using Improved Chemical Entities' 26 August, http://www.hkn24.com/news/articleView.html?idxno=54333, date accessed 25 October 2011.

IMS Health (2010) 'Pharmerging Shake-up: New Imperatives in a Redefined World', http://www.imshealth.com/imshealth/Global/Content/IMS%20Institute/Documents/Pharmerging_Shakeup.pdf, date accessed 9 August 2011.

Jung, C.-H. (2004) 'Transition of Patent System in Korea: History of Strengthening Patent', *Journal of Science and Technology Policy* 14(3), 79–107.

KFDA, *see* Korean Food and Drug Administration.

KHIDI, *see* Korean Health Industry Development Institute.

Korean Assembly Special Committee Report for KOR–US FTA (2007) *Analysis of the Economic Impact of KOR–US FTA* (Seoul: Republic of Korea).

Korean Food and Drug Administration (2007) *Regulation on Evaluation of Drug Safety and Efficacy, no. 2007–20.*

Korean Food and Drug Administration (2010) *Food and Drug Statistical Year Book 2010* (Seoul: KFDA).

Korean Health Industry Development Institute (2007) *Study on the Establishment of Pharmaceutical Industry Development Plan* (Seoul: KHIDI).

Korean Health Industry Development Institute (2008) 'A Development Plan for Cooperation between Foreign and Local Pharmaceutical Companies', *Health Industry Policy Issue Report* 5 (Seoul: KHIDI).

Korean Health Industry Development Institute (2010) *'Analysis on Pharmaceutical Industry'*, http://el.khidi.or.kr/hermes/, date accessed 25 October 2011.

Korean Pharmaceutical Manufacturers' Association (2010) *Pharmaceutical Industry Statistics Report* (Seoul: KPMA).

KPMA, *see* Korean Pharmaceutical Manufacturers' Association.

Kwon, H.-Y. and B.-M. Yang (2010) 'Issues with Orphan Drug Pricing in South Korea', *Korean Journal of Health Economics and Policy* 16(2), 17–37.

Lee, Y.-J. (2007) 'Striking a Balance between Patent Rights and Access to Medicines in Developing Countries: The TRIPS Agreement and Beyond', *Korean Journal of Industrial Property* 24, 189–234.

Ministry of Health and Welfare (2010) *Statistics for Health Insurance and Health Policy* (Seoul: Ministry of Health and Welfare).

Nam, H.-S. (2006) 'Pharmaceutical Monopoly System and KOR–US FTA Negotiations', *Health Insurance Forum* 5(3), 15–27.

National Health Insurance Corporation (2011) *NHI Statistical Year Book 2011* (Seoul: NHIC).

NHIC, *see* National Health Insurance Corporation.

OECD Health Data (2011) http://www.oecd.org/document/16/0,3746,en_2649_34631_2085200_1_1_1_1,00.html, date accessed 2 January 2012.

Park, Y.-G. (2007) 'Harmonizing and Prospect of the International Patent System', *Korean Journal of Industrial Property* 24, 103–43.

World Bank (2012) 'Data Republic of Korea', http://data.worldbank.org/country/korea-republic, date accessed 1 December 2012.

12
Neoliberalism, Intellectual Property Rights and the Turkish Pharmaceutical Industry in the 2000s

Ipek Eren Vural

The strengthening of intellectual property regimes has been an important dimension of the neoliberal restructuring process observed in the global political economy over the last three decades (Harvey, 2007, pp. 34–5). A common factor underpinning both the global neoliberal restructuring process and the strengthening of intellectual property rights (IPR) in the developing world, most clearly under Trade Related Aspects of Intellectual Property Rights (TRIPS), has been the increased structural power of transnational capital (Gill, 1991). Many national policy outcomes in the area of pharmaceutical IPR have also been shaped by the dynamics of particular class struggles in developing countries (Eren Vural, 2007a). As a result, there are significant variations in the strength and standards of IPR provided for pharmaceuticals in different polities (Watal, 2000). At a practical level, such variations present different potentials for meeting public health needs and for local production capabilities. Theoretically and globally, this heterogeneity reveals how the operations and political strategies of transnational capital both impact upon and are mediated by class relations and struggles within and across developing countries.

In this chapter, I analyse the impact of neoliberal restructuring and the strengthening of IPR on the Turkish pharmaceutical industry. I argue that, since the mid-1990s, Turkey's ongoing integration into the EU has been the dominant political framework and dynamic that has reinforced neoliberal restructuring processes. It has also largely driven the creation of a stronger

---

This chapter draws on fieldwork conducted in Ankara and Istanbul in 2011. The author would like to acknowledge research funding provided by the Middle East Technical University of Ankara, within the scope of BAP-04-01-2009-02 and express gratitude to all interviewees from the pharmaceutical industry that invested time and effort into this work. Invaluable comments by the editors significantly enriched the text.

pharmaceutical patents regime than is required under TRIPS. Furthermore, the overarching significance of European integration for Turkey in general, and its subsequent evolution into a platform for stronger IPR protection for pharmaceuticals in particular, should be understood in terms of a hegemonic class project that has been pursued by Turkish conglomerate capital. This dominant class in the Turkish power bloc aims not only to more fully integrate its primary constituents and the Turkish economy within transnational circuits of capital (Ercan, 2002) but also to consolidate the pace of neoliberal reform.

As is the case with the wider European integration process (Bieler and Morton, 2001), in Turkey the pace and substance of policy outcomes on neoliberal restructuring and strengthening of IPR should be viewed as being shaped by intra- and inter-class struggles. In particular, the policy outcomes related to Turkish pharmaceutical IPR have been influenced by the two principal factors of the political capacity and power of local pharmaceutical capital and the compatibility (or not) of its policy interests with those of the powerful Turkish conglomerate capitalist class engaged in pursuing European integration. I will argue that while the integration project facilitated the establishment of a TRIPS-plus Turkish IPR (Sell, 2007), contestations and divisions between local and transnational pharmaceutical capital, within the wider dynamics of class struggle underlying European integration, have so far prevented an intellectual property regime that would completely undermine public health goals and local generics production. Nevertheless, on some other aspects of pharmaceutical patenting there has also been a convergence of interests between these competing fractions of pharmaceutical capital to gain stronger protection on medicines. I will also highlight how patent protection has transformed the material bases of the interests of Turkish pharmaceutical capital and modified relations both within that grouping and with transnational capital.

I argue that neoliberal policies, TRIPs and European integration have together served to significantly increase both the presence and market power of transnational capital in the Turkish pharmaceutical industry over the last three decades. Especially during the 2000s, neoliberal restructuring of the healthcare sector, the integration project and the new intellectual property regime resulted in a wave of transnational entry which, unlike previous waves of market entry, has focused on acquisition of Turkish generics firms. This has been accompanied by a contraction in the market share of locally produced drugs and the emergence of a new form of dependency on formulation imports, exacerbating an historical dependence on imports of active pharmaceutical ingredients (APIs).

Finally, I will trace how increased transnational competition and the strengthening of IPR have resulted in the intensification of research and development (R&D) activities by a handful of remaining local generics firms. While a significant proportion of R&D concentrates on incremental innovation, with a strategic focus on export of generics into developed country markets, its scope remains limited.

Neoliberal restructuring and new IPR in Turkey

The abolition of patent protection in Turkey in the 1960s (alongside a series of regulatory incentives throughout the import substitution era) bolstered the growth of local pharmaceutical (and other) manufacturing. Local pharmaceutical capital in Turkey, however, remained dependent on foreign technology and imports of APIs (from either transnational firms or other foreign unpatented sources). While one group of Turkish pharmaceutical manufacturers (the internationalized fraction of local capital) relied primarily on technology transfer and licensing agreements with transnationals, the domestic-focused fraction relied on foreign firms in other non-patenting countries, mainly from Eastern Europe, for their purchases of technology (Kirim, 1986). The product portfolios of this latter group of firms were dominated by copied versions of on-patent drugs (Kirim, 1986). Overall, not only was the dependence of the Turkish pharmaceutical industry on foreign technology and imports of APIs a determinant of the performance of the respective sectors in the liberalization period, it also informed the respective policy positions they adopted and alliances formed in the conflict over Turkey's position on IPR.

The 1980s marked a shift towards economic liberalization and an export-oriented model of accumulation. From the mid-1990s onwards the revival of the European integration process reinforced the neoliberal transformation of Turkish society and economy. The most important societal force sustaining both these processes was Turkish conglomerate capital, which had emerged as the hegemonic fraction in the Turkish power bloc during the 1980s. In stark contrast to the small- and medium-sized firms that formed the majority of Turkish capital, conglomerate capital consisted of a group of firms that combined different functions in the total circuit of capital (money, production, commerce) within the organizational form of holding companies (Ercan, 2002). Even from the mid-1980s, however, conglomerate capital came to view liberalization and the European integration process as important means of integration into transnational circuits of capital and entrenchment of the pace of neoliberal reform. This group was, therefore, the most important force behind the government's application for EU membership in 1987. During the 1990s it took a leading role in facilitating the rapprochement between the EU and Turkey that was necessary for the formation of a customs union. But, most importantly, throughout this period this group of capital succeeded in (re)constituting European integration as a hegemonic project (Eren Vural, 2007a).

Prior phases of restructuring in the Turkish pharmaceutical industry, in the 1980s and 1990s, have been examined in detail elsewhere (Eren, 2002; Eren

Vural, 2007a, 2007b). It can be noted that liberalization of trade and investment regimes, coupled with the customs union initiated in 1996, resulted in the first wave of transnational entry into the pharmaceutical industry. This had largely focused on imports into Turkey and strengthening collaboration with local pharmaceutical capital, with the consequence of transnationals gaining an increased share in market sales, as well as a rising share of original and licensed products in terms of sales volume and value (Eren, 2002). These initial phases of liberalization also saw the dislocation of the nascent local API production and deterioration in the trade balance of that sector. Local producers of APIs were unable to compete with cheaper imports, leading to soaring growth in importation and a dramatic fall in net pharmaceutical exports, largely caused by the elimination of export incentives. The manufacturing specialization of the Turkish pharmaceutical sector was thus readjusted towards formulation drugs, despite the growth of imports in that area as well (Eren, 2002).

In the 1990s the consolidation of economic liberalization policies and further influx of transnationals into the pharmaceutical industry resulted in the intensification of demands for pharmaceutical patent protection. This pressure coincided with the ongoing TRIPS negotiations and eventually culminated in the introduction of the Turkish Patent Decree of 1995 and extension of patent protection to pharmaceuticals in January 1999. Initially, the legal framework underpinning pharmaceutical patent protection was shaped by Turkey's international obligations under TRIPS itself. Following the conclusion of the EC–Turkey Association Council Decision no. 1/95 between the EU and Turkey in March 1995 and the resulting customs union in 1996, European integration became the determinative framework for evolving policy on pharmaceutical patents. It is exactly because of this overarching integration project that most of the flexibilities present in TRIPS have not been exploited in Turkey. This has involved a failure to establish positive conditions for compulsory licensing and exhaustion of IPR or a more restrictive scope (and procedures) for patentability. Turkey has also failed to properly exploit the transitional periods that TRIPS afforded. In fact, analysis of post-TRIPS changes in the IPR legislation, as well as its particular implementation in the field of pharmaceuticals, reveals that Turkey provides much more stringent protection for pharmaceuticals than required by TRIPS (see Table 12.1).

The policy process that produced these pharmaceutical patent standards and associated measures was shaped by the relative political capacities of the two segments of Turkish pharmaceutical capital mentioned earlier, and the particular stance of politically dominant Turkish conglomerate capital vis-à-vis the European integration project (Eren Vural, 2007a). Indeed, the political capacity of both the internationalized and the domestic-focused segments of Turkish pharmaceutical capital to effect policy should be assessed in respect of their relationship with, and constraints imposed

Table 12.1 Overview of pharmaceutical IPR in Turkey

Aspects of the pharmaceutical patent regime	
Duration of patent protection	Non-extendable 20 years
Length of transitional periods allowed before patent protection became effective	Three years: patent protection for both pharmaceutical products and processes became effective in January 1999
Provision of secondary patents	Patents are granted on formulations, and combination as well as second use
Exceptions to patent exclusivities	Research and experimental use (Article 75 Turkish Patent Decree) Individual prescriptions Bolar exception
Compulsory licences	Granted where no offer for licensing has been made and on grounds of: a) failure to put to use/work the patented invention (Article 96) b) dependency of the subject matter of patents (Article 79) c) public interest (Article 103) (AIPPI, 2008)* Government is not allowed to expropriate patents (AIPPI, 2008). No compulsory licences granted so far in Turkey for the domestic manufacture and supply of pharmaceutical products (AIPPI, 2008). Decree is still not compatible with the 6 December 2005 decision of the TRIPS Council.
Exhaustion of rights	National exhaustion of rights principle preventing parallel imports
Data exclusivity	The term of exclusivity is six years, tied to the duration of patents, starting from the first date of marketing authorization in any country of the European Customs Union
Patent linkage	No
Supplementary protection certificates	No

*The Council of Ministers decides the granting of the compulsory licence when the subject matter of the patent concerns issues like public health or national defence. Where the non-use of the invention or its insufficient use in terms of quality and quantity causes serious damage to the country's economic or technical development, this will also be deemed to involve public interest.
Source: author's own compilation.

by, the wider interests and power of global transnational capital. In particular, the high levels of external dependency of both segments of Turkish pharmaceutical capital on foreign sources of technology and APIs restricted these firms' ability to exploit or advocate the use of TRIPS safeguards and limited their political capacity to form alliances that would have helped to counteract a strong interpretation and implementation of TRIPS. Thus, in the 1990s, the internationalized fraction of Turkish pharmaceutical capital gave in to pressures from transnational pharmaceutical capital and changed its position in favour of patent protection. Although domestic-oriented firms maintained their resolve against protection, the competing interests and policy objectives of their more powerful national counterparts meant that their influence was limited. As a result, rather than focusing on achieving wider policy objectives, such as permanent safeguards on conditions for compulsory licensing and parallel imports, the domestic-oriented firms tended to pursue objectives that achieved only short-term benefits, such as the length of transitional periods.

In this instance, and despite their weakened political influence, during legislative discussions of patent law in the run-up to 1995, the domestic-oriented fractions of local pharmaceutical capital succeeded in convincing the legislative committees of the necessity of longer (namely, ten-year) transitional periods, a provision subsequently adopted in the Decree Patent Law of 1995. This move, however, led the European Commission to declare that the ten-year transitional period might cause problems for Turkish membership of the customs union (*Cumhuriyet*, 1995; Yalciner, 1999). In other words, the longer transitional periods demanded by domestic-oriented pharmaceutical firms came directly to threaten the wider interest of Turkish conglomerate capital with respect to EU membership. As a result of this pressure, the government issued a second executive decree (19 September 1995), which reduced the ten-year period provided for both pharmaceutical products and processes to a total of only three years. It is clear whose political capacity was effective in mediating accession to TRIPS-plus standards, in fact determining the manner in which Turkey's legal and policy regimes would be constrained thereafter.

Neoliberal restructuring in the pharmaceutical industry in the 2000s

In the 2000s the intensification of neoliberal restructuring of the economy proceeded in tandem with progress towards European integration. In 1999 Turkey was announced as one of the candidate countries for full membership of the EU, with accession negotiations initiated in 2005. The elevation of the Justice and Development Party to power in 2002 and its continuing strong hold in office signalled the rise of a new conservative–liberal hegemony, with conglomerate capital as the most powerful fraction. Neoliberal policies implemented during this period have been both more expansive and more intense than in earlier periods. Ongoing contestation over IPR and reforms of the healthcare system were the most important dimensions of neoliberal restructuring in the pharmaceutical sector.

Following the conclusion of the Customs Union Agreement with the EU, Turkey's integration into the EU was again the dominant variable framing struggles over pharmaceutical IPR.[1] An important issue was the provision for data exclusivity, which affords market exclusivities to originators of pharmaceutical test data that prove the safety and efficacy of a new drug that may or may not be protected by patents (Correa, 2002). While the transnational pharmaceutical lobby suggests that additional exclusivities allowed by data exclusivity compensate for the high cost of data generation, the main impact on generics producers is delayed market entry (Correa, 2002). The EC–Turkey Association Council Decision 2/97 (OJ L 191, 21.07.1997) detailed the legislative harmonization undertaken by Turkey to comply with customs union requirements, and included provisions on data exclusivity. This effectively meant that TRIPS-compliant alternatives to data exclusivity—including its rejection (Correa, 2002)—were foregone. In the early 2000s pharmaceutical transnationals had started to build up their lobbying for provision of data exclusivity, primarily aiming at securing market exclusivities for drugs patented before protection became effective in Turkey in 1999. When these lobbying activities fell on deaf ears, a group of EU-based transnationals filed a complaint with the European Commission, in October 2003, through the agency of the European Federation of Pharmaceutical Industries Associations (EFPIA) (EC, 2004).

The policy process around data exclusivity reveals important insights about the realignment of intra-class relations within Turkish pharmaceutical capital. In particular, it highlights how patent protection transformed the material bases of interests in local pharmaceutical capital and modified relations both within that fraction and with transnational pharmaceutical capital. In a 'strong' patent environment, the material conditions of market presence of all local firms are altered (that is, all local firms become more dependent on transnationals for access to technology), with subsequent modifications of their interests and identity (production of generics became the main area of activity of all local firms). The outcomes of these changes were clearly observed throughout the policy process on data exclusivity. Deep-running conflicts about data exclusivity between local and transnational pharmaceutical capital resulted in political reorganization within the industry itself. Thus, in 2003 transnational pharmaceutical firms split from the Employers Union of the Pharmaceutical Industry (EUPI) (which, since the 1960s, had been the primary business association coordinating their joint political action with the internationalized fraction of the local pharmaceutical capital defined earlier) and set up a separate association (Association of Research-Based Pharmaceutical Companies). The EUPI was then reorganized to represent the interests of predominantly local generics producers.

Unlike the policy process that governed pharmaceutical patents, local pharmaceutical capital adopted a united stance on the terms and conditions of data exclusivity. Its goals included: provision of transitional periods until the end of 2007; restriction of the term of exclusivity to the shortest available within the EU member states; and the inclusion of the term of data exclusivity within that of the patent (Isveren, 2004). The outcome of the data exclusivity policy process reveals that, while a united policy stance by local pharmaceutical capital achieved more favourable outcomes, even this possibility was effectively constrained by the overarching goal of European integration and the perception—real or otherwise—that Turkish policy was not a threat to this project (Eren Vural, 2007b). The Turkish Pharmaceutical Licensing Regulation issued in 2005 introduced data exclusivity for pharmaceutical products (Ministry of Health, 2005). Under this regulation, the term of data exclusivity is limited to six years (the shortest duration of exclusivity prevailing in the EU at the time), beginning on the first day of marketing authorization in any country of the European Customs Union (ECU). Although in line with the demands of the pharmaceutical transnationals and the EU, the Regulation provided retroactive protection to products registered in any country of the ECU between 1 January 2001 and 31 December 2004, it also excluded from coverage those molecules for which generics applications were filed in Turkey prior to 31 December 2004. The term of protection provided by data exclusivity is also treated as part of the total patent duration (20 years), which means that the period of data exclusivity cannot be used to extend the patent term.

The EU integration process continues to shape Turkey's IPR, including its implementation and enforcement. During EU accession negotiations, IPR were conspicuously included as an independent chapter (Council of the European Union, 2005). This served to generate new controversies, especially over issues like the provision of additional exclusivities for certain pharmaceutical products in the form of supplementary protection certificates, and extension of the data exclusivity period up to ten years, in line with the most recent European regulation (Directive 2004/27/EC). Local pharmaceutical capital, however, resisted provision of supplementary protection certificates and extension of the data exclusivity period, and its stance was upheld by the Ministry of Health during negotiations, with compliance in these areas deferred until Turkey's full membership of the EU (Ozkan, 2008; Interview 5). Lobbying activities by transnational firms continue to focus on both of these issues. The business associations of transnationals both in Turkey and abroad (for example, the Association of Foreign Capital, and the Research-based Pharmaceutical Manufacturers Association) emphasize how the incompatibilities generated by the two sticking points described above are undermining protection of IPR in Turkey (compare BASCAP, 2011; PhRMA, 2011; YASED, 2011, p. 43).

The European integration process has also been influential in spurring an attempt by the Turkish Patent Institute to draft new patent legislation. These efforts have spanned the last decade, but intense divisions over its content have so far precluded its enactment. Analysis of some of the provisions of the draft legislation is, however, instructive, revealing that, despite the contestation on some aspects of the IPR discussed above, in other instances there has also been a convergence of interests between local and transnational capital in Turkey towards stronger patent rights. Furthermore, the stronger protection that may result from such a convergence of interests may also involve potential trade-offs for public health concerns. The issue of availability of secondary patents is one of those instances. The patentability criteria as defined in Articles 6 and 7 of the current Patent Decree Law 551 (Council of Ministers, 1995) are very broad, and, even though there are no specific novelty or industrial applicability exemptions (which set the legal basis for the provision of exclusivities on formulation, combination and second indications patents), in practice the Turkish Patent Institute (TPI) has been processing secondary patent applications by both foreign and national applicants (Interview 5).

This practice became more entrenched following membership of the European Patent Office and the ratification by Turkey of the European Patent Convention (EPC) in 2000. Local generics manufacturers initially opposed secondary patents, but such opposition has been restricted to the level of private complaints to the TPI, and so far has not been contested in law courts (Interviews 2 and 5). However, as local generics manufacturers have increasingly engaged in incremental innovation and started to file more formulation and combination patents, opposition to secondary patents has to a large extent subsided.[2] As a result, the draft legislation included a redefinition of patentability criteria by TPI experts to include industrial and novelty exceptions of the type allowed in the EPC (Provisions 54.4 and Provisions 54.5, EPC, 2010). Both transnational and local generics firms supported this move.

Similarly, the TPI experts proposed an abandonment of the national exhaustion of rights principle in the current Patent Decree Law 551 (Article 76, Council of Ministers, 1995), which prevents parallel imports by third parties of legally distributed patented pharmaceuticals in favour of an international exhaustion of rights principle that allows parallel imports by third parties of products, as defined above, from anywhere in the world. This was fiercely opposed by a powerful coalition of both transnational and local actors. Transnational pharmaceutical firms are natural opponents of the international exhaustion of rights principle, as it restricts patent exclusivities and prevents differential pricing strategies in various national markets. Turkish firms with global manufacturing operations also feared the parallel importation (or arbitrage) of their lower-priced exports back into the home market (Interview 2). Further, other firms were threatened by the prospect of lower-priced Indian and Chinese imports that might be spurred by international exhaustion of rights (Interview 2). Indeed, Turkish generics pharmaceutical firms feared that cost-competitive and lower-priced exports of on-patent original products from India and China would restrict their own sales of same or similar products under licensing agreements, and even constrain growth in generics formulation sales (Interviews 1 and 3). This belief has found support in many government ministries in Turkey, nearly all of which expressed negative views about the proposed inclusion of the international exhaustion of rights principle in the draft legislation (Interview 5).

Meanwhile, almost all local generics firms and government ministries are in favour of a regional exhaustion of rights principle that could allow parallel imports by third parties of patented original products between the EU and Turkey. The demand for a regional exhaustion of rights principle, however, has so far been opposed by EU-based pharmaceutical firms. Indeed, the EU specifically excluded parallel imports from the scope of the 1995 Customs Union Agreement (EC–Turkey Association Council Decision 1/95, Annex 8), deferring a decision on the regional exhaustion of rights principle until Turkey's full accession.

Neoliberal healthcare reform and the pharmaceutical sector

During the 2000s, healthcare reforms were introduced under the Health Transformation Programme (Ministry of Health, 2003). They constituted another important dimension in the restructuring of the Turkish pharmaceutical industry, endorsing the creation of private healthcare markets and private service delivery and, on the financial side, aiming to broaden the public financing of private healthcare provision. Following the reforms, healthcare financing was centralized through the unification of three hitherto separate public healthcare insurers under the newly established Social Security Institution. The Institution then emerged as the monopsony public purchaser of healthcare services and pharmaceuticals (one buyer facing numerous sellers) from both public and private healthcare providers. The institutional market for healthcare services was further expanded through the initiation of a contribution-based general health insurance system in 2006 and extension of health insurance coverage to lowest-income groups—Turkey's Green Card holders.

The net effect of these reforms was to expand access to healthcare services and the market for healthcare provision, generating an ever-growing public budget for such provision. Social security coverage of the population, including health insurance, increased from 84 per cent of the population in 2004 to 96 per cent in 2011 (Boston Consulting Group, 2011). With an average annual growth rate of 8.8 per cent for health expenditures over the period 1998–2007, Turkey ranked first among all OECD countries in

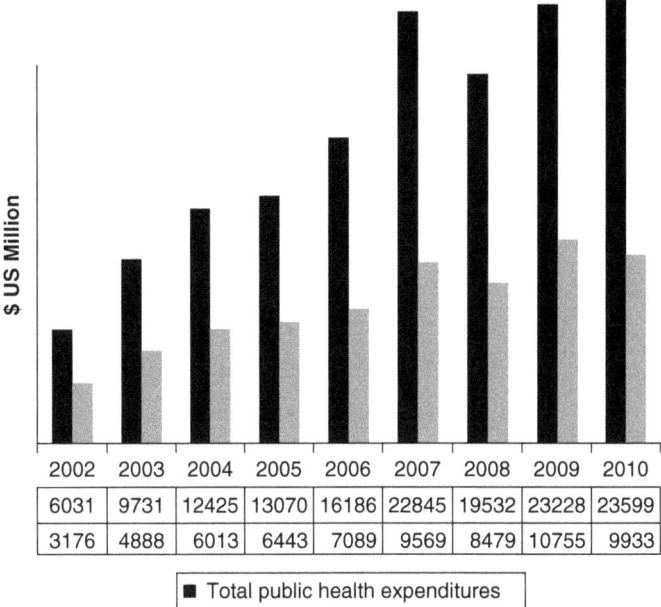

Figure 12.1 Total public health and drug expenditures, 2002–2010, in US$ million
Source: S. Turkoglu, 2008, Ministry of Finance, http//www.bumko.gov.tr: December 2009 Budget Realisations, Detailed Expenditures and December 2010 Budget Realisation, Detailed Expenditures, *Monthly Bulletin*, Social Security Institution, May 2011. Absolute Turkish Lira values in these sources are converted into US dollars using the indicative selling exchange rate values announced by the Turkish Central Bank on the final working day at the end of each year. Total public health and drug expenditures include expenditure by the Social Security Institution, government ministries and Green Card expenditures.

terms of real growth in per capita health expenditure (OECD, 2010, p. 105). Total public health expenditure increased from US$6031 million in 2002 to US$23,599 million in 2010, with an annual compound growth rate of 18.5 per cent (Figure 12.1).

In relation to pharmaceuticals, the impact of neoliberal healthcare reform has translated into double digit growth rates in public pharmaceutical expenditure and pharmaceutical market sales, as well as guaranteed growth potential for the generics formulation sector of the industry. Total public pharmaceutical expenditure increased from US$3176 million in 2002 to US$9933 million in 2010, with an annual compound growth rate of 15 per cent. In 2010 the share of pharmaceutical expenditures within total public health expenditure stood at 42 per cent (Figure 12.1).

Prescription market sales increased in value from US$4. 4 billion in 2003 to US$9.8 billion in 2010, with a compound annual growth rate of almost

232 IPR and Neoliberal Restructuring in Turkey

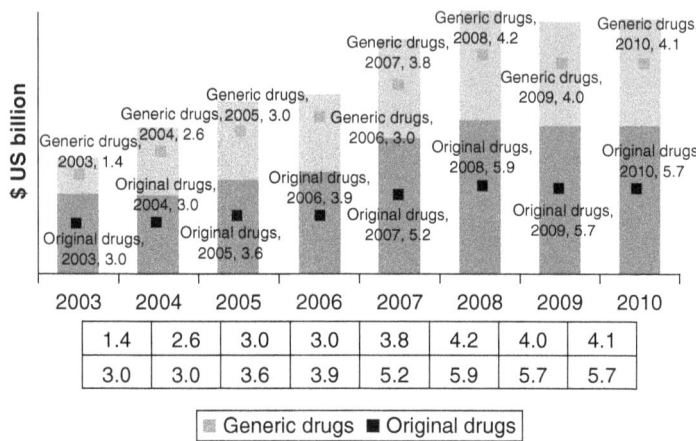

Figure 12.2 Turkish prescription market sales, 2003–2010, in US$ billion
Source: *Business Monitor International*, cited in Deloitte (2010) *Turkish Healthcare Industry Report*. The 2003 value is calculated from IMS, IEIS value in Turkish lira, converted into $US using the selling exchange rate value announced by the Central Bank of Turkey on 31December 2003. Respective value shares of the generic and original drugs were calculated by sales value market shares provided by the IMS, IEIS data.

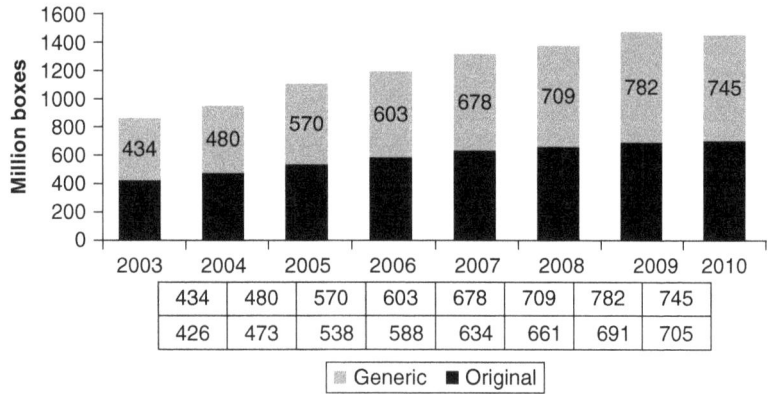

Figure 12.3 Turkish prescription market sales, 2003–2010, in volume of million boxes
Source: IMS, IEIS cited in Deloitte (2010) *Turkish Healthcare Industry Report*, p. 12. 2003 and 2010 value is directly calculated from IEIS, IMS data, combining prescription market sales volume data and shares of generic and original drugs in prescription market volume sales.

12 per cent (see Figure 12.2). Similar growth was seen in sales volumes, which increased from 860 million boxes in 2003 to 1.45 billion boxes in 2010 (see Figure 12.3). Turkey rose from being the eighteenth largest pharmaceutical market in the world in 2003 to twelfth largest market in 2008 (IMS, cited in

Deloitte, 2010). Within the EU, Turkey emerged as the sixth largest market (Pricewaterhouse Coopers, 2010).

Against the background of increasing pharmaceutical expenditures, in 2007 the Social Insurance Organization started to devise intricate measures for cost containment in its purchases of pharmaceuticals. These measures included a 'positive list', compulsory discount rates for both original and generic drugs, and a reference price system for generics. Although since late 2009 these measures have become more stringent, analyses of market sales for original and generic drugs during the 2000s reveal strong growth in value and volume for both groups. For example, generic drug sales increased in value from US$1.4 billion in 2003 to US$4.1 billion in 2010, with an annual compound growth rate of 16 per cent (see Figure 12.2). Their share of total sales value increased from 32.2 per cent to 37.1 per cent. In terms of sales volume, generic drug sales increased from 434 million boxes to 745 million boxes, with an annual compound growth rate of 7.9 per cent, the share in sales volume increasing from 50.5 per cent in 2003 to 51.4 in 2010 (see Figure 12.3). The value of sales of original drugs increased from US$3 billion in 2003 to US$5.7 billion in 2010, with an annual compound growth rate of 9.4 per cent (see Figure 12.2). The share of original products in sales value, however, declined from 67.8 per cent in 2003 to 62.9 per cent in 2010. In terms of sales volume, sales of original drugs increased from 426 million boxes to 705 million boxes, with an annual compound growth rate of 7.4 per cent, while their shares in sales volume declined from 49.5 per cent in 2003 to 48.6 in 2010 (see Figure 12.3).

Together with the impact of stronger IPR and liberalization of investment and services regimes, neoliberal restructuring of the healthcare sector also contributed to a second wave of transnational penetration into the domestic pharmaceutical industry. As opposed to the first wave of transnational penetration, which focused mainly on imports into Turkey and collaboration with local generics firms, this second wave of transnational entry has been characterized by acquisition of local generics firms by transnationals. A total of 18 takeovers took place between 1999 and 2011, with both large and small generics firms targeted (Table 12.2).

Transnational acquisitions of local firms have so far primarily aimed to capture a share of sales in the growing generics market. As documented elsewhere (Chaudhuri, 2010), there is a strong tendency among the transnationals to expand their operations into the generics sector as a strategy to compensate for sales losses incurred as a result of expiry of patent monopolies on blockbuster drugs and declining productivity of pharmaceutical R&D. Acquisitions of local firms allow transnationals rapid market access and use of established sales forces, as well as acquiring companies' reputation, production facilities and product portfolios. As detailed above, healthcare reforms significantly expanded both the pharmaceutical market and public pharmaceutical expenditure. This ensured strong growth for the generics

Table 12.2 Transnational entry and acquisitions in the Turkish pharmaceutical market, 1999–2011

Year	Local target firm	Origin of acquirer	Detail of acquisitions
1999	Ilsan, Iltas	Hexal (Germany)	Information not available.
2000	Ibrahim Ethem Ulagay	Menarini (Italy)	Majority share sold.
2003	Fako	Actavis (Iceland)	Total shares sold: in 2003 79% of the shares were sold for US$63 million and in 2006 the remaining shares were sold for US$20 million.
2005	Hexal, Hexal Ilsan	Novartis (Switzerland)	Following the merger between Hexal and Novartis, Hexal Ilsan was controlled by Novartis, which subsequently traded in Turkey under the name Sandoz.
2006	Biofarma Pharmaceuticals	PiLS-CVCI (US/UK)	100% takeover, valued at US$200 million.
2006	Munir Sahin Ilac	PiLS (UK)	100% takeover.
2006	Taymed	White Swan BV (Netherlands)	100% takeover.
2006	Deva holding	East Pharma Sarl (Luxembourg)	Majority share: 52% of shares were transferred.
2007	Eczacibasi Saglik Urunleri, ve Eczacibasi Ozgun Kimya	Zentiva (Czech Republic)	75% of shares acquired, valued at US$610 million.
2007	Roche's Gebze production plant	Sandoz International (Germany)	100% share, Novartis's generics production extension.
2007	Saba Ilac	East Pharma holding (Luxembourg)	96% of shares, valued at US$14 million.
Date unknown	Med Ilac	Teva (Israel)	100% acquisition.

2008	EBV Saglik	Ebewe Pharma (Austria)	100% acquisition.
2008	Dr Feridun Frik Ilac Sanayii	Is Girisim (Turkey)	17% acquisition, valued at US$17 million dollars.
2008	Yeni Ilac	Recordati (Italy)	100% acquisition, valued at US$62 million.
Date unknown	Rasyonel Ilac	Alfa Wasserman (Italy)	100% acquisition.
2009	Eczacibasi Zentiva	Sanofi Aventis (France)	Majority share.
2011	Dr Feridun Frik	Recordati (Italy)	100% acquisition, valued at US$ 130 million.

Source: Compiled by the author from Pricewaterhouse Coopers (2010) and Sol Portali (2009).

sector, which was without doubt instrumental in spurring a number of acquisitions by the transnationals.

The acquisition of generics firms for the purpose of gaining access to neighbouring markets has so far been a minor factor. One example of this motivation, however, may have been at play in the acquisition of Eczacibasi, which was historically the pioneering local generics firm. In 2007, 75 per cent of Eczacibasi's shares were bought by the generics firm Zentiva, which was itself acquired by one of its shareholders, Sanofi Aventis, in 2009. Following the takeover, Zentiva became the unifying brand for Sanofi's European generics operations. In 2011 it was announced that the Turkish plant would become an important centre for Sanofi's generics exports (Pharma Letter, 2011). There are signs of a growing number of bids by transnationals for the remainder of the larger market-leading Turkish generics firms, which often have extensive production units and capacities, or a specialized focus on certain therapeutic groups. There have been bids by Pfizer for Abdi Ibrahim and a bid by Eli Lilly for Mustafa Nevzat, signalling the appeal of Turkish firms to foreign transnationals as a basis for generics exports into Europe and other neighbouring markets.

Strengthening of IPR and transnational entry, however, arose at the time of (and possibly caused) increasing import dependence in the local industry, as well as contraction in the market share of locally produced drugs. During the 1990s, successive waves of liberalization further consolidated the dependency of the local pharmaceutical industry on imported APIs. During the 2000s, the strong growth in formulation imports generated a new form of dependency. The growth in the value of imported formulation

Table 12.3 Pharmaceutical imports and exports, 1980–2010, in US$ million

	Total			APIs		Formulation	
	Imports	Exports	Ex/imp	Imports	Exports	Imports	Exports
1980	93	4	4	91	2	2	2
1985	149	13	9	137	10	8	3
1990	470	90	19	386	23	18	67
1995	660	61	9	496	24	25	37
1996	979	105	11	717	56	27	49
1997	982	98	10	668	39	32	59
1998	1180	129	11	769	61	42	68
1999	1337	128	10	785	67	41	62
2000	1511	140	9	828	69	683	71
2001	1534	132	9	836	83	698	49
2002	1716	180	10	874	94	842	86
2003	2419	88	4	1231	21	1188	66
2004	2710	331	12	1379	145	1330	186
2005	2845	282	10	1409	65	1436	217
2006	3036	313	10	1433	66	1602	247
2007	3524	358	10	1660	69	1863	288
2008	4360	421	10	2057	85	2303	336
2009	4533	310	7	1300	11	3233	299
2010	4032	356	9	1028	31	3004	325

Source: Compiled from Republic of Turkey, Ministry of Health, Health Statistics Yearbooks, 2004, 2008, 2010.

drugs is greater than the growth in total pharmaceutical imports and in API imports combined (see Table 12.3). The value of imported formulation drugs increased from US$683 million in 2000 to US$3004 million in 2010, with an annual compound growth rate of 15 per cent. This compares with an annual compound growth rate for total pharmaceutical imports and API imports over the same period of 10 per cent and 2 per cent, respectively (see Table 12.3). The share of formulation drug imports in total pharmaceutical imports increased from 45 per cent in 2000 to 53 per cent in 2008, and up to 74 per cent in 2010. Meanwhile, the share of APIs in total imports declined from 55 per cent in 2000 to 47 per cent in 2008, and 25 per cent in 2010.[3]

The growing dominance of imported formulation drugs can also be observed in the composition of market sales volume and value, which indicates that imported formulation drugs are replacing locally produced products (Boston Consulting Group, 2011). While in 2005 imported formulation drugs constituted 15 per cent of sales volume and 42 per cent of sales value, in 2010 the shares of imported formulation drugs in sales volume and value both increased, to 23 per cent and 52 per cent, respectively (see

Table 12.4 Percentage of imported and locally produced pharmaceuticals in the Turkish pharmaceutical market, 2005–2010

Sales Value	2005	2006	2007	2008	2009	2010
% of Imported Pharmaceuticals	42	46	48	58	52	52
% of Locally Produced Pharmaceutical	58	54	52	50	48	48
Sales Volume						
% of Imported Pharmaceuticals	15	17	18	20	22	23
% of Locally Produced Pharmaceutical	85	83	82	80	78	77

Source: Calculated from 2011 IMS Dataview, IMS Health, www.imshealth.com.

Table 12.4). Increased import dependency of the local pharmaceutical industry can also be observed in the export to import ratio of the industry, which is approximately 10 per cent (see Table 12.3). Excluding the energy sector, the pharma trade deficit constitutes 10 per cent of Turkey's total trade deficit (Boston Consultancy Group, 2011).

Despite increasing dependency on formulation imports, there has also been some growth over the last five years in exports of formulation drugs. The value of these exports increased from US$71 million in 2000 to US$325 million in 2010, with an annual compound growth rate of 16 per cent (see Table 12.3). To a large extent this growth in formulation exports is indicative of the attempts by the handful of remaining local firms to increase their R&D and expand into generics export markets, mainly as a result of increased transnational competition in the domestic market.

R&D activities in the generics sector

Strengthening of IPR, increased domestic competition, and market penetration and acquisitions by transnational firms have all led local generics firms aspiring to survive towards R&D. R&D carried out by local firms differs depending on company size and scope of activities. While most firms are engaged in the formulations sector, a handful of remaining firms engaged in API production have extended their R&D towards development of new production methods. The largest investors in R&D among domestic firms invest around 5–10 per cent of their sales annually on R&D, and employ on average 100 to 150 personnel. Many have separate R&D centres. Another indicator of the greater focus on R&D by domestic firms is apparent in their formation of in-house IPR departments that employ staff with industrial, chemical engineering or pharmacology backgrounds and specialization in IPR law. These in-house units train the staff in R&D laboratories—for example, in how daily development practices may generate minor innovations that can be patented. These units also develop patenting strategies, trace molecules going offpatent for further product development, and identify molecules that are on patent but whose patents may be challenged or circumvented. Meanwhile, firms with more modest R&D activities invest around only 2 per cent of their sales annually in R&D and employ from 10 to 20 personnel; often they do not have separate R&D centres or budgets and work with external patent offices.

While a series of state-sponsored financial incentives that developed within the framework of neoliberal restructuring in the 2000s prepared the ground for foreign acquisitions, they also allowed local firms remaining in the industry to use restricted yet growing funds for R&D. The most important incentive has been growing pharmaceutical sales and public expenditures resulting from expansion of the institutional market. This was backed up by a favourable pricing regime for pharmaceuticals, which by international standards, at least until 2009, provided highly generous ceiling prices and allowed additional exchange rate profits for both original and generics producers. Finally, a series of financial incentives (for example, the state covers up to 60–75 per cent of R&D costs on a project basis) and income tax immunities for R&D, as well as social security subsidization for R&D personnel, have been instrumental in the growth of Turkish pharmaceutical R&D expenditure.

Sudip Chaudhuri's research (Chaudhuri, 2007, 2010) on types of R&D activities carried out by Indian pharmaceutical firms presents a valuable categorization that can be used in most developing countries. He develops a fivefold categorization of R&D activities, which descends in order of the value-added gains made by local firms. These are: (1) R&D for new chemical entities; (2) modification of existing chemical entities to develop new formulations and compositions, that is, incrementally modified drugs; (3) R&D for development of generics and exports into regulated markets; (4) R&D for challenging patents; and (5) research for the development of non-infringing processes.

In the Turkish pharmaceutical industry there are apparently no R&D activities by local firms directed to the development of new chemical entities. The high cost of research for new chemical entities, lack of necessary know-how and technical competence are referred to by local firms as the most significant barriers to activities in this area. Although some indicate that their collaboration with foreign partners could enable such work, so far there are no tangible achievements. Since local firms as yet carry out no new molecule research, clinical research activities have also remained restricted. Some local firms already undertake the coordination of the clinical studies carried out by their licensors in Turkey (Interview 3). Still, in the coming years, in view of the development of new combination drugs, which has emerged as one of the most common forms of incremental drug innovation, and as R&D activities gear up for penetration into export markets, clinical research by local firms is also likely to increase (Interview 3).

Modifications of existing chemical entities for the development of new formulations and compositions appear to be the most important dimension of local R&D. These activities aim for 'incremental innovations' that 'provide benefits to patients, such as reducing side effects, increasing convenience or enhancing comfort in ways that enhance compliance with treatment' (OECD, 2008, p. 195). These efforts have been accompanied by increased incidence of patenting activities by local firms. Given this, the majority of the patents applications by local generics firms focus on pharmaceutical form patents, formulation patents and combination patents (Interviews 1, 2, 3 and 4; Mutlu, 2008). Although there has been an intensification of patent applications by local pharmaceutical manufacturers over the period 2004–2010, on average their share in the total number of applications is still only around 5 per cent, and massively surpassed by the growth in foreign applications (see Figure 12.4).

Rather than achieving price premiums at product launch, patents on incremental innovations are used by local firms to generate market exclusivities. An important outcome of R&D-driven incremental innovation by Turkish firms has been product differentiation. This is used as a means of attaining competitive advantage. Furthermore, in Turkey almost all pharmaceuticals are marketed under trademarks (sustained by substantial advertising and promotional expenditures), which delivers another type of product differentiation. Once a particular pharmaceutical product is included in the positive list of the Social Security Institution (again, the dominant purchaser), marketing activities by pharmaceutical firms to increase sales of products are directed towards two targets. First, marketing is directed

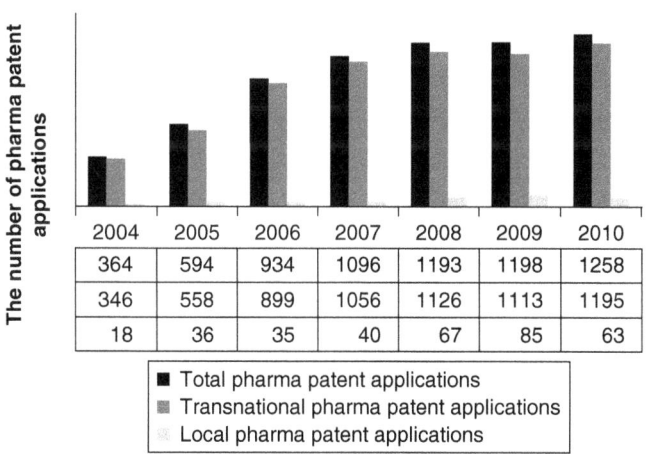

Figure 12.4 Pharmaceutical patent applications to the Turkish Patent Institute, 2004–2010

Source: Unpublished and processed data for 2004–2008 were received from the Turkish Patent Institute. Raw data for 2009 and 2010 were received from the Turkish Patent Institute and processed by the author.

at physicians to convince them to prescribe a particular product within a therapeutic group. Second, it is directed at pharmacists, alongside offers of discounts and promotions to encourage dispensing of the particular product. This strategy works very well for incremental innovation, allowing local firms to target specific patient groups and develop unique properties for products, as well as gaining the niche monopolies delivered through the patents.

When patents and incremental innovation are coupled with marketing activities directed at physicians, this acts to shift sales in a certain therapeutic group towards the new product (Interviews 1, 2 and 3). Moreover, such incremental drugs often become unsubstitutable at the lower end of the distribution chain. In Turkey, pharmacists have the right to substitute higher-priced products with lower-priced products on the grounds of efficacy. As new incremental drugs do not have any equivalents in the market, once prescribed by physicians, pharmacists can no longer substitute the given product with another one. This not only ensures larger sales volumes for the products concerned, but also alleviates the need to provide discounts and promotions to pharmacists to ensure greater sales.

In some cases, when incremental innovation is achieved on molecules that are still on patent in markets such as Europe (but not in Turkey, because they were marketed before 1995), the ability to gain secondary patents grants domestic manufacturers exclusivities both in Europe and in Turkey (for example, valsartan, EP 1994 926 B1[4]). Incremental innovation can thus increase Turkish drug exports too.

The development of generic formulations for blockbuster drugs, including process validation, bioequivalence tests and generation of other data for licensing dossiers, is a more typical R&D activity undertaken by Turkish generics firms. As in the case above, the development of generics formulations may be directed towards either local or export markets. While these firms still predominantly export to semi-regulated markets in the Middle East, the ex-Soviet Republics (in particular the Turkish Republics) and North Africa, over the last five years or so there have been significant investments in R&D for exports of patent-expired drugs to developed country markets (Interviews 1, 2 and 3). Access to developed country markets, however, necessitates satisfaction of those countries' regulatory and quality standards (Chaudhuri, 2007, 2010). Local generics firms are, therefore, required to meet bioequivalence tests and provide information on manufacturing facilities, processes and standards, as well as having their manufacturing facilities approved by the authorities of the targeted developed export market. In response, there has been an upsurge of investment by local producers in production plants that satisfy European standards, as well as in having their manufacturing plants approved by those authorities.

Among the targeted regulated markets, Turkish firms have a clear preference for European markets over the US market (Interviews 1, 2 and 3). This is understandable, not only in view of Europe's geographical proximity, but also because of closer harmonization of Turkish technical requirements and regulations with those in the EU. This harmonization process has been in train since the 1980s. Even so, some local firms specializing in therapeutic groups in which there is less competition, due to the higher costs and technology-intensive nature of production (such as with oncology products), have also successfully penetrated the US market. But this represents an exception rather than a general tendency.

Local firms usually enter export markets through partnerships developed with and by foreign firms. These can also involve R&D collaborations for product development. In such circumstances the necessary R&D to develop products, as well as pilot production and final production of the product, invariably takes place in Turkey, while registration of products in export markets and their distribution are carried out by the foreign partner (Interviews 1 and 3). Collaboration with foreign firms for product development allows the essential guidance and expertise of foreign firms, facilitating easier market penetration for Turkish exports. It also provides other important forms of know-how with respect to R&D activities directed at foreign markets. To gain such know-how Turkish firms have also employed foreign personnel, especially Indian scientists, who, according to local company executives, have considerably more experience and insight in generics product development and research (Interviews 1 and 3).

While foreign collaboration for product development is an increasingly popular strategy for Turkish firms, similar collaborations with and outsourcing to local universities have remained limited, and where they do exist they occur on a short-term contractual level and pertain to the product or process validation (Interviews 1, 2 and 3). On a limited scale, Turkish generics firms also challenge patents in both the US and Europe. One Turkish firm with its US partner, for example, successfully challenged a patent in the US held by Sanofi Aventis on oxaliplatin, a chemotherapy drug (Interview 1). Another Turkish firm challenged in the EPO a patent (EP 0973527B1) held by Abbott covering Klaritromisin MR, and managed to have that patent invalidated (Interview 2). In the US, a successful patent challenge may allow a foreign generics (or other) firm to be the first generics entrant to that market (Chaudhuri, 2010), while in Europe it may allow the firm to file its own patents and attain exclusivities. Still, the scope and returns of these patent challenging strategies remain marginal for Turkish generics firms as compared with generics manufacturers in other countries, such as India (Chaudhuri, 2010).

Overall, it seems that Turkey's generics industry has become divided in the strategies it pursues. Following the strengthening of Turkish IPR laws, R&D and foreign collaboration have emerged as the primary means for introduction of new products into the Turkish and foreign markets, rather than pure copying and reliance on low cost. Meanwhile, for small-sized local pharma firms that cannot fund such R&D, purchases of product dossiers from foreign sources, especially Indian manufacturers, alongside importing activities for formulation and resale, have emerged as a more cost-conscious and realistic alternative (Interview 4).

Conclusion

This chapter has revealed that a neoliberal restructuring process in Turkey has been reinforced by ongoing EU integration. Together, these drivers have led to the strengthening of Turkey's IPR. All these processes have significantly increased the presence and market power of transnational pharmaceutical capital. This expansion of power and presence has sustained a period of acquisitions of local generics firms and contraction in the market share of locally produced drugs, as well as growing import dependence of Turkey's residual pharmaceutical industry. While European integration has served as a platform for the transposition of stronger IPR, the process has been subject to extensive contestation among local and transnational pharmaceutical capital. Despite such contestation on some aspects of the IPR, we can also discern a convergence of interests between competing fractions of pharmaceutical capital towards stronger IPR protection. Furthermore, stronger IPR have made R&D the primary means of generating and launching new products, and have intensified R&D activities among a handful of remaining local generics firms. These firms have mainly concentrated on incremental innovation and exports to developed country markets. The impact on the Turkish pharmaceutical industry, however, has been towards increasing import dependency overall.

Notes

1. While recognizing the ongoing powerful lobbying by US-based pharmaceutical transnationals and the conditionalities imposed by the US government in favour of stronger IPR protection, this argument proposes that EU integration processes are also being used to augment the influence of these pressures.
2. A self-contradictory attitude is prevalent among local generics firms against the enforcement of second indication patents, which are predominantly filed by transnationals. While domestic firms support the redefinition of patentability criteria, they also complain about the irreversibility of the damage caused by the provision of exclusivities for indication patents, despite the absence of the necessary legal framework under the current Patent Decree (Interview 2).
3. The growth in imports of formulation drugs has increased significantly over the last two years, which may be due to the negative impacts of the global financial crisis on local production.
4. Valsartan EP 1994 926 B1: Valsartan is the name of a formulation that regulates high blood pressure; the reference is to a European patent granted to a Turkish firm on a modification of that formulation.

References

AIPPI, *see* Association Internationale pour le Protection de la Propriété Intellectuelle.
Association Internationale pour le Protection de la Propriété Intellectuelle (2008) 'Turkey Report Q202. The Impact of Public Health Issues on Exclusive Patent Rights', https://www.aippi.org/download/commitees/202/GR202turkey.pdf, date accessed 28 February 2012.
BASCAP, *see* Business Action to Stop Counterfeiting and Piracy.
Bieler, A. and A. D. Morton (eds) (2001) *Social Forces in the Making of the New Europe: The Restructuring of European Social Relations in the Global Political Economy* (Basingstoke: Palgrave Macmillan).
Boston Consulting Group (2011) 'Partnering with the Government to Globalise the Turkish Pharmaceutical Industry', Pharmaceutical Manufacturers Association of Turkey, http://www.ieis.org.tr/YAYINLAR/Partnering_with_Government_to_globalize_TR_pharma_industry.pdf, date accessed 4 December 2011.
Business Action to Stop Counterfeiting and Piracy (2011) 'Promoting and Protecting Intellectual Property in Turkey', http://www.iccwbo.org/uploadedFiles/BASCAP/Pages/Promoting%20and%20Protecting%20Intellectual%20Property%20in%20Turkey%20-%20final.pdf, date accessed 2 January 2012.
Chaudhuri, S. (2007) 'Is Product Patent Protection Necessary in Developing Countries for Innovation? R&D by Indian Pharmaceutical Companies after TRIPS', Working Paper Series, No. 614, September 2007 (Calcutta: Indian Institute of Management), http://ictsd.net/downloads/2008/08/sudip-wp-india-rd-trips-sept-2007.pdf, date accessed 4 November 2011.
Chaudhuri, S. (2010) 'The Indian Pharmaceutical Industry After TRIPS', in S. Chaudhuri, C. Park and K. M. Gopakumar (eds), *Five Years into the Product Patent Regime: India's Response* (New York: UNDP).
Correa, C. (2002) *Protection of Data Submitted for the Registration of Pharmaceuticals: Implementing the Standards of the TRIPs Agreement* (Geneva: South Centre).
Council of the European Union (2005) *Negotiation Framework* 3 October 2005, www.ec.europa.eu/enlargement/pdf/st20002_05_tr_framedoc_en.pdf, date accessed 6 December 2011.
Council of Ministers (1995) 'Patent Haklarinin Korunmasi Hakinda Kanun Hukmunde Kararname', KHK/551 27 June, *Official Gazette* no. 22326, Republic of Turkey.
Cumhuriyet (1995) 'Ilacta On Yillik Gecis Sureci Sorun Oldu', *Daily Newspaper* p. 10.
Deloitte (2010) *Turkish Healthcare Industry Report, Republic of Turkey Prime Ministry Investment Support and Promotion Agency,* http://www.invest.gov.tr/en-US/infocenter/publications/Documents/HEALTHCARE.INDUSTRY.pdf, date accessed 5 November 2011.
EC, *see* European Commission.
EC–Turkey Association Council Decision (1996) 'EC-TURKEY No: 1/95 of 6 March 1995 on Implementing the Final Phase of Customs Union', *Official Journal of European Communities* L35, 1–46.
EC–Turkey Association Council Decision (1997) 'EC-TURKEY No: 2/97 of 4 June 1997 on Establishing the List of Community Instruments Relating to the Removal of Technical Barriers to Trade and the Conditions and Arrangements Governing their Implementation by Turkey', *Official Journal of European Communities* L191, 1–67.
EPC, *see* European Patent Convention.
Ercan, F. (2002) 'The Contradictory Continuity of the Turkish Capital Accumulation Process: A Critical Perspective on the Internationalisation of the Turkish Economy'

in N. Balkan and S. Savran (eds) *The Ravages of Neoliberalism: Economy, Society, and Gender in Turkey* (New York: Nova Science).

Eren, I. (2002) The Transnationalisation of the Turkish Pharmaceutical Industry, PhD Thesis, University of Sussex, Institute of Development Studies.

Eren Vural, I. (2007a) 'Domestic Contours of Global Regulation: Understanding the Policy Changes on Pharmaceutical Patents in India and Turkey', *Review of International Political Economy* 14, 105–42.

Eren Vural, I. (2007b) 'A Political Economy of the Recent Changes in the Pharmaceutical Patent Policies across the Developing World and Turkey', *METU Studies in Development* 34, 337–85.

European Commission (2004) 'Report to Trade Barriers Regulation Committee: TBR Proceedings Concerning Turkish Practices Affecting Trade in Pharmaceutical Products', European Commission Directorate General for Trade, 13 September 2004, non-confidential version, http://trade.ec.europa.eu/doclib/html/119478.htm, date accessed 5 November 2011.

European Patent Convention (2010) 14th edn, http://www.epo.org/law-practice/legal-texts/epc.html, date accessed 7 September 2011.

Gill, R.S. (1991) *American Hegemony and the Trilateral Commission*. Cambridge Studies in International Relations: 5 (Cambridge: Cambridge University Press).

Harvey, D. (2007) 'Neoliberalism as Creative Destruction', *The Annals of the American Academy of Political and Social Science* 610(1), 22–44.

Ims Health (2011) IMS Dataview, http:www.imshealth.com.

Ims, Ieis (2010) Turkish Pharmaceutical Market-Consumption, http://www.ieis.org.tr/asp_sayfalar/index.asp?sayfa=220&menuk=12, date accessed 30 November 2011.

Isveren (2004) ' "IEIS" inca hazirlatilan Rapor Ankara da tertiplenen bir toplanti ile tanitildi', http://tiskweb.com/isveren_sayfa.asp?yazi_id=882&id=51, date accessed 11 March 2013.

Kirim, A. (1986) 'The Transnational Corporations and Local Capital: Comparative Conduct and Performance in the Turkish Pharmaceutical Industry', *World Development* 14, 503–21.

Ministry of Finance (2009) General Directorate of Budget and Fiscal Control Monthly Budget Implementation Results, December, Detailed Budget Expenditures, http://www.bumko.gov.tr/TR/Genel/BelgeGoster.aspx?F6E10F8892433CFFA79D6F5E6 C1B43FF9B71935287F9CB97, date accessed 8 March 2013.

Ministry of Health (2003) *Transformation in Health Program* (Ankara: Ministry of Health Publications).

Ministry of Health (2004) *Health Statistics Yearbook* (Ankara: Ministry of Health Publications).

Ministry of Health (2005) 'Regulation on Licensing of Pharmaceuticals', *Official Gazette* 25705, 19 January.

Ministry of Health (2008) *Health Statistics Yearbook* (Ankara: Ministry of Health Publications).

Ministry of Health (2010) *Health Statistics Yearbook* (Ankara: Ministry of Health Publications).

Mutlu, O. (2008) 'Jenerik Ilacta Fikri Haklar ve Sanovel', *Guncel Eczacilik*, 14–17 June.

OECD (2008) *Pharmaceutical Pricing Policies in a Global Market*, OECD Health Policy Studies, http://www.oecd.org/document/36/0,3746,en_2649_33929_41000996_1_1_1_1,00.html, date accessed 6 January 2012.

OECD(2010) *Health at a Glance: Europe 2010* (Paris: OECD Publishing), http://dx.doi.org/10.1787/health_glance-2010-en, date accessed 22 February 2012.

Ozkan, S. (2008) 'Ilacta Patent Korumasi', *Sinai Mulkiyet Haklari Uygulamalari Egitimi*, 17 November, Turk Patent Enstitusu, Ankara, www.tpe.gov.tr/dosyalar/haber/P2_serkanozkan.pdf, date accessed 29 February 2012.

Pharmaceutical Research and Manufacturers Association of America (2011) Special 301 Submission Hearing Statement, http://user1927995.sites.myregisteredsite.com/sitebuildercontent/sitebuilderfiles/phrma.pdf, date accessed 11 March 2013.

Pharma Letter (2011) 'Turkey to Become Sanofi Generics' Unit Zentiva's R&D Base' 28 June, http://www.thepharmaletter.com/file/105388/turkey-to-become-sanofi-generics-unit-zentiva's, date accessed 4 December 2011.

PhRMA, *see* Pharmaceutical Research and Manufacturers Association of America.

Pricewaterhouse Coopers (2010) 'Ilac Sektoru Birlesme ve Satin Almalari: 2006–2009 Donemi Incelemesi', http://www.pwc.com/tr_TR/tr/publications/Assets/Pharmacy09_TUR.pdf, date accessed 8 January 2012.

Sell, S.K. (2007) 'TRIPs-plus Free Trade Agreements and Access to Medicines', *Liverpool Law Review* 28, 41–75.

Social Security Institution 2011 Monthly Statistical Bulletin, May, http://www.sgk.gov.tr/wps/wcm/connect/55106ae1-247f-457d-8fda-04a616a8b60c/2011+MAYIS+AYI+AYLIK+%C4%B0STAT%C4%B0ST%C4%B0K+B%C3%9CLTEN%C4%B0.pdf?MOD=AJPERES, date accessed 8 March 2012.

Sol Portali (2009) 'Hapi Yutmak ne Manaya gelir' 21 July, http//:haber.sol.org.tr/ekonomi.hapi-yutmak-ne-manaya-gelir-haberi-15939, date accessed 27 March 2012.

Turkoglu, S. (2008) New Regulations and Principles of Reimbursement in Turkey. ISPOR Antalya Presentation, http://www.klinikfarmakoloji.com/index.php?q=taxonomy/term/3&page=3, date accessed 8 March 2012.

Watal, J. (2000) *Access to Essential Medicines in Developing Countries: Does the WTO TRIPS Agreement Hinder it?* Science Technology and Innovation Discussion Paper Number 8, Center for International Development (Cambridge, MA: Harvard University Press).

Yalçıner, U. (1999) 'Gümrük Birliği ve Türkiye de İlaçta Patent Koruması', *İktisadi Kalkınma Vakfı Dergisi*, 143, *Ocak-Nisan* 89–92.

Yased (2011) *Protection of Intellectual Property Rights in Turkey: Impact on Foreign Direct Investment* (Istanbul: YASED).

Interviews

Interview 1, local company executives, 25 August 2011, Istanbul.
Interview 2, local company executive, 7 September 2011, Istanbul.
Interview 3, local company executives, 16 November 2011, Istanbul.
Interview 4, local company executive, 1 December 2011, Istanbul.
Interview 5, patent expert, Turkish Patent Institute, 26 July 2011, Ankara.

13
Conclusion: TRIPS, Drug Production in the Global South and Access to Medicines

Hans Löfgren and Owain David Williams

The Trade Related Aspects of Intellectual Property Rights (TRIPS) Agreement, which inaugurated a global regime of minimum intellectual property rights (IPR) standards, marked the high point in the neoliberal tide as it surged across the pharmaceutical sector. The introduction and enforcement of pharmaceutical product patents, hitherto uncommon in the Global South (and also not recognized in many developed countries), was often accompanied by the privatization or closure of state-owned drug firms and an opening-up of the drug sector to foreign investment. IPR standards have been further extended and deepened post-1995 through bilateral and regional trade agreements. While the TRIPS agreement has advantaged the interests of the multinational pharmaceutical companies (MNCs), the variable degree of implementation of this agreement in different countries reported in this volume is one factor limiting that advantage. For the contemporary movement for access to affordable medicines, however, the question is whether the weaknesses in the global IPR regime itself and the resistance described in this volume are likely to be sufficient to secure such access worldwide.

The aspiration to access to affordable medicines for all did find an early and promising expression in the 1970s and 1980s. During this period, many states in what was then known as the Third World supported local generics manufacturers through industry and regulatory policies to meet the need for low-cost medicines. The context was that of an import-substitution model of industrialization, and weak patent protection was one of its central features. The United Nations Conference on Trade and Development (UNCTAD) championed the New International Economic Order (NIEO) and produced many reports focused on the pharmaceutical sector (see, for example, Lall, 1975). At its meeting in Colombo in 1976, the Non-Aligned Movement criticized the MNCs 'as an instrument of northern domination' and a momentum was building for medicines to be defined as public goods (*Editorial Note*, 1995). In 1975, the Director General of the World Health

Organization (WHO) told the World Health Assembly of the 'urgent need to ensure that most essential drugs are available at a reasonable price', and WHO's first essential drug list, published in 1978, envisaged a shift of basic medicines 'from the private sphere into a public health commons' (Greene, 2010). In 1981 the WHO established an Action Programme on Essential Drugs, and played a lead role in the development of national drug policies premised on increased public sector financing and 'even closer regulation by the state' (Murray et al., 1995). Yet few, if any, developing countries were able to develop innovative capacities (Ballance et al., 1992; Chudnovsky, 1983).

This aspiration for essential medicines to be considered public goods accessible to all could not, however, withstand the rise of the neoliberal ideology which infused the global political economy of pharmaceuticals in the 1990s. The role of the WHO was overtaken by 'the far wealthier and more influential World Bank, and the WHO's mission [had] been dispersed among other UN agencies' (Silver, 1998). Notwithstanding the life and death significance of affordable generics, the self-serving corporate discourse proclaiming product patents a prerequisite for pharmaceutical innovation was accepted as common sense within the policy elites. Two features of the evidence reported in this volume, however, indicate that this victory is far from total.

First, the use value of medicines—the prevention, alleviation or cure of ill-health and disease—is such as to ensure that corporate control will always be resisted. While TRIPS marked the highpoint of neoliberalism, it also triggered a global counter-movement which sought to protect and extend local production of affordable generics and define access to essential medicines as a *human right*. Central to this renewal of the drug policy aspirations of the Third World period was the campaign for access to anti-retrovirals for HIV/AIDS. Second—and ironically in the era of neoliberalism—some governments of the South sought to pursue this right on their citizens' behalf by demanding expanded market competition in such medicines so as to bring down drug prices. The global IPR regime promoted by the MNCs as the guarantor of good governance in pharmaceutical market was thus unmasked as the protector of their anti-competitive, monopoly rents.

Strategically as well as ideologically, it is clear from this volume that TRIPS and IPR are not the sole determinants of the political economy of global drug production. Factors such as historical industry trajectories, social inequalities and corruption, inadequately funded and organized public health systems, shortages of trained health workers, and ineffectual regulatory regimes contribute to poor access to essential medicines.

The significance of circumstances other than TRIPS is particularly evident in the chapters on China and Cuba. China has recognized product patents for pharmaceuticals since 1992, with full TRIPS compliance achieved ten years later, and its enforcement is considered credible. China also provides for data exclusivity for six years (beyond what is required under TRIPS). But the impact of TRIPS compliance is dwarfed by the effect on market demand of economic growth and the rolling out of universal health insurance. China has also recently instituted a national list of essential drugs and amended its legislation to provide greater scope for compulsory licensing and parallel imports, and signalled other changes to expand access to cheaper generics. As in the developed countries, universal health insurance and an increased public share of health financing will increase the demand for medicines. This will be accompanied by an increased emphasis on cost-effectiveness assessments and more effective price controls. In the unique case of Cuba, full TRIPS compliance has had no negative effect on its successful biotechnology industry. In a system in which all participants in the innovation system operate within the public sector, product patents are *de facto* awarded to the state itself.

The effect of the TRIPS agreement has also been blunted somewhat by other developments in recent years. The Doha Declaration of 2001 was a major achievement for 'access to medicines' (World Trade Organization, 2012). There have also been other positive developments, such as new funding for R&D and supply through philanthropic foundations and public–private partnerships. But the overall pattern is mixed; the growth in pharmaceutical patenting, including 'evergreening' through trivial product modifications, is particularly disconcerting. Patented products as yet constitute a small proportion of pharmaceutical markets in the South, but their relative share and therapeutic significance will inevitably increase in coming years. On present trends, the pricing of patented second and third generation HIV/AIDS drugs will significantly reduce the number of patients able to afford adequate treatment.

The chapter on India shows how far resistance to TRIPS can be taken within the framework of that agreement and within the constraints of the global political economy. Of course, this chapter details the pricing strategies of MNCs marketing on-patent products in this market, exposing their brazen business model as one of supplying patented drugs at exorbitant prices to the upper middle class. But the author also shows that India has a remarkable history of civil society engagement with drug policy and IPR, and has made more extensive use of TRIPS flexibilities than probably any other country. Particular attention has focused on Section 3(d) of the Indian Patents (Amendment) Act 2005, intended to prevent the awarding of patents for new uses or slightly modified versions of known molecules, unless a 'significant enhancement of efficacy' can be demonstrated. The objective is to prevent the unwarranted extension of monopoly pricing through patenting of trivial modifications (evergreening). India's issuing of its first compulsory licence of a drug marketed by Bayer in March 2012 is also of great significance. At the time of writing, Bayer is challenging this decision; similarly, the rejection of Novartis' claim for a modified version of an anti-cancer medicine has been fought in the courts since 2006. With a domestic industry with unique capabilities, India is now the fulcrum of global political and social struggles over pharmaceutical policy and access to medicines, as evidenced by these high-profile cases.

While some drug firms in India engage in discovery-oriented research, this volume has identified a lack of R&D capabilities across the case study countries (notwithstanding some exceptions) to take up the promise of enhanced innovation contained in arguments for IPR. The same countries show little capacity to avail themselves of the benefits of advanced technologies developed in other countries by importing them and applying them to their own. There is evidence of pockets of innovative capabilities also in China and Brazil, but, even in the large emerging economies, local firms are principally engaged in production and supply of basic generics. In Brazil the 'majority of APIs, the building blocks of any pharmaceutical product, be it on or off patent, are imported... only a handful of local firms are engaged in innovative research or chemical production' (Sweet, herein, p. 67). (Again, Cuba is an exception, having successfully developed an entirely state-operated innovative biotechnology sector.) At the same time, the MNCs are moving into generics markets on a broad scale and are in the process of integrating innovation-oriented industry segments in the South through acquisitions, investments in R&D centres, and outsourcing arrangements. A recent study of firms in China, India, Brazil and South Africa identifies 'a highly integrated global industry when it comes to innovation', but this integration is occurring within global networks dominated by the MNCs (Rezaie et al., 2012, p. 13).

The political economy of pharmaceuticals has been shaped significantly by the TRIPS Agreement since its inception. That agreement, and the Doha Declaration, purported to balance free trade and market ideology with public health by including flexibilities such as compulsory licensing to expand domestic production and permission of exports of low-cost generics. While some of these flexibilities have been exercised to increase access to affordable medicines, we believe that the patenting system has continued to impede the development of drug production and access to medicines in the Global South.

In the Third World era, political aspirations to ensure access to essential medicines for all were integral to programmes oriented towards national self-sufficiency, import-substitution industrialization and public sector production. But it was never the case that drug firms in the developing world could challenge the dominance of the MNCs in R&D. In the contemporary political economy of pharmaceuticals, the global integration of the innovation and production systems ensures that R&D capacity remains highly skewed in favour of the MNCs seeking to maximize monopoly rents through patent protection. The global debate since 2000 has been increasingly focused on alternative R&D funding mechanisms which require a radical restructuring of the industry. Positions range from the view that only minor tinkering with the patent system is required, to arguments for less reliance on intellectual property rights within a new global framework for health research, to models that do away with patents altogether (see, for example, Expert Working Group on Research and Development, 2012; Pogge et al., 2010). We believe that the studies included in this volume support the case for a radical policy perspective, entailing abolishing the patent system. This keystone of neoliberal ideology seems to us to constitute the most significant present obstacle to the human right of access to affordable medicines. Future research and political mobilizations need to be focused on extending the resistance to the IPR regime identified in this volume to a realistic programme for an alternative global political economy of pharmaceuticals.

References

Ballance, R. H., J. Pogány and H. Forstner (1992) *The World's Pharmaceutical Industries: An International Perspective on Innovation, Competition and Policy* (Aldershot: Edward Elgar).

Chudnovsky, D. (1983) 'Patents and Trademarks in Pharmaceuticals', *World Development* 11, 187–93.

'Editorial Note' (1995) *Development Dialogue* 1995(1), 2–4.

Expert Working Group on Research and Development (2012) Research and Development to Meet Health Needs in Developing Countries: Strengthening Global Financing and Coordination: Report of the Consultative Expert Working Group on Research and Development: Financing and Coordination (Geneva: World Health Organization).

Greene, J. A. (2010) 'When Did Medicines Become Essential?', *Bulletin of the World Health Organization* 88, 483–4.

Lall, S. (1975) *Major Issues in Transfer of Technology to Developing Countries: A Case Study of the Pharmaceutical Industry* (New York: United Nations Conference on Trade Development Secretariat).

Murray, M., N. Gasman and G. Tomson (1995) 'Health and Drug Policies: Making Them the Top of the Agenda: A Strategy Paper', *Development Dialogue* 1995(1), 5–24.

Pogge, T. W. M., M. Rimmer and K. Rubenstein (eds) (2010) *Incentives for Global Public Health: Patent Law and Access to Essential Medicines* (Cambridge, UK; New York: Cambridge University Press).

Rezaie, R., A. McGahan, S. Frew, A. Daar and P. Singer (2012) 'Emergence of Biopharmaceutical Innovators in China, India, Brazil, and South Africa as Global Competitors and Collaborators', *Health Research Policy and Systems* 10(1), 18.

Silver, G. A. (1998) 'International Health Services Need an Interorganizational Policy', *American Journal of Public Health* 88, 727–9.

World Trade Organization (2012) 'The Doha Declaration Explained', http://www.wto.org/english/tratop_e/dda_e/dohaexplained_e.htm, date accessed 25 April 2012.

Index

Note: Locators followed by 'n' refer to notes.

Abbott, F. M., 19, 29, 187
Abbott Laboratories, 19, 44n4, 44n7, 113, 115, 121, 212, 241
Abdel Fadil, M., 92, 103
Abdel Latif, A., 98
Abdool Karim, S. S., 186
active pharmaceutical ingredients (APIs), 2, 10, 19, 35, 37–40, 43, 65–6, 71, 92, 103, 125–6, 141, 156, 163, 170–1, 196, 199, 222–4, 226, 235–7, 249
Adly, H., 99, 105
Aftab, S., 170
Ahlquist, G., 142
Ahmed, S. I., 98, 171, 172
Akita, T., 135
Akram, M., 99, 106, 169, 170
Alavi, R., 154, 156
Al-Gedadi, N. A., 147, 159
al-Hofi, N., 101
Ali, I., 174
Allotey, J., 136
Alkem, 116
anti-cancer drugs, 20, 119, 155
  erlotinib, 119
  herceptin, 120
  imatinib, 118
  sorafenib, 20
Almeida, E. N. D., 37
Amann, E., 37
Amin, T., 35, 95, 99, 123
Ananto, E., 142
Antons, C., 143
Anti-Counterfeiting Trade Agreement (ACTA), 5, 22
anti-HIV/AIDS drug, 119
  tenofovir disoproxil fumarate, 119
anti-malarials, 2, 128
anti-retroviral drugs (ARVs), 2, 16, 18–21, 33–4, 144, 185–6, 193–4, 197–8
  efavirenz, 19, 33, 144
  lamivudine, 144

nelfinavir, 19
nevirapine, 144
  treatment of victims of the HIV/AIDS, 16
Antitrust and Fair Trade Act, 211
ANVISA, 35–40, 43
Army Welfare Pharmaceuticals, 171
Arya, E. K., 138
ASEAN Common Technical Dossiers (ACTD) for prescription, 139–40
Asif, M., 176
Askes (Asuransi Kesehatan), see National Health Insurance scheme
Askeskin (Asuransi Kesehatan bagi para miskin), 138
Association of Southeast Asian Nations (ASEAN), 139, 147, 156, 159, 161
AstraZeneca, 6–8, 113–15
Avafia, T., 14, 16, 18, 193
Awan, M. U., 176
Azevedo, R., 36
Azmi, I. M., 154, 156

Babar, Z. -U. -D., 142, 143, 147, 160, 172, 173, 174, 175, 178
Badrawi, H., 97, 98
Bahgat, H., 93, 94, 96, 97
Baker, B. K., 14, 16, 18
Bale, H. E., 102
Ballance, R. H., 1, 247
Banda, C., 193
Barbosa, D., 35
Basso, M., 35
Baumann, A., 62
Beall, R., 5, 18, 20
Beardsley, T., 75
Bedford, A., 146
Berdissi, W., 101, 102, 105
Bermúdez, J. A. Z., 44n6
Bezerra, C. A., 37, 38
Bieler, A., 222
'Bionexus' status, 161

251

biotechnology patenting, 74–5, 77
Bird, R., 33
Bland, B., 142
Blatt, C. R., 39
Bloom, D. E., 147
Boehringer Ingelheim, 44n7, 113, 193–4
Bolar-type exception, 191
'branded generics,' 8
Boldrin, M., 6
Bond, P., 187
Boulet, P., 17
Bower, D. J., 9
Braithwaite, J., 6, 14, 15, 187
brand-name drugs, 56, 58
Bravo, E. M., 75
Brazil
  compulsory licensing: for ARV efavirenz, 33; free-of-charge treatment programme for all HIV/AIDS, 34; harmonization of IPR to the minimum standards, 33; off patent ARVs, 34; universal access to HIV/AIDS medicines, 34, 43
  economy of production, 39–42, 43; competitors, 40; consistency, 42; government support, 42; import and trade balance, 41; on-patent medicines, foreign multinationals, 40; Pfizer's agreement, 41; PROFARMA, publicly funded programme, 42; public programmes, 39; Sanofi-Aventis' acquisition, 41; trade deficit and import, 41
  legal conflicts, 35–6; ANVISA and INPI, 35; procedural disputes, 35–6; Roche or Aventis applications, 35
  legal framework, 30–2; adoption of TRIPS, 31–2, 44; Brazilian patent-granting agency, 30–1; factors, patent standard, 30–1
  market liberalization and regulation, 36–7; ANVISA, benchmarks, 38, 43; APIs, 37, 39; bioequivalence and pricing rules for generic medicines, 38–9; crisis of legitimacy, 37; generics law, 38–9; price controls/sanitary and surveillance, 37; public procurement, 37–8; Sistema Única de Saúde (SUS), 37
  pipeline patents, 34–5; INPI standards for innovation, 34
  TRIPS compliance/flexibilities, 31
  WTO's Uruguay Round of negotiations, 30
BRIC (Brazil, Russia, India, China and South Africa), 22, 134
Budlender, G., 188
Burrel, T., 187, 190, 193

Cadila Healthcare, 115–16, 126, 128
CancerVax, 84–5
Cassier, M., 31, 34
Centre for Biomolecular Chemistry (CQB), 73
Centre for Chemical Biology, 73
Centre for Genetic Engineering and Biotechnology (CIGB), 70, 72–3, 82–4
Centro de Immunología Molecular (CIM), 71–3, 84
Certificado de Autor de Invención (certificate of authorship of invention), 77
Chakraborty, S., 33
Chandler, L. L., 161
Chataway, J., 105
Chaudhuri, S., 9, 111–31, 162, 178, 233, 238, 240, 241
Cheek, M. L., 79
Chequer, P., 34
Chien, C., 6
China, 11
  adoption of TRIPS: counterfeit drugs, 50; foreign pharmaceutical patents, 51; 2000 Patent Law, 50; 2008 Patent Law, 50; protection for product patents, 50; resolving disputes over patents, 50; SIPO, 50; system of judicial protection, 51
  Article 35 of the Implementing Regulations of the Drug Administration Law 2002, 11–12
  drug expenditure as a percentage of GDP, 57

economic growth and healthcare reform, 51–4; demographic structure, 52; health and economic indicators, 51; healthcare financing, 53; healthcare services, 52–4; market-oriented reforms, 52; out-of-pocket payments, 53; prescription drugs, 53; private financing, 52; rise in health expenditure, 51; urban and rural programmes, 52
health expenditure on pharmaceuticals, 55
multinational firms: availability of IPR, 63; effect of TRIPS compliance, 64; ownership structure, 64–5; pattern of trade, 65–6; pharmaceutical price index, 63–4
patent protection, 49
prescription drugs, 54–9; concern about rising prices, 58; 'countervailing power' of larger buyers, 54; drug expenditure, 57; drug types, 58; generic drugs, 56; global brand-name drugs, 55–6; high-quality global products, 55–6; IP protection, 54–5; national list of essential drugs, 58; NCMS, 54; overprescribing, 54; pharmaceutical expenditure, 54; public funds to healthcare sector, 58; segmented markets, 58; TCM, 56; trends in market share, 56
supply of pharmaceutical products, 59–63; biologics, 62–3; comparisons of R&D capability, 61; concentration indices of market, 59–60; cross-subsidization, 61; indicators of pharmaceutical industry, 60; local and global firms competition, 62; mean profit rate, 60; small-scale firms, 59
TRIPS compliance; benefits for consumers, 67; biologics and regenerative medicines, 67; incentives for multinational firms, 67; price of products, 67; TCM industry, 67

TRIPS-compliant IPR legislation in 2002, 49–50
Choi, A. Y., 12
Choi, Y., 137
Chow, G. C., 52
Chudnovsky, D., 247
Chui, M., 142
Cipla, 115–16, 124–6, 158, 190, 200
Clark, R. Lee (US cancer specialist), 72
Clinton, P., 126
Committee on Economic Social and Cultural Rights, 18
Competition Act, 189, 194
competition law, 19, 194
compulsory licensing
anti-competitive, 194
Brazil: in 2001, 19; for ARV efavirenz, 33; free-of-charge treatment programme for all HIV/AIDS, 34; IPR to minimum standards, 33; off patent ARVs, 34; universal access to HIV/AIDS medicines, 34, 43
Egypt: pharmaceutical production, 103
India: market structure and prices of patented products, 124
Indonesia, in 2004, 19
Korea, in 2002, 19
Malaysia, 158–9; in 2003, 19; government-use authorization, 159; importation of patented anti-retrovirals, 158; WTO's Doha Declaration, 158
Natco Pharma, 20
right to export, 19
South Korea, 208–10; Fuzeon, 210; Gleevec, 209–10; influenza A (H1N1) outbreak in 2009, 210; KODC, 210; Tamiflu, 210; TRIPS Agreement in 1995, 205; US Patent Act, influence of, 207
Thailand, in 2008, 19–20
Compulsory Licensing for Patent Implementation, 21
contract research and manufacturing services (CRAMS), 7
Coombe, M., 79
Coovadia, H., 186

Correa, C. M., 8, 10, 13, 14, 16, 17, 19, 22, 30, 31, 33, 34, 36, 43, 95, 195, 227
'cost-plus' system, 93
Cuba
  biologicals, 79–81; biosimilar product, 80; IPR for vaccines, 80; material limitations of TRIPS, 79–81; National Drug Regulatory Authority, 80; terms of drug regulation and patents, 80
  biotechnology patenting, 74–5
  biotechnology sector, 72–3; CECMED, 72; development programmes, 72–3; 'learning region' approach, 73; recombinant interferon production, 72; Western Havana Scientific Pole, 73
  case studies, 81–6; CIGB's Heberbiovac HB, 82; combined DTP-HepB-HiB product, 83; Cuban CIMAVax-EGF cancer vaccine, 81; Cuban HiB vaccine Quimi- HiB, 83; Cuban pentavalent vaccine, 81; EGF-r anti-cancer vaccine, 84–6; GLP/GMP/GCP, 83; pentavalent DTP-hepB-HiB vaccine, 81–2; process of natural HiB antigen, 83; vaccines, 82; YMBiosciences, 84
  1981 Cuban interferon pilot project, 74
  'full-cycle' nature of biotechnology centres, 74
  GMP/GLP/GCP, 74
  government's 'revolutionary' commitments, 74
  localized IPR regimes, 76–8; 'authorship' of the patent, 77–8; *Certificado de Autor de Invención*, 77; GATT-governed IPR regime, 76; 'institutional' approach to patenting, 77; OCPI, 77; ONIITEM, 76
  non-localized processes, 78–9; dual system of IPR, 79; existence of the US embargo, 78; Helms-Burton and Torricelli amendments, 78; regulatory function of TRIPS, 79
  pentavalent DTP-hepB-HiB vaccine, 71

  pharmaceutical sector, 71–2; biotechnology centres, 71–2; Centre for Chemical Biology, 73; chemical drugs industry, 71; CIGB, 73; CQB, 73; Finlay Institute, 73; raw materials and APIs, 71
  resistance to TRIPS, 75–6; consequences of the US embargo, 76; PCT, 76; synthetic HiB vaccine, 76
  state-operated, biotechnology sector, 74
Customs Union Agreement with the EU, 227, 230

Daftar Plafon Harga Obat (DPHO), 137–8, 143
Daiichi Sankyo, 114–15, 162
Danzon, P. M., 53, 63
data exclusivity, 11–12, 16, 49, 97, 158, 177, 195, 205, 211–13, 218, 225, 227–8, 247
data protection, 158, 178, 185, 194–6
Davis, D., 189
Day, C., 186
Dearing, J., 73
decentralization process, 135, 137, 174
Declaration of Rome, 101
De Coster, S., 147
Deere, C. D., 11, 13, 144
Department of Pharmaceutical Assistance and Strategic Raw Materials (DAF), 44n5
Dep Hukum dan Ham, 140
'Developing Tools for Access to Patent Information,' 17
Dessouki, A., 92, 94, 103, 104, 105
disclosure standards, 13, 187, 190
DiMasi, J. A., 6
Ding, J. A., 154
Doha Declaration, 2, 5, 10, 16–17, 22, 144, 158, 177, 185, 188, 192, 211, 219, 248–9
Draft National Pharmaceuticals Policy, 123
Drahos, P., 6, 13, 14, 15, 30, 187
Druce, N., 195
Drug Act, 171–2, 174
Drug Control Authority, 155–6

Drug Control Organization, 171–2, 174, 176–7
drug regulatory authority, 172, 180
Dukes, G., 29
Dutfield, G., 14

East Asian financial and economic crisis, 159
EC–Turkey Association Council Decision no. 1/95, 224, 230
EC–Turkey Association Council Decision no. 2/97, 227
Egypt
 accessibility and availability of medicines, 93–4; 'cost-plus' system, 93; 'Egypt's retail drug prices, 94; 2008–2009 NHA, 94; pharmaceutical market, 93–4; pricing system, 93; sources of supply, 93–4
 compulsory licences, 103
 2004 Egyptian Industrial Modernisation Centre report, 102–3
 generics industry, 103
 impact of TRIPS, 96–8; IPR-related cases before 1 January 2005, 96–8; Lipitor patent application, 97; olanzapine generic medicine, 96–7; Pfizer against Delta and Memphis, 97; Pfizer against EIPICO, 97; registration of olapex, 96
 Law N. 82, 2002, on the protection of IPR, 98–102
 patents granted post-TRIPS, 95–6; generic alternatives, 95; HIV/AIDS, 96; i-MAK, 95; INN, 95; National Burden of Disease Study, 95; respiratory failure, 96
 pharmaceutical sector, 92–3; decline from 1974, 92; dependence on multinationals, 92–3; Misr for Chemical Productions, 92
 R&D in, 103–4; concept of 'self-sufficiency,' 103–4
 technology transfer and policy, 104–6; international technology transfer, 104; Minapharm's experience, 104–5; MOH, industry and the research sector, 106; R&D, 105; South African Bureau of Standards, 105
 TRIPS-compliant in January 2005, 91
Egyptian Industrial Modernisation Centre report, 102–3
El Ahmady, O., 99
Elbe, S., 146
Ellison, S. F., 54
El Said, M. K., 11
El-Zanaty, F., 100
Employers Union of the Pharmaceutical Industry (EUPI), 227
European Federation of Pharmaceutical Industries Associations (EFPIA), 227
European Patent Convention (EPC), 229
Ercan, F., 222, 223
Eren-Vural, I., 93, 221–42
evergreening, practice of, 3, 31, 36, 178, 248

Farag, M., 98
Faridah, A. Y., 155
Fayyad, S., 92, 94
Feinsilver, J. M., 75
Finlay Institute, 72–3, 82
Fitzgerald, J. F., 44n6
Flynn, S. M., 7, 158
Foong, P. Y., 159
Fowler, E., 33
free-market liberalization, era of, 140
free trade agreements (FTAs), 5, 11–12, 17, 21, 33, 79, 152–63, 167, 178–80, 187, 195, 205, 212–13, 218–19
 bilateral and regional, 5
Frymark, T. 102
Fuzeon, 209, 210, 217

Ganji, S. K., 15
Garrett, L., 145
Generalized System of Preferences (GSP), 16
generic drugs, 1, 5, 39, 49, 56, 137–8, 140–1, 154, 157, 160, 162, 198, 206, 213, 216–18, 232–3
Geng, L., 50
George, E., 106

Gerdtham, U., 51
Germano, S., 144
Gilead Sciences, 19, 34, 119
Gill, R. S., 221
GlaxoSmithKline (GSK), 44n7, 99, 112, 121, 154, 177, 193–4
Gleevec, 206, 209–10, 217
Global Influenza Surveillance Network (GISN), 145
Godwin, J., 11
Gomes, L., 36
González, C. P. V., 44n6
Gopakumar, K. M., 117, 118, 119, 130n5, 162
Good Laboratory Practice, Good Manufacturing Practice and Good Clinical Practice standards (GLP/GMP/GCP), 74, 83–4
Grace, C., 125
Gray, A., 186, 195, 197
Greene, J. A., 247
Green Light Committee Initiative (GLI), 102

Hamed, M. R., 92, 94, 105
Hanim, L., 19
Harvey, D., 221
Hason, A. K., 48, 49
Hassali, M. A., 147, 152–63
Health for All (HFA), 169
Health Insurance Organization (HIO), 94, 100–1
Health Policy Task Force (HPTF), 169
Helfer, L. R., 14, 15
Helms Burton Act, 85
Hermann, R. M., 13
Heywood, P. F., 137
Himont Pharmaceuticals, 171
Ho, C. M., 19, 20
Hogerzeil, H. V., 18
Holbrooke, R., 145
Hollis, A., 2
Hsiao, W. C., 52
Hsieh, C. -R., 48–67
Huang, Y., 54, 61, 63
Hubbard, T., 2
Hunt, V., 4, 7
Husada, R., 134–47
Hu, X., 62

Iizuka, T., 53, 54, 63
India
  market and prices, 116–24; anti-cancer drugs, 118, 119; anti-HIV/AIDS drug, 119; competition in generics, 124; competition of new drugs, 118; compulsory licensing, 124; 'Draft National Pharmaceuticals Policy, 2006,' 123; MNC monopoly drugs, 121–3; Natco Pharma, 124; new drugs, 118–19; patented drugs, classification, 116–17; patent status of new drugs, 117; pricing policies, 120; reintroduction of product patent protection, 116; TRIPS flexibilities, 118
  multinationals, 112–16; access to low-cost reliable products, 115; Aurobindo–Pfizer deal, 115; emerging markets, 112; financial capacity to take over, 115; growth in generics, 115; M&As and tie-ups, 113–14; monopoly, 115; multinationals in the generics market, 112; Pfizer, GSK and Merck, 112–13; post-TRIPS situation, 113; takeover of Dabur Pharma by Fresenius Kabi Oncology, 115; takeover of Ranbaxy by Daiichi Sankyo, 115; takeover of Shantha Biotechs by Sanofi-Aventis, 115; telmisartan, 113
  R&D strategies; 'analogue research,' 127; development of biotechnology, 126–7; development of NCEs, 125; efforts, 126; expenditure with poor returns, 128; lack of the skills and funds, 126–7; MMV, 128; NCE for marketing, 128; for new chemical entities, 126–8; objectives, 125; potential conflict, 127–8; start-to-finish model in NCE research, 126
  TRIPS-compliant patent protection, 111
Indian Patents Amendment Act 15 2005, 191

Indonesia
  healthcare system and medicines, 134–9; *Askeskin*, 138; decentralization process, 135; deficiencies, 135; DPHO, 137–8; expensive pharmaceuticals, 135; health status and diseases, 136; human resource functions, 136; *Jamkesmas*, 138; location of puskesmas and health centres, 138–9; NELM, 137; outbreaks of polio and measles, 137; public health centres (or *puskesmas*), 134; SJSN Law, 138; unbranded generic medicines, 137
  IPR, 143–5; 1989 Act, 143; ARVs, 144; Doha Declaration, 144; government-use licence, 144; Patent Cooperation Treaty, 143; patent law, 144; ratification of TRIPS, 143
  pharmaceutical industry: era of free-market liberalization, 140; imported APIs, 141; Kimia Farma, 140; prescription drugs, 141; unbranded generic medicines, 141–3
  regulation of drug registration and approval, 139–40; ACTD for prescription, 139–40; GMP certification, 139; NAFDC, 139; PIC/S, purpose of, 140
  unbranded generic medicines: DPHO, 143; low market share, 142; modifying purchasing behaviour, 142; prices, 142–3; promotion of self-medication, 142
  virus case: GISN, 145; LMICs, 145, 146–7; Tamiflu episode, 145–6; 'viral sovereignty,' 146
Information and Decision Support Centre (IDSC), 100, 103
Initiative for Medicines, Access, and Knowledge (i-MAK), 95
'Intellectual Property and the Public Domain,' 17
Intellectual Property Laws Amendment Act, 186
Intellectual Property Organization (IPO), 176

intellectual property rights (IPR)
  availability of, 63
  Brazil: harmonization of IPR to the minimum standards, 33
  China: availability of IPR, 63; TRIPS-compliant IPR legislation in 2002, 49–50
  Cuba: 'authorship' of the patent, 77–8; *Certificado de Autor de Invención*, 77; dual system of IPR, 79; GATT-governed IPR regime, 76; 'institutional' approach to patenting, 77; IPR for vaccines, 80; localized IPR regimes, 76–8; OCPI, 77; ONIITEM, 76
  dual system of, 79
  Egypt: IPR-related cases before 1 January 2005, 96–8
  Pakistan, 176–8; flexibilities under TRIPS, 177; IR legislation, components, 176; Lilly *vs.*Werrick, 177; off-patented products, 177; Patents Ordinance 2002, 176–7; PPO, 177; TRIPS-compliant IPR legislation, 176; US Trade Representative's 'Special 301' Watch List, 176
  related cases before 1 January 2005, 96–8
  South Africa: compulsory licensing, 187; disclosure standards, 187; Doha Declaration flexibilities, 188; PCT in 1999, 187; South African Medicines and Related Substances Control Act No. 101 1965, 187; Southern African Customs Union, 187; strong-arm tactics, 187; TRIPS compliant in 1997, 186
  South Korea, 206–13
  Turkey: European integration, 224; export-oriented model, 223; imports of APIs, 223; liberalization policies, 223–4; local producers of APIs, 224; neoliberal restructuring/new IPR, 222, 223–6; patent law, 226; product portfolios, 223; transnational entry, 223; TRIPS-plus Turkish IPR, 222; use of TRIPS safeguards, 226
  for vaccines, 80

International Centre for Trade and
    Sustainable Development, 105
International Conference on
    Harmonization, 161
International Federation of
    Pharmaceutical Manufacturers and
    Associations (IFPMA), 101
International Medical Product
    Anti-Counterfeit Taskforce
    (IMPACT), 101
international non-proprietary names
    (INN), 44n6, 95
International Standards Organization
    (ISO), 71, 74, 83
international technology transfer, 104,
    106

Jaguaribe, R., 31
Jamshed, S., 174, 175
Jamkesmas (Jaminan Kesehatan Masyarakat), 138–9
Jawara, F., 30
Jhamtani, H., 19
Joint United Nations Programme on
    HIV/AIDS, 5
Jonsson, B., 51
Jorge, F. M., 31
Jung, C. -H., 207

Kadah, M., 104
Kaddar, M., 80, 82
Kahn, T., 200
Kaiser, J., 83
Kaitin, K. I., 6
Kamradt-Scott, A., 145
Kanavos, P., 8
Kaplan, W., 10, 71, 103, 196
Kaplowitz, D. R., 78
Kassem, M., 104, 105, 106
Kesic, D., 29, 41
Kieny, M. P., 146
Kimia Farma, 140
Kirim, A., 223
Khan, F. J., 169, 170
Khan, H. I., 177, 178
Khan, N., 167, 170
Khor, M., 16, 19, 20, 158, 159

Korean Food and Drug Administration's
    (KFDA), 12, 204, 210–13, 218
    regulations for cosmetic products in,
    211
Korea Intellectual Property Office
    (KIPO), 209–10, 213
Korean Pharmaceutical Affairs Act, 12
Korea Orphan Drug Centre (KODC),
    210–11
Kudrin, A., 159
Kuhn, R., 5, 18, 20
Kusumadara, A., 143
Kwa, A., 30
Kwon, H. -Y., 204–19

Laboratory for Synthetic Antigens (LAS),
    73, 83
Lacanà, E., 62
Lage, A., 74, 84
Laing, R., 10, 71, 103, 196
Lall, S., 246
Laskar, R. H., 179
Law N. 82, 2002, on the protection of
    IPR
    Egyptian Patent Office, 98
    multinationals: attack through
        counter-propaganda, 100–1;
        biosimilar Reiferon Retard,
        criticism of, 100–1; IDSC survey,
        100–1; IFPMA, 101; making drugs
        unavailable, 100; Reiferon Retard,
        100–1
    non-IPR factors, 101–2; GLI, 102;
        NCD, 102
    registration in transitional phase,
        98–100
'learning region' approach, 73
Li, Y., 50
Lindstrom, B., 11
List and Ceiling of Drug Prices (DPHO),
    143
Liu, C. M., 49
Liu, G., 58, 59, 61, 62, 65, 66
Liu, Y. M., 53
Leahy, J., 41
Lee, K., 145, 146
Lee, S. H., 12
Lee, Y. -J., 211
Leila, R., 94
Lek, C. S., 155

Levine, D. K., 6
Lewis-Lettington, R., 193
Löfgren, H., 1–23, 152–63, 246–50
Lopez-Calva, I. F., 39
Love, J. P., 2, 5, 19, 20, 197
low and middle-income countries (LMICs), 2, 145, 146–7
collective action, 18
Lupin, 116, 126, 128
Lustig, N., 39
Lybecker, M. K., 33
Lyn, T. E., 21

Mahal, A., 58
Mahmoud, I. E., 100
Malaysia
compulsory licensing, 158–9; Doha Declaration, 158; government-use authorization, 159; importation of patented anti-retrovirals, 158
domestic generics industry: 'Bionexus' status, 161; generics from India, 162; healthcare spending, 160; NKEAs, 161; Pharmaceutical Inspection Co-operation Scheme, 161; rationale for using lower priced generics, 161
domestic production and regulations, 159
dual system of public and private health services, 152
financing the healthcare system: medicines policy, 154; out-of-pocket payments, 153; primary care services, 153; private healthcare services, 153; social insurance, 153
IPR, TRIPS and FTAs: bilateral and regional FTAs, 156; bilateral investment treaties, 157; data exclusivity, 158; Patents Act 1983, 156; Patents (Amendment) Act 2000, 156; 'Special 301 Watch List,' 158; TPP—proposed regional trade pact, 157; TRIPS-plus provisions, 156–7; US–Malaysia FTA, 157
pharmaceutical industry: domestically owned companies, 154; Drug Control Authority, 155; expenditure by the public sector, 155; MOPI, 154; Pharmaniaga, 155; production of APIs, 156
pricing and distribution of medicines, 159–60; increasing drug prices, 160; NEDL, 159–60; prices of innovator and generic brands, 160
Malaysian Organisation of Pharmaceutical Industries (MOPI), 154, 157, 160
Malik, M. A., 167–80
Malik, U., 172
Mankind, 116
Mara, K., 101
Mathipa, K., 188
Matthews, D., 14
Mayosi, B. M., 186
McAfee, K., 77
Meads, G., 136
Medicines Act, 16, 187, 189, 193, 197
Medicines for Malaria Venture (MMV), 128
Medicines Patent Pool, 198
Mehanny, M., 99, 106
Mehboob, A. B., 172
Mello e Souza, A., 19
Merican, I., 159
Mezzera, M., 170
Micara, A. G., 5, 17
Milstien, J. B., 80, 82
Mirza, Z., 175
Misr for Chemical Productions, 92
Mohamed, S. K., 100
monopoly drugs, 121–3
Mooraj, Z., 175
Moreira, M. M., 30
Mozeson, M., 126
multinational corporations (MNC), 2–10, 12–16, 18, 22, 93–4, 101–2, 104, 111–13, 115, 117, 119–22, 124, 127–30, 246–9
Munos, B., 6
Munoz-Tellez, V., 14
Musungu, S., 14
Mutlu, O., 239
Muzaka, V., 14, 16, 18

Naidu, G. R., 159
Nam, H. -S., 207
Narciso, S., 142

Natco Pharma, 20, 124, 209
National Agency of Food and Drug Control (NAFDC), 139–40
National Burden of Disease Study, 95
national drug policy, 175–6, 199
national drug regulatory agency (CECMED), 72
National Drug Regulatory Authority, 80, 172
National Essential Drugs List (NEDL), 159–60, 197
National Health Accounts (NHA), 94
National Health Insurance (NHI), 137–9, 204–6, 211, 213–16, 218
National Health Insurance scheme, 137–8, 143
national health policy (NHP), 169–70
National Key Economic Areas (NKEAs), 161
National List of Essential Medicine (NELM), 137
National Office of Inventions and Trademarks (ONIITEM), 76
National Social Security System (SJSN) Law, 138, 142
Nature, 78
new biological entities (NBEs), *see* new chemical entities (NCEs)
new chemical entities (NCEs), 116–17, 125–9, 130n5, 204, 212
New Cooperative Medical Scheme (NCMS), 54
Newhouse, J. P., 51
new molecular entities (NMEs), *see* new chemical entities (NCEs)
Nishtar, S, 167, 168, 169, 171, 172, 173
Nolan, P., 29, 41
Non-Communicable Disease Alliance (NCD), 102
non-governmental organizations (NGOs), 16–17
non-patentability, extent of, 194, 207–8
Núñez, J., 76
Nunn, S. A., 43

Odell, J. S., 15
Oliveira, A. M., 31
Oliveira, N. B. D., 36
on-patent products, 7–8, 16, 18, 40, 56, 223, 230, 248

Organization of Islamic Conference, 156
Orsi, L. F., 31
out-of-pocket payments, 52–3, 153, 168, 186, 209
overprescribing, 54, 67
Ozkan, S., 228

Packenham, R., 37
Padma, T. V., 162
Pages, R., 78
Pakistan
   FTAs, 178–9; impact of, 179; most favoured nation status, 179; signatory SAFTA, 178
   health system, 167–8; communicable diseases, 168; endemic diseases, 168; HIV, 168; institutional reform, 167; large population, 167–8; malnutrition-related conditions and reproductive health, 168
   IPR and medicines, 176–8; flexibilities under TRIPS, 177; IR legislation, components, 176; Lilly *vs.*Werrick, 177; off-patented products, 177; Patents Ordinance 2002, 176–7; PPO, 177; TRIPS-compliant IPR legislation, 176; US Trade Representative's 'Special 301' Watch List, 176
   medicines regulation, 171–2; central drug regulatory authority, 172, 180; Drug Act 1976, 171; Drug Control Organization, 171; drug regulatory authority, 172
   pharmaceutical industry: Army Welfare Pharmaceuticals, 171; Himont Pharmaceuticals, 171; imported machinery and equipment, 170; local production of raw materials, 171; PPMA, 170
   pricing, 172–4; chronic shortages and non-availability, 173; generics drug policy, 174; global consultation fee, 173; local generics, 174–5; maximum retail price, 174–5; national drug policy, 175–6; WHO and HAI pricing, 173
   social protection, 168–9; healthcare funding, 168; HFA, 169; HPTF,

169; medical reimbursement schemes, 169; national programmes, 170; NHP, 169–70; private practitioners, 170; Social Security programme, 168–9; *Zakaat* (Islamic system of charitable contributions), 169
Pakistan Patent Office (PPO), 178
Pakistan Pharmaceutical Manufacturers Association (PPMA), 170
Panjaitan, R., 141
Paragraph 6 system, 144
Park, C., 119
Park, Y. -G., 208
Paris Convention on Intellectual Property, 194
Parmet, W., 189
Patent Cooperation Treaty (PCT), 76, 87n4, 143, 187
Patent Law, 49, 50, 144
Patents Act, 116, 125, 143, 156, 162, 176, 187, 189, 191–3, 207–8, 210, 216, 248
Patents Ordinance, 176–7
Paul-Raj, A., 155
Pauly, M. V., 53
Peng, Xiao, 103
Perera, S., 175
Pérez, I., 76
Pesticide Control Act, 208
Pfizer, 6, 8, 44n7, 92, 97, 112–15, 113, 121–2, 126, 216, 235
Pharmaceutical Affairs Law, 208, 212
Pharmaceutical Inspection Convention and the Pharmaceutical Inspection Co-operation Scheme (PIC/S), 140
Pharmaceutical Inspection Co-operation Scheme, 140, 161
Pharmaceutical Research and Manufacturers of America (PhRMA), 6
pharmaceutical sector
  Brazil, 36–7; ANVISA, 38, 43; APIs, 37, 39; bioequivalence and pricing rules, 38–9; crisis of legitimacy, 37; generics law, 38–9; price controls/sanitary and surveillance, 37; public procurement, 37–8; SUS, 37

Cuban: biotechnology, 71–2; Centre for Chemical Biology, 73; chemical drugs industry, 71; CIGB, 73; CQB, 73; Finlay Institute, 73; raw materials and APIs, 71; vaccine production and biotechnology industry, 71–2
Egypt, 92–3; decline from in 1974, 92; dependence on multinationals, 92–3; Misr for Chemical Productions, 92
Pakistan, 178–9; impact of, 179; most favoured nation status, 179; signatory SAFTA, 178
South Africa, 196–7; Essential Drugs List, 197; issue of local production, 196–7; Pricing Committee, 197; shape and size, 196–7
South Korea: attractive markets, 215; foreign manufactures, 216; generic drugs, 217; industry outputs, 214; over-the-counter and prescription-only medications, 215; Positive List System Policy, 213, 216; reimbursement benefits, 216; SDP Policy, 213–14; supply monopoly abuse, 217; TRIPS Agreement and -plus measures, 213
Turkey, 230–42; access to neighbouring markets, 235; imported and locally produced drugs, 237; imported formulation drugs, 236–7; imports and exports, 235–6; insurance coverage to lowest-income groups, 230; prescription market sales, 231, 232; public health and drug expenditures, 231; R&D activities, 237–42; reference price system, 233; Social Insurance Organization, 233; social security coverage, 230; transnational entry and acquisitions, 233–4
Pharmaniaga, 154–5, 159
Pilla, V., 20
Pingle, S., 112
Piramal Healthcare, 115, 128
Pirmansah, A., 135

Plahte, J., 70–87
PNF Bineka Kimia Farma, or Kimia Farma, 140
Pogge, T. W. M., 2, 250
political economy of pharmaceuticals
  compulsory licences, 18–21; Brazil in 2001, 19; Compulsory Licensing for Patent Implementation, 21; Indonesia in 2004, 19; Korea, in 2002, 19; Malaysia in 2003, 19; Natco Pharma, 20; right to export, 19; Thailand, in 2008, 19–20
  conformity and alignment, 11–15; bilateral and regional TRIPS-plus measures, 11; China, 11; developed country governments and MNCs, 14; failure of many LMICS, 13; IPR ratchet, 14; Korea, 12; Malaysia, 12; 'soft diplomacy,' 14; South Africa, 13; sustained resistance, 14–15; 'TRIPS-minimalist' countries, 13; Turkey, 12
  drug markets in global South, 6–9; access to medicines, 9; 'branded generics,' 8; competitive alternative product brands, 8; CRAMS, 7; 'emerging markets' (pharmerging markets), 7; future of supply of medicines, 9; lifestyle noncommunicable diseases, 7; on-patent or branded generic products, 7; patent-protected 'blockbuster' drugs, 6; R&D productivity crisis, 6
  government strategies, 9–11; ability to produce or import generics, 10; impact on local generics sectors, 10; TRIPS-compliant standards, 11; 'TRIPS maximalism,' 11
  strategic environment, 3–6; ACTA, 4; bilateral and regional FTAs, 5; Doha Declaration, 5; economic globalization, 3; IPR system, 4; monopoly prices, 3; product patents, 6; pseudo-generics, 4; R&D productivity, 4; right to produce generics, 5–6; TRIPS-plus provisions, 4–5
  strategies of resistance, 15–18; Access Coalition of NGOs, 16; amendment to TRIPS, 16; ARV treatment of victims of the HIV/AIDS, 16; collaborative South–South strategies, 15; collective, 15; collective resistance, 17; G20/G21 and Group of 77, 15; GSP, 16; LMIC collective action, 18; patient activist groups, 16; trade law and patenting, 17; WIPO, 17
Positive List System Policy, 213–14, 216
PROFARMA, 42
'progressive realization of rights,' concept of, 188
pseudo-generics, 4
public health centres (or *puskesmas*), 134

Quach, U., 74, 75, 76, 77, 87n3
Quental, C., 42
Quraeshi, Z. A., 174

Ranbaxy, 114–15, 125–8, 162, 178, 196
Rasiah, R., 156
Ratanawijitrasin, S., 74
Razak, A. D., 159
Reichman, J. H., 19, 20
Reid-Henry, S. M., 72, 75, 82
Reidpath, D. D., 136
Reinhardt, U., 61
Remedi Pharmaceutical, 155
Revised Drug Strategy, 17
Rezaie, R., 8, 249
Riera, L., 84
Roffe, P., 31, 33
Rostom, O., 99
Roulot, D., 101
Rushton, S., 2

Samaroo, H. D., 161
Sampurno, H. D., 135
Santoro, M. A., 49
Sanusi, D., 141
Science, 78
Seiter, A., 161
self-medication, promotion of, 142
self-sufficiency, concept of, 103–4, 249
Sell, S. K., 2, 5, 6, 11, 14, 15, 16, 21, 30, 79, 185, 222

Separation of Drug Dispensing from Prescription (SDP) Policy, 213–15
Shafie, A. A., 152–63
Shimotake, J. E., 48, 49
Sierra, G., 77
Silver, G. A., 247
Simoens, S., 142, 147
Singhvi, A., 33
Sistema Única de Saúde (SUS), 37
Smith, B. D., 4
Smith, R. D., 157
Smith, S. R., 157
Snyder, C. M., 54
social health security network, *see* Jamkesmas (Jaminan Kesehatan Masyarakat)
social insurance, 2–3, 153, 204
Social Insurance Organization, 233
Social Security Organization, 153
Social Security programme, 168–9
'soft diplomacy,' 14
Solvay Pharma, 115
South Africa
 constitutional framework: concept of 'progressive realization of rights,' 188; post-apartheid, 188; test of reasonableness, 189
 healthcare: state or out-of-pocket payment, 186
 IPR: compulsory licensing, 187; disclosure standards, 187; Doha Declaration flexibilities, 188; Medicines and Related Substances Control Act, 187; PCT in 1999, 187; Southern African Customs Union, 187; strong-arm tactics, 187; TRIPS compliant in 1997, 186
 patent regime, 189–95; 1997 amendments to the Medicines Act, 193; anti-competitive compulsory licence, 194; Bolar-type exception, 191; competition law, 194; compulsory licensing, 192; data protection, 194–5; disclosure, 190; exceptions, 191–2; exclusions from patentability, 191; government use, 192–3; industrial applicability, 190; inventiveness, 189; lack of transparency, 191;

novelty, 189; opposition procedures, 191; parallel importation, 193; Patents Act, 191; patent standards, 189; revocation of patent, 193–4; uses of invention, 190; voluntary licences, 193
 pharmaceutical sector, 196–7; Essential Drugs List, 197; issue of local production, 196–7; Pricing Committee, 197; shape and size, 196–7
 post-TRIPS prospects, 197–200; compulsory licensing, 197; generic medicines, 198; local firms, 199; Medicines Patent Pool, 198; National Drug Policy for South Africa, 199; private sector market share, 198, 199; SAGMA, 200
South African Bureau of Standards, 105
South African Medicines and Related Substances Control Act, 187
South African Patents Act, 191
South Asian Association of Regional Cooperation (SAARC) countries, 172–3, 178
South Asian Free Trade Agreement (SAFTA), 178
Southern African Customs Union, 13, 187, 195
Southern African Generics Medicines Association (SAGMA), 200
South Korea
 anti-trust law, 211–13; Antitrust and Fair Trade Act 2011, 211; data exclusivity, 212–13; TRIPS-plus, 211
 compulsory licensing, 208–10; Fuzeon, 210; Gleevec, 209–10; influenza A (H1N1) outbreak in 2009, 210; KODC, 210; Tamiflu, 210; TRIPS Agreement in 1995, 205; US Patent Act, influence of, 207
 healthcare system, 205–6; NHI, 205, 206; NHIC, 206; private provision, 206
 IPR, 206–13
 KIPO, 209
 KOR–US FTA, 205
 1961 legislation, 207

South Korea – *continued*
  member of WTO, 207
  NHI, 204
  parallel importation: KFDA regulations for cosmetic products in, 211; NHI's Pharmaceutical Benefit Scheme, 211
  patentability, 207–8; extent of non-patentability, 207–8; novelty, 207; Patent Act 2011, 207; Patent Act Amendments of 1986, 208; Pharmaceutical Affairs Law, 208
  patent linkage, 213; coordination between KFDA and KIPO, 213; generic drugs, 213
  pharmaceutical sector: attractive markets, 215; foreign manufactures, 216; generic drugs, 217; industry outputs, 214; over-the-counter and prescription-only medications, 215; Positive List System Policy, 213, 216; reimbursement benefits, 216; SDP Policy, 213–14; supply monopoly abuse, 217; TRIPS Agreement and -plus measures, 213
  post-TRIPS prospects: combination drugs, 218; FTAs, 218
'Special 301 Watch List,' 158
Srinivasan, S., 20
State Intellectual Property Office (SIPO), 21, 49, 50
Strategy and Plan of Action, 18
Sulej, J. C., 9
Sun, 116, 124, 126, 128, 130n5
Sun, X., 54
Sutherland, D., 41
Sweet, C., 40

Tageldin, M. A., 105
Tahirkheli, M., 175
Tamiflu, 33, 145–6, 210
Tarn, Y. H., 154
Third World, 246
Tempest, B., 7, 112
Thatte, U., 169
't Hoen, E. F. M., 1, 29, 33
Thorsteinsdóttir, H., 87n3
Tigre, P., 36

Torrent, 114–15, 126–8
Trademarks Act, 176
Trade Preferential System, 156
Trade Related Aspects of Intellectual Property Rights (TRIPS), *passim*
traditional Chinese medicine (TCM), 56–8, 60, 62–3, 67
Treatment Action Campaign (TAC), 16, 188, 194
TRIPS flexibilities, 3
TRIPS-plus measures, 211
  bilateral and regional, 11
TRIPS-plus provisions, 4
Tunsarawuth, S., 144
Turkey
  IPR, 222, 223–6; economic liberalization policies, 223–4; European integration, 224; export-oriented model, 223; imports of APIs, 223; local producers of APIs, 224; patent law, 226; product portfolios, 223; transnational entry, 223; use of TRIPS safeguards, 226
  neoliberal healthcare reform, 230–42; access to neighbouring markets, 235; health insurance coverage, 230; imported and locally produced drugs, 237; imported formulation drugs, 236–7; imports and exports, 235–6; prescription market sales, 231; public health and drug expenditures, 231; R&D activities, 237–42; reference price system, 233; Social Insurance Organization, 233; social security coverage, 230; transnational entry and acquisitions, 233–4
  neoliberal restructuring, 226–30; abandonment of the national exhaustion of rights principle, 229; Customs Union Agreement with the EU, 227; data exclusivity conflicts, 227–8; EC–Turkey Association Council Decision 2/97, 227; EFPIA, 227; EPC, 229; generics firms, 230; influence of EU integration, 228–9; 'strong' patent environment, 227; threat of lower-priced imports, 229;

Turkish Pharmaceutical Licensing Regulation, 228
R&D activities: foreign collaboration, 241; generic formulations for blockbuster drugs, 240; local firms, 237; new formulations and compositions, 238–9; partnerships, 241; patent applications, 239; patents on incremental innovations, 239; positive list, Social Security Institution, 239; sales of products, 239–40; state-sponsored financial incentives, 238; value-added gains, 238
TRIPS-plus Turkish IPR, 222
Turkish Pharmaceutical Licensing Regulation, 228
Turkoglu, S., 231

unbranded generic medicines, 137–8, 141–3, 147
UN Covenant on Economic, Social and Cultural Rights (CESCR), 18
United Nations Conference on Trade and Development (UNCTAD), 13, 104–5, 105, 135, 144, 190, 246
United Nations Development Programme (UNDP), 13
United States Trade Representative's (USTR), 14, 16, 44n2
Uruguay Round of General Agreement on Tariffs and Trade (GATT), 6, 70, 76
US Food and Drug Administration (USFDA), 9, 95, 130n5, 131n7, 204, 216
US–Malaysia FTA, 157
US Patent Act, influence of, 207
US Trade Representative's 'Special 301' Watch List, 176

Valente, V., 38
value-added gains, 238
Vaughan, V. S., 33
Vawda, Y. A, 185–201
Velasquez, G., 17
Verez, V., 83
Vijay, B., 38

'viral sovereignty' of Indonesia, 146
Vivas-Eugui, D., 11
voluntary licences, 18–19, 123, 185, 193–4, 198
Vosgerau, M. Z., 39

Wagstaff, A., 53
Wang, R. Y., 55, 58
Watal, J., 15, 221
Way, A., 100
Weyland, K., 37
Williams, O. D., 1–23, 246–50
Wilson, D., 112
Wondemagegnehu, E., 74
World Health Organization (WHO), 13, 15, 17–18, 83, 87, 93–4, 96, 101–2, 104–5, 135, 137, 145–6, 153, 167, 169–70, 173–4, 206, 246–7
World Intellectual Property Organization (WIPO), 14, 17, 22
led technical assistance programmes, 14
World Trade Organization (WTO), 1–2, 5–6, 14–18, 29–31, 33, 43, 48–9, 66, 97, 116, 123, 135, 152, 156, 158, 176–7, 185, 187–8, 207–8, 248
Wright, R., 93, 94, 96, 97

Yalciner, U., 226
Yang, B. -M., 204–19
Yang, Y., 54, 61, 63
Yasir, M., 175
Yee, A., 41
Yeung, G., 59, 60, 61, 64
Yip, W., 52, 58
YMBiosciences, 84–5
Yon, R., 159
Yu, C. P., 153
Yu, M., 59
Yu, P. K., 10, 11, 14, 15, 17
Yu, X., 53, 59
Yusuf, S., 170

Zaman, H. H., 154
Zaman, Q., 179
Zakaat (Islamic system of charitable contributions), 169
Zehr, L., 85
Zhang, J., 41

GPSR Compliance

The European Union's (EU) General Product Safety Regulation (GPSR) is a set of rules that requires consumer products to be safe and our obligations to ensure this.

If you have any concerns about our products, you can contact us on

ProductSafety@springernature.com

In case Publisher is established outside the EU, the EU authorized representative is:

Springer Nature Customer Service Center GmbH
Europaplatz 3
69115 Heidelberg, Germany

www.ingramcontent.com/pod-product-compliance
Lightning Source LLC
Chambersburg PA
CBHW071615100426
42873CB00004B/52